IN SEARCH OF WINE

IN SEARCH OF WINE

A Tour of the Vineyards of France

Charles Walter Berry

Series Editor: Jancis Robinson

SIDGWICK & JACKSON

LONDON

This edition published in 1987 by
Sidgwick & Jackson Limited
First published in 1935
by Constable & Company Limited

Copyright © 1935 by Charles Walter Berry
Foreword copyright © 1987 by Jancis Robinson

Map on page viii by Neil Hyslop
ISBN 0–283–99485–1

Printed by
Anchor Brendon
for Sidgwick & Jackson Limited
1 Tavistock Chambers, Bloomsbury Way
London WC1A 2SG

With a thought to
B A C C H U S
in particular
and a Humble Recognition
of the Wisdom
of Others

CONTENTS

IN SEARCH OF WINE

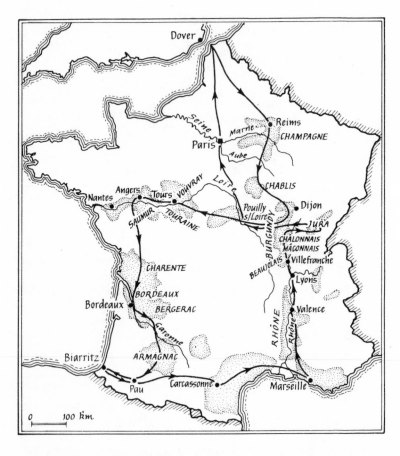

Map showing Charles Walter Berry's route through France, 1934

INTRODUCTION

Along with his more dashing second cousin Francis Berry and their partner Hugh Rudd, Charles Walter Berry put wine merchants Berry Bros. on the international map. Walter made wine trade history by venturing into the cellars of those who supplied him, staying in hotels (of which he could write in his journal: 'A good night – no mosquitos') in order to understand better the product he was selling and to survey, in unparalleled depth for the time, the French *vignoble*.

In Search of Wine records Charles Walter Berry's famous eight-week tour of France in the autumn of 1934. He was perhaps most respected by his contemporaries – fellow connoisseurs such as H. Warner Allen and Ian Maxwell Campbell – for his unusual ability to judge very young wine. It was a particularly useful attribute on this journey from cask to caskful of '33s and '34s.

He was also an observant traveller, diligently making note of local grape varieties (including the relatively high proportion of hybrids planted then), local recipes and even the news of the moment. In Bordeaux, just after tasting each of the sixty casks of Château Le Prieuré 1933 he had bought (while Alexis Lichine – who added his name to this Margaux property after he bought it in 1951 – was still selling advertising space as a junior on the *International Herald Tribune*), he records his disgust at the assassination of King Alexander of Yugoslavia in Marseille the previous day.

The author's idiosyncratic, almost playful approach to travel and story-telling also allows us to form a strong impression of the Surbiton pioneer himself and, not least, the *badinage* with his succession of co-travellers. Charles Walter Berry eventually managed to find three suitably like-minded and well-constituted companions whose wives would release them to fill in for his chauffeur ('who could not be spared from home for so long a period'). His companions were, successively, his own son Reggie, Ian Maxwell Campbell's son Lorne and 'the Sec', Samuel Thresher of Williams & Humbert. They had a high old time, revelling in running jokes (some of them truly terrible) and shared criticism of their fellow diners, occasionally coming dangerously close to breaking into music hall ditties in unsuitable settings.

In *The Story of Berry Bros & Rudd*, the author Tom Johnson describes Charles Walter Berry thus:

> Walter was stocky and fair, a guardian of the home base who held narrow, classic views in the matter of drink. Not for him a superb single malt or old rum or Calvados or even vintage port ('because the fermentation is artificially cut short'), but simply good wine, more good wine and then cognac. Despite an inherent shyness, he was a brilliant salesman . . . and like most good salesman, knew how and when to buy.

In this unique record of the wine world of the 1930s the author is modest but definite about his own tasting impressions, writing after his account of the still-fermenting Château Cheval Blanc 1934: 'We shall certainly have a say in the purchase of the *totalité* of this famous wine!' The firm's confidence had been bolstered by the Repeal of Prohibition in the USA the year before, and presumably its purchasing budget helped by a substantial investment in the exceptional 1928 vintage in Bordeaux.

The journal also portrays Charles Walter Berry, in his typically self-mocking style, as something of a dandy. On one of his wartime experiences (he was injured when parachuting from an observation balloon) he wrote: 'How proud I was when walking, fully equippped, along the Strand to Charing Cross station, adorned like a pukka A.B. [able bodied seaman]. I think the little brown gaiters appealed to me most.' Yet contrary to this character portrait, he also appears to have

[x]

been far from shy with the women he met on his travels. Gentle joshing comes across as a favourite pursuit.

In Bordeaux he met a succession of names still prominent in wine circles today: Messieurs Danglade, Cruse, Eschenauer, Cordier, Schyler and Calvet. Of this last visit he observes happily: 'Madame Jack Calvet, his daughter-in-law, did the honours with perfection – in fact, before we parted she almost promised to accompany me on my next balloon trip.'

A few days earlier he had, 'after a good deal of knocking and patience', gained entrance to Château Mouton-Rothschild where he found young Baron Phillipe (*sic*) de Rothschild 'taking the keenest interest in everything that went on, making alterations to his *chais* and his house, and endeavouring to make everything as perfect as possible'. The Baron let slip he was working on a wine to be called 'Château Mouton Cadet'.

As recompense for their travels, Berry and his companions were entertained royally, being able to compare the relative merits of Château Lafite 1878 and 1875 *chez* Cruse, 1904 Corton Grancey *chez* 'my dear old friend Louis Latour' and the 1880, 1884 and 1892 *chez* Perrier-Jouët. 'Off-duty' meals tended to conform to a pattern of Berry's beloved Champagne *nature* during, and as good a cognac as could be found after.

Charles Walter Berry records so much detail that few readers will fail to find some fact or judgment to titillate them on every page. From Beaujolais he records a ranking of the crus which suggests that St Amour and 'Chanes' (Chénas?) only fairly recently enjoyed anything like the *réclame* of the then top three villages Moulin-à-Vent, Fleurie and Morgon. From the Rhône he reports the recent demise of Château Grillet: 'The property belongs to an *avocat* who appears to take no pride in this estate . . . a thousand pities, say all wine lovers; but that is his affair.' In Marseille we learn how an 'oat-board' may be used to complain to a hotel's management about damp sheets. And from Sète we have a detailed account of the manufacture of French vermouth, so vital to the cocktails of the period.

This book is itself a cocktail, composed of a hundred and

one often disparate ingredients which Charles Walter Berry has done little to shake together. Read fifty years on, it is none the worse, and arguably even more entertaining, for that. It is a true period piece from which the modern wine lover can learn much.

JANCIS ROBINSON
May 1987

LETTER-PREFACE

from

H. WARNER ALLEN

4th July, 1935.

Dear Walter,

I cannot think why you have conferred on me the honour and pleasure of writing this preface. What can I say about your knowledge of wine? What can I say about that delicacy of taste, that sure judgment and that mature experience, which on the one hand enables you to perceive with prophetic divination the promise of a glorious maturity in the crudity of youth, and on the other hand impels you to spurt into wines, however highly thought of, if they do not rise to the true standard of excellence, the mitigating tastelessness of those windy waters which Mr. Chesterton so rightly condemns?

By a chance, just before I read the proofs of your last chapter, I picked up an ancient volume published nearly forty years ago—*The Works of Max Beerbohm*. In that fine flower of his pen, *Dandies and Dandies*, the one and only Max writes of Beau Brummell and tells of his derring-do. How he went to White's, to routs, to races; how he played battledore and shuttlecock in a moonlit garden; how he eloped with a young Countess from a ball at Lady Jersey's.

It was even whispered that he once, in the company of some friends, made as though he would wrench the knocker off the door of some shop. But these things he did, not, most certainly, for any exuberant love of life. Rather did he regard them as healthful exercise of the body and a charm against that corpulency which, in the end, caused his downfall.

That corpulency—the words call up an image of the Coffee Mill of 3, St. James Street where you to-day preside over the

[xiii]

finest wines in Europe and where nearly 150 years ago Brummell came not only to furnish his cellar but also to watch the inroads of the demon fat. In point of fact he seems to have resisted the enemy gallantly.

One would wish to hear Max's comments on Brummell's weight recorded in the Register of Berry Bros. & Co. In 1798 he starts gaily with 12 stone 4 lbs. despite the handicap of 'Boots and Frock'. It must have been a terrible moment when he passed the rubicon of 13 stone. On October 19th, 1801, in half-boots he weighed 13 stone 1 lb., but he was not easily to be defeated. Who can tell what dandiacal abstemiousness is betokened by the next entry in the register: April 20th 1802, 12 stone 5 lbs., still in half-boots.

Boots and Great Coat accounted for something in the 13 stone 10 lbs. which he weighed on November 16th, 1811, the Comet Year: evil times were near and four years later with the same impedimenta he had dropped to 12 stone 10 lb. In the following year he fled the country and the historian believes that he never returned from his exile. Your records show that he did indeed return, shorn of his glory, and for the first time weighing less than 12 stone. On July 26th, 1822, his weight in boots is given as only 10 stone 13 lbs., so cruelly had poverty and failure diminished his presence.

I cannot resist referring to another point of history. Long ago Augustin Filon, the faithful friend of Napoleon III and the Empress Eugenie and the tutor of the ill-fated Prince Imperial, told me that he had found conspiring on behalf of the Bonapartists among the best amusements of his life. How he would have loved the description of Napoleon III conspiring in your cellars with an English journalist over two good bottles. The picture of the future Emperor searching the bins and peeping into empty casks for an eavesdropping spy is delightful.

I do not think that anyone before you has made so complete a survey of the vineyards of France. Not even in French is there any book which provides the wine-lover with such a wealth of information. From experience I know how delightful are many of the wines you brought back with you from your tour. The discoveries that you made have been shared with your friends, and the French Government should at once confer on you its highest honours for the generosity with which you have spread abroad the glories of fine wines little known in this country.

Good wine needs no bush and your book needs no praise of mine to commend it to all good fellows the world over.

Your humble Servant in the Fellowship of Wine,

H. WARNER ALLEN

AUTHOR'S FOREWORD

THE difficulties of the preliminary arrangements attendant on such a tour as a Tour of the Vineyards of France, in search of wine, were not easily overcome. The wrench of leaving the office for so long had to be stoically faced, and then there was the difficulty of finding someone sufficiently interested and leisurely who could, or would accompany me.

Owing to an accident in 1917 I am precluded from driving myself and as my chauffeur could not be spared from home for so long a period, the most important point of all, in order to insure the pleasure and success of the tour, resolved itself on the choice of a genial and interested companion, having œnological propensities.

I set to work and invited, with all sorts of inducements, friends and friendly clients to accompany me, with the result that eventually I almost gave up in despair, for 'they all with one consent began to make excuse' . . . I will admit, invariably in a charming manner. This one said : 'I am building a house and therefore cannot leave.' Another had an invalid at home and could not quit. This one was expecting something to happen and could not be absent. The lure of the rod prevented others . . . that of the 'long tails' many another. The excuses indeed were legion, but through them all I could trace that dominating influence so forcibly portrayed in the twentieth century in the piercing and agonizing cry—'MY WIFE . . . WON'T LET ME'.

The desire to find one such companion for eight weeks was not to be gratified ; nevertheless, I suffered little on this account, as will be realised in the context. I had, as it were, a relay of 'chauffeurs', all genial, thoroughly companionable, and above all, keenly interested.

In compiling this record of these eight weeks I have had my

mind set on two fundamental purposes; to share any knowledge I may have gathered, and to do so in as simple and happy a way as possible. I therefore cordially invite any one who feels so disposed to join me in going over the ground again and sharing with me, not only the tasting and drinking of many a bottle of good wine, but also the pleasures and amusement of observation and reminiscences which occurred on the way.

It is my wish to take you, tolerant reader, day by day, whatever the weather; should you find the journey somewhat fatiguing I conjure you to take a rest at some of the 'milestones' and continue the journey when refreshed: if, however, the trail should prove irksome or monotonous, please forgive me for wearying you. I would, however, plead with you, out of the vinous consideration of your heart, not to throw away the 'ticket' but pass it on to someone who perhaps may find, if not amusement or interest, yet some few remarks on wines and vintages that may prove of service to him or her in making 'choice' through life's journey. Undoubtedly the names of many well-known wines and well-known shippers do not appear, in fact they are conspicuous by their absence. No slight is intended, for it was inevitable that on such a journey I could not find the time to see everyone, and this is a faithful record of each day's experience.

As a result of the publication of *Viniana* I received, and continue to do so, many a letter of regret and disappointment, a disappointment tinged with the taste of 'sour grapes'. 'Why, Oh! Why, Mr. Berry, did you tell us of these fine wines, knowing full well and with your tongue in your cheek that it is not possible to procure them? . . . you cause one's mouth to water, without the means of an antidote. . . . Was it kind?'

To these expressed regrets I had but one reply, explaining that I presumed to believe that many would have been glad to revel with me in the pleasures of a happy retrospect: this usually had the effect of appeasing them, especially if I could find a 'good old bottle' to partake of and enjoy with them.

With the 'amende honorable' on my mind and in order to provide information on French Wines and Brandies which are procurable, I have undertaken this tour, at the same time endeavouring to establish more firmly, if possible, the roots of this particular 'BERRY' in the soil of the Wine-producing areas of La Belle France.

At the close of each chapter will be found an epitome of vintages and suggestions, which I trust may prove useful.

In conclusion I would ask, and that sincerely, that when we are privileged to enjoy the greatest of GOD's gifts to mankind, that we join forces and echo with one of the greatest sons of France, to wit, François Rabelais—'Oh ! how good is GOD to give us of this juice.'

C. W. B.

BACCHUS

In *Viniana* I quoted Plutarch as follows :

'Bacchus was not more esteemed for being the first inventor of wine than for inventing the ivy crown, which so powerfully corrected its inebriating qualities.'

This gave rise to some little controversy ; first that I was incorrect in stating that the wreath was of ivy leaves whereas it was of vine leaves ; secondly, supposing the wreath was of ivy, what could have been its immediate bearing ?

I set to work to make some enquiries, the result of which resolved itself into the fact that there has been considerable dispute as to what the leaves actually were. I am still of the opinion that Plutarch knew what he was talking about ; for the easiest mistake for anyone to fall into (and he or she would do so without giving it a thought) would be that Bacchus, if he had a wreath of any kind, would surely have one of vine leaves.

I came across a book entitled *History of Ancient Wines* of which the following is an extract :

'Previously to the introduction of the second course, the guests were provided with chaplets of leaves or flowers, which they placed on their foreheads or temples, and occasionally also, on their cups. Perfumes were at the same time offered to such as chose to anoint their face and hands, or have their garlands sprinkled with them. This mode of adorning their persons, which was borrowed from the Asiatic nations, obtained so universally among the Greeks and Romans that, by almost every author after the time of Homer, it is spoken of as the necessary accompaniment of the feast. It is said to have originated from a belief that the leaves of certain plants, as the ivy, myrtle and laurel, or certain flowers, as the violet and rose, possessed the power of dispersing the fumes and counteracting the noxious effects of wine. On this account the ivy has always been sacred to Bacchus, and formed the basis of the wreaths with which his images, and the heads of his worshippers were encircled; but, being deficient in smell, it was seldom employed for festal garlands; and, in general, the preference was given to the myrtle, which, in addition to its cooling or astringent qualities, was supposed to have an exhilarating influence on the mind. On ordinary occasions the guests were contented with simple wreaths from the latter shrub; but, at their gayer entertainments, its foliage was entwined with roses and violets, or such other flowers as were in season, and recommended themselves by the beauty of their colours, or the fragrancy of their smell. Much taste was displayed in the arrangement of these garlands, which was usually confided to female hands; and as the demand for them was great, the manufacture and sale of them became a distinct branch of trade.

To appear in a disordered chaplet was reckoned a sign of inebriety; and a custom prevailed of placing a garland confusedly put together on the heads of such as were guilty of excess in their cups. Several passages of the Fabliaux show that, so late as the twelfth and thirteenth centuries, the above-mentioned decoration of the banquet was still in vogue; and in this country, the ceremony of crowning the wassail-bowl was retained to a comparatively recent period. At present the only relics of the usage in question that I am aware of, are to be found in those wreaths of ivy or flowers, which, in some countries, serve as the signs of taverns, or houses where wine is sold.'

In Lloyd's *Encyclopaedia* it is definitely stated that the garland of Bacchus was made of *either* vine leaves or ivy leaves.

It is well known that the Ancient Romans when at feast had placed in certain parts of the feasting chamber a Piscatorium, where, when over-feasted, they could empty their overloaded stomach by sickness and thus be ready to proceed with the feast. It may be that the Ivy represents much the same kind of idea.

An excess of alcoholic beverage could be corrected to a large degree by sickness, and such could and would be produced by decoction of Ivy. The emptying of the stomach would not clear the brain, which effect would possibly be hastened by intense sickness. As already indicated, the Ivy infusion produces intense sickness and sweating. It is likely, therefore, that these two qualities combined would relieve anyone who was suffering from alcoholic excess.

Further, excessive and continuous absorption of wine, especially new wine, and to a particular type of person, gives

[xxii]

acute rheumatism. Ivy decoction is used even to-day as a homeopathic remedy for this disorder.

Going back 500 years before Christ, when drugs were crude and mostly herbal, it seems quite a reasonable deduction that the garland around the head of Bacchus might have been Ivy, representative of a *correction* which he was able to give to those of his followers who had taken excess.

Under classical myths, I read the following :

'Bacchus figures in perennial youth with a crown of IVY or VINE leaves around his temples, and holding in his hand *a spear bound with* IVY.'

At the very kind suggestion of Mrs. Alice H. Henry, a daughter of the late Sir Lauder Brunton, I wrote to Doctor Cotton, the head of the Herbarium at Kew Gardens, to inquire if he could throw any light on the subject. I received a reply, together with a note by a member of the staff—Mr. N. Y. Sandwith. This note is very interesting, and I consider adds another point in favour of IVY leaves.

Mr. Sandwith writes that :

'The Ivy ($\kappa\iota\sigma\sigma\acute{o}s$) was always regarded by the classical Greeks as an inseparable adjunct of Dionysus (Bacchus). They even imagined that it was imported into Europe from Asia, along with the Bacchic cult. . . .'

and he continues :

'The "Bacchae" of Euripides is full of references to the Ivy, the Dappled Fawn Skin, and the Wild Women, which were regarded as the three sinister emblems of the alien Bacchus by all ascetic and conservative Greeks. Thus we even have the Greek epithet $\kappa\iota\sigma\sigma\acute{o}-\pi\lambda\eta\kappa\tau\sigma s$ which means "struck" or "frenzied" with the ivy-rod of Bacchus (*i.e.* with wine). The Ivy was sometimes actually called $\Delta\iota\sigma\nu\acute{v}\sigma\iota\sigma\nu$ and the god was sometimes called $\kappa\iota\sigma\sigma\acute{o}s$, Ivy ! It is therefore obvious that Ivy and Intoxication came to be regarded as inseparable concepts. An Ivy-bush came to be a common tavern sign and hence the proverb—"good wine needs no bush".'

In the Vatican there is a colossal statue of ANTINOUS the favourite attendant of the Emperor Hadrian (A.D. 117-138).

It is in the character of Bacchus and is undoubtedly IVY-CROWNED.

THE WISDOM OF OTHERS

ADAM

'IN THE Island of Madagascar . . . the natives believe that the four rivers of paradise consisted of milk, wine, honey, and oil : and that Adam, who required no sustenance, having drunk of the wine and tasted of the fruits, contrary to the command of God, was driven from the Garden and subjected to the punishments which were thus entailed upon him and his posterity.'

SAMUEL MOREWOOD

DAVID

(*d.* 1015 B.C.)

'HE CAUSETH the grass to grow for the cattle, and herb for the service of man : that he may bring forth food out of the earth ;
And wine that maketh glad the heart of man, and oil to make his face to shine, and bread which strengtheneth man's heart.'

PSALM 104, V. 14-15

SOLOMON

(*d.* 953 B.C.)

'I AM come into my garden, my sister, my spouse : I have gathered my myrrh with my spice ; I have eaten my honeycomb with my honey : I have drunk my wine with my milk : eat, O friends : drink, yea, drink abundantly, O beloved.'

SOLOMON'S SONG 5, I

[XXV]

HOMER

(*d. circa* 850 B.C.)

'THE WEARY find new strength in generous Wine.'

PYTHAGORAS

(*d.* 500 B.C.)

'PYTHAGORAS, WITH all his stoicism, is said not to have been insensible to a well regulated indulgence in the use of wine.'

MOREWOOD

DARIUS

(*d. circa* 486 B.C.)

'HE DESIRED no greater encomium should be engraved on his tomb, than that he was able to drink a large quantity of Wine, without being inebriated.'

ATHENAEUS, Lib. X.

AESCHYLUS

(*d.* 456 B.C.)

'AESCHYLUS (IF Plutarch in his Symposiacs merit any Faith) drank composing ; and drinking, composed.'

RABELAIS

SOCRATES

(*d.* 399 B.C.)

'SOCRATES TAKES an opportunity of calling for Wine, and proposes drinking it in small glasses, not that he was averse to a liberal and

[xxvi]

free use of Wine on that occasion, but that by drinking small glasses, they would be gradually more animated, and incited to repeat them more frequently, by which means they should continue revived, and longer happy together. This he beautifully compares to repeated gentle showers, which enliven plants and flowers, raise them, display their various beauties and diffuse their fragrancy, which by heavy and repeated rains droop, lose all their virtues, and are oppressed ; as the body and mind are, by repeated draughts in large glasses.'

BARRY

HIPPOCRATES

(*d.* 377 B.C.)

'HIPPOCRATES, THE father of physic, recommends a cheerful glass.'

MOREWOOD

'HIPPOCRATES WAS the first who applied Wine to medical uses.'

BARRY

PLATO

(*d.* 347 B.C.)

'PLATO, WHO strictly restrains the use of it, and severely censures the excess, says that nothing more excellent or valuable than Wine was ever granted by God to mankind.'

BARRY

DIOGENES

(*d. circa* 323 B.C.)

'DIOGENES, THOUGH so rigid a philosopher in self-denial, drank wine with more than common gratification : and though he threw away

[xxvii]

his water bowl as superfluous, when he beheld a man drinking water
out of his hands at a brook, yet, it is affirmed, that he never refused the
wine goblet, when presented to him at another's expense.'

MOREWOOD

ALEXANDER

(*d.* 323 B.C.)

'ALEXANDER, IN his Indian expedition at the siege of Petra, directed
thirty pits to be made as reservoirs for snow, which were covered with
straw, to defend it against the external air : with this his wine and
water was cooled.'

CHARLES MYTELLEN, Apud Athen. Lib. III, Cap. 21

ASCLEPIADES

(Lived about 100 B.C.)

'ASCLEPIADES, A physician, who practised at Rome, ninety-six years
before the Christian era, successfully administered wine, with every
remedy, to all his patients, and wrote a treatise on its virtues, in which
he observed that the Gods had not bestowed a more valuable gift on
man.'

MOREWOOD

LUCULLUS

(*d.* 57 B.C.)

'LUCULLUS . . .WHEN on his return from his Asiatic conquests, he
bestowed, as a donative to his soldiers, above a hundred thousand
Amphoræ of Greek wine.'

BARRY

CICERO

(*d.* 43 B.C.)

'NOR DO I refer this so much to the gratification of the palate, as to its more salutary influence on your FOOD and SPIRITS, and disengaging your mind from any anxious cares : These are most effectually promoted by a free conversation ; nor is it ever more delightfully animated than in these convivial suppers ; on which account, we have more justly distinguished them by that *name* than the Greeks, by a term only expressive of the *Powers of Wine*, as we then indeed enjoy life together.'

CICERO, Lib. IX. EP. XXIV. 3

HORACE

(*d.* 27 B.C.)

'THUS EVERY guest may drink and fill
As much or little as he will ;
Exempted from the Bedlam rules
Of roaring prodigals and fools.
Whether, in merry mood, or whim,
He fills his goblet to the brim ;
Or better pleased, to let it pass
Is cheerful with a moderate glass.'

HORAT. SAT. Lib. II. VI. 67

PLUTARCH

(*d.* 46 A.D.)

'PLUTARCH NOT only expressed the same sentiments (as Plato), but attempts to explain its mechanic operation in producing these effects, by gradually opening some peculiar canals, and avenues to the soul, which then gently admit some of the milder parts of the

[xxix]

Wine into them, which if intemperately taken would be irregularly
diffused through the whole body.'

SYMPOSIA, Lib. IV

SENECA

(*d.* 65 A.D.)

'SENECA THOUGHT the senses ought not to be overcome, but the cares
of life might be lightened, by an exhilaration of the spirits.'

MOREWOOD

ST. PAUL

(*d. circa* 67 A.D.)

'DRINK NO longer water, but use a little wine for thy stomach's sake
and thine often infirmities.'

I TIMOTHY 5. 23

PLINY

(*d.* 79 A.D.)

'VINUM SETINUM was particularly esteemed for its light, grateful and
permanent qualities : and Pliny, among other praises which he bestows
on it, says it was the favourite Wine of Augustus ; nor is it im-
probable that this is the wine so much recommended by St. Paul to
Timothy, for strengthening the stomach ; as these vineyards were
but at a small distance from the Appii Forum, and the ruins of the
tavern, where he first met his friends from Rome, are still remaining,
and have been often mentioned by late travellers.'

BARRY 1775

[xxx]

GALEN

(Lived *circa* 140 A.D.)

'GALEN, ALTHOUGH he called wine the nurse of old age, was against its abuse.'

MOREWOOD

PALLADIUS

(*d. circa* 400 A.D.)

'PALLADIUS GIVES several particular forms, which were used by the Greeks, of improving the flavour, colour, and strength of their Wines and to give to new wine the qualities of old wine. He mentions one so effectually useful to this purpose, that it was said to be communicated to the Cretans by the Pythean oracle; in which, among other ingredients, the Hepatic Aloes has a considerable share.'

Lib. XI. DE RE RUSTICA

RHAZES

(*d.* 932 A.D.)

'RHASES, A Mahommetan, says no liquor is equal to good wine.'

MOREWOOD

OMAR

(*d. circa* 1310 A.D.)

'AND MUCH as Wine has played the Infidel,
And robbed me of my Love of Honour—well,
I often wonder what the Vintners buy
One half so precious as the Goods they sell.'

OMAR KHAYYÁM

[xxxi]

PETRARCH

(*d.* 1372 A.D.)

'WHEN PETRARCH urged URBAN V. to remove to Rome, his Holiness found the Cardinals opposed to leaving Avignon. Demanding their reason, they replied,

"Il n'y a point de vin de Beaune en Italie, et sans vin de Beaune notre vie sera malheureuse."

They speak the truth, said Petrarch, for they adore it "comme le nectar des dieux ".'

WELD

HAFIZ

(*d. circa* 1390 A.D.)

'I AM neither a judge, nor a priest, nor a censor, nor a lawyer; why should I forbid the use of wine?

'Do not be vexed at the trifles of the world; drink, for it is a folly for a wise man to be afflicted.

'That poignant liquor, which the zealot calls the mother of sins, is pleasanter and sweeter to me than the kisses of a maiden.

'The only friends who are free from care are the goblet of wine and a book of odes.

'The tulip is acquainted with the faithlessness of the world; for, from the time that it blows till it dies, it holds the cup in its hand.

'Give me wine! Wine that shall subdue the strongest; that I may for a time forget the cares and troubles of the world.

'The roses have come, nor can anything afford so much pleasure as a goblet of wine.

'The enjoyments of life are vain; bring wine, for the trappings of the world are perishable.'

[xxxii]

HENRY V

(*d.* 1415 A.D.)

'THE STRONG and foaming wine of Champagne was found so injurious that HENRY V. was obliged, after the battle of Agincourt, to forbid its use in his army, except when tempered with water.'

LETTER OF F. MICHEL, T. G. SHAW

RABELAIS

(*d.* 1553 A.D.)

'BOTTLE ! WHOSE Mysterious Deep
Do's ten thousand secrets keep,
With attentive ear I wait ;
Ease my mind, and speak my Fate.
Soul of joy !   Like Bacchus, we
More than India gain by thee.
Truths unborn thy Juice reveals,
Which futurity conceals.
Antidote to Frauds and Lyes,
Wine, that mounts us to the Skies,
May thy Father Noah's Brood
Like him drown, but in thy Flood.
Speak, so may the Liquid Mine
Of Rubies, or of Diamonds, shine.
Bottle ! whose Mysterious Deep,
Do's ten thousand secrets keep,
With attentive ear I wait ;
Ease my mind, and speak my Fate.'

SHAKESPEARE

(*d.* 1616 A.D.)

'O, THAT men should put an enemy in their mouths, to steal away their brains !'

OTHELLO, II, 3

THOS. RANDOLPH

(*d.* 1630 A.D.)

'SACKE IS the life, soul and spirit of a man, the fire which Prometheus stole, not from Jove's kitchen, but his wine-cellar, to encrease the native peat and radicall moisture, without which we are but drousie dust or dead clay. This is nectar, the very Nepenthe the Gods were drunk with: 'tis this that gave Gannymede beauty, Hebe youth, to Jove his heaven and eternity. Doe you thinke Aristotle drank perry? or Plato Cyder? Doe you think Alexander had ever conquered the world if he had bin sober? He knew the force and valour of Sacke; that it was the best armour, the best encouragement, and that none could be a Commander that was not double drunk with wine and ambition.'

ARISTIPPUS, 'THE JOVIAL PHILOSOPHER', 1630

DEAN ALDRICH

(*d.* 1710 A.D.)

'THERE ARE, if I do rightly think,
Five reasons why a man should drink:
Good wine, a friend, or being dry—
Or any other reason why.'

VOLTAIRE

(*d.* 1778 A.D.)

'HE (CANDIDE) said to Pangloss: "Oh! get me a little wine and oil; I am dying".'

IN SEARCH OF WINE

A tour of the Vineyards of France

CHAPTER I

DOVER TO REIMS

ON the 18th day of September in the year of Grace 1934, we left Dover by the Townshend Ferry, with our baggage tucked in the small car, which, to agree with its number plate, we christened the 'Little Auk'. I would advise this way in preference to all others, and I say this advisedly from experience, as it saved much tribulation.

On the way over, Neptune being in a very considerate mood, I thought I would while away a part of the time in an endeavour to solve the crossword puzzle in the day's issue of the *Morning Post*, when, on turning over the pages of the paper I caught sight of a column headed in large print—'WINE 3300 YEARS OLD'. I called out to my friend Lorne, who was my first companion and chauffeur—'Here's a pretty to-do . . . here we are in search of the wines of 1934, yet barely made, and the first thing that is brought to our notice is wine some three thousand, three hundred years old, which His Majesty, Pharaoh Akhenaten himself must have enjoyed with his friends, or maybe by himself.'

'By the way, Lorne,' I said, 'have I ever shown you wine a couple of thousand years old ? No ? Well if we survive this tour, you must remind me and I will show it to you.' The wine I referred to came from the collection of the celebrated Dr. Sambon, the Cancer Research Expert. It was found, in a small amphora, which unfortunately was broken, in the cellar of Florus' villa, which was destroyed in the memorable earthquake of Pompeii in A.D. 63.

'It has retained its flavour and character unchanged,' said Dr. Sambon, 'indeed it has the peculiar aroma of the modern Campanian wines which I know well, but, though it certainly is the residue of some choice wine of rare vintage, it would be difficult

B.W.

to decide whether it is oldest Falernian, or some of Florus' own product from his Vesuvian vineyards.'

Now, I must introduce Lorne to you . . . his surname is Campbell, a 'Smith' from the other side of the Tweed, and such a good one. He is a young and intelligent Scot, full of enthusiasm for the lore of old wine and for the knowledge of newer vintages. It was most appropriate that Lorne, as I will refer to him, should have joined me ; for it was with his father, as young men, that we lived together in Bordeaux in the years 1891-1892 ; each of us endeavouring to assimilate as much knowledge as possible appertaining to the Vine and its culture, and incidentally of the French language. Where I failed miserably, young Campbell, as he was then—now, Colonel Ian Campbell, C.B.E., T.D., succeeded gloriously, as did his two eminent brothers, now Members of Parliament—

Vice-Admiral Gordon Campbell, V.C., D.S.O., M.P.
('the mystery V.C.').
Sir Edward T. Campbell, M.P.

Colonel Campbell is one of the leading lights of the Wine Trade, and the benefit of his erudition is enjoyed by ninety-nine per cent. of those interested in this ancient and interesting pursuit.

I so well remember that it was in the year 1892 that we were in Bordeaux, for it was in January of that year that the Duke of Clarence died, and I attended a memorial service in the Protestant Church in Bordeaux. In the evening I went to a dinner party, which had been previously arranged, at which were a number of ladies—young ladies, and others not so young. In the course of the dinner I was asked, in French, what I had been doing during the day ; I explained in the best way I could in broken French that I had 'assisté' at the memorial service.

'Were many there,' asked the lady of the house. 'Oh yes,' I said, . . . 'All the English Colony I think, and I sat "au derrière d'une charmante jeune fille".' At that there was loud and uproarious laughter. My mistake was explained to me, so now you know why I remember the year 1892 in Bordeaux so well.

We duly arrived in CALAIS . . . somehow or other I never arrive in Calais unless I think of 'MARY'. She evidently had a

[2]

'tender heart' in spite of the fact that, at school we were taught to learn of her as 'Bloody' Mary.

These thoughts soon passed, owing to the insistence of the Customs' Officer requiring the largest and most inaccessible trunk to be opened for inspection. However, we had nothing to declare and therefore feared, as the Yorkshireman would say, 'Nowt'.

Before proceeding on our way, we thought it well, not only to fill up the Little Auk with petrol and oil, but to attend to our requirements as well. We therefore made for the dining-room of the Terminus Hotel, and partook of a light 'déjeuner'.

We did not wish for anything out of the way to drink, so were content with a White Graves, which was passable, especially when helped with Perrier Water. I glanced round at other tables and noticed that most diners were indulging in wine, either Graves, Claret, Burgundy, and, at one table, Cyder.

At the next table to us they were all drinking Claret : Julien (for we knew his name and remembered the Continental greetings on the Quay) with a Padré, his wife and three daughters ... uncle Julien was in for a lively time I could see.

The first slight annoyance was when I removed a considerable piece of cord, or thick string from my mouth, inadvertently left in the omelette. We had a long time to wait for the Salad, but it was so good that we remarked—'Better late than never.' I then introduced a 'cheese' to Lorne that made him open his eyes ... it was given to me by that excellent connoisseur and gourmet, Mr. H. C. Levis. I beg of you to try it. . . . 'exquis ! ! '

> Half—good Roquefort⎫ with a suspicion of
> Half—good butter   ⎭   Armagnac.

Mix this all up together into a thick paste (being careful not to add too much Armagnac, which will spoil it) then spread it on hot toast, or biscuit (we had the former) and it would have made the heart of Lucullus rejoice. We then had a cup of coffee which the boy spilt on the cloth. This simple incident reminded Lorne of an occasion in Cologne when he was there with his father, a boy had a similar misfortune. The head waiter was furious, so the Colonel remarked, as he would do (so unlike some Colonels)

[3]

that mistakes would happen : 'But', said the head waiter, 'they *must not* happen here.' And the poor lad was ejected. (How typically German.)

We quit the dining-room, more complete inside, but having left about one hundred francs behind. As we left the Quay we could not help but remark on the large number of anglers, with lines and nets. I have often watched them in order to while away the time. . . . I suppose they do catch something sometimes, but I have never seen a fish landed here by rod and line.

On the way to ARRAS, where we intended to stay the night, we soon found ourselves in the country ; pasture and arable land ; plenty of roots . . . 'good for partridges' said Lorne . . . terrible fellows, these peaceable Scots, always wanting to kill something ! I am sure he wished he had a gun handy.

In passing through ARDRES, we were struck with a sudden sight of cherished familiar colours, but we did not stop to inquire the reason . . . nevertheless, in passing, it was pleasing.

Red, White and Blue. . . .

A White Horse, led by a man in Blue, and ridden by a boy in Red. I wonder what it meant. . . . I wish I had asked.

All that we noticed about this town were the red tiles of the houses, and the number of cafés, at the tables of which many men were consuming much beer, but beer had no particular interest for us.

Lorne thought he saw a Magpie, and seeing him somewhat elated I inquired the reason : he was shocked at my ignorance. 'Don't you know', said he, 'that that bird, the Magpie, is the bird of the Campbells ? '

I didn't, I confessed, and told him they were welcome to it. We shall hear more of them later on.

'What village was that?' I asked, as we passed between a number of small dwellings. 'That', said Lorne, 'is Courbet.' How we laughed over this. . . . We passed through several Courbets, and it was some time before we realised that, instead of the name of the village or town, it was only the name of the Advertising Agent ! such as we see in this country—'Boro', etc., etc. However, there was a fine view to greet and to please us

[4]

from this so-called 'Courbet'. I suppose it is the job of Courbet to look for fine positions ! !

We then reached ST. OMER ; what memories as we passed down the Avenue and saw the Trench Mortars . . . and a few miles further on, the village of ARQUES, with a street bearing the name—'Rue MISS CAVELL'.

At WITTES, standing at the door of a very old and dilapidated apology for a house, stood an old and, no doubt venerable dame, for over the door on an old wooden sign were the words—'MOTHER—so and so' but Lorne was driving so quickly that I could not see what particular Mother she was . . . evidently some dear old soul who had well tended our Tommies during the distressful times.

At AIRE there were still many ruins to be seen ; but at LAMBRES most of the town had been rebuilt. All seemed happy and prosperous here ; men, women and children hard at work in the fields.

At BOURECQ and at LILLERS the scene changes, for we have coal mines to the right.

As we passed through the village of CHOCQUES our thoughts paid a flying visit to Peckham, for there was on a bicycle the fattest, smiling, rosy-faced boy I have ever seen. 'Grow fat, and laugh' . . . he looked like it indeed !

There is a military cemetery here, the passing of which never fails to give a feeling of sadness.

'Courbet again', says Lorne, 'like "HOMMES" in the Gare which I once mistook for the name of the station ! ' 'I will tell you one better than that', I rejoined. 'Years ago (in fact 1891) when I was living in Bordeaux with your father, I had been invited to spend the week-end at the Château Le Prieuré, near Blaye. I was instructed to take a ticket for St. Paul, but to be careful to change at St. André de Cubzac. All went well until we arrived at St. André ; I looked out of the window of the carriage (such as it was) but could see no name, while the porter, or guard, was calling out—"Comme vous voudrez" or something like that. Well said I to myself, he certainly is not calling out "St. André de Cubzac" and I settled back as comfortably as possible, to carry on to the next station, when, hearing a tap at the window I saw

Louis, the son of my host, who had come down to meet me. "You must change here," he said : I explained that I had been told to change at St. André de Cubzac ; this was not that, but "comme 'quelque chose'." How heartily he laughed, but he had me out in time, and a jolly good week-end I spent.'

On through BETHUNE, where they are still rebuilding ; what vicissitudes this town has passed through . . . was it not in 1710 that the town was taken by Marlborough. However, it is French again since the Treaty of Utrecht. I have an old bottle on which is a glass button bearing the words—

I H

P A X

1713

Naturally this came to my mind, and my friend Lorne had to put up with a serious dissertation, while endeavouring to point out to me the interesting old fourteenth century Belfry. We continued through the small village of AIX-NOULETTE, where a passing remark—'how pitiable' describes what we thought of it.

We then made a slight détour in order to pay respects to the Military Cemeteries, inaugurated by His Majesty—the approach was disgraceful, but on the summit we were regaled by a lovely view.

These cemeteries are indeed beautiful in their simplicity . . . we were quite struck by a large notice at the entrance, as follows :

'No visitors allowed the worse for drink ; with dogs or with bicycles.' Very excellent prohibitions.

Through SOUCHEZ, with more of these sinister reminders ever before us. . . . Vimy Ridge on the left ; a large German cemetery with the sombre Black Crosses and the old concrete emplacements on the right.

In the distance we have a view of Arras and enter by St. Catherine, going straight to our hotel before a later tour of inspection. Always lock your car, is good advice, for, from a window of the hotel, on my way down, I noticed two men endeavouring to open it. 'Which way shall we go?' asked Lorne. 'If you have no objection I should like to go across to the railway station in order to see a few of the spots I knew so well in 1917.'

On the corner house of one little street we noticed the words 'Cosy Corner', and on the window sill, just as it was left—

1 D.C.L.I. 6 PLATOON
Hair Cutting Saloon.

Rather pathetic, wasn't it !

Somewhat hungry we soon returned to the hotel to dine ; the omelette aux Champignons, and the Poulet were well cooked and served on highly decorated plates, but the wine list was a very poor affair ; there seemed to be no idea of order, for under 'Vin d'Anjou' was listed—Pommery 1930 ! !

We contented ourselves with a bottle of Blanc de Blanc . . . it was quite cheap at 25 francs, and proved very good . . . a clean wine without any apparent acidity.

The mustard was too full of vinegar and garlic was predominant, but the Blanc de Blanc washed the offence away.

At the next table to us was seated a young local swell . . . he had in front of him two empty beer bottles, and was then attacking a bottle of Red Wine, which, by the expression on his face, must have been sour. The thought passed my mind that he would probably want more beer to wash it down, and he did !

The Fine de la Maison was full of caramel and decidedly 'woody', and to cap it all, the coffee was full of chicory.

After a stroll, and a little disgruntled, we returned to the hotel and retired to bed . . . a good spacious bedroom, with bathroom, the door of which would not shut (not that I particularly wanted it to), the same applied to one of the large windows.

In spite of the noise of much rain during the night, I was up at seven o'clock, and well refreshed after a cold bath.

We were in for a good auspicious time I thought, for had I not dreamt of a black cat ; awakened to the Silvery Cambridge bells of the Hotel de Ville, and when getting out of bed almost trodden on a spider scampering across the bedroom.

The first place we passed when leaving ARRAS was BEAURAINS. It was still raining, and a gloomy thought reminded me that it was on the roof of a dilapidated house at Beaurains that I was picked up unconscious after a parachute descent in April 1917. Near ST. QUENTIN we were more intimately reminded of days

[7]

now passed, by the gun emplacements and the still standing Nissen huts.

At LE MESNIL the tree stumps told their tale ; the musings of which were dispensed by a strong smell of roast chestnuts at VERMAND.

It was now raining very hard as we passed by HOLNON, where the roads were flooded, and it continued to do so as we crossed through ST. QUENTIN. Here we experienced some little difficulty in finding the way . . . road signs were certainly wanting, so much so that, in spite of the heavy rain I was obliged to quit the car to inquire the direction. In the best French I could muster I made the inquiry and was answered in perfect English, my bene- factor adding that he was frequently asked the same question by motorists passing that way. We proceeded, but the downpour was like a deluge, and it was only with difficulty that we could see the roadway.

Nearing CRÉPY we saw two Magpies—this meant 'bonheur' I told Lorne, and surely, before long, the clouds seemed to be breaking. I had to explain to Lorne about the Magpies . . . even he, a Campbell, did not know their significance. . . .

1 Pie . . . . RIEN.
2 Pies . . . BONHEUR.
3   ,, . . . MALHEUR.
4   ,, . . . MARIAGE.
5   ,, . . . MORT.
6   ,, . . . CIEL.
7   ,, . . ENFER. . . .

so we must be on the lookout.

At CRÉPY we made a détour, for, to the left of the village is to be found the emplacement of one of Germany's Big Bertha Guns, intended to shell Paris during the War. It was a wonderful sight and a marvellous engineering feat, but the one thing that struck me most was the effect of a direct hit by a French shell, which demolished this warfare giant. We approached the place down a delightful cutting, through a long wood. The emplace- ment itself was fed by a light railway and the actual construction was 'enormous'. The bed of the emplacement was flooded, the concrete surrounds were of great thickness ; one could see by the missing iron nuts and rivets that souvenir hunters had been busy. They must have been weary of their booty, for one iron nut alone would have been of great weight. Serve them right, was the thought which passed through my mind.

The rain had stopped and we continued over the valley of the Aisne to LAON on the approach of which we had a fine view with Notre Dame on the Hill. The ruins of FESTIEUX brought the memory of horrors very near to us, but we carried on through such war time places as BERRY AU BAC with its new church and terrible crater.

At LA NEUVILLE it was raining again, and the numerous war signs were somewhat depressing, but at CHAUFFOUR the sun tried to shine, evidently causing Lorne to express the fact that he was beginning to feel hungry. Sunshine apparently has the effect of sharpening up everything, even the appetite.

Passing through LA NEUVILLETTE which still wore the deep stains of war, we reached REIMS, having passed along the glorious Chemin des Dames.

REIMS ; what thoughts ! I must admit that its martyrdom for the moment crowded out the thoughts of the fine wines we had come in search of.

In material damage during the war ; eighty millions sterling would not cover it ; and Oh ! how many a brave citizen laid down his life for his country. However, this is not the time to ponder on such things, we must go on to our hotel, the Lion d'Or, where we had a little argument about the rooms, which was appeased by the production on my part of a letter from the Management stating that accommodation had been reserved. Otherwise, I fear we should have fared badly. We desired to do little else than wash and take our déjeuner.

On entering the Restaurant we found, seated at a table next to the one we were to occupy, Mr. and Mrs. R. Sterling Clark, who had arrived that day from Paris. Right glad I was to see them and to look forward to their company into the Champagne districts.

Mr. Clark I had known for many years, and had learned how to appreciate the real interest he took in fine wines, not only in fine wines . . . an excellent store of which he possesses, but also in the entertaining 'small' wines of good quality which one comes across in various parts of the Wine-growing areas of France.

Mrs. Clark I had not met before . . . this introduction proved to be the first of those great pleasures which were in store for me. I was a little perturbed in mind for a moment ; I admit this, as 'open confession is good for the soul', but any misgivings were quickly dispelled by the intelligent interest the good lady took in the surroundings, as well as in the fine wines we were to partake of.

For déjeuner we had an excellent sole, and a very tender tournedos, which were washed down to the tune of a bottle of 1929 Crémant de Cramant, recommended by both Mr. and Mrs. Clark. It was excellent, soft and exquisite . . . we thoroughly enjoyed it. I delight in these white grape wines with little mousse.

With the coffee . . . a small glass of Delamain, 1870 Grande Fine ; that also was better than we were expecting, so we were in a very good frame of mind to set out on our mission, without delay.

Déjeuner was hardly finished when I was called to the telephone to hear the voice of my good friend, Louis Budin, of the house of Messieurs·Perrier-Jouët et Cie, insisting that I should come along with my friends ; he would show us the countryside and we were to stop and partake of dinner with him.

This indeed was an auspicious start, and off we went.

To those who read I shall hope to impart the various items of knowledge and interest in the same way and sequence as I gathered them, and not in any way to attempt to write a history on Champagne ; although somewhat different from stereotyped procedure I hope to make it my attitude throughout.

CHAPTER II

CHAMPAGNE

IMMEDIATELY taking advantage of our good fortune we hastened on to EPERNAY, lying in a pleasant valley. On our left we passed the Montagne de Reims, with the famous growths of Verzenay, Bouzy, etc. Monsieur Budin greeted us and immediately forgot his business, and placed himself graciously at our disposal.

We were then shown the different species of grapes, which were now being gathered, the vintage being in full swing. Here were the Pinot, the predominate vine . . . there were the Black Pinot and the Meunier, also a Pinot : this, however, is not a variety to give quality, but a large quantity. In the first growths there are no Meunier . . . in the second growths the best slopes are planted with Pinot Noir, the others with Meunier. In the third growths there is nothing but Meunier.

South of EPERNAY we find the White grapes, the famous Chardonnay, or White Pinot . . . this is also found on the celebrated slopes of the famous Montrachet. At Cramant the soil is of chalk . . . the vines are stumpy in order to allow the plants to absorb more heat from the ground.

In Messieurs Perrier-Jouët's establishment here, we found a large number of workers picking out any faulty grapes, as is customary, and discarding them, so that the clean fruit alone goes to the pressoir . . . no less than 36,000 kilos of grapes go through during the day. The result of this pressing is divided and classified, the premier cuve representing the best quality, after which follow the 1er Taille and the 2me Taille : the residue is then pressed again to supply juice for the peasants and workmen. This is blended with a similar juice derived from black grapes, making a red wine, quite drinkable for them.

In all this work I noticed that only wooden implements were used so that the juice should not come in contact with metal of any kind. During this time the working hours are very long, the heavy and costly machinery being in motion for only about fourteen days. For the remainder of the year it is idle, there being no further use for it. Such a position must necessarily add to the cost of production. .

After all the juice has been extracted the residue of skins and stalks pressed tightly together resembles a mass like cow cake, which could be cut in slabs. This is distilled for 'Marc' and is an old practice in Champagne, as well as in Bourgogne and elsewhere. This Marc is much appreciated by the peasants.

After distillation, the residue is used to 'dress' the vineyards.

The quantity of wine made this year is enormous, in fact too much . . . of the quality we look for good results, though it is a little early yet to justify any definite opinion.

That the wine is healthy is unquestionable as the vines and the fruit were free from disease.

As the grapes are pressed, the juice flows and is pumped at the same time into cuves, where it remains for about 10 to 12 hours. It is then drawn off into small casks or barriques . . . after 24 hours it will be found to be in full fermentation. These casks are then moved as quickly as possible to a resting place in order that the wine should settle before being blended in large cuvées. During removal the spile must be removed to allow the gas caused by fermentation to escape.

Once safely in their chais, the casks are left bung uppermost, with a vine leaf over the bung-hole, secured down by a stone, thus allowing the ferment, if any, to escape, and preventing any dust from entering and coming into contact with the wine : the casks being filled up as soon as the fermentation has stopped.

In the February following, the blending into large cuvées takes place. As soon as the operation has been satisfactorily completed, the wine is drawn off again into barriques, where it remains until the month of May, when it is bottled.

The art of blending is the principal factor governing the production of fine Champagne wine, and in this respect each particular firm has its secret ! All White grape would not be successful, although the finest quality is said to be from the wine made in the somewhat small area in which the Pinot-Blanc is planted—notably at Cramant, Avize and Mesnil—and yet what delightful wines one can enjoy in the country . . . those known as the 'Blanc de Blanc'; for instance . . . that delectable bottle we enjoyed at luncheon at Mr. Clark's instigation. These wines do not travel very well. They lose, somewhat, their limpidity, and further (a great advantage in my personal opinion) they are not nearly so 'mousseux'. You will therefore see the necessity of blending the wine from Black grapes with that of White, and it is the shipper's art that comes into commission, to know what to blend and in what proportion. Incidentally, the 'White' is much more costly, so that in inexpensive wines one must not look for much of it.

The White grape it is said—for elegance; the Black grape for body. In the Marne area 80 per cent. is planted Black grape, and the 20 per cent. balance with the White variety. This information I gathered at Cramant, but I must refrain from tiring you with more about the actual finishing of the wine until we come into contact with it.

There had been heavy rain during the morning, such as we had experienced during our journey from ARRAS . . . this had delayed the gathering. However, it was clear again, and the vendangeurs were at work. Too much rain would be a calamity, so everyone is hoping for sunshine to-morrow.

Monsieur Budin spoke of the difficulty experienced in some quarters with the famous 1911 Wines. We all remember how good they were—were, alas, as they are now practically non-existent! I think one of the finest wines I have tasted, that is Champagne Wine, was the Perrier-Jouët 1911. Those who have read *Viniana* will know what I thought of it, and now for the first time I learned from Monsieur Budin himself of the difficulties that were experienced, especially with the White grape areas. It would appear that there was too much sugar, that is, natural sugar in the wine, and it became necessary to give the greatest care to the blending of the cuves. So the life of a proprietor of vineyards at Cramant (White grape) is not all 'couleur de rose'.

As we motored by in this area we noticed the Heidsieck vineyards, where the large baskets of grapes were being brought in. On the left were those of Messieurs G. H. Mumm et Cie., and further on those of Messieurs Moët and Chandon. In each instance, I remember, I remarked how few were the very old vines. For choice, and without prejudice I would select the vineyards at Cramant, where Messieurs Perrier-Jouët certainly have a large proportion on the most favoured slopes.

I used to love to see the patient old oxen plodding along, as they do up the Douro, but now, to my disappointment, our old friend the horse is displacing them.

We now stopped at a vineyard, and at Monsieur Budin's suggestion we alighted in order to have a few friendly words with the gatherers, old and young alike, of both sexes, at work.

There were something like 250 Italians at work, some picking, some carrying, others sorting, etc., etc., and our host assured us that he had little or no trouble with them. They came year by year, evidently in the same way as the hop-pickers do in our country.

Their last night was a great gala affair, when a dance was arranged and they danced to the accordion until the early hours of the morning. This was at one of the beautiful vineyards at Cramant, and Monsieur Budin bade us take notice of its aspect. It was a fine hill, finely situated. On the crest were woods, following down the slopes were the vines, and on the level where the vines would not succeed were to be seen fields of corn. The soil was mostly chalk, but Messieurs Perrier-Jouët, in conformity with most of the proprietors of fine vineyards, in order to increase the virtue thereof, added quantities of 'compost' as a covering ; this being a special mixture of clay and manure. Being of a somewhat inquisitive nature, I began to make inquiries as to the vines . . . how long they would bear good fruit, etc. : in answer to many questions I gathered that after three years they would expect about half a crop, and even with the third vintage the quality would not be what was desired ; so that, when the vine is young the quality of the wine is not so very good.

At ten years they are considered to be at their best, and will last on without deterioration to any extent, up to twenty-five or thirty years.

Five per cent. of the vineyard was replanted each year, making an average life of, say, twenty years.

We continued our way absorbingly interested in all we saw. Our host pointed to the direction of HAUTVILLERS where the famous monk, Dom Pérignon lies buried, yet his memory lives as fresh and sparkling as ever.

Monsieur Budin explained to us that the remarkable thing about the blind monk was that he would arrange his blends by tasting the fruit itself, and not the juice as is customary . . . 'I should fail there sadly' he added. I, more or less out of fun, suggested he would have no difficulty in placing the juices of grape in their proper order, and be able to tell which was which. He said—'I will tell you of one incident that did occur . . . I would not have mentioned it had you not brought up the question.' Then he told us, in all modesty, explaining that, after all it could not be difficult . . . how an old peasant brought to him one day three baskets of grapes, exactly alike, and asked him to say what he thought of them. He tasted the grapes and after careful consideration, made his classification . . . 1, 2, 3 . . . No. 1 . . . Monsieur Budin placed as an ungrafted Pinot—No. 2 . . . an Hybrid, and No. 3 . . . a variety of Chablis Pinot, the origin of which was not very clear : this particular plant had been studied for years by the peasant in his little 'champ d'expériences'.

Monsieur Budin was correct and, as he acknowledged, rather surprised but very pleased, as it was the first time that he had been given the opportunity of such a tasting, according to the old monk's methods.

Before Champagne was made sparkling, it had a great reputation . . . the still wines of AY and BOUZY vied with the wines of BORDEAUX and BURGUNDY ; this would be towards the end of the seventeenth century.

We learned many things from our erudite friend—such interesting items as . . . to make still Champagne it is necessary to bottle during the declining moon of February. The moon is undoubtedly an important factor.

The quantity of sugar gained by the grapes in a given time is less in a rising moon than in a declining one, therefore the calendar is considered very carefully and tenderly at the time of the vintage. This year there was a new moon on the 9th of September, declining up to the 30th of September : the next new moon appeared on the 8th of October, so that the moon was very accommodating this year.

We passed through EPERNAY which was in the throes of a Fair, and arrived in good time at Monsieur Budin's hospitable house for dinner, which was indeed a princely repast.

With Escargots de Bourgogne, which were excellent (an opinion thoroughly endorsed by Mr. and Mrs. Clark, and Lorne who had not tasted them before), we had wine of the 1921 vintage—Cramant—the same wine, one bottle STILL and the other SPARKLING. How good they were . . . I preferred the STILL wine which seemed better to subdue the exuberance of the Escargots.

Escargots de Bourgogne are not so easily come by in these days . . . in fact most of the edible ones are now reared in 'SNAIL PARKS', the reason being that so much chemical mixture is sprayed on the vine leaves on which the snails thrive, that they become sick . . . and who wants to take advantage of a sick snail ?

Monsieur Budin, knowing my predilection for the White grape, thoughtfully offered to follow with a dish of succulent eggs, a bottle of 1928 Cramant and a bottle of 1928 Mesnil. These were of most excellent quality, quite dry . . . the Mesnil I thought slightly the fuller wine : but here I was in the minority.

With the roast partridge, we had indeed three notable wines, and very glad I was, especially as they proved so attractive to my friends, and they would surely never have such an opportunity again.

Listen . . .   1880 Perrier-Jouët,
                      1884 Perrier-Jouët,
                      1892 Perrier-Jouët.

If I were to tell you in appropriate words what I thought of them, you would smile, so I shall keep my thoughts to myself and rob you of your mirth. I must add, however, that in my notebook, I wrote afterwards, against the 1892, one word which was all-sufficient—CHAMPION ! !

[16]

It was so wonderful that the horrid commercial instinct was difficult to quieten. . . . I wondered if there was any for sale, I dared not ask, being a guest at the table . . . also I felt that there could only be a very small quantity remaining in Monsieur Budin's private cellar for use on special occasions.

There are more ways than one to overcome difficulties, so when an opening arrived, I said in the most nonchalant manner . . . 'You have not many of these treasures left—what a pity it is that the end must come to all good things.'

I was surprised at his reply . . . 'I am not the proud possessor. They belong to my brother-in-law, poor fellow. He is lying dangerously ill.' (In fact he has since passed over to the great majority.) 'I doubt if he will ever drink the sixty bottles that remain to him.' I kept a discreet silence, but on parting, courage, no doubt the result of enjoying such fine wine, came to me and, clothing myself in a boldness which is not habitual, I whispered to my host, while tenderly pressing his hand—'Wouldn't it be a charitable thing if I offered to buy that 1892 Perrier-Jouët Nectar, and thus put temptation out of the way of your invalid brother-in-law.'

He promised to mention it to him . . . he did and—well, I was satisfied ; certainly once again we can repeat—'Fortune favours the brave.'

With the dessert we were offered a bottle of delectable Ch. d'Yquem 1900. . . . What a wine !

However, I preferred to go without dessert and remain faithful to the 1892.

After a glass of very fine old Cognac with the coffee, and a suitable interval for chatting, we were ready, although reluctant to take our way back to REIMS, emphatically indebted to our kind host.

On the return journey I could not help but think over these famous wines and all that Monsieur Budin had told us. I thought of the act of blending and recalled to mind a bottle I had enjoyed with Ronnie Fox, of 1920 Lanson, known as 'Cuvée de Famille'. It was delightful, the whole cuvée was five Hhds., comprised as follows :

[17]

1 Hhd. Verzenay	Red.
1 Hhd. Bouzy	

1 Hhd. Mesnil	
1 Hhd. Trépail	White.
1 Hhd. Cramant	

I have frequently told him how I enjoyed it, but so far it has had no other effect than his genial smile.

I also endeavoured to make my friends jealous by relating the particulars of a lunch we once gave at the office, commencing with a bottle of 1857 Still Sillery, from the cellar of the late Grand Duke Michael . . . which was wonderfully preserved; full of quality and elegance.

'This', said one of them 'was an isolated case' . . . . 'By no means', I assured them, for only a few weeks before we had had (I have looked up the menu to have the particulars correct) the following :

> 1929 Still Champagne, Calmet Blanc,
> 1928 Blanc de Blanc,
> 1928 Cumières—from one vineyard,
> 1874 Sillery (a marvellous bottle, graciously given us by the Earl of Rosebery),

and a magnum of
> 1892 Binet Dry Elite, which was beautifully fresh and enjoyable.

A half-bottle of 1857 Johannisberg was produced as a curiosity ; it was light in colour and had retained its character in an amazing way.

On the following morning Lorne introduced us to Messieurs Krug of Reims, that is, to the partners themselves . . . their wines, of course, being well known to us. A huge sheep dog greeted us when we passed through the large gates and accompanied us up the steps of the portico ; discreetly leaving us in the good hands of his master and mistress.

Madame Joseph Krug is a wonderful lady. The fine work which she did during the war and after has been duly recognised by the French Government, for she is the worthy possessor of two honourable decorations :

    (1) Croix de Guerre.
    (2) Chevalière de la Légion d'Honneur.

In the cellars at Messieurs Krug we saw very much of interest, in addition being shown the places where, during the war period, a school was carried on . . . also an excellent hospital, with yet another part apportioned off for divine service.

At my request, and as I thought it would be of interest to my friends, Monsieur Krug had arranged with Monsieur Charbonneaux to show us his VERRERIES or bottle-making works. This is a sight worth seeing, and I advise all those who go to Reims to make the time to visit such an interesting place.

Forty years ago, the work was done by hand, but now it is done mostly by automatic machinery. None the less, the process from beginning to end is most entertaining.

Bottle-making in France is a very old industry, dating back to the thirteenth century. I have referred to my notes, made when I was visiting Reims many years ago . . . I find that the method is much the same now except that machinery displaces the human factor in many phases of the operation.

In case anyone would care to read the process as it was, I will transcribe my notes instead of describing what I actually saw on this 20th day of September. I feel sure it will prove more interesting. . . .

'The bottles are made by a gang consisting of five persons, the Gatherer, the Blower, the Wetter-off, the Bottle-maker and the Taker-in. The process is in this wise . . . the Gatherer gathers the glass from a tank furnace in the end of the blowing iron. He rolls it on a slab, either of iron or stone, slightly expanding the glass by blowing, and then passes the blowing iron and the molten glass to the Blower, who proceeds to transmit the glass into a mould ; these moulds, invented by Monsieur Carillon, are made of cast-iron, either in two pieces hinged together at the base or at one side, or in three pieces, one forming the body and two pieces forming the neck. He closes the mould by pressing the lever with his foot, and then either blows down the blowing iron, or, by utilising the more modern method, attaches it to a tube connected with a supply of compressed air.'

'When the air has forced the glass to take the form of the mould, the mould is opened and the Blower gives the blowing iron with the bottle attached to it, to the Wetter-off. This individual proceeds to touch the top of the neck of the bottle with a moistened piece of iron, and with a simple tap on the blowing iron, so detaches the bottle that it drops into a wooden trough provided for the purpose. He then grips the body of the bottle with an instrument fashioned with four prongs, which is attached to an iron rod, and hands it to the Bottle-maker, who in turn heats the broken neck of the bottle in the working furnace, or "Glory-hole", binds a band of molten glass around the neck of it and, at the same time, shapes the inside and the outside of the mouth with a special tool provided for the purpose. This is practically the finished article, and is carried off by the Taker-in to the LEHR ; that is the annealing furnace.'

As I have mentioned, most of this work is now being done by machinery, and perhaps it is as well, for the poor wretches who did the blowing in the old style were destined to live but a few years . . . their cheeks presented a pitiable sight, many of them having countless small holes in the sides.

I remember how scared I was when I first saw the Takers-in (generally small boys) at work, for when they took the finished bottles to the annealing furnace, it behoved me to be very much on the 'qui vive' . . . it was alarming to see them, almost naked, running from place to place with red or white hot molten glass at the end of a very long rod, and they carried out these duties in the most unconcerned and, to me, hazardous fashion.

After this, which was a little tiring, especially for the ladies, we were taken by Monsieur Krug to enjoy his hospitality at lunch. As my theme is in reality WINE I must be excused if I have taken (here and in many similar occasions) due and close note of what we were offered to drink. Of course, it goes without saying that we were entirely spoilt. The first wine we had was Krug, 1919 Private Cuvée . . . those who know the wine and have finished their stock will wish me to leave it at that, and, so as not to make them envious, I will be content to tell you that it was

[20]

excellent, and I would have been quite happy to continue the repast to that tune ; but other wines were in store for us :

1904 Krug . . . . STILL,
1904   ,, ... SPARKLING,
1880 Bouzy . . . STILL RED,
1920   ,,   . . .

The 1920 Bouzy was quite attractive . . . the 1880 Bouzy, which we had with the artichokes, although I would not have dared to express the opinion, must have been better many years ago.

Both the specimens of 1904 I enjoyed immensely, although for once in a way I preferred the Sparkling Wine : incidentally 1904 was the year of Monsieur and Madame Krug's marriage. Well, here's to them ! even in the memory of those delightful bottles, and may they have many, many years of continued happiness to look forward to.

We returned to an adjacent room for coffee while the dog, not the sheep dog, but a little terrier, showed off his tricks which were quite entertaining. However, Time, that inexorable master, called to us, and off we were once more.

Our first visit was to the house of H. Lochet, a most important cork factory carried on by a Mr. de Tassigny. It does not sound frightfully exciting to visit a cork factory, but it is certainly 'mildly' so. It is quite an education to see the various processes from the bark to the finished article . . . the cutting off of the bark (a very sharpened knife is required) the shaping, the fastening together of the two halves, for nearly always a Champagne cork is composed of two separate corks cut flat and then rounded off . . . all this is very intriguing.

The most interesting point to me was the sorting and discarding of any faulty corks ; ones which would be likely to produce a 'corked' bottle. Quite a number are thrown aside every day, the sorter being rewarded for each faulty one he detects.

I had a try at it and, although I probably passed two or three questionable ones, I had the satisfaction of detecting a couple and discarding them, to the gratification of the sorter by whose side I was standing. There is a small yellow sulphury mark which can be seen, and when smelt, invariably speaks for itself.

Even after the corks are delivered from the factory to the merchant, they are subject to another very severe scrutiny.

When you notice a very small cork, as hard as iron, you can be sure that the wine has been disgorged for a long time; a large new cork indicates that the second cork has not been long in the bottle. This does not necessarily mean that the wine is young, for it may have been a wine left 'sur pointe' in the original cellar and only recently disgorged, that is, before being shipped. This is no detriment to the old wine—on the contrary it leaves an extra freshness with the wine.

Of this I had recently an excellent example with a quantity of 1906 vintage wine, which had been 'sur pointe' until shipped about eighteen months ago.

From the cork factory we proceeded to Monsieur Krug's establishment in order to taste some wines.

To commence with, although really too early, we tasted a few specimens of the 1934 vintage. An enormous quantity is made; in fact, a great difficulty has arisen, which is to know what to do with it : I understood that, in some places, if one gave two empty casks a third would be filled free.

Avize (White grape) 1934 seemed to me a clean pleasant wine with natural sugar. The Ambonnay from near Bouzy (Black grape) was dark and coarse, and candidly I found difficulty in coming to any conclusion about it. It did, however, open one's eyes to the real necessity of blending.

I believe that I omitted to mention that, in the blending there is always a certain percentage of old wine used and this wine, instead of being stored in casks, which might pass on a woody taste, is kept in magnums and is therefore fresher.

Having discussed the prospects of the present vintage which promises well, we settled down to a serious dégustation. . . .

1929 Krug . . . Inclined to be sweet, a lack of acidity, very
soft and ripe.
1928 Krug . . . Very good. A smell of the Fleur des Vignes—
this should develop well, very well, it seems

> so well balanced, which is after all, what one looks for.

1926 Krug . . . Jolly good ! ! But it shows its age in comparison with the 1928.

This was very interesting and went far to endorse the opinions I had already formed, that the 1926 is an excellent wine for present consumption ; that 1928 will keep longer than the wines of 1929.

We then hied to the Hotel for a wash and brush-up, only to return for dinner at the home of these hospitable people.

With regard to the wine we had at dinner, it was a veritable treat . . . Krug, Private Cuvée, 1900, 1884 and 1911 ; they were all beautiful wines. I have been trying to find a flaw with one of them in order to enhance the description of the others, but it cannot be done.

That guilty fellow Lorne was so emphatic in his praises of the 1911 that Monsieur Krug actually opened another bottle of it as a parting gesture, and a very pretty one too, thoroughly appreciated by all.

The morning of the next day brought us a disappointment, for Mr. and Mrs. Clark were obliged to return to Paris. However, I had the satisfaction of feeling that, in spite of some fatigue which a lady must have experienced, they had both enjoyed their visit and did not consider that the time had been wasted; in fact, they promised to join me later in Bordeaux if circumstances permitted.

My good friend, Monsieur Georges Robinet of the illustrious firm of Messieurs G. H. Mumm et Cie., had kindly extended to me and my friends an invitation to visit their cellars and to partake of déjeuner with them, therefore Lorne and I descended on them and made proper excuses on behalf of the ones who had already left for Paris.

We had already visited some famous cellars, and found the same precise methods followed out here. I have described the making of Champagne up to the time of the wine being ready to bottle, and the operations following this can be well seen in the eleven miles of cellars belonging to the firm of Messieurs G. H.

Mumm et Cie. I will detail them as concisely as possible, which I hope will give some idea of the stupendous work entailed in providing a bottle of bubbly when we take our 'best girl out to dinner'.

1. Having finished its fermentation, which goes on for several weeks, the blended wine is bottled.

2. These bottles are then stored away in a horizontal position in the cellars.

3. In the spring a secondary fermentation begins to take place, causing a deposit to form in the bottle.

4. It will be necessary to remove this, so the bottles are placed on racks, called 'pupitres', at an angle of 55°, that is 'sur pointes'.

5. The bottles are then subjected to 'remuage', each bottle being slightly twisted from the wrist, and this is carried on until the bottle has completed a circle (a small white mark in the punt of the bottle serves as indicator). By this time the sediment has fallen on to the end of the cork : an experienced man can manipulate from 30, even up to 40,000 a day.

6. A clever manipulator extracts the cork and the sediment, which in most instances has, by a simple process, been frozen on to the cork, entailing a loss of only 2 per cent. instead of about 6 per cent. under the old method.

7. The dosage is then added, according to the degree of sweetness required ; if no sweetness is required the bottle is filled up with its own wine and remains a Natural wine—this might be excellent in some years when there is a large quantity of natural sugar or lack of acidity, but more often than not, dry nature has to be assisted.

8. Corking. A fine cork is now used in the place of the original, which has been discarded ; for every Champagne bottle must have had two corks.

9. With the assistance of a special machine the agrafe, or wire fastening is affixed to the bottle. All that now remains is to dress it for the particular market it is required.

10. For this there must be selected Foil, Neck Label and Body Label.

11. Placing in straw envelopes and packing completes a case ready for marking for exportation.

[24]

All this interesting work we witnessed in the cellars of Messieurs Mumm before we partook of the excellent déjeuner that Monsieur and Madame Robinet had prepared for us.

As an introduction, we had a bottle of 1932 Cramant, much more pleasant than I would have thought considering the vintage. This was followed by the Cordon Rouge, 1911, a beautiful wine indeed. It was exquisite . . . I do like the nineteen elevens and, by the look of greed on Lorne's face I think he was enjoying that too.

This was too much, so Monsieur Robinet brought us down to earth again by introducing a Still Red Bouzy of 1928. I hope he did not notice the condition of this particular glass of mine, as we left the table. The same remark might apply to two other wines he offered as interesting, out of the kindness of his heart . . . Ch. Camponac, a Red Bordeaux wine, and 1921 Still White Bouzy.

I did sip these wines, and thought the Red Bouzy of 1928 interesting . . . the Still White was more attractive, but somewhat heavy. I was still lingering after another glass of the 1921 when, to my surprise a magnum of 1906 G. H. Mumm, Cordon Rouge, was produced. Do you blame me for neglecting the other glasses? I did enjoy it and while doing so, Monsieur Robinet inquired if I knew why the legislators in the U.S.A. refused to allow the importation of magnums into New York. To explain, he related that an American gentleman was crazy to visit Reims, not only to see the martyred city, but also to see some of the famous cellars which stretch for miles. His wife was an ardent prohibitionist, and only with difficulty agreed to accompany him, on his solemn promise that he would not taste or drink any of the wine there. He agreed—poor fellow—and as a true man to his word, he carried out his obligation until . . . yes . . . until the temptation was too much, for, dining with Monsieur Robinet, the sight of a MAGNUM OF 1906 was overpowering and he succumbed ! ! !

I was quite able to understand this fall from grace, for surely that magnum was more tempting than a bushel of apples !

Monsieur and Madame Robinet ; Lorne joins with me in sincere thanks for your generous hospitality and can assure you that the remembrance of your charming family circle flanked by those beautiful wines of 1911 and 1906 will be with us, if possible, beyond the grave : if so, we shall hope to be, by their virtue, one of those little stars that 'TWINKLE'; with all due deference to Saint Vincent, the vignerons' patron saint.

It was getting a little late in the afternoon, and as we had promised to dine with a very old and revered friend at his country house near COURTISOLS, I allowed Lorne no respite, and urged him to look 'slippy' as we had between forty and fifty miles to go on a road unknown to us.

We found Monsieur and Madame Armand Walfard at home ... it was some years since I had seen them. What a pleasure to descend suddenly upon old friends in this way. There they were, a veritable Darby and Joan, enjoying the sweets of a well-earned retirement : retirement, yes, but no restraint on an insatiable gluttony for work.

We had a run through the vineyards before dinner as we were anxious to see them, and it would be dark after the meal.

The evening being a little fresh we conjured our old friend not to venture far, and to show how his intellect is not impaired, he did not hesitate to obey.

Of his La Vesle wine, which is a most attractive proposition—Still White Champagne, he sells principally in France some 120 to 150,000 bottles annually ; a nice business for a retired gentleman. In addition to this he has a hobby in breeding trout, and told me that he sold on an average 25,000 fish yearly. Sitting down in the seclusion of his attractive dining-room, we four just enjoyed ourselves, talking of the past more than of the present or the future. The dear old couple evidently firmly believe in the old adage—'sufficient unto the day, etc.'

Whilst we were thus passing the time we were entertained with wines which proved to be most interesting. In the first place we had a bottle or two (I am not quite certain) of his Vesle wine, a Still Vin Natur de la Champagne. . . . I found it most attractive ; very inexpensive I learnt, and very enjoyable. This was quite a young wine—in fact, these wines can be consumed quite young. However, to show us an older wine from his property, a bottle of the 1929 vintage was produced ; it really was, without endeavouring to say something polite to our host, exactly as we described it to him—'Excellent quality . . . very good indeed.'

To my delight a bottle of 1911 Binet then made its appearance, but it soon stood by, a void of little interest. Its place was taken by a magnum—Oh! those insidious magnums, of Binet Dry Elite. This was a surprise and a treat. It was one of those magnums which had been mixed up together (three different vintages) during the war, and no one could tell until the cork was pulled what the vintage was. This brought to my mind an occasion at the Savage Club when I was entertaining about a score of good fellows, and I regaled them with these magnums, promising a reward of a bottle of FINEST CHAMPAGNE COGNAC to anyone who would correctly state the respective vintages of the three magnums. I held the corks, the only clue.

I was not ruined by the expense of the Brandy, for only one person gave the correct solution, and that was Major H. R. Rudd; clever fellow.

'Well,' inquired my dear old friend, 'what do you make of this?' 'Well,' I said, 'the last I had proved to be 1906.' 'And so is this', said he, gleefully producing the cork. . . . I wonder if I should have guessed right . . . I doubt it. It seemed so very fresh, I think I should have been inclined to say 1911, and yet it was not the same as the bottle which was introduced to us a few minutes earlier: the freshness would have deterred me from saying 1904; so there might have been the possibility of a victory if I had carried on.

Thank you so much, Monsieur Walfard, for that magnum ! ! Have you read what I said to our old mutual friend, Georges Robinet? Yes; good; and be pleased to accept the same, both of you, you dear old friends.

The next morning early, we were off to AY, the centre of one of the most famous wine-producing areas of Black grapes in the Champagne. Incidentally, King Henry IV took a pride in calling himself the Lord D'Ay. As we proceeded we were remarking on the fine view on our right, when our attention was distracted by the noise of many lorries, speeding along behind us. We thought fit to allow them to pass; they contained numbers of empty casks being rushed to the vineyard proprietors, for the

[27]

quantity of wine being made this year had upset all calculations on the score of casks to hold it.

Nearing AY, we could see on our right, the renowned HAUTVILLERS, looking very perky and picturesque, tucked away on the hill-side.

We passed an old man, quite blind. . . . I wondered if, by second sight, or through some mystery, he could imagine the lovely views around him. They were gathering grapes close at hand . . . instinct must have led him there, for he was enjoying the fruit someone had given him, a little girl I'll be bound, for they are very tender to a 'poor old man, and blind too'.

We continued along the undulating road to BOUZY; the road was certainly very dusty, and on inquiring what effect this microbic dust would have on the fermentation, I was assured NONE.

While craning out of the car, to catch sight of some of the pre-phylloxera vines, two nasty wasps flew in, distracting our attention. No doubt, owing to the recent rains and more rottenness in some bunches of grapes they had been enticed from their retreats.

These rains were responsible for much 'pourriture', so much so that it was necessary to employ eighty sorters for every fifteen gatherers, which almost doubles the expense of labour.

Monsieur Bollinger, whom we had had the pleasure of meeting, was carefully scrutinising the baskets as they were brought in to the sorters, a dozen or more of whom were seated at their work along the roadside.

'I will show you something', said Monsieur Bollinger, and with justifiable pride he led us to what is probably the last small vineyard of old French vines, some of them one hundred to one hundred and twenty years old, but he said, with a slight sadness in his voice . . . 'the time will come'.

Monsieur Bollinger expressed the opinion that some of the wines of 1932 will prove to develop well; this will be most interesting. So far, I have not come across any, except that good bottle of Cramant 1932, with which Monsieur Robinet introduced his beautiful wines.

On leaving BOUZY we made our way across to AY, being

desirous to see the cellars, the stocks and the Château of Messrs. Ayala, of which we had recently heard such good reports. They were certainly in no way exaggerated . . . the cellars are very, very large. The chalk seams (or strata) stretch in a direct line all the way from AY to FOLKESTONE.

The stocks of wine are very important and I was much impressed with some cuvées of 1926 and 1928 vintages. With such wines as these the famous house of Ayala should soon be known all over the world. A most pleasant bottle of Vin Rosé 1928 attracted me very much—so soft and clean.

We then went across to the Château, that is the Château d'Ay, of the seventeenth century. What delightful views, and what a pleasant avenue of Linden trees, forming a screened verandah. Messieurs Ayala are very proud of this famous estate, and justly so. I cannot help but feel from the kind reception I had at their hands that they would welcome any interested friend of mine equally so.

We must tear ourselves away from here, although reluctantly, for had we not engaged to lunch with a number of friends at the 'Auberge Bellevue' in the Commune of Champillon? The proprietor had been duly warned on the telephone, so we were expecting good fare at his justly celebrated rendezvous.

The Auberge Bellevue lies between Reims and Epernay, and is run by Talochard, otherwise Monsieur Cogne. It is a little out of the way, but what a treat when you arrive! Looking from the balcony windows facing, can be seen a thousand hectares of vineyards and a delightful view of the Valley of the Marne . . . indeed a panorama ! !

But this is not all. You have come to partake of the cooking of a real August Escoffier ; for Monsieur Cogne is a masterpiece in more ways than one . . . by the menu, which I will show you in a minute, you will understand that he is in *one* way—in another way it is by his proportions. Judge for yourselves what they really are, his girth—well, it would take you some time to get round him : his weight one hundred and sixty-eight kilos (approximately 26 stone and a half), and his smile the largest thing about him.

He frequently goes to Brides les Bains for a cure ; on the last

occasion a facetious friend thought fit to write to him. . . .   He
addressed the envelope :

MONSIEUR COGNE,

168 KILOS,

à BRIDE LES BAINS. . . .

and the letter was duly received.*   (See page 31).

Nevertheless, he is a very energetic man, up betimes in the
morning in order to do his own marketing.   On this errand he
never fails to take his faithful dog, who, sitting by, eyes him all
the time and, as soon as he sees his master 'shut eye' at the wheel
he pats his hand and in that way keeps him awake.

While waiting for déjeuner we looked out of the balcony
window and enjoyed the beautiful views, at the same time being
kept amused by two black squirrels playing leapfrog in the same
enclosure as a couple of roosters, who were playing a game of
Hide and Seek around the night coop.   When the heavier of the
two eventually caught his victim he almost killed him . . . he had
evidently been flirting with one of his wives, for he immediately
strutted across the pen and whispered something in her ear.

We must give up these frivolities and turn our attention to the
déjeuner that Monsieur Cogne had prepared for us.   Here is the
menu :

Le Brochet de Marne Sauce verte.	Cramant Natural 1929.
Le jambon du pays, chaud en croûte.	
Les Epinards à la crème.	Le Mesnil brut 1929.
Le Chapon farce au fois gras truffé.	Cumières Rouge.
Les pommes Lyonnaise.	1933 Noir de Noir.
La Salade de Saison.	Ayala 1926, in magnums.
Le fromage de Vigneron.	
Les Fraises Melba.	
Fruits en corbeille	Fine Gde. Réserve
Café.	Guy Gautier.

It was indeed a sumptuous repast.   Everything fitted in so
well.   It was beautifully cooked and elegantly served by two

charming waitresses, one of whom filled our glasses from the magnum, with one hand. So much was my admiration that I was constrained to be photographed arm in arm with her, before departing ! ! I will let you into a secret . . . PEPETTE was her name . . . ask for her when you visit this estimable establishment.

The Cramant and Le Mesnil were excellent. These two would have sufficed as far as I was concerned. The Noir de Noir I did not care for . . . it did not appeal to me in the least. The magnum was also excellent and I do not think it was due either to the size of the bottle or to the waitress, but to the quality of the wine itself. The Champagne Ayala brought to my mind an amusing little incident. My wife and Margaret my youngest daughter were in Scotland, and I had told them to be sure, if they came in tired, to indulge in a half-bottle of 'Fizz' . . . Here is the sequel, in a letter from the young lady :

'We took your advice and had the first wine on the list, Ayala, and have come to the conclusion that it's d . . . good ! Congratulations.'

Now, what is one to do with a child like that ?

Before leaving, whom should I meet but my good friend, Mr. Freeman. I had left him at the Lion d'Or in the morning, when I had had the pleasure of meeting his good lady.

Mr. Freeman is probably known to many of you for he masquerades as the NEW PEPYS in *Truth*, and the following is an extract from his diary of September 22nd, which appeared in the issue of *Truth* of October 3rd, 1934 :

'September 22.—Upp betimes to coffee and rolls (But Lord !

---

* The following is a reference to gentlemen who would not come under the category of 'Pharaoh's lean kine' :

At The Coffee Mill, St. James's Street.
GEORGE DRUMMOND, *Jnr.*—25 st. 12 lbs.—1850.

At Maldon, Essex.
EDWARD BRIGHT. Aged 29—44 st.—1750 (*circa*). Ancestor of our late accountant, Mr. Clifford Bright. It is said that seven men were with ease buttoned within his waistcoat !

Born at Leicester.
DANIEL LAMBERT—52 st. 10½ lbs. Died in 1809. Reference is made to this gentleman's waistcoat as being in the Museum at King's Lynn, with a girth of 102 inches ! (He only drank water . . . moral !).

What noble coffee !) Then into lounge to await our company's assembling. Here whom sh^d I see but my good friend Mr. Berry, the vinter of St. James's St., and into discourse with him. Is, he tells me, here on a businesse round of the vineyards and like to be somewhile before he is done with them. Soe presented him to my wife, whom he did assure of having always suspected for an angel, her meek endurance of the things I say ab^t her, and now he sees her he knows it. Whereat she enraptured, but I smiled inwardly, wishing he c^d see her in the privacy of our home sometimes with her publick smile off.'

The pronunciation of the name 'Pepys' has always been a stumbling block to me and probably to many others. It occurred to me that I would like the NEW PEPYS to meet the present 'chief corner stone' of the illustrious family, so I invited them as fellow guests to a banquet of The Knights of The Round Table Club ; very interesting was the conversation, the result of which was the following extract from a letter I received from The Earl of Cottenham :

'There is a tradition that the family originally came from Italy. The name unquestionably exists in that country, the two well-known Italian authors, Guglielmo Pepe or Peppe, 1611, and Baron Antonio Pepi, 1750-70, testifying to the fact.

'It is thought that some of the family moved into France and settled for a generation or two at Languedoc, which supposition is supported by the name "Pepyons" occurring in the "Armorial Général de la France", Hozier, Paris, 1768, Registre 6, in an ancient contract of marriage in the Province of Languedoc, dated 1292, and in "Le Cabinet Historique", III, p. 12, also by Hozier, in the Bibliothèque Nationale at Paris, the name "Pepie" occurs.

'The first mention of the name in English manuscript—so far as can be ascertained—occurs in the "Rotuli Hundredorum" (Edw. I, 1273), and is as follows :

"Richard Pepis holds one messuage and one rood of land of the same G. He pays a halfpenny for the lot."

'The name has been misspelt in seventeen different ways :

(1) Pepis.   Rolls of the Hundreds, 1273.
(2) Pepy.   Inquisitiones ad quod damnum, 1439.

(3)	Pypys.	Will of Laurence Pypys, 1511.
(4)	Pipes.	(Ditto).
(5)	Peppis.	Will of John Peppis of Branktre, 1518.
(6)	Peppes.	Will of Margaret, wife of above, 1519.
(7)	Pepes.	Will of Thomas Pepes of Cottenham, 1520.
(8)	Peppys.	Will of John Peppys of Debden, 1552.
(9)	Peaps.	Will of John Peaps of Cambridge, 1636.
(10)	Pippis.	Will of Anna Pippis of Cambridge, 1639.
(11)	Peapys.	Magdalen College, Cambridge, Records, 1653.
(12)	Peps.	Samuel Pepys, marriage register, St. Martin's in the Fields, 1655.
(13)	Pypes.	Admon. of Wm. Pypes' Estate, 1656.
(14)	Peypes.	Letter of Edw. Montagu to Chief Justice Pepys, 1656.
(15)	Peeps.	Extracts from 'Coffee House Paper', Samuel Pepys' Diary.
(16)	Peepes.	Marriage Licence, John Peepes and Mary Gibson, Apr. 1683.
(17)	Peyps.	Burial register of Samuel Peyps, St. Olave's, Hart Street, 1703.

'The accepted spelling of the name "Pepys" was adopted generally about the end of the seventeenth century, though it occurs many years before that time.

'There have been numerous ways of pronouncing the name, as "Peps", "Peeps", and "Peppis". The Diarist undoubtedly pronounced it "Peeps", and the lineal descendants to his sister Paulina, the family of "Pepys Cockerell", pronounce it so to this day.

'The other branches of the family all pronounce it as "Peppis", and the latter pronunciation is almost certainly correct because of two facts, that in the earliest writing it is spelt "Pepis", and that the French form of the name is "Pepy".'

We were a little tired by the time we returned to the Lion d'Or and were glad to have a quiet and simple dinner with a bottle of the wine I enjoy so much, the Blanc de Blanc : which always recalled the fact that before Champagne was sparkling, it had a great reputation, the Still Red Wines of Ay and Bouzy vieing with the famous Wines of Bordeaux and Burgundy.

1865.⎫
1874.⎭ Excellent wines . . . Fruity, full colour.

1868.⎫
1870.⎭ In spite of the body—finesse.

1874. A grand wine, full bodied.

1880. A big wine of good quality.

1884. More elegant.

1889. Somewhat lighter . . . of fine quality.

1892. Exceptional ! ! !

1893. Very good, but too ripe.

1898. Rather hard in its early stages, but developed very well.

1899. Here was a wine ! !

1900. Vied with the 1899 . . . perhaps not so fine.

1904.⎫
1906.⎭ Very good indeed, and still sought for by connoisseurs.

1911. Proved to be excellent.

⎡Made under great difficulties, but some have turned
1914. ⎨   out fine wines. How well I remember some fine
1915. ⎪   bottles of 1914 Pol Roger and Bollinger among
⎣   others.

1919. Very good, and still is.

1920.   Ditto.

1921. Very ripe. Has matured more quickly than the last two.

1923. I did not care for very much.

1926. Very good indeed, and very forward.

1928. Excellent !

1929. Also very good. Probably will not last as long as 1928.

1933. Has fine prospects.

1934. There is an abundance. The quality remains to be seen.

Note.—In 1910, 1¼ million bottles of bad wine were produced, and in 1904, 96 millions of fine wine were produced. . . . So with the large quantity we may expect much.

As 1892 was to 1893, so I consider :
                      1899 to 1900,
                      1920 to 1921.
                      1928 to 1929.

My suggestions for what they are worth can be summed up as follows :

Should a cellar contain old wines, that is, up to 1906, use them and enjoy them. They are fine now, and are not likely to improve, bearing in mind that some people like the wine young, therefore keep them for those who know better.

The 1911 can be kept for some time as the 'bonne bouche' without misgivings, always remembering to put them away in the lowest or coolest bins available in the cellar.

I would almost suggest drinking the 1914's and 1915's before the 1911's.

Naturally the remarks on these old wines will not appeal to a great many as the existent quantity is so limited.

We then come to wines which may be found in a great many places. Of the three vintages—1919, 1920 and 1921 I cannot help but think it would be wise to use the 1921 first. In the year of 1921 we enjoyed a very hot summer . . . the grapes became very ripe and a rapid maturity is the natural result. These wines are most enjoyable at present, therefore indulge in them, even if you leave 1919 and 1920 a little longer.

I do not wish to convey the impression that the 1921's will not be so good for the next few years, but I cannot see that they will improve.

To those who have 1923 wines, I would advise using them.

The wines of 1926 are of very fine quality, and although holders need have no misgivings, they are not likely to make very 'old bones'.

We now come to the two excellent vintages of 1928 and 1929. Somehow, I think if the Champagne shippers had had the courage of their convictions, they would have shown their 1929 wine before the 1928 . . . it is so very forward. However, they are both of excellent quality, and we can look forward to many a good bottle in the years to come.

CHAPTER III

CHABLIS

RAIN greeted us when we ventured outside on Sunday morning, 23rd September, but we would brook no delay. We had bidden 'au revoir' to my good friend, the NEW PEPYS, who was in the lounge of the hotel with his too-indulgent lady, both looking the picture of health and happiness ; for the good sparkling wines of Champagne had done them no harm.

We had thought of paying a visit to the ancient Church of Saint-Remi, the building of which was commenced in 1039, but on second thoughts we did not feel justified in allotting any time to it, especially as we had been there on former occasions. There is a delightful touch connected with Saint-Remi, Archbishop of Reims, 530 A.D., that he was much attached to his vines, and in his will took particular pains that they should pass into worthy hands.

Just after nine o'clock we were off, but as Sunday was a 'dies NON' we intended to jog along comfortably as far as AUXERRE, stay there the night, and reach CHABLIS early on the Monday morning.

In spite of the rain the chasseurs were out—quite a number of them—after partridges, Lorne surmised, seeing strips of clover . . . a real Sherlock Holmes, isn't he ?

Close to LA POMPELLE we saw the great crater, a horrid reminder . . . and near by, left as it was at the end of the war, a small area of the actualities ; I cannot believe that just outside Reims the people require so vivid a recollection impressed upon them. . . . Barbed wire, steel helmet erected on stone work, British Tanks which had been captured and used against the French. . . . No ; I didn't much care for it. However, the sun was now trying to shine over the village and disperse the gloom.

As we continued our way, I think it was at CHALONS S/MARNE, we became alive to the fact that the memory of 1914 was very much in evidence.

Here was being held a National Congress (Union Nationale des Anciens Mobilisés de la Guerre). There was a large concourse of people, flags were flying and the ex-soldiers stationed around the Church were singing from FAUST !

Mr. Watson—I beg his pardon—Lorne, confided to me that he thought a service was about to take place ! ! But I was one up on him, for seeing a man dressed in his Sunday best, carrying two yards of bread under his arm, I ventured to remark—'I believe he is taking it home to eat.'

With such intellectual outbursts we motored on, the Little Auk behaving very well, until our attention was drawn to a very beautiful avenue, which led us to ARCIS S/AUBE, and its picturesque weir.

We reached TROYES in time for déjeuner ; as we crossed the river we noticed that the anglers had also gone to déjeuner, for the lines were still out with no one to hold the rods. At an hotel we fared passing well ; with melon, followed by an omelette, we had a half-bottle of what might be described as 'local Wine' . . . NEUVILLE pétillant, 1929, Cuvée Spéciale, brut, 15 francs. We did not expect much, but seeing it described as 'brut' we risked it, but we were not in the least happy with it . . . it was sweet : Brut by name and Brute by nature ! So, in order to continue in a better frame of mind, we decided to have a bottle of a wine which Lorne thought I would be pleased with, and so I was . . . Crémant de Cramant . . . for it went very well with the veal and ham, etc.

Looking at the Wine List I noticed that the proprietor had the audacity to charge 40 francs for a 'verre' of Marc ; being of a thrifty disposition (?) and not encouraged by my companion from the other side of the Tweed, we made martyrs of ourselves. Toying with the pages of the Wine List, which always interest me, I was somewhat astounded at the rubbish that was offered— Bordeaux Wines of 1912 and 1915 at 40 francs ! I do know of one connoisseur who would probably have indulged in the former, but not for me. I noticed a wine quoted at 100 francs, and believe me, it was a wine of 1907 . . . good, yes, but who would dare proclaim it higher?

These prices quite perturbed me, and unconsciously I found myself looking at the list of Eau-de-Vie, etc.; there was no Cognac on the List, and Marc, at 40 francs the glass, was out of the question. I took courage and ordered Marc of another kind for each of us. 'Lorne must take the rough with the smooth,' I said to myself. . . . Only 4 francs a glass, the bottle duly arrived, in all its glory . . . gold foil on the neck, an elegant label on which the contents were described as—BELNOT MARC, vieux extra, de la Champagne.

The patron came across to have a chat . . . he had had experience in London; his son was now at the Trocadero. He sincerely hoped that France would remain on the Gold Standard and, when I mentioned that I thought it was somewhat detrimental to the Export Trade, he shrugged his shoulders, remarking 'Tant mieux.'

I have seen, I suppose most people have, badly behaved children; there was one at a table close to ours—Ma, Pa and the Baby . . . Oh, such a horrid child. He would persist in helping himself with his tiny fists, off his parents' plates; he did get into such a mess. The climax came when he was carried out, screaming, because he was not allowed to rub his nose in the potatoes !!

After this episode with the méchant, the proprietor continued. He deplored the change in London as compared with Paris . . . his great regret seemed to be that there was no ODDONINO.

English second-class hotels, he declared, were far better than the French second-class.

He found that all meat (with the exception of veal) was better in the provinces than in London and he added that, while the exchange was as it is—approximately 75 francs to the pound, he would, and many of his friends would, spend their holidays in England.

We invited him to partake of a 'verre' of Marc, and were somewhat surprised that he refused. He knew something ! 'I never touch it', he said, 'it tastes of the stalks, which to me proves that distillation does not destroy all, certainly not at the strength this is distilled.'

[38]

The conversation flagged somewhat, so I inquired why the first bottle we had of NEUVILLE brut was so sweet, and the only reply forthcoming was that it was difficult to tell what was inside a half-bottle ! !

Lorne thought it was his turn to say something à propos of never knowing what you were to receive.

He told of how, on one occasion, he was with Mr. Graham of Port Wine renown at a certain hotel in Cambridge. A bottle of 1912 Taylor Fladgate was ordered as likely to be worth drinking, and to their surprise they were given 1922 Martinez. Complaint, and justly so, was made . . . eventually the 1912 Taylor was produced and the waiter asked if he should place it on the ice ! !

We had a quick look around the city, the old capital of 'La Champagne', noticing in particular the quaint old church of St. John. It was in this church, after the treaty of Troyes in 1420, that Catherine of France was married to Henry V. of England.

We had little time to spare, and left about three o'clock for AUXERRE.

The weather was fine and warm, although somewhat cloudy, and passing through St. André, where a factory was in the process of being built, we assumed that business was looking up. We continued through some hilly, woody, rather pretty country, where everyone seemed to trust his neighbour, as we could see no boundary lines between the different properties.

At BOUILLY our attention was directed to the attractive half-timbered houses, and a field set out for 'LE FOOTBALL'.

We encountered some vines here, and wondered what sort of wine was made, also, large quantities of elderberries ; I silenced Lorne at once ! At LE CHEMINOT we disturbed a large covey of partridges, which elated my good friend 'chasseur'.

At CORCELLES we ran into a flock of sheep and a small herd of cattle, which required considerable patience and ingenuity to pass.

We were then at ST. FLORENTIN, with its elegant church (Renaissance), outside of which flags were flying, a band was playing to a large number of people, who evidently were much interested in something.

We crossed the river Armançon, by an imposing-looking

[39]

bridge . . . on through LORDONNOIS and PONTIGNY, where the level-crossing gates were closed against us.

We waited and waited . . . considerable altercation was taking place, which lasted for some time ; meanwhile an engine was whistling away for all it was worth, and when it did come in sight it proved to be an insignificant-looking locomotive pulling along with some difficulty, a couple of passenger carriages and a like number of horse boxes.

By this time the number of motorists waiting the pleasure of the railway was assuming a large proportion, and the chorus of hooters was almost deafening.

Eventually, two porters appeared, pushing an empty truck along the line and, having passed, our patience was rewarded : we had been waiting $8\frac{1}{2}$ minutes ! How long before that the gates had been closed I dare not guess, but, by the impatience of those in front of us, I should think—for hours ! !

As we proceeded we noticed more vineyards . . . the vintage would appear to have been finished.

MONTIGNY-LA-RESLE was a pretty village, in the woods ; the old rusty mauve roofs of the dwellings were quite attractive.

At VILLENEUVE we came into some beautiful country . . . fine hedgerows, the blue of the Scabious, the tints of the bracken throwing off their summer suits, with the sunlight peeping through the trees, made a most appealing picture.

We enjoyed some lovely views, with AUXERRE in the distance. We were now at JONCHE, where a hand-press was already at work by the roadside. . . . I hope the peasant will make good wine and enjoy it.

We had climbed some 1400-1500 ft., and the evening light through the avenue of trees was most entrancing ; down this delightful via, were to be seen chasseurs, pêcheurs, vendangeurs, bicyclists . . . all wending their way home to AUXERRE.

As we had ample time, and we might not have another opportunity of seeing AVALLON, we decided to continue our way there, and to return to AUXERRE later. It was necessary to re-petrol and re-oil. . . . How terribly expensive these commodities are—three times the price in England, which makes such a journey very costly.

In spite of threatening weather we went on through the village of AUGY, where the smoke from an engine filled the countryside. The railway companies should be compelled to use CARDIFF coal ! !

At CHAMPS I was much interested in a battle royal between two crows and a hawk. Lorne would not stop to see the end, but I think the taloned one got the worst of it.

We crossed the Yonne, a pretty river just here, and greeted several patient anglers, none of whom had caught anything. From the valley, we climbed again into hilly country, with many a vineyard on either side.

We were nearing VERMENTON, passing considerable cement works. One thing which attracted me in this town was an interesting old sun-dial, but our speed was too rapid for me to take full particulars.

The country was wooded, with houses tucked away in seclusion. They looked enticing, and the inhabitants had but a short distance to go before they were rewarded with beautiful views ahead.

We reached two villages close together, the one LUCY S/CURE, and the other BESSY . . . apart from the beautiful country there was nothing in particular to attract my attention, but Lorne insisted on stopping. Standing erect, he raised his hat and muttered something. On inquiry, I understood him to say that it was an action of respect to his grandmother LUCY and his great-aunt, BESSY.

The country around here is becoming most interesting. We did not feel that we had time to visit the Grotto, at ARCY, or to parley with the anglers in LA CURE, but continued straight on, through a long tunnel that had been cut through the hill-sides at ST. MORÉ.

The cliffs are rocky and picturesque here ; we were passed by many cars in both directions, as it is the main Paris-Nice highway. Incidentally we noticed quite a few carrying the ubiquitous letters—G.B.

At VOUTENAY we were welcomed, or threatened by two peacocks. What a noise they can make ! ! Clouds were on the hills, and the hills surrounded us ; 'A magpie,' said Lorne. . . . 'Perhaps it won't rain after all,' I said.

ı Pie—Rien . . . do you remember ?

We were called to a halt at a level crossing, but did not have long to wait ; in the car immediately in front of us was a kennel strapped on to the luggage carrier, and although, as far as we could see, there were but three dogs in the kennel, they seemed packed, as the saying is—'like sardines in a box'.

I hope you are not becoming tired with this journey, but in order to arrive at our destination, we must go on with it. At SERMIZELLES we found a very pretty village, with an ancient 'tour', one of those delightful old-world places, with purple roofs to the cottages. The clouds had cleared . . . the magpie had brought us luck.

We had now reached AVALLON, and considered ourselves well repaid ; what wonderful views from the Terraces. Large notices at conspicuous corners invite visitors to these Terraces, and right glad we were that we did not turn down the repeated invitation. Such is the memory of this vista that it will live with me for ever.

We found time to see the ancient Tour Gavjard (1438), the Notre Dame de St. Lazare (twelfth century) and the fine old Belfry (1456).

We left AVALLON, with some regret, but our douleur was appeased by a gorgeous sunset.

We really must have a sight of VÉZELAY before returning to AUXERRE, and so we did.

We were making our way quietly along the usual route when we suddenly heard a loud report.

'The man in a car stationed some 200 yards in front of us has shot himself', I said. 'No', replied Lorne, for by this time we had reached the car to find that the motorist, evidently a tired chasseur, was having a final shot at a passing bird, while seated in his car.

At BLANNAY we turned from the main road and had a fine view of VÉZELAY in the distance.

We passed through a village, the name of which I had noticed on a signboard—ASQUINS. I muttered something, purposely inaudible, and when Lorne inquired what I said, I replied that I was only ASKING him the name of the village . . . there was silence ! !

Here we are at VÉZELAY . . . a little dark, but we could see that it was marvellous. We must endeavour to come here again—we did. I will leave my impressions until that time, as I fear I am wearying you and you want to get to AUXERRE for dinner.

This is what you are to have for dinner—quite simple—soup, fish from the Yonne—nothing to boast about, a cutlet cooked very well, and a toothsome becassine; these were assisted by a 1928 Pouilly, which was not in the least pleasant . . . it was as dry as the bones Ezekiel dreamt of . . . so we called for a bottle of 1919 Grand Chablis, Vaudésir. I cannot say that I enjoyed it, although I would not have wished to make a fuss. I think it must have been well stretched; it mixed with Perrier Water. For amusement, we had a small bottle of a Sparkling Chablis, which was atrocious, and one of Sparkling Auxerre Rosé—the least said of this the soonest mended. Blanche and Antoinette were very obliging and did their level best to please, but they had a difficult task. Blanche, I may tell you, was very dark, very dark indeed, and, strive all I could against it, the words of a ditty would continue to come to my mind—

> 'Adelaide went to a party,
> Adelaide went home tight !
> Dark rings under pretty eyes,
> Showed Adelaide ADELAIDE night.'

But I was quite nonplussed when, in my limited French, I tried to explain this to her; I was soon tied up in a knot. . . . How they laughed ! !

After a short stroll, we retired for the night and became victims of the unsavoury mosquito.

We were ready for an early departure in the morning. As I was settling the little account I heard a crash; a glass had been dropped ! 'Oh, those careless girls', said the hostess, and opened a door to inquire of the damage. 'What have you broken', she asked. . . . 'Only a glass', replied the dark Blanche. 'You must be more careful', was the rejoinder.

As Blanche looked a trifle sad, I said, 'Une pie—rien . . . deux pies—bonheur.'

[43]

She laughed again and, as she passed through the door, we heard her say, 'I must break another'.

'Oh ! those girls !' said the tolerant lady of the house, and smiled.

At 10 o'clock we were well on the way, and passed a number of soldiers. Evidently manœuvres were being carried out, but it might have been a soldiers' picnic ; for some were smoking and others doing up their puttees.

The country was hilly, and the scenery certainly pretty . . . we enjoyed it.

After passing BEINE we came to an avenue, and many walnut trees. They were so tempting that we alighted and gathered quite a supply to take with us on the way. The greedy Lorne, however, was for cracking one with his teeth. 'Stop that,' I cried, 'you will break a tooth.' The obedient fellow took notice and produced a knife, the blade of which he speedily broke (the shells were very hard). He then found a couple of large stones with which he accomplished the feat !

We were now nearing the precincts of CHABLIS, and entered the village of MILLY, one of the areas entitled to the appellation 'Grand Chablis'.

As the term ' Chablis' has been abused in the past, probably more than any other, it might be well for me to inform you as to exactly what now is, and is not, Chablis.

A fight had been going on for nine years over the question, between the Vineyard Proprietors of Chablis and the Wholesale Wine and Spirit Merchants of the Yonne.

The decision was left with the Court of Cassation, the result being that twenty Communes are entitled to the appellation— 'Chablis', and these are divided into Grand Chablis, Chablis, and Bourgogne des Environs de Chablis.

In accordance with this agreement the appellations—'Chablis-Villages', 'Supérieurs and Petit Chablis' for the better wines are suppressed, and replaced by the one appellation 'Chablis', and for the ordinary wines—'Chablis-Villages' and 'Petit Chablis' are designated as 'Bourgogne des Environs de Chablis'.

It might be useful to know the classification of the Grands Vins de Chablis.

Of the Têtes premiers Crus, we have the Vaudésir, Valmur, Blanchot, Les Clos, Grenouille and a part of Preuze.

Of the premiers Crus: Vaulorent, Fourchaume, Mont de Milieu, Chapelot . . . of the deuxièmes Crus, les Lys, Sechet, Epinotte, les Forêts, and several others. Fine Chablis is a wine that will keep and improve for many years. As far back as the twelfth century we read about them spoken of in these terms.

The vintage had commenced, and everyone was very busy . . . however, not too busy to give us more than ordinary attention.

First, we visited the chais of Monsieur Albert Pic, and then the caves. The previous vintage wines had been moved fifteen days before from the chais. It is necessary to keep them separate, as the fermentation of the new wine might affect the old.

The first consideration was to taste some reserves of 1933 vintage. . . .

LIGNORELLES (Chablis) was very good. There seemed to be a little fermentation, but in spite of this, and having been only recently racked, it tasted very well. These wines are racked five or six times, the proprietor being most anxious that all the sugar is thoroughly fermented out.

GRAND CHABLIS 1933 . . . had good flavour, but still held on to a little sugar.

HELIE . . . A good wine, with body and flavour: it was difficult to taste, owing to the fermentation.

VAULORENT . . . Very good.

LYS . . . harder, but good wine.

MONT DE MILIEU . . . the best, and I was very pleased with this.

We then attacked the 1932 wines . . .

VAULORENT . . . very good.

LYS . . . not so pleasing.

We were not able to taste much of the 1934, but from experience the growers look forward to good wine; in bad years the wines show only from 5° to 6° alcohol, in an average year 8° . . . and in this year 10° and even more, so that we may perhaps look for such wines as were produced in the good years of 1900, 1906, etc. . . . and then, how we will delight to drown the oysters!

In fact, in thirty years we can only recall about half a dozen really good vintages (1900, 1904, 1906, 1911, 1921 and 1929 for example). We do look, nevertheless, for fine wines in 1933, and shall we say, although it is too early to prophesy—1934.

The wines of Chablis must not in any way be confused with the White Wines of the Côte d'Or, Mâcon, etc. . . . they are totally different, in a class by themselves.

The Grand Chablis and Chablis is made from the PINOT-Chardonnay vines and the soil is distinctive. A top layer of gravel, with Kimmeridgian Clay below. If the vineyard proprietors could but arrange the elements all would be well, but, like us, they have to bow to the inevitable, and well do they know how exposed they are to all the changes that occur, and how the promising vintage of 1928 was to a great extent destroyed by early frost, and later on by violent hailstorms.

Before going to lunch we put our lips to an ordinary wine, or rather 'must' of 1934. It had just arrived, and had started to ferment. . . . I would not like to predict its future.

SACY, 1934—seemed too acid for my liking.

We heard LE CHANSON DU VIN, in another variety, which, being full of sugar, was fermenting wildly—'Bourru', I described it, which made my host smile . . . I don't know why !

We then went in to what was described as a simple lunch . . . very enjoyable and all-sufficient.

We had eggs, delicately served, saucissons of all varieties, and tournedos, cooked to a turn.

To accompany these we commenced with an ordinary wine of Sacy grape, 1933 . . . quite Natural and very enjoyable . . . to be followed by 1919 Valmur—very good and still fresh, and 1921 Valmur—excellent.

I happened to mention to our hostess that we had gathered some walnuts by the way, when she inquired if I had ever tried walnuts and honey . . . No ; well, we did . . . slightly too sugary for my taste, but delicious. If anyone has a sweet tooth I beg of them to try this.

To finish, we had a Marc de Chablis, thirty years old—I must confess I did not care for it very much ; but our dear old host seemed to enjoy it thoroughly, and described it as of 'fine quality'. It may have been, but everything is a 'matter of comparison'. We were also introduced to Mirabelle, and a kind of Sloe Gin, made after the flesh had been removed from the fruit, and some old Cognac; 'This last for me', I said—'Every time!'

On the 18th May, 1934, particularly at BLANCHOT, the vines were subjected to a heavy frost, which completely stripped them, so that it was necessary to prune them back to the starting point again. The premiers Grands Crus were more affected than the mediocre ones. Evidently the hot summer made some amends, for by the second week in July new bunches of grapes were formed on the vines; these, however, will contain a lesser degree of sugar.

Before starting on our way to DIJON where much work awaited us, we thought well to take Monsieur Bailey's offer (the son-in-law of our host) to have a look over some of the vineyards. On the slopes we could see where heavy rains had washed away considerable soil which would have to be replaced.

Monsieur Bailey told me, which I thought was very interesting, that when the vine growers of the Aube wished to send delegates to Paris to argue that they should be included in the 'Champagne' area, they approached those of Chablis, asking them to join forces.

Chablis rightly refused, on the ground that they were more akin to the Province of Bourgogne. I also learned that unscrupulous merchants—such do exist, you may be surprised to learn—had actually been making inquiries as to how much a Chablis merchant would charge to receive White wine from 'elsewhere', take it into his chais, and send it back as Chablis ! Would you believe that such villainy existed ?

Think what we have escaped !

About half-past three we bade farewell to our good and hospitable friends, with many an expression of sincere thanks.

As we motored along we saw vines on each side, mostly on the slopes—the greater part of the gathering had been finished.

Through FLEYS with its quaint old Church . . . then at a very sharp turn we nearly ran into a flock of sheep; what silly things sheep are ! We continued through TONNERRE, TANLAY and PLIMELLES, but I cannot tell you what happened along this road

[47]

as I was guilty of playing a little game called 'SHUT EYE'. However, I was fully alert as we passed by the boundary dividing the Yonne from the Côte d'Or. Here, a horse, somewhat nervous of the appearance of the Little Auk, careered all over the road, much to our consternation. However, we steered clear of all difficulties, to arrive at LAIGNES, in the midst of a crowded market day.

At CERILLY we noticed in a meadow a number of small cattle (SCHWIZ). They were the prettiest cattle I have ever seen, if such an adjective can be used. Their mousey coats were most attractive ; I have heard young ladies exclaim 'How sweet', when I would have said 'What a foolish remark', but I would have forgiven them here. They were grazing, and as I watched them I called to mind something I had read—I think in one of Mark Twain's works; if not, in one of E. V. Lucas's—for nothing escapes his notice—that cattle when grazing always face the same way. These did certainly . . . I made a point of taking notice as we proceeded. It is nearly always so—make a note and remember to observe, and you will be surprised how true it is. I suppose it has to do with the breeze and the direction of the blades of grass. I took a great liking to these little mousey-coated creatures.

Up a long winding road we were soon at CHÂTILLON S/SEINE. We passed through several villages, without anything in particular to attract our attention, except perhaps that they always seemed to remain old and stationary . . . it was the rarest thing to see a new house being built.

We had some fine scenery to enjoy as we skirted the forest of CHÂTILLON.

The sun was beginning to set and the reflections were most pleasing, in addition to which we were frequently entertained by the clever dogs bringing the sheep into the folds.

Many fruit trees lined the road sides as we approached ST. SEINE L'ABBAYE ; the country was very picturesque. We arrived at the town down a very, very steep hill, complete with a number of hair-pin bends.

Through the town we climbed again, and were rewarded with a view of a most glorious sunset. After SUZON we enjoyed some of the most delightful scenery ; winding roads, forest views, rocky hills somewhat reminiscent of the Cheddar Gorge, and on to DIJON, where we arrived about 7.30, at La Cloche . . . perhaps a little tired, but quite happy.

SUMMARY OF CHABLIS

1870.	A remarkable wine.
1875.	Very abundant, but not very good.
1878. 1881. 1884.	Very good.
1886.	Milder.
1888. 1893. 1895.	Excellent.
1899.	Very little, but good.
1900. 1904. 1906. 1911.	Very good.
1915.	Good.
1921. 1926. 1929.	Excellent.

I do not suppose there exists any quantity of wine in private cellars older than 1900.

Do not keep the fine wines of 1900, 1904 and 1906, but drink them while they are so excellent.

The 1911 may keep longer even than the 1921's which are so ripe and excellent at the present time. I believe the 1926 Grand Chablis will continue to improve, but as soon as a slight darkening of the wine is noticeable, my advice is—drink it.

There need be no hurry over the 1929's, which are so good and will continue to improve, but do not delay too long before considering the 1933; always remembering that the quantity available of the fine wines is strictly limited.

CHAPTER IV

BURGUNDY AND POUILLY S/LOIRE

As we arrived at the hotel a terrible-looking ruffian greeted us, which caused us to remember how necessary it was to lock the car while we entered the hotel to make inquiries about the rooms we had reserved.

It was not long before we had had a good wash, and went in to dine. What should we drink—was the all-important question. We were thirsty and, remembering the fine dry wines of Chablis, which we had so recently left, we ordered a bottle of Chablis Vaudésir, 1926. We were not very successful, for the first bottle was corked, and so was the second—no question about it. The third was good, and we enjoyed it, more or less.

This reminded me of a letter from a gentleman, as follows :

'Two bottles of the Champagne are being returned as "corked" in fact, the corks were most difficult to get out.'

The menu was not exciting ... perhaps we expected too much.

As we were finishing with a glass of Fromy's 30 years old Cognac, which was good, we were much amused by the conversation of three strangers.

'What does "La Cloche" mean ?' asked one ... 'I think it is a bell' ... 'No', replied the second—'a "cloche" is a clock.'

'You are both wrong,' chimed in the third. 'It's a pendulum ! !'

On the following morning, Tuesday, the 25th September, we made our way to see our good friend Emile Siredey, of Maison Regnier, and were much interested in visiting the vast cellars ... the first containing the new wine—that is, 1933 ... another, the old wine, and then—older, and oldest.

We were much intrigued by the methods—old and new—of removing the sediment from the bottles. It is claimed that the wine in no way suffers . . . I wonder? I cannot but think a discriminating palate might detect the operation.

The weather had now cleared, for it had been raining when we started, and we went off in the smiling sunshine to partake of déjeuner.

The 'Châteaubriant' was selected, and we fared extremely well. With a paté, and some Jambon d/Dijon cooked in White wine, we had a bottle of 1923 Meursault, Goutte d'Or . . . good quality and clean. This lasted us with the fish—good size, river trout, weighing 1½ lbs. at least . . . they deserved the good Meursault.

Pheasant en casserole followed. Very good it was, and with this we indulged in a bottle of 1923 Mazis Chambertin—an excellent bottle of wine. It was made from the vieux cépages, and reminded me somewhat of Romanée Conti. The Eau de vie de Marc (Chambertin) did not appeal to me, in spite of its being 1889.

After déjeuner we paid a visit to the nearest vineyards on the Côte d'Or. In order to arrive there we must pass by FIXIN (pronounced 'Fissin') where we saw an old peasant on the roadside pressing the grapes for his two or three casks of wine.

Admirers of the great Napoleon would not miss FIXIN, with its Parc de Noisot.

Here will be found much of interest; a replica of the Emperor's house at St. Helena, containing many interesting things.

In particular that beautiful work of Rude 'Réveil de Napoleon'.

I was constrained to buy a large number of post-cards relating to Napoleon, and send them to my good lady at home, for she almost worships the man. I suppose many others do as well . . . he certainly was a genius.

After our short spell of sight-seeing at FIXIN, and enjoying the wonderful view from the heights—with Mont Blanc occasionally peeping over from behind the Jura, we quitted and commenced more serious business.

At Mazis-Chambertin (Gevrey) we entered an interesting chai, where the wine was being made in the old-fashioned way —the juice running into casks of a capacity of some seven thousand litres. The working hours were long—from seven to seven . . . the vendangeurs were surely very tired when the time came for them to call a halt.

On one of the walls of this chai was inscribed a record of each vintage, a few details of which I noted in my little book.

The 31st August was the earliest date on which the vintage commenced, and this was in 1893.

A few others are interesting :

1863. 4th October . . . Passable.⎫ The first and the last
1931. 13th   ,,   . . . ⎭   recorded.
1910. No vintage ; mildew of grapes in July destroyed all
       in three days.
1928. Good—two vintages—
      29th September, 1st florissant,
      29th October,   2nd   ,,
        By reason of the hail, 6th June.
1879. 22nd October. Bad.
      No pressing for 1st wine (red).

This year the vintage commenced on the 24th September, and was in full swing at Chambertin.

The designation 'Gevrey-Chambertin' is in common use . . . it is well to remember that all Chambertin is Gevrey, but all Gevrey is not Chambertin, and further, that the words 'Grand Chambertin' are not strictly correct.

The famous Clos de Bèze is, in fact, divided with Chambertin. It is one vineyard of some 27 hectares, divided in equal portions. Lower down we come to the Chapelle-Chambertin.

The monks of the Abbey de Cîteaux planted the Clos de Vougeot, and those of the Abbey de Bèze, not to be outdone, planted the Clos de Bèze. Gossip has it that this irritated the monks of Cîteaux, who approached the owner of the other half of the field (or champ) on which was the newly planted Clos de Bèze, and having purchased it proceeded to plant it with vines, calling their new acquisition by the name of the previous owner —Bertin : that is the Champ de Bertin, or, as it is known the world over—Chambertin. (This took place as long ago as the twelfth century.)

The vines are the Pinots, sometimes called the Petits Noiriens, or NOIRIENS—two ways of speaking of the same vine.

We then made a survey of that delightful little commune of Morey St. Denis, the birthplace of many a beautiful wine, with the celebrated Clos de Tart, and Bonnes Mares in the vicinity.

The district is all agog with fine vineyards : Chambolle on the left, with the celebrated Les Musigny ; Les Amoureuses.

It is indeed wonderful that here we have some of the finest wines the world produces and yet, almost within a stone's throw on the other side of the main road, only the commonest wine is made ; from a Gamay grape, because the Pinot will not flourish, and if it did, the soil, etc., is such that the yield would be of very mediocre quality.

This was a good insight for several days' work to come, along the Côte d'Or.

We therefore left our friend, with grateful thanks, and were glad of a little repose before adjourning to one of the many taverns for a simple dinner, when we actually were content to partake of the vin compris—blanc—en carafe, and found it very drinkable.

The next day we arose early, and were rewarded with the sight of a wonderful red sky . . . we hoped that it would not prove the truth of 'Red sky in the morning is the shepherd's warning, etc.'

We called on an old friend at Nuits St. Georges . . . unfortunately he was laid aside with an attack of lumbago, and we were deprived of the pleasure of meeting him, and of obtaining some first-hand information.

The reports of the vintages which we received from our old friend's associate were not very encouraging. He certainly could be classed among the pessimists.

'Yes', he said, 'there are a few 1929's left, but they are expensive. The ones we have are mostly of the Côte de Beaune.'

This did not interest me very much as I am more attached to the wines of the Côte de Nuits . . . 1930, 1931 and 1932 he classed, with an appropriate gesture, as 'rubbish'.

Of the 1933 vintage, he was not proud . . . in fact, he referred to it as 'very light, and not much good'.

I then inquired of the prospects of the 1934 vintage, and Sir Pessimist impressed upon us that the greatest discrimination would have to be used in selecting any of the wines, owing to the fact that, in his opinion, the 'taille', that is, the pruning, was not carried out by many proprietors, sufficiently hard.

We were glad to be out in the fresh air, and to make our way to Beaune.

I had become mildly excited at the prospects of seeing my dear old friend, Louis Latour, and his family. What he does not know about Burgundy wine, from the planting of the vine to the draining of the bottle, is not worth knowing, and he has such a charming way of imparting his knowledge.

Before lunch I begged leave to pay a visit to the Hospices de Beaune. I am ashamed to say that, during all my visits here, I had never made time to go there. Please don't miss it . . . it is more than 'well worth while'.

The Hospital of Beaune, or as it is habitually spoken of, the Hospices de Beaune, is an ancient building—full of interest . . . a few hours spent in visiting the various apartments would give sufficient data—useful and interesting data—to fill a book on its own. I would therefore seek your indulgence to be allowed to be as brief as possible.

It was about the middle of the fifteenth century that the Chancellor, Nicolas Rolin, and his wife, Guigone de Salins, conceived the charitable idea of building a hospital to the Glory of God, and for the amelioration of the suffering of the poor and destitute.

In spite of the fact that he came from Autun, Beaune was selected for the honour.

The architecture is Flemish, and the 'tout ensemble' is both attractive and picturesque.

The courtyard is 250 feet across, and is surrounded by a gallery, access to which can be had by asking.

The ancient well presents a picture by itself, and, having taken an interested look at this, we entered the Grand Salle . . . all so clean . . . with the cubicles skirting each wall.

The ancient pewter utensils, used by the poor old folk at their meals, took my fancy, for to see the way they fondled them, and tucked in, did one's heart good.

The mural decorations in their simplicity attract attention : on all sides will be seen the initials 'N' and 'G' entwined, representing Nicolas and Guigone. The word 'Seulle' catches the eye, also the simple device of a solitary bird on a branch. It is quite natural to seek an explanation.

My good and erudite friend, Monsieur Louis Latour, explained to me when I saw him afterwards that, when marrying his second wife (Guigone de Salins), the Chancellor Nicolas wished her to understand very plainly that she should be his one and only 'love', or 'star' of their common life. This was not altogether unheard of . . . even a few years later, the Duke of Burgundy—Philippe le Bon—wrote, in the same strain after his marriage with Isabelle of Portugal . . . 'AULTRE N'AURAY'.

The two letters 'N' and 'G' are evidently the initial letters of Nicolas and Guigone.

The bird means, in all probability, 'solitary as the sparrow on the branch', and was very likely adopted by Guigone de Salins after the death of her husband. Nicolas Rolin was born in 1380, and died on the 18th January, 1461.

Guigone de Salins died in the garb of a Sister of the Hospices, on the 24th December, 1470.

The refectory reminded me of what one sees in our old Abbeys. The Chapel is indeed beautiful, but must be seen to be appreciated. The various wards are all in apple-pie order and kept scrupulously clean. In the grand and spacious hall, and in the court, the annual sale of the Wines of the Hospices takes place. Wines are offered after each vintage (in November) and when the vintage is a success, very fine wines come under the hammer ; for many an excellent vineyard has been left as a legacy to the Hospices. It is, in a great measure, from this source that the income is derived.

The kitchen was a picture ; the steel implements were so highly polished that you could see your face reflected in every direction.

Should anyone intend to pay a visit to the Hospices, do not fail to see 'Bertrand' . . . he is delightful—do not be scared at his vacant and yet inquiring look, for he will do you no harm ; he is the 'Tourne-broche de la cuisine'.

There is much to see and enjoy of past ages : the offices, the apothecary, the museum.

In the museum you will see a remarkable picture—'Le Retable' of the last judgment, painted on wood. It is not only a marvellous conception, but marvellously executed. As you examine it, from a little distance, use a magnifying glass which is provided, and scrutinise the details, for instance the work and colouring of the jewels is astounding !

On one side of the picture can be seen Guigone de Salins, Isabella of Portugal, Philippotte and four Apostles, and beneath them is the way to hell : horrible scenes !

On the opposite, or left-hand side of the picture, will be recognised Eugénie IV, Duc Philippe, Nicolas Rolin, his son, Bishop of Autun, and four other Apostles. Beneath is the happier side— the righteous ones on the way to enter heaven.

In the centre is to be seen St. Michael weighing the souls. Here is seen an angel standing at the entrance, pointing the way to the Marble Halls . . . this is most inspiring. The memory of this wonderful work will surely live with me as long as the fragrant memory of many a fine bottle of wine emanating from the Hospices de Beaune (Rolin) and the Hospices de Beaune (Salins).

One corner of the picture depicts hell itself, and the wicked being cast down . . . What a warning to naughty vignerons !

' Lorne, I think it is time we were going.'

We lunched at Château de Corton Grancey where, besides being regaled with recherché wine and food, we had the pleasure of meeting a number of charming and interesting people ; all, I believe, sons and daughters, or in-laws, of our very genial and hospitable host and hostess, Monsieur and Madame Louis Latour.

The memory of this family gathering will long remain with me, especially as Lorne did the talking. . . . Well, he is a linguist, and, encouraged by the smiles of the ladies, he got well away with it.

The wines we were offered, and did not refuse, were 1928 Corton Charlemagne (Blanc) which had fruit and body, perhaps a trifle on the sweet side, owing to the exceptional maturity reached that year ; there is no doubt that the 1928 vintage has produced excellent wines.

To follow, we had a red Corton, Clos la Vigne-au-Saint, also 1928, and also very attractive.

To follow this was 1923 Romanée St. Vivant, a very fine wine, perfectly sound, and will keep for years . . . that is, if the owners will give it the chance.

As the pièce de résistance, Monsieur Latour treated us to a bottle of 1904 Corton Grancey . . . 'Thank you so much, my generous host'—It was kind and a kindness well appreciated. This you will readily understand when I confess I was terribly disappointed when I saw the decanter was empty.

But, what a wine ! And of what a vintage, and served in the best conditions—this being the bottle's only journey in life ! Body—yes, but so soft that I thought all the body was a depth of elegance. And what flavour !

But I must not continue in this strain or I shall be called over the coals for making the 'mouth to water'.

After coffee and very fine Cognac, which was enjoyed on the terrace, with a fine view looking towards Switzerland, we bade au revoir to the hospitable family, not forgetting to throw a kiss to the sweet little grand-daughter Marie-Claire who had retired upstairs to take her afternoon's sleep.

The slopes of the Côte d'Or, facing East and South East, are always delightful . . . I think those of the hill of Corton mostly so—they are the highest and the most beautiful. Although classified as a wine of the Côte de Beaune, the Aloxe-Corton (pronounced 'Alose') is almost adjoining the Côte de Nuits, and has the good fortune of benefiting by the virtues of both.

What beautiful wines I can remember having enjoyed from the Clos du Roi (Corton). Le Grand Monarque knew well what he was doing when he decided that here was THE wine fit for the illustrious King of France—hence 'Clos du Roi'.

We must not forget the Corton Charlemagne—yes, your thought is quite natural and correct . . . the great King-Emperor had the closest associations with the vineyard. A record shows that in 775, he actually possessed it.

There is not much depth of soil, partly chalk . . . this becomes washed off during a storm, and much labour and expense is required to replace it.

The vines are American roots, with the PINOT grafted on. The greatest care is carried out in the planting. As we proceeded up the hill, we could notice the different plants—at the foot of the hill, the RIPARIA, the best of which is the Gloire de Montpellier, then the RIPARIA RUPESTRIS, and finally, the CHASSELAS BERLANDIERI (there is more chalk here).

These are known by numbers such as 3309, 41B and 16149. I am becoming very technical . . . it is foolish of me. I promise not to be so uninteresting again—anyhow, not until the next time.

One of the favourite wines of Voltaire was the Corton Grancey, the property of Monsieur Louis Latour.

Monsieur Lebault, a President of the Parliament of Bourgogne held at DIJON, was a former proprietor of this famous growth, in fact it was a descendant of his, le Comte de Grancey, who gave his name to the property. He lived a considerable portion of his life on the Estate, and was generously inclined to make gifts of his wine to his friends, Voltaire in particular being one of the fortunate recipients. Greuze was a visitor . . . it was here that he executed that fine picture of Madame Lebault.

In the centre of this fine vineyard I noticed several long sticks with leaves on them : on inquiring, I learnt that the vendangeurs of a neighbouring vineyard had gone a little too far and had gathered the produce of three rows of about 300 vines apiece by mistake, and when the guilty one recognised what he had done, he placed these signs at the end of the rows to indicate that he was ready and willing to pay for his trespass.

We then returned to some serious work in the chais.

Being anxious to taste some samples of the 1933 vintage, my host very kindly consented. It was the vintage we had heard so recently spoken of, not in the most encouraging way.

The first wine was the Corton Grancey . . . I endeavoured to examine it most critically, and my remarks were : 'Very good ; cannot find anything amiss'.

The next was a Chambertin of 1933. It was a big wine, of a different character.

Then we tasted 1933 Romanée St. Vivant which had finished its fermentation in November, 1933. It was very soft, and appealed to me immensely.

Here the vintage in 1933 had been late . . . the quantity small, but very well succeeded.

On the cellar wall I noticed the following terse remark, written by one Olivier de Serres, the first writer on Agriculture in the sixteenth century :

' The object of vine growers is to gather their grapes en perfection de bonté, that is, when the grapes have reached the maximum of their qualities.'

As we passed along I noticed that some vine leaves, on taking on their autumnal tints, were turning red . . . others golden, and on inquiring, I found that the common ones turned red, and the fine ones—golden.

The Clos de Chapitre at ALOXE is also a good vineyard, although it does not aspire to the pre-eminence of its neighbour.

On examining various bunches of grapes, I found signs of the cochylis, but, I am glad to say, not so bad as to affect the wine.

Nicotine is used largely as a preventative for this disease.

The grapes were so full of juice that the carriers were wet through, from the juice that exuded through the baskets they were carrying.

We then visited the celebrated Romanée Conti. This growth again can thank Louis XIV for its great popularity . . . for did he not give out in public that he had recovered from his illness and felt so much better after a diet on this wine ?

Apart from this it is a very fine vineyard and deserves all the popularity it enjoys.

When I was told that the vineyard dates back to the Roman Age, I smiled, but undoubtedly it does go back a long way.

The planting is very irregular. The vines last for between thirty and forty years, and from these stocks other vines are reared, by a special process—much too intricate for me to try to explain.

Before entering the chais of Romanée Conti we had a look around. We were overlooking Vosne Romanée, while higher up the slope was Romanée (tout court) not so good.

As you may imagine, I was still quite anxious to taste some of the 1933 wines.

Grand Souchot, and the Echezeaux I found light in colour, of good quality, but somewhat astringent.

The Grands Echezeaux were fuller, and better quality.

La Tache was very good indeed, or so was my impression. This wine from 1933 becomes the property of the owners of Romanée Conti.

Richebourg was the next. Very typical I found this . . . with rather a dry finish. It did not appeal to me very much.

Then came the Romanée Conti—all 1933 . . . such an elegant wine . . . fine flavour and much quality to develop.

When we left here I could not help noticing some vendangeurs resting, and at the same time helping themselves to the grapes they had been picking.

'You must lose a large quantity by this method of consumption,' I inquired.

'Indeed, you are right,' replied my host; 'we calculate that, at Château Grancey, the vendangeurs consume during the vintage, no less than ten thousand francs worth of grapes.'

No wonder that they are continually absent for a short time !

Before returning to DIJON, we expressed the desire to visit the ancient Château of Clos Vougeot. It proved most interesting . . . the building is thirteenth century, and the outhouses of an earlier date.

The four very, very old presses interested us immensely. They were most impressive, made of Cîteaux Oak, and required ten men on each arm to manipulate.

I do not intend to describe the interior of the Château with full details, but I should like to mention the Grand Salon—a marvellous sixteenth century chimneypiece.

What did attract my attention here was the fine view of the vineyards from the windows. The Petit Salon was also attractive, of the time of François 1er, and decorated with the arms of Bretagne.

In this room was a beautiful picture which made me envious . . . 'La Jeune Captive'.

This old Château belongs to a former socialist deputy, Monsieur Camuzet; who, however, does not occupy any of the rooms.

But we must not delay our return to DIJON. It was becoming dark, and we had a rendezvous for dinner.

We had invited Monsieur Siredey to join us at the 'Trois Faisans'. Out of the natural kindness of his heart he had been to see the proprietor of this famous restaurant during the day, and arranged for an excellent repast in a small private room. This was the menu :

CAVIAR
GRENOUILLES - - 1928 MEURSAULT, Goutte d'Or
    (the best I have tasted) (Excellent !)
ROGNONS - - - 1923 GEVREY CHAMBERTIN
    à la Champigny. (La Combe au Moine)
                                beautiful wine.

ARTICHAUT
FOIE GRAS TRUFFÉ - COGNAC, HENNESSY

We were very satisfied and very happy. The way in which Lorne attacked one of the bottles of Gevrey Chambertin caused me to inquire if he had hollow legs—just by way of a joke.

'Yes,' said he, carrying on the joke, and added—'also blotting-paper in my boots for this occasion.'

We spoke of Chambertin, and I was much interested to learn that the thrush is very fond of grapes . . . so much so, that it is customary to plant, at Chambertin in particular, White grapes for the first ten metres from the crest of the hill ; so that the birds who live in the woods on the summit should not so readily see the grapes, as if they had been black ones.

Before quitting, I remembered an incident which I related, much to the amusement of the sommelier : A friend of mine was partaking dinner at Grantham, and had ordered a bottle of Burgundy. When it was brought to the table he noticed that it was on the cold side . . . he therefore called the waiter and asked him to be good enough to warm it.

The result was almost incredible. . . . After a short time the waiter returned, all smiles, with the Burgundy, steaming—and in a saucepan ! ! !

I gathered that he was about to inquire if it was warm enough, but he did not get as far as that !

The next day we were favoured with fine weather, and had a royal time, for had not Monsieur Coquet more than kindly placed his valuable services at our disposal?

The weather was so fine and hot that I actually sported my Panama!

The first visit we paid was again at Gevrey; we were much interested in tasting the new wine of 1934 . . . of course it was much too early to form an opinion, but we decided that it was good—with 12°.

We then tasted the 1933. In spite of what I had been told the previous day, I found the wine good, and 'tendre' . . . that is, elegant. It was very forward, and would be ready for bottling early in 1935. If one can judge of the 1934, I should think they will be ready to put into bottle in the spring of 1936.

A 1933 Petite Chapelle had body but was dry.

1933 St. Jacques had more fruit, albeit a little rough.

1933 Charmes Chambertin pleased me much more. Fine flavour and not so dry.

Evidently discrimination was necessary in considering the wines of 1933.

We then went to MOREY ST. DENIS which adjoins Gevrey, and is responsible for many excellent wines.

We here met a delightful old gentleman—a most enthusiastic proprietor, who showed us over his cellars with justifiable pride. His son was imbued with the same zeal, but perhaps with a trifle more commercial instinct.

We proceeded to taste the following wines, against which I will place my impressions:

1928 *Charmes Chambertin* . . . A good wine, but surely should have been in bottle by now. However, it will come round more quickly for drinking, with maybe less body.

1933 *Chambolle Musigny* (2 cuves) . . . the first of 6 Hhds. 13° . . . very good indeed, but keep a discreet silence.

The second of 4 Hhds. was equally good.

1933 *Charmes Chambertin.* 15 Hhds. also 13°. *Very* good, is my note.

1933 *Gevrey Chambertin.* 7 Hhds. I did not like this . . .NO!

I was impressed with the first two, and already was desirous

[62]

of possessing them, but the proprietor wished to see the three lots disposed of together and thus make room for the new vintage; but not at any price would I have the 7 Hhds.

The price he asked for the other two was out of the question. We therefore left it like that.

'Would you care to see an excellent wine of Morey 1932'? he asked. 'Such a wine does not exist', was my rejoinder.

'I'll show you one', and forthwith he produced a wine that certainly was not bad, and at the price, good value.

He generously bade us take a bottle of Charmes Chambertin 1926 with us for lunch, which we did, promising to drink to our old friend, Morizot.

Before going, I ventured to make an offer for his 6, 4 and 15 Hhds., but he ridiculed it. You will learn the sequel towards the end of the tour. I think Papa, as the son spoke of him, would have seen the generosity of the offer, but his offspring looked at the proposal in a different light.

Our good friend, Monsieur Coquet, then took us to visit some friends of his at Nuits St. Georges, where, before partaking of the excellent déjeuner they had prepared, we carried out a further tasting duty.

Monsieur Rodier was happy to show us, while we were in his vast caves, some 1933 wines of Nuits, in which we had expressed a certain amount of interest.

1933 *Nuits Chamottes* . . . Quite good.
1933 *Nuits* . . . Better, more fruit.
1933 *Nuits Porrets* . . . I did not care for.
1933 *Nuits Boudots* . . . Better.
1933 *Nuits Vaucrains* . . . Very good.

At déjeuner we had an ordeal. . . . They were too kind! However, we survived it and were able to carry on without the slightest difficulty.

These are the wines offered at this Bourguignon lunch:

1932 *Bâtard Montrachet*.
   (Leave out the first 't' in Montrachet when speaking of this wine.) Good. This, with excellent river fish.
1930 *Côte de Beaune*. 12°.
1930 *Côte de Nuits*. 13°.

I preferred the Nuits but could see that the Côte de Beaune
will be ready earlier for consumption.

1933 *Gevrey Chambertin.*

1933 *Clos des Lambrays* . . . this last was most attractive.

These young wines were followed by :

1928 *Morey, Clos des Lambrays.*

1929   ,,   ,,   ,,

    I admit I preferred the 1929 . . . it had more fruit.

We then opened a bottle of 1926 Charmes Chambertin, which
had been given to us during the morning. It was perhaps a little
disappointing, but had considerable flavour.

1898 Clos des Lambrays . . . This was a WINE ! Very, very
fine. I thought how Stephen Gwynn would have rejoiced with
this beautiful wine ; his merry twinkle over a glass of good wine
must always be a refreshing memory for anyone who has shared
a fine bottle with him.

Naturally, fine wines were then brought into open discussion,
each member of the party exclaiming on some beautiful 'bottle'
they had enjoyed at some time or other. I do not think that
anyone surpassed the wines I once was privileged to find placed
before me by that young and enthusiastic connoisseur, Mr.
Eustace Hoare.

It was some twelve months ago, and how vividly it remains in
my memory. I shall refrain from discussing the wines, after the
rebukes I have received from some unhappy people who had
read *Viniana*, but I cannot, even for their sake, fail to mention
them :

        1904 MONTRACHET ! !

        1911 CHAMBERTIN ! !

        1904 CLOS DE VOUGEOT ! ! !

        1893 MUSIGNY.

        1865 CHAMBERTIN ! ! ! ! ! ! !

        1896 TAYLOR—It smelt very good.

We all stood and drank a silent toast—to the God of Wines,
and the Goddess of our wonderful repast and then retired to a
delightful library, and indulged in a petit verre of fine Cognac ;
out of interest we were shown the Eau de Vie de Marc, which

is made in the Public Still—I was content to smile my appreciation while our good friends of the house of Monsieur Bahèzre puffed away at all sorts of remarkable pipes. Cause and effect . . . I wonder !

Our next visit was to be at the Montrachet—we approached with a feeling of reverence, for has not the wine been described as 'divine'?

The Chevalier facing . . . the Bâtard on the left of the famous Le Montrachet generally referred to as Grand Montrachet, and the Demoiselle, lying apart, is quite small.

There used to be a guide who showed the tourist this country-side, and would delight in pointing out the vineyards of the Montrachet in this wise . . . true, or not, it is a 'jolie histoire':

'Voisinage dangereux. . . . Ici le Chevalier, là la Demoiselle et plus bas de l'autre côté, c'était inévitable, regardez le Bâtard-Montrachet !

'L'Aîné, le Chevalier, la Demoiselle, le Bâtard, ils sont tous de la famille des Montrachet. Mais si l'un est roi, les autres ne sont que princes du sang.'

We arrived at Chassagne immediately . . . called on Monsieur Colin Bouley, the régisseur of Monsieur le Général le Marquis de Laguiche, who shares, with the Baron Thénard, the most important portion referred to as 'le "Grand" Montrachet'.

This area is but small . . . in 1933 the Marquis made but one half cask. What a calamity for a wine known all the world over for its fine qualities !

This year (1934) there will be about twelve casks. I wonder how many I shall be fortunate enough to secure ? We shall see later.

It was not possible to taste it, for, in fact, the vintage had not yet commenced, but by hook or by crook, I intended coming along this way again before returning—then we shall see what we shall see !

Monsieur Colin Bouley was most anxious for us to taste the 1929 Le Montrachet of the Marquis. Oh ! What a wine.! A wine such as the young subalterns in the Guards would describe as 'one which "got you a bit forrerder" '.

I am quite sure the Marquis will have no objection if I quote from one of his letters. I do so, for it is a privilege and pleasure to let others know that there are such men living who take infinite care and pains, and justifiable pride in the making of their wine :

'This wine, having a very high degree of alcohol and a lot of sugar, would not be able to be bottled before a certain number of years. It would be at least three years, but that would depend on the fermentation, which I absolutely refuse to cause to be more rapid by means which are in current use in the wine business.

'Our wine is essentially an article of luxury, and even if I should be the only one to drink it I should always keep the old quality up ; perfectly natural, without any manipulation, a great deal of keeping power and a flavour entirely of its own.

'I have at the same time also in view in writing to you to invite you to come and see me during one of your travels if you pass through our region, because here I could let you taste the whole series of Montrachet for years back. You would thus see the successive transformation of my wines. I do not speak of the 1870, which was remarkable, but which has become maderizé, but since 1894 there are some curious wines and some very good ones, above all the 1906 for example. This long life is due precisely to the manner in which we make our vintage and treat the wine. One can never arrive at the same quality if it is manipulated.'

We spoke of the fine wine of Meursault, but the only reply we were vouchsafed was very terse :

'Le Meursault n'est pas Le Montrachet ! !'

Nevertheless, it can be very good indeed. Well do I remember the 1915 and 1923, in particular the Meursault Perrières.

Monsieur Coquet pointed out to us his vineyard at Bâtard-Montrachet, very pleasantly situated, and where excellent wine is made. He then took us to CHAGNY, having given us so much of his valuable time, and equally valuable assistance, that we were quite at a loss to express our thanks adequately. I hope he will read this and then know how very grateful we were.

At CHAGNY we waited for the motor-bus in order to go to DIJON. . . . It was a shabby old bus, but one or two incidents which occurred made the journey, at least, amusing.

We had a fine view from MONTHELIE, along the road which runs between walls on the way to the well-known districts of Volnay and Pommard.

As a little relaxation from vinous thoughts I will tell you what happened in the bus . . . all so simple and yet amusing.

In the first place a Sister of Mercy entered, wearing one of the enormous white hats; every time she moved someone was struck in the face, so that, on each of these occasions we enjoyed a little scene of 'french politesse', commencing with a thousand apologies on the one part, and ending with a 'pas de quoi' in different tones on the other part.

Sitting on a seat alongside of us were two women, somewhat fashionably dressed—their finger-nails were of burnished silver . . . I knew of the scarlet runners, but the silver touch was new to me !

At the next stop the bus was detained while a would-be passenger hurriedly gulped down his beer. He then, with a spring, seized the handrail, jumped on to the bus, and went sprawling on the floor, much to the consternation of the other passengers.

We were gradually becoming 'full inside' when four passengers arrived, carrying fairly large baskets of freshly gathered grapes. These baskets were placed upon the floor of the bus, but during this procedure a small bunch fell out of one basket . . . Oh ! The fuss this caused. It was quite close to us, and we were admonished for moving our feet, as we might have trod on them. The two silvered queens seemed anxious to assist, and as they bent forward in their anxiety to find the elusive bunch, they knocked each other on the head. The 'politesse' departed for a minute ! I imagine that the thought of damaging the 'silver' prevented further turmoil.

Eventually the bunch was discovered and placed within the basket, the owner of which, evidently not wishing to cause further commotion, deciding to rest it on his knees. He was wearing quite a decent suit when he did this. . . . The juice of the grapes was exuding so much that, when he alighted from the bus, the suit was by no means—decent—but, there is a silver lining behind each cloud. . . . He had recovered the lost bunch, and was taking it home in triumph !

I could continue like this indefinitely, for the journey occupied nearly two hours, but I will have consideration, and desist.

We arrived at the hotel somewhat jaded, but a bath soon put us to rights, and we betook ourselves to one of the many taverns to enjoy a quiet and simple tête-à-tête dinner ; with a truite meunière, and a Châteaubriant garni. We indulged in the Vin Rosé en carafe, and thoroughly enjoyed it.

The only thing that might have taken away our appetites, but it didn't, was the sight of a pair of hairy legs belonging to a fleshy young woman at the next table. . . . Good wine stables one for anything !

The next day was Friday, 28th September. Before we kept our appointment with Monsieur Siredey, we made a most important call at the bank, and then paid a short visit to the museum, which was very interesting, but much like most museums ; however, I was intrigued with the tombs of the Dukes, and the relics of Philippe le Hardi, Jean Sans Peur, Philippe le Bon and Charles le Temeraire ; the sight of which brought back the memory of many a history lesson.

Duty called us, and we were off to taste a number of wines, the details of which may prove of interest to some. I will therefore give the names of the wines and my remarks in the order in which they arrived :

1929 Hospices de Beaujeu . . . A pleasant, inexpensive wine.

1929 Côte de Beaune . . . Good, clean wine.

1929 Côte Chalonnais, Mercurey . . . Good.

1929 Beaune . . . Did not care for . . . A suspicion of acidity at the back.

1928 Pommard . . . Typical, but soft.

1928 Gevrey Chambertin . . . A little disappointing in the after-taste.

1933 wines next came on the scene.

1933 Hospices de Beaujeu . . . Fair body, and sugar.

1933 Moulin-à-Vent . . . Good.

1933 Santenay . . . Not quite so pleasing.

1933 Volnay . . . Did not care for. Flavour falls away.

1933 Aloxe Corton . . . Very good indeed—fine colour.

1933 Pommard . . . A little troublé.

1933 Nuits St. Georges . . . Good, very forward.

1933 Corton . . . Good.   Sugar and flavour.

1933 Chambertin . . . Grand wine—plenty of fruit.

These 1933 wines had only recently been racked, so were not sampled under the best conditions.

The consensus of opinion was that the 1934 wines would not be superior to those of 1933.

We then tasted, at my request, two White Wines which were very interesting, and decided me to visit the Province from which they came.

The POUILLY S/LOIRE (which must not be confused with the Pouilly Fuissé) known as the Blanc Fumé, I found quite attractive—dry, with a pleasant flavour, perhaps a goût de terroir, and with some body. . . .   We will hear more of these in due course.

This was certainly a good morning's work and we deserved our lunch at Nuits St. Georges, whither we wended our way, having been strongly recommended to pay a visit to the Croix Blanche.

We were well repaid for taking this journey. . . .   Our 'simple' repast was as follows :

HORS D'ŒUVRES.

SMOKED HAM SAUSAGE.

TROUT—We had seen them alive a few minutes before.

HAM—This was a treat . . . Braised Ham Nuitonne, Stuffed Tomatoes . . . The Sauce was said to be made with the Grands Vins de Nuits.

A GIGOT then made its appearance . . . I could not tackle it for fear of never being able to look an ewe in the face again.   The Sauce served with this was excellent—Champignons, Onions, etc. . . . I tucked into this and actually, to

With this we were content to enjoy a White Clos de Vougeot, 1929 vintage . . . which was a very good flavoury wine.

follow example, wiped the plate
with bread and ate it—yes—not
only ate it, but thoroughly enjoyed it. . . .

Last—A curious CREAM CHEESE,
with sugar. As we did not think
it would go well with the wine,   Fine, 25 years old—
we indulged in an excellent   Coffee.
Camembert. . . .

What more could anyone want, except perhaps the smile of
'Mariette' and the good lady of the house, both of which we
were certainly treated to.

There were two little quotations printed on the menu, which
are well worth repeating :

'Si le vin avait été malfaisant, on n'aurait pas attendu 4000 ans
pour s'en apercevoir.'—Dr. E. Perrier.

The other was from Rabelais, as follows :

'Il y a trop de vin pour dire la messe ; pas assez pour faire
tourner les moulins, donc il faut boire.'

We had been told that we should find it good, and *we did*.
I said to Lorne—'I shall try to return here one day', and *I did !*

After this sumptuous déjeuner we proceeded to Beaune in
search of Madame de Marcilly, for I had heard that she had good
vineyards, and knew how to make good wine.

We had a little difficulty in finding her house. At one street
corner we asked a little boy, about ten years of age, if he knew
the name. He was sweetly apologetic—'No, gentlemen', he
said. 'I only wish I did, and then I should have had much
pleasure in directing you.'

However, when we did find the house, nobody was at home :
'Tant pis pour nous', was our remark.

Lorne thought he would like to see AUTUN, as we had time to
spare, so—why not ? Off we went. A little game for one, that
I have played before after lunch, kept me busy, for I had no idea
that we had passed through Pommard and Volnay; in fact, we
were nearing the Cathedral City when Lorne considerately
drew my attention to a company of soldiers on the march.

We took a gentle tour round the city, the general view of which was pleasing—a little disturbing perhaps, by virtue of the number of priests one sees walking about.

Some of the old Roman fortifications still exist, and are very interesting . . . the Porte d'Arboux taking my fancy.

The Temple of Janus I voted an atrocity, but I have no doubt that its history allows it to take on quite a different aspect.

The Cathedral, St. Lazare, was very fine indeed, and was well worth a visit.

'Paterfamilias' was with his children, and had entered, when one of them commenced to play with the Holy Water, on which, in the sacred edifice, he was immediately given a sound box on the ears—this reminded me of an event my father used to tell us. On one occasion he was at the Cathedral at Cologne (I think it was), when he noticed that the flower sellers were wont, when their stock began to droop, to hasten into the Cathedral and revive the flowers by dipping them in the Holy Water at the entrance.

As the day was drawing to a close we deemed it was time to hurry back to DIJON . . . some of the roads were very pleasant, reminding us of the joyous English country lanes. The sound of the cigales (grasshoppers) was almost deafening in places, so much so that we stopped the car to listen to them, not being quite sure whether it was something amiss with the car, or the cigales.

Near MELIN we came across a motorist whose lights had failed, and were able to give him a lift. He was deeply grateful.

As we passed along the Côte d'Or, the evening air was permeated with the smell of new wine, and country song.

We then had to think of dinner, in spite of our sumptuous déjeuner, so decided to go opposite, to the Châteaubriant, where we had fared so well on a previous occasion.

We had a good meal and took the opportunity to taste some wines that were more or less new to us.

First of all was a Pouilly S/Loire; after my previous remarks about the wine, perhaps you are not surprised . . . 1928 wine . . . it was excellent—light and full of flavour. I thought, however, I detected a slight suspicion of sulphur. This may have been so, as on inquiry I found that at Pouilly S/Loire this sulphur expedient is resorted to, as in the Bordeaux district.

We then had a 1923 Grand Pouilly, Blanc Fumé—in brilliant condition . . . a trifle sweet but very good.

Seeing a wine on the list we had not met before, we decided to have a bottle of Ch. de Sancerre, 1923. I cannot say that I enjoyed it—it was somewhat heady.

We finished up with a Grande Fine, 1874.

Monsieur Bony, the proprietor, joined us and, as he was very anxious to reciprocate, we were persuaded to taste 1926 Eau de Vie de Marc. How they delight to boast about their Marc . . . candidly, I detest it.

This particular Marc was not so bad. We understood that after distillation it had been kept two years in new casks, and then transferred to old ones.

The public distiller does the work ; each proprietor is entitled to 19 litres, free of duty, after which he pays a tax, and in addition a luxury tax.

We bade the host 'good-night' and, after a short stroll, were very glad to 'turn in'.

The next morning we took our leave of La Cloche, and thanked the hall porter, Guazzoni, for his many little services and kind attention. It is well to make note of these things when they do happen. By the way, he was an individual of some local importance at the moment, for had not his photo been published in the papers as giving evidence in the notorious Stavisky-Prince affair. It would appear that Prince immediately before his death had been a guest at the hotel.

Monsieur Siredey and his friend, the Comte de Tourbet, called at the hotel to bid us farewell, and kindly gave us a few introductions to important people in other areas, which proved most useful.

The last word we heard of the 1934 Burgundy wine was that the alcoholic degree seemed to be increasing . . . the last sample tasted at Chambertin had given 14°.

Lorne was very anxious to revisit those interesting towns of AVALLON and VÉZELAY, so I gave way to a very natural desire, in addition to which a day without continual tasting would be a relief.

On this side of DIJON we saw but little of vineyards—a few near SOMBERNON, on the slopes of the hills, and again in the vicinity of VITTEAUX. I imagine an ordinary wine would be made for local consumption.

There was a dangerous descent into VITTEAUX, a town of about a thousand inhabitants. They were, however, repaid very well for any hills they had to climb, for the scenery in the immediate vicinity was beautiful indeed. At the end of an avenue of poplars, a great many of which were numbered (I hoped their days were not numbered, for they were very stately), was a level crossing, the protecting gates of which were closed against us, but we had the satisfaction, if you will, of catching up with a car that had passed us some time earlier, going at a speed of not less than 70 to 80 m.p.h.

It was not charitable to smile, was it?

We were eventually allowed to pass. Over the Canal de Bourgogne there was little of interest, save a very curious old church, perched on the utmost summit of a hill. When I come to think of it, it may have been the ruins of some ancient abbey.

'Two magpies', said Lorne ... Now we were in for 'bonheur' and surely enough, as we passed through PRECEY our good fortune was to see the prettiest young woman I can remember to have ever seen.

'Did you see that?' asked Lorne. 'Indeed I did', I replied. 'What a beautiful Madonna she would have made.'

The country was not very interesting about here ... one or two fine avenues after we passed CLERMONT. The trees were planted irregularly ... somewhat unusual ... and of a large variety—Ash, Acacia, Sycamore, Walnut, among others.

As we passed through ROUVRAY we had to make several detours on account of the Fair which was taking place ... evidently a great day for the people of the district.

At the small old village of CUSSY LES FORGES, which as far as we could see boasted of one long street only, an electric light was suspended in the centre of the road to show the way to modern innovations.

Another four miles, and we were at AVALLON, and immediately proceeded to take our déjeuner at the Chapeau Rouge.

[73]

The lunch was quite simple . . . a great falling off from the day before. Seeing Blanc Fumé, 1929 vintage, on the list we decided to have a bottle in spite of the extravagant price of thirty-five francs a bottle. It was a good wine, but not so good as the 1928 we had at Dijon.

The cork broke . . . this happens fifty per cent. of the times a cork is extracted. The fault lies entirely with the stupid cork-screws provided . . . they are more like gimlets with narrow thread, than as a corkscrew should be, with a wide thread. It was not the fault of the waitress . . . she did her best, most mechanically. As she stood against the wall when we entered, I took her to be a large wax doll, and when she came forward I remarked to Lorne that it was a clock-work waitress—the very short and very rapid steps were truly remarkable.

There were many people in the restaurant and, as in most provincial towns of France, one could judge that the 'inside' care was of much more importance than that of their personal appearance.

Then to VÉZELAY, a climb to reach the town . . . vines to the right and left. The road we had come along was bad . . . it was very noticeable after all the excellent roads we had traversed. We were well repaid when we reached the heights. The panoramic views were magnificent ! especially from the terrace at the rear of the Cathedral.

We rested on the ramparts. . . . All was so still, everything seemed sublime, until the falling chestnuts brought us to ourselves and the realities of life—for, on our right, a little hidden by the spreading trees, were a devoted couple . . . very devoted, and on our left, from a little below, arose the sound made by the washerwomen as they beat the harmless linen.

Standing on these ramparts in contemplative silence, I thought of many a little episode of life, but one, like a recurring and never ending decimal, would continue to make itself heard.

I was a very small, and maybe naughty, boy, and on this occasion was being taken by my nurse for a walk along the front at Brighton. . . . I can just remember it—it was on the upper walk between the old chain pier and Kemp Town. Seeing a stone on the pavement I picked it up, and when nurse wasn't looking (probably paying attention to a younger brother) I dropped it over the railings. As bad luck would have it, it fell on the hat of an elderly gentleman ! The sequel you may imagine. I was very sore for several days after, and had to take my meals standing ! !

It is strange why that incident should have come into my head after all those years. I have wondered why, and I have come to the conclusion that it was brought to life by the fact that I had thrown some of the chestnuts over the ramparts without considering where they were likely to fall.

Before we quit VÉZELAY, we had to take a peep at the Cathedral. It is both wonderful and interesting. Without going into details, imagine that here on the crest of the hill is one of the largest churches in France, with a length of nearly three hundred and fifty feet, with a proportionate height ! The building dates back to the eleventh century, and was one of the meeting places of the Crusaders. Richard, Cœur de Lion, made this church his rendezvous when he set out on the third Crusade.

This appealed to me very much, particularly so as I have the honour of being a Commander of the Venerable Order of St. John of Jerusalem.

It was here that the saintly Abbot of CLAIRVAUX preached for the second Crusade. I wonder if you will bear with me while I transgress for a moment, and give you a few words I wrote on this, some time since ?

> '. . . the thund'ring sound of this,
> And the general calamities
> To the Christian heroes, fell upon
> The Soul of Bernard, learnéd Abbot
> Of CLAIRVAUX, with such effect to cause
> The righteous chord within to vibrate,
> That like unto Peter the Hermit . . .
> Of old he did echo forth at home
> And abroad the grim necessity
> Of a new Crusade ; exhorting rich
> And poor, high and low, to the service

Of our Lord, in the endeavour to
Wrest the Sepulchre and other of
The Holy Places from the power
Of the Infidels.
True sincerity did place so fine
So powerful an edge upon his
Eloquence that far the greater part
Of those who heard him plead straightway
Subscribed their names unto the service
Of the Cross, women were astonishéd
Their sons and husbands did not so much
As hesitate to obey the call,
But left their homes and occupations
For a service in the holy cause ;
To prevent so great an exodus
They contrived all manner of schemes
To avoid contact with St. Bernard.
Many men were hid in places dark
Not to regain the bright light of day
Until the priest and his followers
Had taken their departure.'

Standing here at VÉZELAY, I could quite understand that the holy St. Bernard, with his eloquence, together with the background of this 'merveilleuse basilique', was able to do all that is claimed for him.

'Come on, Lorne', I said at last—'we must be off, but on the way I should like to see the much spoken of bridges at SAINT-PÈRE and at PIERRE-PERTHUIS.' Accordingly, to SAINT-PÈRE we went, and what a reward awaited us !

Near by the higher bridge was an old—in fact, twelfth to thirteenth century—castle, which was most interesting . . . tucked away among the rocky surroundings.

At the bridge we jumped out of the car and for ten minutes or more breathed in, and overwhelmed ourselves with, the scenery. The silence was gently tempered with the rippling sound of water passing under the ancient bridge, which remained hundreds of feet below.

Saturated, as it were, with this scene, we turned to go, when, facing the other way, we beheld another view—vézelay in the distance, standing proud and majestic in its lofty isolation.

'Lorne', I said (and every letter was a capital), 'isn't it BEAUTI-FUL !' We saw eye to eye !

The scene changed as we progressed. . . . At usy we were reminded of our own villages, with the green, the playground not only of little boys and girls, but of turkeys, geese, ducks, piglets, etc., etc.

'Look', exclaimed Lorne. 'At what?' I inquired. 'Surely', he added, 'you saw the heather on the right ?' He was pleased for quite a long time, in fact, until we reached AVALLON.

Having deposited our belongings at the Hotel, we took a stroll along the famous terraces before dinner. The views are certainly fine and extensive. We also enjoyed the entertainment (untaxed) of many children playing their games—one very bandy-legged little boy was the most energetic. . . . How he kept his balance was astonishing. I delight in watching children, and also in hearing the funny little things they say—yes, I can remember one or two little things which amused me very much. . . .

The little girl who could not find her pyjamas, called over the banisters—'Mummy, I got no 'jamas . . . must I go to bed raw ?'

Another one, saying her prayers, to nurse—

> 'Gentle Jesus, meek and mild,
> See how they run !'

My little nephew, Peter, aged six years, sneezed while saying his prayers to his mother one evening, and continued—

'Excuse me, God . . . no one died !' . . . and then carried on as if nothing had happened.

Another, a little older, had been to church with her mother (the parson had preached of the Heavenly Host all clothed in white). On the way home she seemed a little quiet, so her mother inquired what she was thinking about—'I was thinking', she said, 'what a lot of washing Mrs. God must have to do !'

We went in to dinner at the Hotel de la Poste. This was the hotel, I understand, where Napoleon stopped after his escape from the Isle of Elba. Perhaps that was why it was a little expensive ! But I forgive them, for it was the first one we had been to where we had butter offered to us without asking for it. I like butter, and plenty of it. . . . Butter and olives are the finest things to take if you wish, or if it is necessary, to drink a little more than you would in the ordinary way.

We had some grilled Perch, à la meunière, from the local streams. They were excellent, and reminded me of the first time I had enjoyed them in this way. The late Earl of Warwick had kindly invited me down to his fishing, near Leicester. We were not very successful with the trout, but later caught quantities of Perch, and regaled ourselves with them, cooked in this way, at breakfast.

To wash them down, we ordered a carafe of Chablis, 1933 . . . a small insignificant wine, but very drinkable.

The next item on our menu was Champignons and Truffes à la crème, and to follow, an excellent duck. With these we had Still Champagne nature . . . it was very good. I do enjoy these wines, not extravagant in price, but delectable.

It is almost incredible, but the best Cognac to be offered was the Martell XXX—quite good for Brandy and Soda, but, for a fine liqueur after a good dinner—'I ask you, Lorne, is it reasonable ?'

The next morning we were up early. I could not help but notice a card displayed in several places, which showed that, as in England, our good neighbours had suffered a little from the drought. On the cards was printed the following :

'Ne gaspillez pas l'eau, vous risquer d'en manquer.'

Before nine o'clock we were on our way—a pleasant morning, a little fresh. A number of chasseurs were out on the country roads, which were so bad that we had another excuse to go via VÉZELAY.

'Lorne', says I . . . 'three magpies', so we crossed our fingers until we saw two more together. We were lucky, for we did not have to go far before we uncrossed them ! Stupid, you will say, but it all adds a little fun on the journey.

At DORNECY were a few small vineyards, with the vendangeurs hard at work.

At ARMES, as we crossed the river Yonne, we noticed several anglers . . . so far we had never seen a fish landed !

At CLAMECY we passed a pillion rider ; the first we had seen. I think the high price of oil and petrol must have had something to do with this, because I think the French girls are equally courageous with ours.

At MOULOT we caught sight of another industry . . . basket-making, which was carried on by the roadside. We were travelling quickly, and it may have been simply a community of Gipsies at work.

At VARZY our attention was attracted by the old Church . . . the two turrets, complete with clock and barometer. On inquiry, we were informed that it was twelfth century. We had not the time to stop and look over it, but it appeared very interesting.

A pretty little sight somewhat amused us as we left the small town . . . a small dog pulling along a pram, with His Majesty, the baby, inside.

From here, the scenery was picturesque, vines and work being carried on. All appeared pleasant, except the men . . . they had been too busy for a week to find the time to shave ! !

We were now climbing up a hill, maybe one mile long, and I noticed again, as I had noticed so often before, the ease with which the women as well as the men on bicycles negotiate these steep hills—no pushing the bike up hill as is generally seen with us.

We crossed over the Mazon, and felt a spot of rain, although the sun was shining. . . . We looked out for a rainbow.

At LES BERTINS we turned off the National road in order to go to POUILLY S/LOIRE, where we were anxious to make use of one of Monsieur Siredey's introductions.

At first the road was not so good, but on passing NANCY it developed into one with a fine surface.

When I saw a couple of cats sitting among a number of baby chicks, I thought to myself—yes, anything is possible ! And yet I was unable to break a dog of chasing sheep. What a moral ! Begin young, no matter whether it be in reference to mankind, beast, bird or fish—but it is not so easy as it might appear.

[79]

The abundance of sloes in the hedgerows was very noticeable. I am surprised that one never comes across French Sloe Gin . . . I must make some inquiries.

We had, on our left, a fine view of the river Loire, but the water was very low.

On arrival at POUILLY S/LOIRE we made inquiries for Le Comte de La Chesnaye, an introduction to whom we had been given by Le Comte de Tourbet.

The Count was away, but would we see Madame ? Certainly we would, and after waiting a short time we were ushered into her room. It was evidently the mother, not the wife, of the Count, and she graciously introduced herself as Mme la Comtesse d'Ennery de La Chesnaye.

The dear old lady, very charming, had passed some eighty-five summers, I believe, but her enthusiasm for the wines of the country was unbounded. I am greatly indebted to her for the information I am able to give in reference to the wine of Pouilly S/Loire, and in particular the celebrated Blanc Fumé, so little known in this country.

She told me that the record of the vineyards dated back to the time of the Romans, adding that, a few days before the battle of Fontenoy in 841 A.D., the troops of Charles the Bold crossed the ford at Mesves, a mile or two from Pouilly, and burnt the vines.

The vines flourished easily in those days, the spring frosts being rare, and new vineyards soon sprang up, not only on the hill slopes but on the plains.

The extension, however, did not take place until transport became easier, first by the canals and later by railroad . . . especially between 1860 and 1890, when very large quantities of grapes were sent to Paris.

In some years, about 1880, a special daily train of thirty wagons freighted with grapes, left for Paris markets, and that would last a month and sometimes longer.

When the grapes were too ripe, or when a storm damaged them, it was found necessary to make wine with them.

These late vintages of very ripe grapes produced fine wine, free from acidity, and very soft, which made the reputation of the Muscadet Wines—the name given to the Chasselas of Pouilly.

[80]

To-day the grapes are no longer required for Paris, and the whole produce is made in to wine.

The phylloxera scourge destroyed the entire vineyards between 1890 and 1900, and the whole area had to be replanted.

In 1925, the 'appellation d'origine' was legally given—'White Wine of Pouilly S/Loire', provided that the wines were made from the Chasselas grape.

Pouilly Fumé and Blanc Fumé de Pouilly are wines from stock of the same name, and nothing else. Blanc Fumé, quite an exceptional wine, comes from the stock blanc fumé, derived from the Sauvignon, so much prized in the Bordelais.

The grape is very small, and the bunches very compact. When eating the fruit, the same 'goût de fumé' is detected as in the wine made from them.

The Blanc Fumé is a wine sought after by connoisseurs, and is generally rather high in price. This unique vine will not give good results in all soils. It ripens late, and the proprietors desire to see a touch of the 'pourriture noble' in order to make a perfect wine.

The vintage, on an average, commences about the first of November.

Chalk or chalky clay is the best soil in which to plant.

In a year when the grapes do not ripen well, an unpleasant acid wine is the result.

The vineyards of Pouilly are not very extensive, covering about one thousand hectares, in which are the communes of ST. AUDELAIN, GARCHY, ST. MARTIN, TRACY, ST. LAURENT and MESVES.

The quantity varies very much in different years. In 1905 when the vines were in full strength the récolte was 100,000 hectos.

In 1929	-	-	70,000 hectos.
In 1932	-	-	40,000 ,,
In 1933	-	-	20,000 ,,

As a matter for guidance, I might mention a few of the best known growths—such information is always useful . . . Les Nues, Château du Nozet, Les Foletières, Les Chaumes, etc., etc.

Certainly I understood that whereas in other vine growing areas the production was excessive . . . Pouilly S/Loire suffered from under production . . . this does seem regrettable, for Blanc Fumé can be such an excellent wine.

Madame La Comtesse hoped for great success in 1934. Owing to the hot summer the vintage was expected to commence at least a fortnight earlier than is usual, and bar accidents, an excellent wine should be made.

When the wine is made it does not require much time to mature . . . it can be bottled in a year and will be ready to drink two years after.

The most remarkable years were the Comet year, 1811, and 1870 . . . this latter, the dear old lady told us, was still very good. I had not the cheek to suggest that we should try it, if she had a bottle or two tucked away.

As already mentioned, the phylloxera arrived in 1895. On replanting, the vines of Mâcon were tried on an American root, but they were not successful.

At present a good American stock is used, with Blanc Fumé or Muscadet grafted on. There is very little red wine made.

After thanking the Comtesse for her kindness, and for all the information she had so unsparingly given us, we left in the care of her régisseur, and visited her vineyards and chais, where we were privileged to taste several wines :

1933 Muscadet . . . Good body—peculiar coarseness at back.

1933 Blanc Fumé . . . Very good—clean, 13°.

1933 Muscadet and Blanc Fumé—Blended . . . I was not impressed.

1933 Blanc Fumé—5 pièces . . . interesting and will make good wine. Could detect the true smell of Blanc Fumé.

On walking through the vineyards we could see that the grapes were ripe, with a suspicion of 'pourriture noble', so we should be able to look forward to some really good Blanc Fumé. The Comtesse expected to make 20 to 25 pièces of 200 litres, of Blanc Fumé, and about 80 pièces of Muscadet.

On leaving POUILLY S/LOIRE we made for SANCERRE for lunch, speaking on the way of the charm of the dear old lady. It was very hot and many a picnic was being enjoyed by the countryside.

The water in the Loire was very low, and many bathing tents were on the sand.

Over the canal, and then a steep climb to SANCERRE : vines were to be seen on either side, but the vineyards did not seem well kept . . . full of weeds. Perhaps this was unavoidable, for when the grapes are ripening it is not advisable to plough.

On entering the hotel I thought I saw my old friend Raven-Hill . . . just the sort of place one would expect to find him, enjoying a glass of good wine, but when I approached him I found my mistake, and had to apologise to Monsieur Josselin. It is said that every man has his double . . . here was surely a case in point.

'Lorne', I said . . . 'à propos to Raven-Hill, he wrote to me on one occasion after we had dined together in the City, that he had had an extraordinary dream, in which I demonstrated to him that, by the aid of the water diviner, or dowser's twig, I could tell if the wine was all right before I drew the cork ! He said it was the most vivid dream that could be imagined, and felt that he ought to record it by a sketch. This sketch you must ask me to show you when I return.'

We were content with a simple lunch, and thinking it wise to sample the wines of the country we ordered a bottle of Sancerre, Sauvignon de Chavignol, 1929 vintage. It was very light, pleasant, but had not much flavour.

We followed this with a bottle of Sancerre Pinot 1929 ; which was like a miniature Beaujolais . . . hard and dry. Not caring for this we thought we would try a Sancerre Rosé, Fricanbault 1929, but we were no more successful. To accompany these wines we enjoyed Whitebait from the Loire, a Pheasant and Cheese. The cheese was very hard, which caused Lorne to inquire—'What is this ? Cheese !' I replied—'All but(t).' He declared he would never eat cheese made from goat's milk again.

'We must make a move', I said.

The first thing we noticed was a game of pat ball, played between four girls and a lad of about sixteen ; the ground was rough on the crest of the hill, where the giggling girls had the poor lad 'on a bit of toast'. Up and down the hill he ran after that ball. 'To what lengths immature love will go', we remarked,

[83]

as we strolled on to the terrace, planted with Cedar trees, to enjoy a most wonderful view overlooking the Loire. Before leaving Sancerre we thought it well to purchase a small glass, so that when we felt it necessary to indulge in a 'petit verre' the necessaries would be at hand.

Shortly before three o'clock we dragged ourselves away from very pleasant surroundings.

At COSNE we had the difficulty of manoeuvring through the market which was taking place . . . a part of the difficulty is occasioned, I fancy, by the fact that the hoot of the motor-horn is not discernible, mingling with the continued mooing of the cattle.

At NEUVY S/LOIRE we came across much traffic on the road—evidently a main thoroughfare.

On the way from BONNY to BRIARE we passed an interesting old church on the left. There were many small vineyards, and we also noticed quantities of blackberries. A hare darted and dodged across the road, to our amusement, just before we passed along the fine avenue of Plane trees which leads to BRIARE. Here we left the Paris road, with a fine park and château on the right.

We were nearing GIEN. The river was very low, and many people were sitting about on the sand of the river bed.

There is an excellent bridge at GIEN, with fine bastions. We counted a dozen anglers, but never a fish did we see caught.

The only excitement was when a hook was caught in a rock. I could almost see the smile on the face of the little fish as they continued to sport and jump all around.

I was uncertain as to how the name of the town GIEN should be pronounced. I therefore took advantage of the presence of two ladies on the bridge—particularly as they appeared to be natives. Raising my hat as politely as I could I made the inquiry. By the answering look I guessed they thought I was only 'up to Wednesday night', but I straightened out the difficulty, and they explained that it was ZHYAN. I thanked them and then, in order to improve the shining hour, I told them a little 'histoire' of when I was a small boy at school. It was impressed upon us that if we did not understand anything which

[84]

was said to us, we should ask for an explanation. A short time after this, the 'head' was giving a talk, and speaking of something I did not understand. I raised my hand, and instead of being asked what I wanted he said—'Don't be long'. Blushingly I replied that I did not wish to leave the room, but as I did not understand what he was talking about, I was wanting to ask for an explanation.

'Cavey' (for that was the name we gave the 'head') looked at me for a moment. . . . It was a long one for me . . . then, putting his hand in his pocket, he drew out a sixpence and presented me with it, remarking—'Good boy, Berry, always ask if you don't know.'

This explanation amused but satisfied the two young ladies. Perhaps they did not write me down 'AN ASS'.

When we went back for the Little Auk on the other side of the road, we found a couple of roughs, tenderly stroking it . . . moral—never leave your car unlocked !

The afternoon was very hot, and when in the open country we missed the shade of the trees. In spite of this we came across several picnic parties—the young folk all enjoying a romping game, such as 'blind man's buff' or 'touch'. . . . I would have wished to join in, especially with one party, but it was really too, too hot !

At OUZOUER S/LOIRE we saw a gendarme leading off a small boy, who had evidently stolen a bicycle. . . . I cannot tell you which of them appeared as the more important.

'Whatever are you so elated over, Lorne', I inquired. . . . 'I've seen', said he, 'and I know it's true, a man who has actually shaved !'

'Maybe he cannot grow a beard', I replied. 'No', said Lorne, 'I know he has, for I could see the remains of the soap still in his ears !'

We were soon passing in between meadows . . . with here and there a few vines. On the roadside was a huge walnut tree, and a number of men were beating it; but the country after the morning might be described as dull.

As we proceeded we realised that there was a bicycle race taking place, probably for some professional cup. Through the

[85]

little villages were large numbers of expectant and interested groups . . . the competitors, each numbered, wore a variety of colours, the significance of which I was unable to determine.

At LES BORDES we passed the result of a motor accident. There was indeed great excitement !

The road was good, probably the reason why it was chosen for the race. At ST. MARTIN D'ABBOT all the inhabitants seemed to be out to see the cyclists pass.

As we neared ORLÉANS we noticed many more vines, and from CHECY we had a glimpse of the Cathedral in the distance. CHECY itself boasts of a beautiful thirteenth century church, and a twelfth century belfry.

Through BRIONNE we went, and the race had ended. . . . I do not know who won, except that the crowd were acclaiming one cyclist dressed in red, and another in green . . . across the back of one of them being printed—PEUGEOT-HELYETT.

It was 5.30 when we reached the Cathedral City . . . an ancient one, dating back to the time of Julius Caesar.

We decided to look at the Cathedral, which was most impressive. We were attracted by the War Memorial, with the inscription—

'To the Glory of God and to the Memory of One Million Dead who fell in the Great War, 1914-1918, and of whom the greater part rest in France.'

The Memorial was embellished with the Arms of Great Britain, her Dominions and Colonies.

This, outside the Chapel of Jeanne d'Arc ! ! Food for thought.

At the hotel we found the mail awaiting us and among the papers was a telegram from Reg., saying that we were to expect him about ten o'clock.

Reg.—I must introduce to you as my eldest son, and one of my partners. He was coming to ORLÉANS to relieve Lorne, whose business in the old country required his attention.

Before going to the station to meet the train, we decided to have dinner at the hotel—the last with Lorne, who was due to leave in the morning.

With a mild consommé and a Loire salmon we had a bottle of

[86]

1926 Chavignol . . . it resembled a fairly good White Mâconnais without much quality—nevertheless interesting.

With a roast pheasant, we indulged in a bottle of 1928 Chinon, 1ère Côte. It was nothing very special . . . perhaps a little sour, maybe not sufficiently matured.

As I was anxious for Lorne to taste a bottle of Bourgueil, that delectable wine with the raspberry flavour of which he had heard me speak, but so far had not come across, we decided to disregard the 1928 Chinon and order a bottle of 1923 Bourgueil: St. Nicolas de Bourgueil—we were well repaid for our perseverance. . . . It was very good and very flavoury—that is, of the subtle raspberry flavour.

I have tasted others more pronounced, but this was very good . . . perhaps it was more flavoury a few years ago.

A little incident occurred at this hotel which I would like to mention:

At a table near us were Mother, Father, two little sons and a little daughter—all very well behaved.

One little boy evidently was not very strong, so towards the end of the meal he was given a seat on Daddy's knee. The other boy began to be a little restive . . . perhaps a little jealous, so he had a seat on Daddy's other knee. As there were no more knees the little girl sat where she was—such a little darling—no jealousy . . . but she chatted and played with the little boys. It was a pretty picture. After they had retired I asked the waiter to go out to buy a box of chocolates which I sent up to the little girl, with a few words of admiration at her conduct. One of her father's cards came back on which was written: 'Un gros merci de la petite fille de Robert Decoppet', by which I could see that I had given the little one pleasure. I was more than repaid.

After the coffee and 'Fine' we went down to the station to meet Reg and, so as to appear thoroughly important, we took the car with us.

He turned up to time, having come by air to Paris, and on by train to Orléans . . . a little tired, a big bit thirsty, and in the best of spirits.

[87]

SUMMARY OF BURGUNDY.

1865. Very fine.
1868. „   „
1869. Probably the finest known.
1870. Coarse, good quality.
1874.⎫
1875.⎬ Very good.
1877.⎮
1878.⎭
1881. Good—little too dry.
1885.⎫ Very good.
1886.⎭
1887. Excellent.
1888. Disappointing.
1889. Very good.
1893. Good.
1895. Excellent.
1898.⎫ Very good.
1899.⎭
1904. Very fine indeed.
1906. Very fine.
1907. Very good.
1908. Good.
1911. Excellent, full, fine and soft.
1914. Promised more than it could perform.
1915. Excellent.
1916. Good.
1919. Very good.
1923. Excellent.
1924. Good.
1926. Very good.
1928. Fine.
1929. Good—buy with discrimination.
1930.⎫
1931.⎬ Leave alone.
1932.⎭
1933. Promises very well—will probably mature quickly.
1934. Should be good, but it is not wise to prophesy.

Should a cellar contain any rarities, that is, any older than 1888, it would be advisable to have friends to gather round and enjoy them—if the bottles are full (that is, not ullaged) they might be wonderful, provided they are of a fine vintage.

I had a bottle of 1869 Clos de Vougeot a short time since. . . . It was magnificent—bottled velvet ! !

May I take an opportunity here to give a word of advice. . . .

If any cellars contain such old wines, the owners should have the bins overhauled, placing aside the slight ullages for personal use and throwing away the ullages.

The full bottles should be in a bin by themselves . . . thus will one be able to avoid the great disappointment of offering a friend a bad or inferior wine, when it had been hoped to give him or her a treat . . . a beautiful bottle.

Those who are fortunate enough to possess such wines as 1904, 1906 and 1907 may still rest comfortable in the knowledge that they are likely to remain 'superb' for some time. . . .

1911 . . . Drink before the 1904, 6, 7. Specimens I have recently seen cause me to say this.

1914 . . . No—Pricked, most of it, and is it to be wondered at?

1915 . . . These can be kept as best. Will remain excellent wines for years to come.

For those who like Old Burgundies and find their cellars depleted, I suggest to try and find a small quantity of 1915, or the older vintages I have mentioned. See that some 1923 is in the cellar—of fine wines—to use when the old ones are finished.

A little 1926 might be very advantageous and, if circumstances permit, concentrate on 1928, keeping an eye on an early purchase of 1933, remembering that this vintage is likely to mature quickly.

Of the 1934 it is too early to speak, but they promise well—if not great things.

POUILLY S/LOIRE.

The famous vintages have been 1811 and 1870, but these are only memories.

1893, 1900, 1906, 1911, 1919, 1921, 1926,
1928, 1929 and 1933. . . .

[89]

There was so much natural sugar in the 1921 that some of the wine actually fermented after four years in bottle !

I do not suppose many cellars contain these somewhat rare wines, but if any hold 1893 I would suggest using it soon.

The 1911 wine should keep well, also the 1919. The 1921 seems somewhat dangerous—use it.

Probably the 1929 will not last as long as the 1928.

CHAPTER V

ANJOU, TOURAINE, VOUVRAY AND SAUMUR

At 7 o'clock on Monday, the 1st October, I shouted to Reg and Lorne a simple word, which gives much satisfaction to some folks if they get it in first on the first day of the month . . . 'RABBITS' . . . I called out, and wished them well—Lorne on a safe return, and Reg on an enjoyable and instructive tour with his father.

It was not the first occasion that we had been in France at the same time, for Reg had been in the Gunners' during the war, whilst I was in the Royal Flying Corps, altered after to the Royal Air Force, but we had not previously taken a vinous trip together and we were both looking forward to it with enthusiasm.

As for Lorne, we went down to the station at 7.30 to see him off; to be candid, I did not have tears in my eyes or a lump in my throat, but without such an obvious manifestation of grief, I had an unusual feeling at heart that made me sad at parting with such an excellent, considerate, and intelligent companion who had taken me over some 1250 miles—but 'Needs must, etc. . . . ' and off he went to London, while we headed for some vine-growing areas of France which I had never visited before.

It must have been about 8 o'clock as we quitted Orléans . . . the sky was cloudy, but by the time we were in the open country it seemed to be clearing, although there was still a misty atmosphere, which perhaps suggested a hot day in store.

At SAINT AY the mist had cleared, and we were able to see quantities of vines, both on our right and on our left.

These small vineyards were evidently the holdings of peasant proprietors ; for the gathering was taking place and, at the roadside, the small press was at work, hurrying on the making of their wine.

At BAULE the sun was doing its best to shine, but as we passed through BEAUGENCY, with its quaint river way and fine avenue, we encountered so much mist that we could not see the old church which we had been told to look for.

We approached SUÈVRES by an avenue of apple trees . . . no one seems to care about apples . . . I wondered to whom they belonged.

We gathered a few, and after the first bite we no longer wondered why they were not sought after !

The autumnal tints of the leaves on the vines were very attractive, the colour tells its tale, that is to say, as a general rule. On the gamay and inferior varieties, the leaves turn red . . . does this indicate danger ? On the higher class plants—a beautiful and enticing golden yellow !

As we passed a blacksmith's shop, the smell sent our thoughts across the Channel to the English villages. It was pleasant, but we looked in vain for the 'spreading chestnut tree'.

The main road here had evidently been cut through a large estate, because it was hedged on each side by strong walls.

We were now well on the way to BLOIS . . . more avenues of apple trees. The rosy cheeks of the fruit were the only attractive property about them . . . they were very nasty to taste !

BLOIS is a large town of some importance and, as we entered, we were obliged to slow down somewhat, for the Cavalry were out exercising.

On the other side of the town, we noticed a charming estate with the Château La Vicomté for sale. I fear it will remain empty for a long time . . . only a few people want such properties in these days ; besides, it lies low and overlooks the river, which must be responsible for much of the mist that is experienced here.

Near LES GROUETS we passed two lovers on their bicycles. . . . It is good to be so happy, and so young. I recalled a time when, as a young swain, I was teaching Dorcas to ride . . . instead of looking at the handle-bars I was gazing into her face, and fell over an obstruction in the road, hurting my elbow so much that I was obliged to carry my arm in a sling for some time after. Moral— Don't teach girls to ride bicycles !

These two, however, were past this stage and were undoubtedly on the look-out for dangers ahead.

At LES ECURES we crossed a fine bridge and found on the further side some very pleasant scenery which we thoroughly enjoyed.

At VOUVRAY station we passed under the railway bridge ; then crossed LA CISSE, a pretty tributary of the Loire, but we were still some little distance from the town of VOUVRAY.

The wine was advertised in bold letters and in every direction, which reminded me of the Roman proverb that 'Good wine needs no bush'. However, I soon put aside such an uncharitable thought and began to look forward to sampling some of it.

At ROCHECORBON we made use of the introduction which Monsieur Albert Pic had given me, and called on le Vicomte de Cournon at his charming residence, only a short way from the main road. We found the Vicomte at home and very much occupied with his chais and the arrangements for the vintage which had just commenced—being at least a fortnight earlier than usual.

Good wine was to be expected, although somewhat irregular, owing, I understood, to too much cochylis.

The average alcoholic degree varies between 12° and 14°. The wines are usually sweet, and made into sparkling wines. The method known as 'Chaptalisation', that is, the addition of sugar to the must before fermentation, is seldom resorted to, as the grapes are naturally so full of sugar.

Of the vines of the Indre et Loire, there are planted, approximately, one half red—groslot, and the other half—Pinot blanc de la Loire.

The actual area—almost all clay soil—to which the appellation 'Vouvray' is legally applied is but small, comprising STE. RADEGONDE, ROCHECORBON, VOUVRAY, VERNOU. . . .

At the invitation of Monsieur le Vicomte we tasted some of his many wines . . . 1933—12° was sweet. It seemed to me more pleasant than Sauternes—more subtle.

Another sample of 1933 somewhat astonished us, as it had already a taste of maderization. When Reg mentioned this we were told that that was a special wine and this particular goût was looked for. 'Unfortunately', our host added, 'I have but twenty hectos.'

Being unable to understand it, I left it alone, noting it down in my mind as a dangerous wine to handle.

These wines are kept for about twelve months in 'fûts Touraine', containing about 250 litres. The large casks, or cuves, had the name of 'demi-muids', of 600 litres.

We were then ushered into one of the private rooms, and were regaled with the following wines of Vouvray :

1919 (bottled 1920) pétillant. This had a slight deposit and would be difficult to handle.

1931. This was not very sweet. One of the best wines of 1931 I have seen.

1926. This was almost fine.

1933. Good quality . . . sweeter than the others.

At LE PONT DE CISSE we took our déjeuner out of doors . . . a remarkable arrangement of tables, surrounded by hedges, gave the appearance of the Hampton Court Maze. The table legs were formed of tree-trunks, mostly natural ones.

Cockles were a specialité, but did not appeal to me. Stewed eels followed, after which we were able to commence in reality. . . . With a partridge, well cooked, we had a bottle of Vouvray Pétillant (14 fcs.) which was very enjoyable—not too sweet . . . and, I understand, made from their own vineyards.

The service was perhaps the slowest I have experienced, during which time we listened to the squalling of a little child named Françoise—I felt like strangling it . . . but these were only passing thoughts !

A Siamese cat amused us, but we had nothing to feed it with.

Our table, fortunately, was not under a chestnut tree. Close by, a family moved away in the middle of their lunch, because of the annoyance caused by the falling nuts on their table.

We learned indeed the truth of the old adage—'Patience is a virtue.' Nevertheless, we were compensated with the delightful surroundings . . . everything would have been happy but for that kid—more squalling and more smacking went on ! I shall hate the name of Françoise ! !

However, everyone else seemed happy . . . some playing ping-pong . . . and as we moved off we could hear the vendangeurs a-singing.

We passed through VERNOU, with its pretty terraces, along a wooded road and some open country to CHANÇAY.

My good friend Stephen Gwynn had given me a letter of introduction to Monsieur and Madame Chevalley, who had a property here. Unfortunately, after finding our way to the avenue of laurels which led to their pretty retreat, we were disappointed at finding that they had left for Paris the day before. We were therefore unable to meet these charming people or to taste their wines.

We then went in search of a Monsieur Pequignot, at the Villa le Vigneau. It was a curious circular climb . . . impossible for a car which Reg minded *pro tem.* ; I struggled up to the top where the vineyards were situated, in an excellent position.

Dogs barked at me all the way up . . . I was glad that they were either chained or in cages. When I reached the summit I found that the grapes were already being pressed, and the little community was very busy.

Monsieur Pequignot assured me that his wine was the best cru of Vouvray, but beyond this I failed to derive any information. He directed me to Monsieur Vavasseur, the Mayor.

I made my retreat as politely as possible, regretting my loss of time, passing down the slopes where were to be seen pomegranates and figs.

I immediately called on the Mayor, at his chais, at his office and at his house, but unfortunately he was 'not at home'.

Leaving here we made our way to TOURS. This must be a busy town, for we found the streets crowded with people.

We went straight to the Hotel, and soon settled down, with a good appetite, to dinner.

With an agreeable menu, we called for local wines.

Petit Bourgueil en carafe ; it seemed to be old, but passable.

We also had a White Wine en carafe, called 'Azay le Rideau', which Reg described as 'sour' . . . and he was not far wrong, yet the way he swilled it away with Perrier Water made me envy such a thirst.

A 1928 Bourgueil to follow was quite good, and we found more than a suspicion of that intriguing raspberry flavour, in spite of the fact that a much scented lady sat at the next table. These wines, it must be remembered, will not last long.

We felt impelled to taste the Marc de Touraine, which we left in the glass . . . and we called for an 1893 Armagnac, which was clean, good and soft.

We were not much impressed. Our waiter seemed to be 'a few over the eight' and, on taking a stroll, we could not help but notice the number of dirty people there were about the streets and the boulevards.

We were glad to retire, but I had not bargained for the mosquitoes. I heard them during the long hours of the night, making a devil of a noise . . . evidently in triumph at having bitten me ! I would not turn on the light, fearing that others would come in, and, seeing that I was slaughtering their pals, would revenge themselves on me.

Tuesday, the 2nd October . . . I was up early, rejoicing in the prospects of a fine day. The valet brought in the café complet . . . like them all, he stepped over the clean boots outside the door —he would never think of placing them inside ! However, 'it is an ill wind, etc.' and I was, in a measure, repaid, for when I opened the door I was rewarded with the sight of a beautiful creature in an amazing dressing-gown, passing along the corridor. I suppose it would not have been 'comme il faut' to have given a morning salutation.

I attacked my coffee, but found I had been served with salt instead of sugar : I called to Reg to inquire how he fared . . . it was like playing a game of hide and seek, for between us we must have had a dozen doors—where one would have sufficed, there were two !

We left early, and to our surprise a slight drizzle had commenced. When we passed ST. CYR it commenced to rain heavily. At LA RICHE we noticed many anglers already at work, or play, if you prefer—from boats. We did not envy them . . . they would soon be drenched if the rain continued.

When we passed the Pont de Bresne the weather began to clear, and at LANGEAIS it was quite bright.

Here a man had actually caught a fair-sized fish. The way he was describing it to his friends reminded me of an occasion when an angler, after having finished a bottle of Scotch, was returning home 'fishless' across a meadow, and sighted a scarecrow with outstretched arms. Going up to it, he said, in such a tone as you can well imagine—'You're a liar . . . a d—— liar ! There never was a fish as big as that.'

A large advertisement of Chenard Walcker cars called to remembrance my first motor tour in Scotland. It was many years ago, and I remembered how we all enjoyed it . . . nevertheless, I was quite happy with the Little Auk.

The sun was shining as we passed through LA CHAPELLE, where there is an attractive old chapel. The scene, however, was totally spoilt by the creation of a 'convenience' outside the walls. This happens very often . . . another instance of French propriety. It certainly should be removed.

Having passed the village we came across many more small vineyards.

As we intended to visit ANGERS we left SAUMUR on our left, meaning to return here later.

At ST. MARTIN DE LA PLACE I happened to look out of the car as we were passing a young woman. She greeted me by putting out her tongue, for no reason I imagine, except perhaps that she thought we were not attractive . . . correct, maybe, but not polite ! I like to make excuses for all such slips ; there were quantities of apples on the roadside . . . maybe they were crab apples, and she had taken a bite from one. We will be pleased to leave it at that !

At LES ROSIERS there seemed to be but one street, and this was designated as a 'one-way' street. 'Perhaps', said Reg, 'there may be a back way.'

We passed by ST. MATHURIN with its quaint old houses facing the river.

'Did you see two magpies ? ' I asked Reg. 'Yes', he replied, 'and a Buchanan cat chasing them.'

At LA BOHALLE we got out to watch considerable excitement, caused by five men and two women netting the river, but the only fish that were caught, as far as we could see, were small ones. It was not our lot to join in those shrieks of joy when a 'monster' is trapped.

We soon reached ANGERS, and made our way to the magnificent Establishment—Maison Cointreau . . . famous the world over.

We stopped to inquire the way of one who appeared a gentlemanly and considerate sort of person ; he seemed grieved that we were so ignorant . . . 'Rue de la Roe', he said, barking at me—'comprenez ?' He said it so rapidly, and, thinking that if I did not understand he would take me for a fool, I replied—'Oui, wow wow—' 'C'est ça', he said, and we both continued our respective ways.

However, we soon found this illustrious house, and had the very great pleasure of meeting Monsieur André Cointreau and Monsieur Bertin.

I am sure Reg would wish to join with me in expressing our grateful thanks for all their kindness. They immediately forsook their work, and placed themselves at our disposal.

It is a wonderful establishment . . . my feeble words of admiration would not enable you to conjure up in your minds the vast stills, cuves, etc., etc. . . . all containing those delightful liqueurs that ladies love so much. Personally, I think there is only one liqueur, and that is Fine Champagne.

However, I am in the minority, so I will admit that, of all the others I have ever tasted, I feel I would give the preference to Cointreau, for quality and flavour. I must find out one of these days if, with all their up-to-date methods and opportunities, they cannot produce a good quality Sloe Gin. There are quantities of Sloes to be had . . . perhaps the Gin is the difficulty ; we shall see.

Having inadequately expressed our thanks for so much courtesy and attention, we started for SAUMUR.

The first obstacle we met was a horse harnessed to a cart, in the centre of the road. There was no driver, and the folk on the road sides were watching open-mouthed. Reg hooted, and when he did so, the gentle creature turned his head round and, immediately pulling to the right, allowed us to pass. We acknowledged his action as we do when we pass an A.A. or R.A.C. man on the road.

No sooner had we passed than we were hemmed in by a herd of cows, but they were not so responsive in spite of the hooting. We were running parallel with the Loire. I suppose at times there is some water in the river . . . here, sand for ballast was being removed from the river bed. We arrived at SAUMUR in time for lunch . . . Champignons and Lamb were on the menu, so we had them to the accompaniment of a bottle of Côteaux de Saumur (10 fcs.). It was poor quality, but dry. All the other wines on the list were sweet. We tried, for experience, a wine described as Rosé du Pays (7 fcs.), and we wished we had not.

We were interested to note on the list a Bourgueil mousseux. I had no knowledge of such a wine ; but, at the moment, neither of us seemed sufficiently courageous to sample it.

At 2 o'clock we set out for CHINON, via DAMPIERRE and SOUZAY ; at the village of PARNAY Reg drew my attention to an Alsatian dog and a kitten enjoying a boisterous romp.

On the right the houses built in the rocks gave a picturesque appearance. As we crossed the bridge at CHINON we enjoyed a very happy view of the ancient castle.

It was at CHINON that François Rabelais was born, about 1495. This was impressed upon us when we came across an excellent Statue raised to his immortal memory. We ventured to call on a Monsieur Beauvillain, whose name and address had been given to us by M. Maurice Roblin of Tours, and right glad we were that we did, for we found him at home, and most willing to give us much information, and further, to allow us to taste some Chinon wines.

1928 Chinon, bottled in 1931, was of good quality, with a dry finish. This was the wine which pleased me most.

We had a look at the outside of the Maison de Rabelais, rue de la Lamproie. . . . It is a pretty, comfortable square house, with a front grille. A small, artificial well of water is in the front approach. . . . The water is so green that it gives the impression as being now just as it was left in the sixteenth century by Rabelais—highly probable, as he had little use for water, me-thinks !

On leaving CHINON we passed many vineyards ; the vintage had barely commenced, so the hanging branches of grapes afforded a pleasant sight.

To BOURGUEIL we directed our way, over the bridge crossing the Loire to PORT BOULET . . . the country was not particularly interesting.

BOURGUEIL itself is a quaint, rather dirty-looking market town, with narrow streets, or so it appeared to us. We went straight on to ST. NICOLAS for we had heard of the good wines of Bourgueil St. Nicolas.

As we neared our objective we stopped in order to taste a few grapes. The vintage seemingly was not yet finished.

They tasted good, but not so sweet as others we had tasted.

At one vineyard we decided to exchange a few words with one of the vendangeurs. Loudly he sang the praises of the wines of St. Nicolas . . . he was, indeed, an enthusiast. This vineyard, he told us, was one of the best . . . all Breton vines on stony soil. It was an abundant vintage, and excellent wine was looked for. He was not allowed to talk with us for long, as shouts from the other vendangeurs were urging him to hurry up and not delay the gathering.

At ALLONNES we saw the peasant proprietors already making their wine. By the time we reached SAUMUR it had commenced to rain.

There was not much water in the river, but we were informed that in winter it would be full and that the large sandbanks that formed the bed shifted their positions every year.

The view was extremely fine, and when the sun endeavoured to put in an appearance, the scene down the river in the sunlight could be expressed as a perfect picture.

My good friend Mr. Sterling Clark had asked me to taste some wine—a pretty Bourgueil which he had still lying in SAUMUR. We therefore collected a bottle, and arranged to taste it at dinner at one of the hotels.

It was not the most ideal spot to taste it, as the dining-room smelt atrociously of fish. However, we did the best we could.

We commenced with a wine of BRÉZÉ, Clos de Treilles, 1er Grand Cru 1930 (25 fcs.). It was of good quality, soft, not very sweet, and it reminded me somewhat of a Rhine wine of medium quality.

We then had the bottle of Bourgueil 1928. It was quite sound, but was served rather too warm. It still possessed that delightful raspberry flavour or fragrance, but not so pronounced as it was eighteen months before.

There seems to me no doubt that these wines should be consumed young, and not left to age.

Altogether it was not a very successful dinner . . . the Cerebos salt holder contained pepper, much to my annoyance, and to make matters slightly more irritating the large bowl of flowers on the table contained mostly dead dahlias.

There was no good Cognac, so we selected Quetch, a prune liqueur, which was, at least, interesting.

The next morning I awoke to the endless sounds of church bells. The good people of SAUMUR evidently require much summoning to their devotions.

On raising myself in bed on my elbow, I could see that there had been much rain during the night, but that the clouds were dispersing, and the old river was winding its way silently down stream towards the Bay of Biscay.

Some of the fish, I mused, will not pass this way again after running the gauntlet of so much tantalizing bait.

When I ventured out to the bank, leaving Reg to fetch the 'Little Auk', I found it was raining, and my early hopes of a fine day were not so well founded.

A somewhat extraordinary thing occurred. In mentioning it I do so to warn others—always check your bills and your change, even at a bank, those institutions which we rather look upon as infallible.

I presented a letter of credit, and asked for fifty pounds, at the day's rate of exchange. As I glanced across the desk at the clerk making his calculations I noticed the 'rate' at which he was calculating. I immediately, on a scrap of paper, multiplied the figure by fifty.

When the francs were passed across to me I politely asked leave to check them, and, not making the amount correct, I inquired of the rate of exchange, which was as I had taken down. I counted up again, and then handed them across to the cashier, asking him to satisfy himself that I was ninety francs short. He agreed, without any suspicion of an apology, muttered 'erreur', and handed me what I took to be ninety francs, which on check-ing, I found to be eighty ! On demand he gave me the other ten francs . . . *verb. sap.*

On one occasion at a restaurant, an item of 1.50 was entered on the bill as 15.0, and on another occasion, seeing caviare on the 'carte' at 22 francs, I decided to be extravagant, but was a little annoyed when I discovered on the bill that I had been charged 30 francs . . . carelessness, no doubt ; but, again I would say— *verb. sap.*

Alas, how often has one found the 'date' added in the total ! !

But I think you will agree that the limit was reached when the waiter upset the soup on the cloth, apologised, and proceeded to cover it up with a clean serviette. On the bill I was charged for a 'couvert neuf' !

On the way to visit Maison Veuve Amiot, we passed by the Cavalry School, which, from the little that one could see in passing, well deserves its great reputation.

As Vouvray was the principal wine of Touraine, so Saumur is considered to be of Anjou.

We were fortunate in having introductions to Maison Amiot. The gentleman who received us so graciously was the grandson of the original Madame Amiot.

The cellars of this establishment are very spacious, cut through rock and chalk, and are well deserving of a visit.

The wine was blended in huge glass-lined tanks, and everyone was very busy, which made us appreciate the time which the principals were extending to us.

The grape that is used for the White Wine is the Pinot de la Loire, and the process of making is practically the same as in the Champagne district.

We noticed one man, in particular, hard at the work of 'remuage' and we were told that he could manipulate by that rapid shake from the wrists up to 40,000 bottles a day.

It is almost incredible. I hope for his sake, when he meets St. Peter, that his hands are not shaking ! !

Wages are gradually coming down, which in due course should have its effect on the price for the wine.

Monsieur Amiot allowed us to taste some of the wines :

Brézé (Côteaux de Saumur) was slightly pétillant. I should think about 2 per cent. of sweetness, which I understood was not added, but natural. . . . It was a very attractive wine at a reasonable price.

A Vouvray was the next to be tasted. This was too sweet for my taste, although the quality was better than the Brézé . . . this also was pétillant.

The Still wine weighs about 11° alcohol. It would be thought that this would be sufficient to hold the wine under all circumstances, but our experience is that a journey frequently causes it to fall out of condition.

Saumur Muscatel was the next. For those who like such wines it would appeal, but I found it too sickly.

We then tasted a wine from the Côteaux du Layon 1929 . . . a still, natural sweet wine—11° to 12°. Being 1929, it had already been bottled, but I gathered that the younger wines were still in cask and could be shipped in bulk, which would mean a considerable saving in Freight and Duty. Bottled wines are subject to a Duty of 6s. per gallon, against those in bulk of 4s. per gallon ; that is, not exceeding 25°, whereas the wines of the higher strength not exceeding 42° are subject to 10s. and 8s. per gallon respectively. Sparkling wines pay 16s. 6d. per gallon, Empire wines have a preferential duty.

We were then offered a Still Wine, Rosé 1928, Cabernet d'Anjou grape . . . attractive to look at, and to the taste pleasant and soft, although a trifle sweet, like a medium Sauterne. I thought the quality of this natural wine particularly good, and as there were but four hundred bottles I deemed it wise to arrange for their removal. Monsieur Amiot very kindly invited us to lunch, when we had another bottle of Brézé Grand Vin, pétillant, a little sweet, but good quality ; these wines should be consumed before they become too old as they soon lose their freshness and take on an 'earthy' flavour.

A bottle of 1923 Crémant du Roi (Veuve Amiot) was interesting ; this particular wine I learned had a proportion of wine from Champagne in its composition.

CHABICHOU was a curious cheese we had at this meal. . . . It is made from goat's milk, which was not difficult to believe.

[103]

After lunch we went up to see the Château de Saumur, with its interesting Museum (Reg being particularly attracted by the skeleton of 'Flying Fox').

The Château is built on an eminence which seemed to command the town ; its very domineering position is quite impressive.

It requires the expense of a little energy in order to reach the summit, but when you do, you are rewarded with the beauty of surrounding scenery ! Should you ever visit Saumur you must not miss this scene.

We took a last look at this delightful view. I cannot imagine a better, especially as we saw it, illuminated by a rainbow with snatches of retiring mist in the distance.

One of the bridges over the river—for there are two—is well worth consideration. I believe it is regarded as one of the finest structures of its kind in France.

We paid our respects to the well-known firm of Maison Bouvet Ladubay, and had a sight of their extensive caves which, with those of Maison Ackermann Laurence, compete as show places for visitors.

As we now had a little time before dinner, the indefatigable Reg suggested that we should have a run over the south-western area of Saumur.

It was pleasant after the rain, along a good road bordered by vineyards on each side where the vintage was in full swing.

Passing DISTRE we entered more open country. At MONTREUIL-BELLAY there is a fine castle. In the early days this was a fortified town, but the fortifications were destroyed when the town was taken after a long siege, by Geoffrey Plantagenet.

We then turned to the right, making for DOUÉ, which is an interesting town, with its eleventh century church. Leaving DOUÉ, we passed down a very fine avenue, and after BAGNEUX we had a fine view as we approached SAUMUR.

At dinner we decided to be brave, and ordered with a well-cooked meal a bottle of 1922 Champigny Rouge and one of 1929 vintage. The sommelier was anxious to warm the wines, but for us this was out of the question : he seemed surprised !

The older wine was quite bright, without deposit. . . . It was slightly pétillant, and had an old taste and a flavour of faded violets.

The 1929 had the same sort of flavour but, after its older brother, seemed a little crude. Perhaps the quality was not so good.

We topped these up with a glass of 1878 Sazerac, which was enjoyable.

At one or two tables from us, a honeymoon couple were dining; an embryo cavalry officer and a flaxen jeunesse, certainly not out of her teens. They were evidently deeply in love with one another; surely the consummation of such a union will give rise to another generation. Whoever they are, may they be blessed with a 'quiver full', to their continued happiness and to the glory of La Belle France.

A walk before turning in, I suggested to Reg, but he was for the latter straight away.

As I crossed the road to lean over the parapet and gaze on the ambling Loire for a minute, a paper boy, who evidently had one last paper to dispose of, came running along, the while shouting at the top of his . . . voice ! How grateful I felt that this nuisance had been stopped in London.

I slept fairly well, in spite of the fact that outside my window were cross-roads; with much motor traffic the hooting was almost deafening. I dreamed of the 'silent' work of Mr. Hore-Belisha, and wondered, in my reverie, if by chance he had ever slept here.

Summary of the Vintages of the Wines of Touraine and Anjou

CHINON AND BOURGUEIL.

1893, 1906, 1911, 1921, 1923, 1926, 1928, 1929, 1933.

The best wines—particularly in Chinon and Bourgueil—are made from the Breton (pronounced BEURTON by the vignerons), also called Cabernet.

In good years, the degree varies from 10° to 13°.

The general opinion was that the wines of 1934 would not be so good as those of 1933, but it was early days to tell.

[105]

The consensus of opinion gives us the finest vintages of recent years—the 1921 and 1928. The 1921 wines are perhaps commencing to show their age too much : a little 1928 in a cellar would do no harm.

The good years are 1919, 1923, 1926 and 1929 (particularly Red Wine).

The vintage of 1933 is spoken of as 'very good', and it is hoped that the 1934 will be another good year. The vintages to leave alone are—1930 and 1932.

CHAPTER VI

CHARENTE

(*Cognac*)

Thursday, 4th October, 1934. . . . This is the anniversary of my mother's birthday, and quite rightly we woke to a happy smiling morning.

My mother, one of the 'four pretty Miss Saw's of Plymouth', who passed away a few years ago at the good old age of 83½, was one of the sweetest creatures that the good Lord ever gave breath to. . . . She was a saint if ever there was one, and when taking my evening walk I often think of her, and occasionally I have tried to remember even one solitary instance when she spoke a cross word to any of us, and I have been defeated !

We were a large family—there were thirteen children born alive, and three more that might have been, and yet, with all this, we never heard a cross word . . . and such patience ! She undoubtedly deserves a monument. God rest her peaceful soul !

With thoughts of the darling, and with the bright morning, we were happy on leaving Saumur for the Brandy district, viâ POITIERS.

At FONTEVRAULT we saw a very quaint well, but had not the time to alight and examine it . . . carrying on to STE. HILAIRE, where there was a fine view to please us.

At LOUDUN a large dog was rolling in the middle of the road, and we were forced to pull up while he finished his gymnastics.

At ANGLIERS the vintage was still proceeding . . . in fact, this was the case along the length of the journey, more or less in patches.

We had somewhat of a climb at POLIGNY, but the bicyclists carried on. They do not seem to mind the hills . . . 'Habitude', chimed in Reg.

The approach to POITIERS is very picturesque, with the hill-sides dotted with houses . . . many actually built in the rocks.

POITIERS, and Edward, the Black Prince, always hold a fascination for me. I remember on one occasion, I paid a visit to War-wick Castle, and one of the interesting objects to be seen in the Hall is the armour of the Black Prince. I recollect how disappointed I was . . . it was silver bright, whereas I had always learned that he was so-called from the colour of the armour he wore.

For tourists who are not on the same bent as we were there is much of historical interest to be seen in the vicinity. For us—no . . . we were off to find a reasonable place in which we could have our lunch. We selected the Hotel du Palais . . . here was quite a good list of wines, Red Bordeaux of 1920, 1924 and 1928. I thought it a little early to offer 1928's . . . White and Red Burgundies of 1915, 1919 and 1920, but alas, no 1923's—what a fall from grace—and the prices were reasonable.

The list also included Rhône wines, Alsatian wines and Italian wines . . . the proprietors deserve success.

We considered under the circumstances that it was incumbent upon us to try the local wines. We therefore made martyrs of ourselves, and ordered a Vin du Pays, Loudun Blanc, 15 fcs., and a Muscadet, 16 fcs. The first was a very dry, clean wine, which we enjoyed . . . the Muscadet was somewhat hard and unsympathetic, but probably of superior quality.

We then had a bottle of Ch. de la Noé de Bel-Air, 1er Grand Cru 1933. It sounded very grand but did not appeal to us ; in fact, it was hardly ready to drink.

Before leaving POITIERS we had a look at the Cathedral St. Pierre. It is a fine building, with a most interesting entrance. We hurriedly passed along to visit the Baptistère St. Jean and its small museum. This is indeed worth a visit, dating back to the time of the Gauls, certainly fourth century. The exhibits were most interesting, but unfortunately I had no time to make a note of them . . . you'll understand when I let you into a secret —a charming young lady showed us round, and occupied most of my attention !

We were soon on our way to ANGOULÊME . . . I was perhaps

guilty of 'shut-eye' for a moment, when Reg exclaimed—'Did you see that funny-looking magpie ?' I think its mother must have been guilty of flirting with a corbeau—perhaps the sinister-looking fellow which has just flown in front of us.

We had a little difficulty with the car, but this was soon overcome. There had been much rain, and a considerable storm, for branches of trees were frequently met with on the roads, especially between VIVONNE and LES MINIÈRES.

At VILLEGATS there was a fine view—more trouble with the car ... 'Grit in the jet', explained Reg, but it was all Greek to me !

At HAUTE SANGLE we encountered another storm . . . much rain and lightning.

At MANSLE the car stopped—no petrol. Fortunately we were outside the house of Madame Eden, sage-femme ! who also dealt in petrol, and off we went quite happily.

We crossed the Charente, and at TOURRIERS had a sight of some vines.

It was still raining, nevertheless we continued up the steep hill into ANGOULÊME—all agog, with the fair in full swing.

We had decided to stay at Les Trois Piliers, and alighting there found that they were expecting us.

Nobody could have been more attentive, and we had good accommodation. We were not so happy with the dinner . . . however, it makes one appreciate what one gets at home—and, for me—at the office, when Sergeant Dufty does his best . . . and excellent it is !

I frequently smile when remembering an occasion when the Sergeant asked permission to go off early.

'Going straight home, I hope, Sergeant ?'

'Yes, Sir, I am going home to nurse the baby while the wife goes to the pictures.'

'What is she going to see, eh ! Sergeant !'

'Oh', says he . . . ' "The light side of love" or something like that.'

With this repast we ordered a bottle of Pouilly 1926 (25 fcs.). . . . It was dark in colour and horrible to taste, so we helped it down with Perrier Water.

[109]

Cold plates for hot soup seem to be the regular thing, but it always annoys me, and being annoyed and a little tired, I found fault with everything.

'Reg', I said, 'we will get out of this after a glass of "Fine".'

We had what appeared to us as the best they had to offer—1900. It made me shudder . . . dark, and of poor quality.

'We must have a walk around the fair', I suggested. The noise and the laughter soon dispelled the gloom, and we watched the roundabouts and sideshows until it was time to retire.

I was much struck with one exhibit, and that was a cage full of birds . . . crammed so full that the little birds must have found it difficult to breathe, let alone to sing . . . and yet some were chirping. I must ask my good friend Jacques Delamain, the famous ornithologist—'pourquoi les oiseaux chantent ?'

It was raining when we went to bed, and it was raining when we awoke in the morning, although the heavy clouds seemed to be clearing somewhat.

I had opened wide my French windows and the rain during the night had swamped the floor of the room—I had slept through it all !

In spite of the rain we thought it necessary to have the Little Auk well 'preened', so we were not away until after 10 o'clock, making for JARNAC. Passing through HIERSAC we left CHATEAU-NEUF S/CHARENTE on our left ; which brought back to me the memories of my life there some forty-four years ago. Reg brought me to myself by exclaiming—'Did you see that weasel run across the road?'

I had not.

There are many vineyards here, and the vendangeurs were very busy. This continued to be so at JARNAC, where a cattle market was taking place.

We went straight to find our good friend Jacques Delamain; if I mention any names here or elsewhere, it must be understood that it was simply because they were of people and places I met on my trip, and does not suggest for one minute that there are not others better known and equally estimable.

Having paid my respects to my old friend and arranged to see him on the morrow, we moved off to Segonzac . . . there are some excellent vineyards around here in the heart of the Grande Champagne.

'Two magpies', said Reg as we went along. 'Bonheur', I exclaimed, 'we shall see something worth seeing !'

We were nearing SEGONZAC . . . vines everywhere, and on the left—GENTÉ, the place where the famous Brandy, as referred to in *Viniana*, came from.

At SEGONZAC I made use of an introduction from my old friend G. D. Atkinson (who knows a good thing when he sees it), to Monsieur Albert Frapin. This will cause dear old Jacques Delamain to smile . . . the reason you will learn later.

We paid a visit to a veritable nest-egg of Old Brandies—marvellous ! . . . some of them upwards of one hundred years old, and Oh ! so good. But we shall hear more of these later.

It was a pleasant, secluded spot, where one could conjure up all sorts of 'spirits'. Old Monsieur and Madame Renaud lived here, jealously keeping an eye on their wonderful properties. One rather gathered that the old gentleman would much prefer to see in his chais these remarkable Cognacs than a corresponding amount shown in his pass-book—*and so would I*, under similar circumstances !

Monsieur Renaud's son André looked after the chais and their contents and, therefore, we were not surprised to find them in apple-pie order. He had married Monsieur Pierre Frapin's daughter, and therefore we had an excellent introduction.

As it was approaching the luncheon hour Monsieur Frapin very kindly invited us to partake of this meal at his charming house—Le Moulin.

Through an intriguing and pleasant private drive we wended our narrow way to this mansion, situated on the hill, in the midst of such scenery as one would hardly expect in the Champagne district.

I will admit that I felt very guilty at descending on Madame so suddenly, but her gracious manner soon put us at ease.

As a 'vin ordinaire' we had a pleasant little wine—'Vin du Pays', from the family Estate of Chez Piet. It was certainly the best beverage wine I have tasted in the Charente, and on inquiry I learned that it was 1928 vintage (which was so good nearly everywhere) and that the plants were the 'St. Emilion', which term is a corruption of Sémilion.

With one of the most tasty déjeuners we enjoyed a Red Bordeaux wine, 1917 Ch. Branaire . . . it was a good specimen of a vintage that has sometimes not been spoken of in the highest terms.

Ch. d'Yquem 1906 to follow, and for those who like rich, luscious wines this must have been delectable. Now I come to think of it, I believe a pêche Melba was served with it and I fell a victim to Madame's entreaties and thoroughly enjoyed it. Needless to say, I was glad when the fine Brandies arrived . . .

1906 Gabloteau—very fine and very elegant.

1856 Chabran—a little coarse after the elegance of the 1906.

Madame Frapin insisted that we should return to dinner and, although out of sheer modesty I said that I thought it was not possible, Reg turned the tables on me and accepted for both of us . . . in reality I was very glad for we not only fared sumptuously, but enjoyed most delightful company and conversation. I remember how intrigued I was with Madame Frapin's French bulldog. He really was rather a dear, and the way in which he tried to find in which hand the sugar was, was most entertaining.

Monsieur André Guerin was of the party and accompanied us in the afternoon to some of Monsieur Frapin's fine Estates and Establishments.

I would like to congratulate Monsieur Frapin on having the services of a young man so intelligent and so industrious. Between the two of them we, that is Reg as well as myself, were able to pick up much useful and interesting information.

One of my great desires was to see the famous Gabloteau vineyard, for the 'fine' Champagne from which I have more than ordinary regard.

It is certainly one of the finest and best cared for vineyards that I have seen.

Deep chalky soil is a feature of this, the first large vineyard after the phylloxera, and I should think this still remains the largest.

The Folle Blanche has been replaced by the St. Emilion and

[112]

the Colombard, for the reason that the proprietors were not satisfied with the over-maturity of the fruit of the old stock. When properly ripe, too many rotten grapes were to be found. The reason of this is undoubtedly the 'pourriture grise', a species of rot that affects the grapes before or at maturity, in some years, and causes them to shrivel and dry up, with a resulting loss of yield and uncleanliness in the wine. Therefore, the proprietors hasten to gather the grapes when they see the 'trouble' coming on. The 'pourriture noble' is an entirely different thing. It leaves the grape plump and juicy, and only turns it to a brown colour, which is not particularly pleasant to look at, but no ill effects come from it as regards quality.

At Gabloteau I revelled in the aroma, and yes, in the flavour of 1900, 1902, 1904, 1906 and 1914 . . . exquisite specimens ! It is a pity they are so expensive. . . . Had I been a rich man and could have felt justified, not one but even two of those casks would have found a new home. A cask of such Brandy appeals to me far more than all the bins of Vintage Port which are laid down for future generations.

I grant that there are many 'cons' to contend with, not the least, the 'wood'. The evaporation is natural, and adds to the cost, but the 'wood' . . . a split stave will cause a woody taste. I thought I detected a 'goût de Bois', otherwise I would have been happy to enshroud my soul in any of these 'spirits'. They were so 'fine', so delectable, so light and fragrant.

I understood that the early distilled Brandy would often prove the best (in the same way that a brewer always looks upon the October brew as being the best). At Gabloteau, the wine was distilled twice . . . the first process at 28° and the second at 70° Gay Lussac. For the first few years one has to reckon on an average loss by evaporation of approximately 7 per cent. to 8 per cent. the first year, and afterwards not so much. The ideal thing would be to have one cask (of well-seasoned oak) and a smaller one from which to keep it filled . . . but this would be somewhat of a luxury !

The next morning we started about 9 o'clock for JARNAC. The first things that Reg saw were three magpies, but I assured him that he must have counted the same one twice over. We then espied a bird which we did not know, but later, when trying to explain it to the great ornithologist, we learned that it must have been a 'Grive'—a wild thrush which, by the erratic way it flew, is considered the only bird which gets drunk from eating too many grapes !

Jacques Delamain, out of his enthusiasm, had many interesting Brandies to show us.

After tasting a few more or less ordinary Cognacs, we were shown a 1906 Grande Fine de St. Preuil, and were immediately faced with the difference—comparisons are odious ! This Cognac of St. Preuil was a trifle too dark for my liking, but the next sample of 1906 Grande Fine was pale, and very, very good . . . . no suspicion of extraneous matter. I liked this and inquired from whence it came. 'Segonzac', he replied—thereby hangs a tale ! !

I gathered that the ideal strength at which to keep Brandy was at proof, but of course it often proves a difficulty should one's chais be too hot or too damp. At the riverside, with much dampness in the atmosphere, it is inclined to get weaker and weaker, and even in a very small way increase in bulk, whereas, on the slopes of the hill, where the sun plays on the chais, the strength may be maintained, although the quantity may be gradually reduced.

Monsieur Delamain complained bitterly that Brandy which they knew as 'Trop-pleins' was allowed to be described as 'Cognac', when obtained by single distillation, not in pot still and by double distillation which is the usage of the country. 'Trop-pleins' is only applied to the wines which, during a very plentiful year, are in excess of what the vignerons can fill into their casks when pressing the grapes. These 'trop-pleins' find their way at low prices to buyers who can supply casks, and will prove either a dead weight on the market, or a source of good profit to individual distillers when prices rise again, with no corresponding quality. The description 'Cognac' enables these inferior Brandies, which never age well, to compete with the true and finished product, to the detriment of the good name of Cognac.

As a very interesting treat we were offered Grande Fine

Champagne of the year 1777. I found it much more interesting from the point of view of its age than for any other reason.

We then tried an 1812 Fins Bois . . . the price was more reasonable, and I thought it would be commercially interesting, but on tasting it I found that it had a peculiar varnishy taste that certainly would not appeal to connoisseurs.

We then sampled 1914 and 1922 . . . . I thought the 1914 quite attractive.

1929 Grands Fins Bois distilled at 20° was already taking a good shape.

The Grande Fine of 1929, in comparison, was more delicate.

1893 Grands Fins Bois interested me, especially when I gathered that there was NO Grande Champagne in that year.

We were then shown an 1875 Grands Fins Bois, which appealed to me so much on account of its cleanness and quality that I was, perforce, obliged to arrange for it to take a journey !

The Grande Fine recommenced after the phylloxera in 1895.

We tasted a Fins Bois of 1893, which was very dark in colour, and had what my friends described as 'Rancio'. I suggested that someone had added too much caramel, but I was assured that it was not so . . . the colour was entirely from an old oak cask and the Brandy had been kept in a chai perhaps a little subject to the heat of the summer. This word 'Rancio' is used to describe a special character of fullness and fatness in some Brandies. Its origin is certainly an excess of wood in the earlier stages of the life of the Brandy, which, in the course of years, mixing with the natural essential oils, gives the Brandy softness and age, with sometimes a touch of 'rankness' (rance, rancio), accompanied by colour darker than the normal one.

As a matter of fact I did not dislike it, although my predilection is for pale, fine, light Brandies.

I jokingly said to my good friend, 'Is that all you have to show me?' He smilingly crossed the tasting-room and returned with a sample, asking me what I thought of it. Assuming as important an air as possible, I turned the Brandy round in the glass, smelt it, tasted it . . . when Reg chipped in and suggested that it would make an excellent Brandy for Brandy and Soda.

Jacques Delamain replied that at the moment it was ideal for that, but it would develop into something 'extra'.

It appeared that it was a blend of fine Brandy, only three years old . . . one half Grande Fine, blended with Fins Bois.

The last sample that we tasted here was a Grande Fine Champagne, from near Segonzac, of 1922. It had indeed a good flavour, but I did not get excited about it.

We then went off with our genial friend to partake of lunch with him.

In several places we noticed, as I had noticed elsewhere, quantities of flowers, something akin to a yellow marguerite. . . . I had been too shy to ask what they were, for fear of showing my ignorance, but, after sampling all these Brandies, the spirit encouraged me and, in answer to a somewhat subtle inquiry, I learned that they were the flowers of the Jerusalem artichoke, and that the vegetable was used as food for pigs and cattle.

I do not suppose many of you good readers have ever had the pleasurable opportunity of meeting Madame Delamain. Well, I am sorry for you ; for her delightful company and intellect is on a par with that of her husband's . . . which is saying much.

Before entering the house we took a little tour around the Estate, and seeing in a cage a few love-birds (indicative of those who lived inside the house)—called BUDGERIGARS, I took advantage of the opportunity to explain the crowded state of a cage of little birds at the Fair, at ANGOULÊME . . . in spite of which, the little feathered ones were singing.

'In such misery as that', I asked. ' "Pourquoi les oiseaux chantent ?" '

I thought I was one up, but I believe, although I pretended not to understand, that the query came back as a boomerang . . . the rascal insinuated that there were some people who could not grasp the difference between a song and a cry !

We enjoyed an excellent lunch in our host's charming dining-room, with a view of the wooded country 'en face'.

In defiance of all the unkind things I have said of their 'vins du Pays' I was actually offered a red wine of the district—1912. Exceptions prove the rule, and indeed it did here. I have frequently wondered how much he was pulling my leg !

A 1908 Barsac, not very sweet, was good, and then we regaled ourselves with a little excellent Burgundy—1915 Corton. Once again I repeated what beautiful wines were made in the Côte d'Or in the year 1915.

During the enjoyment of coffee, and a glass of superfine 1834 Grande Fine, I made a point of inquiring why the Folle Blanche plant was losing some of its great popularity. Monsieur Delamain tried to explain to me, and I hope I have it correct, that in the first place, that is, after the phylloxera, the Folle Blanche did not appear to be affected by the 'pourriture grise' in spite of the fact that the bunches of grapes were more compact . . . but as time went on it was realised that the St. Emilion plant, with fruit not so compact, withstood the 'pourriture grise' more effectively.

In Armagnac you will find a third of the vines are still Folle Blanche, and the other two-thirds divided between the Jurançon, the Blanquette and the Colombard.

I made some inquiries ; as I thought—'here's the opportunity to ask about the American stock on which the French vines of the Grande Fine Champagne are grafted.'

When the grafting on to the American stock came into practice —early in the 'eighties—as the only remedy against phylloxera (which had invaded and destroyed the vineyards in 1878 and after) the varieties of American vines which were used at first were 'Vitis Riparia' and 'Vitis Rupestris', and later, crosses between the two kinds. But this American 'blood' proved unsuitable for the chalky hills of the Grande Champagne, the soil of which contains a very high percentage of chalk (sometimes between 50 per cent. and 70 per cent.).

To find a suitable stock a mission was sent to U.S.A., and a vine was found growing wild on the chalky soil there. That vine—'Vitis Berlandieri'—was brought back to France, but its cultivation proved to be difficult. However, when crossed with the two other American kinds, it gave hybrids which had a root system powerful enough to prosper on the dry chalk hills. The first seedlings of Berlandieri hybrids were obtained in 1887, I understand, at the Station Viticole of Cognac, and after that, the replanting of the Grande Champagne was only a question of

time. But this explains why, in 1893, the new vineyards of the
Grands Fins Bois gave for the first time a plentiful vintage, whilst
the yield in the Grande Champagne was practically nil, as the
vines planted were still too young. The replanted vineyards of
the Grande Champagne began to give Brandy in 1895 and 1896
only.

After lunch we were to take a tour in the district, and this was
where a little fun began !

I must explain that for several years my good friend Jacques
Delamain had promised me that he would show me a 'nest egg'
of the most marvellous old Brandies that existed . . . and at long
last the time had arrived.

It was a great secret, as the owner guarded his stock with the
utmost jealousy, and evidently took a delight in seeing his fine
' spirits' remain in his chais.

The psychological moment had arrived, and off we went. At
last, in a hushed voice he said, with a warning finger, not to make
any noise—'Here we are !'

Indeed, we were to see a fine collection, and we were introduced
to some of the most excellent Brandies ; (by this time Reg had
dug me in the ribs). The following are my notes :

1870-1875.	1st Puncheon—very good nose, trifle bitter.
	2nd „ cleaner.
	3rd „ curious—did not like.
	4th „ slightly fuller.
	5th „ very much like No. 4.
1874.	6th „ very good *indeed* . . . a wonderful Brandy, but they are all A 1 except No. 5.
1878.	A number of Puncheons . . . very good, but not quite so fine.
?1858.	The date was uncertain, but what quality. Who cares about dates when this is *the* goods !
1858.	(Certain.) Little darker, but—oh ! so good. The difference in colour is explained by the 'wood'.
1858.	Another Puncheon, just as delectable as the last.

I must explain that I did not very much like the somewhat
foetid smell of this particular chai, but was assured that it was

natural to it.   Nevertheless, I took each sample in turn to the open, to taste.

The strength of these Brandies was a natural one of 30° to 32° Sykes. Very soon the owner will have to put on his thinking cap, and then. . . . He may be persuaded to sell, for the danger point will come in nine or ten years' time when the alcoholic degrees become as low as 40° under proof.

I expect all of you have grasped the situation. This was the very place we had visited the day before ! I did not smile . . . took it all very seriously, and neither Reg nor I 'let on'. I wish I could see my dear old friend's face when he reads this ! !

It was somewhat of a struggle to leave here, but off we had to go. I noticed around here that Walnut trees were quite a feature in the vineyards.

There is much romantic history attaching to these parts, especially for the English visitor, for it is about here that Edward, the Black Prince, reached farthest south . . . all in the Grande Champagne. I have it in my heart to forgive him for not continuing further afield.

From St. Preuil there is a finer view than could be expected in the district.

ST. MÊME we passed, locally known as 'Les Vertus' . . . so much laughter accompanied the explanation that I was unable to grasp the meaning.

Here in the valley we find American vines, the Riparia, and Rupestris as stock for grafting, for it thrives well in damp soil. But at a little distance, where we have the stony soil, the chief root is the hybrid Berlandieri 1202, which grows well on the chalk.

We were again at ST. MÊME, and ready for a little sight-seeing. Jacques Delamain's brother Robert . . . a bird of the same delightful feather, and a keen archæologist, insisted that we visit some ancient and very interesting caves . . . limestone. We had a Limoges potter with us, who was, as you may imagine, extremely interested.

From here, we paid a visit to a little village 'GRAVES' (Charente), with its old church ; however, crossing into the Fins Bois at BASSAC, we found a truly old-world atmosphere.

The Church here is remarkable—commenced in the Roman period (1009), and finished some two hundred years later. At times it was in the hands of the Protestants, and at others, in the hands of the Roman Catholics. It was built as a fortified Church, and at the time of the historical battle of Jarnac, 1569, it was in peril of definite destruction. But it is well worth a visit, if the 'spirit' calls you to these parts.

The cloister dates back to 1685 ; it is in a very dilapidated condition, almost so bad as to cause our archæological pride to shed a tear !

Through one of the old houses at the back of the adjoining courtyard we were allowed to pass, and entered an enchanting and secluded garden which led down to the river, on the banks of which grew the Catalpa trees—very sightly.

After an enjoyable cup of tea with Madame Delamain, whom we could not fail to revisit, we made our way back to ANGOULÊME, the sunset promising a good day for the morrow.

At the Trois Piliers we partook of our dinner and washed down a Jambon d'York, which Reg declared had come viâ Denmark (it was certainly not a patch on our EPICHAMS), with the contents of a carafe of Champagne nature, for which we were charged the very reasonable price of 10 francs.

A Fine Champagne, 2nd Empire ! ! completed the meal. I will not make any more comment on the 'Fine' or the 'Empire'.

Some Brandies are naturally, from contact with the wood, dark ; I am forcibly under the impression that they lack the exquisite flavour and the ethereal touch of the pale variety.

I remember, on one occasion, a delightful veteran of some 85 years old, asked me to send him three dozen fine, pale Brandy, adding—'Pray, don't think I have taken leave of my senses . . . I am confident it will see me out, but then, Mr. Berry, what pleasure I shall have to know how my executors are able to regale themselves . . . a little return for all the trouble they will be put to !'

If I remember correctly, my only rejoinder was—'A most noble and spirited sentiment, Sir.'

It might, however, be well for me to repeat here much that I have already said in reference to Brandy, Cognac and Grande

Champagne, particularly as I took advantage of the opportunity to instil it further into Reg.

Brandy can come from anywhere, not only from France, provided always that it is a spirit distilled from Wine : it is different with Cognac ; this also is a spirit distilled from Wine, but made in the Charente district of France, and no other is entitled to be so described. Cognac is subdivided roughly into seven classifications . . .

1. GRANDE CHAMPAGNE.
2. PETITE CHAMPAGNE.
3. BORDERIES.
4. FINS BOIS.
5. BONS BOIS.
6. BOIS ORDINAIRES.
7. BOIS COMMUNS.

Cognac is distilled from the wine of the White grape, in a 'Pot' still. It requires eight to ten Hogsheads of wine, according to the strength of the wine, to make one Hogshead of Cognac.

The word 'Champagne' is occasionally a stumbling block, no doubt by reason of the accustomed use of the word in referring to the sparkling wine of Reims. 'Champ', a field, is a space, cultivated or not, where there are no trees ; by extension of the meaning of the word to large spaces, the name 'Champagne' or 'terre de Champs' has been given to whole districts, hills or high plains, dry, sparsely timbered, with a subsoil of chalk or limestone. These are exactly the characters of both the Champagnes of the Charente, and of the hills and plains of the old French Province of Champagne.

In both is found the same nature of soil, which is chalky, and the same rather bare, arid landscape !

Before retiring I thought I would take a stroll around the Fair, which was being held in the immediate vicinity of the hotel.

There seemed to be an unusually large number of people, probably on account of the Elections Cantonales to be held on the morrow.

I always find it amusing to stroll round the Fairs, in spite of the deafening noise of the Roundabouts, etc., etc. The first show which caught my eye was placarded as 'Daisy'—'without legs or arms ; she eats, drinks, sews, writes, etc. . . . Has received diploma for painting.' However, it did not say by whom awarded !

'L'Enfant Phoque' was next to it . . . not much business being done here as the place was shut.

Numbers of wild animals in the travelling menagerie, shooting galleries, and merry-go-rounds galore !

My attention was called forcibly to the large number of very young children and even babies being dragged about among the crowd. One little lad, a bright little chap, was crying, and I saw his mother give him two sous to buy some sweets. It immediately brought to my mind a little incident in my own family life, which was rather amusing. . . . My eldest brother, Harry, had been a good boy—I am not suggesting that he was ever otherwise !— (he must have been six or seven years old) and his mother had given him a penny to buy some 'bull's eyes'. When he came back he was crying bitterly. . . . 'Why, Harry, dear boy, what *is* the matter . . . what are you crying for ?' said his mother. 'He wouldn't let me have any. He only laughed at me,' he wailed. 'That is funny', his mother said . . . 'To which shop did you go ?' 'I went to the butcher's', whimpered Harry . . . 'and he wouldn't give me any !'

It must have been many a long year since I thought of this, but on seeing this rosy-faced boy off to buy his pennyworth of sweets, it was brought back to my mind.

Lotteries seemed to be the most popular side show ; although I must admit that the sweet-making fascinated me . . . yards and yards and yards of it, never-ending . . . twisted into all sorts of fantastic shapes. And when the operator commenced manipulating it like skeins of wool, the little ones in the crowd stood spell-bound.

It was not so late after all when I retired, for the clocks had to be put back one hour !

My sleep was considerably broken by the roaring of the menagerie lions, and when I heard firing the next morning I really thought that they had escaped, but not so . . . it was merely rocket signals being let off on account of a particular aerial contest.

It was a beautiful morning when we left ANGOULÊME soon after 8.30; on our way to my old friends at Chateau le Prieuré, St. Genès.

We passed through the village of HIERSAC rather before 9 o'clock of a Sabbath morning, and the first thing that greeted us was the sight of slops being emptied out from the windows. ... 'Would you believe it, Reg', I asked. 'Yes, I would believe anything here', he said.

I agree that the people certainly did some funny things.

We passed many chasseurs, and a little further on, seated by the roadside, we caught sight of one plucking a goose. His dog was beside him and from the look on his face I am convinced that no other dog would dare to try and 'retrieve' this man's booty.

At JARNAC we were stopped at the level crossing, at the approach to which we found the Fire Brigade hard at work. A little copse was smouldering and one small tree, the Phoenix perhaps, was still warm.

Such fires are handled in the proper manner in JARNAC. There must have been, without exaggeration, some fifty firemen or other officials!

Some of these carried on their backs vast bugles, which they blew without any encouragement; I think this must have been with the idea that it helped on the good work. Unfortunately, it had the contra effect, as, whatever duty was being performed, the workers immediately stopped, in order to listen in admiration.

There were many vineyards around here ... on through COGNAC, with Martell's building to greet us, we went on to MONTIGNAC ... here we noticed a signboard on the left to GIMEUX, which unhesitatingly brought to mind the generosity of Madame Frapin, in opening for us after dinner a bottle of her 'family' Brandy from GIMEUX, which was Grande Champagne of 1840.

Between STE. FOY and PERIGNAC we came across many beaters. What a sight they would have been for Lorne, but Reg had it to himself.

Near by, a spotlessly clean goat—white as snow—had my attention instead.

PONS, with its many bridges, is quite attractive and interesting, with its ancient Church and Archway.

As we passed through BELLVIRE we overtook a car which looked as if it had been made in the year 'dot', fit for any veteran race. It is extraordinary how they get along . . . this one was not doing more than about three or four kilometres an hour, and making a terrible noise all the time. It reminded me of one we saw a few days before at GENSAC, not on the road, but in a garage, where it was kept as a museum piece. While we 'admired' it our genial host persisted in pulling the cork of a bottle of Champagne, 1921 Moët and Chandon, Dry Imperial. It was a pleasant surprise to find *Dry* Imperial and not *Brut* Imperial.

While still discussing this remarkable evidence of past activity we overtook something even more remarkable . . . 'Darby and Joan' on a motor-bike—I am certain that their joint ages must have been upwards of one hundred and fifty years ! It was indeed a happy sight.

Taking down notes in a car every now and then requires practice, otherwise they become impossible to read—this I have found to my regret !

Passing by this energetic couple, we evidently went over a bump in the road, which caused me to drop my small piece of paper.

'You should hold it firmly', said Reg, 'like a nettle . . . then you will come to no harm !'

This brought to my mind the old rhyme—

'If you gently touch a NETTLE,
It will sting you for your pains,
Grasp it like a man of mettle—
And it soft and silk remains !'

It is curious that the word 'Nettle' should bring to mind, not only this, but an incident connected with a nettle, which appealed to me as a reminder of—'Out of the mouths of babes . . . etc.' It was related to me by Mrs. Lucas of her grandchild, Lavinia, who had evidently been stung with a nettle (the child being five years old).

'Grannie', asked the child . . . 'What is the good of nettles?'

To which Grannie replied that she really did not know but that they must have some use as the Good God had made them.

A minute's silence ... 'Grannie, I do think that God must have an awe-ful sense of fun !'

About here we espied one magpie ... 'That's nothing', said Reg, and we almost immediately passed a dead rabbit on the road, squashed to nothing.

'Going down from Nottingham to Doncaster', added Reg, 'during last Doncaster week, Barbara counted no less than one hundred and forty-three dead rabbits lying about the roadway !' I am not going to vouch for either the accuracy of Barbara's arithmetic, or Reg's memory.

At ST. AUBIN, the vines commenced to put in an appearance, and near EYRANS a small Still was at work on the roadside.

I now caught sight of the 'Trois Moulins' and recognised a place where, upwards of forty years ago, I passed many a happy time with the family of my dear old friend Louis O'Lanyer. Some of the family still live at Chateau Le Prieuré, St. Genès, whither we were wending our way, in order to pay a long promised visit.

What a pleasure it is to meet the friends of one's youth. Here they were ready to greet us, the two younger daughters—Daisy, that is Mdlle O'Lanyer, as happy and as charming as ever ... and Blanche—now Madame Pierre Cayrou, equally charming as her sister, and as beautiful as ever, in spite of a year or more of anxiety over her husband's health. Thank God, he is much better, and they can now look forward to many years of continued good health and happiness.

Pierre Cayrou soon came in ... a worthy husband for an equally worthy woman.

I shook him warmly by the hand, and would have liked to have kissed the ladies, but modesty withheld me. I hope they will read this so that, perhaps, one never knows, on the next occasion they will make the advance.

Time soon passed, recounting many incidents of happy youth. I could not help reminding Blanche of an occasion when my mother was visiting Le Prieuré, and she was a baby girl. During this time my mother found much pleasure in seizing every opportunity of nursing the sweet little flaxen-haired creature. Madame O'Lanyer (who was to me as a second mother in her attentions and kindness) was anxious to express to my mother when she was leaving how very grateful she was for her care and fondness for her little one, and said, in an emotional voice— 'Dear Madam Berrie . . . I thank you for your great kidneys (kindness) !'

We spoke of the little black horse, Charbon . . . how he bolted through the vineyards with me, much to the consternation of everyone, but I escaped with little more than a few bruises.

At lunch we enjoyed the Prieuré wine of 1929. It was exceedingly pleasant; Pierre Cayrou looks after the vineyards with particular attention.

1926 Ch. Brane Cantenac to follow was almost a fine wine. Some of the wines of 1926 are developing much better than was anticipated.

In the afternoon I took a stroll in order to cast a glance at some of the spots in the close vicinity, recalling to memory much that had given me pleasure.

I made a point of going as far as the cemetery, in order to stand bareheaded in silence in front of the imposing vault containing the earthly remains of generations of the family—

O'Lanyer de L'Estaing

where my old friend has found his last resting place.

I trust that it will be a great many years before the occasion arises to re-open the vault.

On returning to Le Prieuré I found my old (boy) friend, Louis, the eldest of the family. He had heard I was coming, and considerately made the journey to shake me by the hand.

A little grey, perhaps, but otherwise just the same, with the same merry twinkle in his eye. We spoke of our early days . . . the boxing matches, the tennis, Estelle, the étang, the bathing pool in the river, billiards, naughty little episodes in Bordeaux, and a hundred and one things. It is wonderful how the time passes with such reminiscences.

Louis is a gentleman at large. He has a small vineyard of his own, breeds dogs, and spends what time he can 'à la chasse'.

After tea, we had a walk round the park, and paid a visit to the chais, etc. I found everything very much as in bygone days, although machinery had been installed, and had supplanted manual labour. The sight of the old fouloir brought back to my memory how I assisted in treading the grapes, and dancing with the vendangeurs, to the airs from a violin and penny whistle.

I understand that the harmony between proprietors and vignerons is not as it was—when all was peace. Now they indulge in bickerings and grumblings due, I gather, to communistic influence.

During the war time Monsieur O'Lanyer had forty German prisoners to house in the rooms of the old Prieuré, and in return they worked in the vineyards. The family spoke of them in very good terms.

Being in the chais, I expressed a desire to see the new wine. The totalité of the 1933 wine which we had secured was in Bordeaux, and I would see it there.

The maître de chais came forward . . . surely I knew that face. . . . Yes, it was Alfred, who was a boy on the vineyards at the time of my sojourn in 1891-2.

He looked well and happy, and was, I gathered, quite a 'good chap'.

We tasted the red wine in three different stages of fermentation, so it was not possible to form any opinion, but it promises well.

White wine from one vat was tasted, which made me splutter all over the place, much to the amusement of the ladies.

The beautiful stables are now used for motor-cars, etc., facing which is a grass plot, netted in . . . the scene of former tennis playing, but now derelict.

How I could remember countless games . . . I inquired about a dapper little man who used to join us—the Comte de Saint-Legier, proprietor of the well-known Pauillac Château of Grand-Puy-Lacoste—but he also has 'taken wings'.

Before going back to the house, Pierre Cayrou and I ventured out of the gates, and took a walk along to the Mairé, in order to learn the result of the Elections Cantonales.

As far as he was concerned, the right man was evidently elected, for he joined me with a contented expression on his face . . .

46 for, and 32 against, in a total poll of 78, out of many hundreds; is this apathy or laziness?

Before dinner we stood out on the balcony, listening to the old Prieuré church bells. Across the river we could see the stately Château Ducru Beaucaillou, and also Château Lynch Bages. Not long before this I had had a bottle of 1895 Ch. Ducru Beaucaillou . . . it was excellent! I threw across an acknowledgment.

I was so pleased with the 1929 wine of Le Prieuré, that in spite of the desire to open some famous bottle, I insisted on having it again . . . Light and elegant, and when thirsty, one could drink a lot.

After dinner we sat in the hall, admiring the beautiful tapestries, and keeping up a continuous chatter.

My friends were much amused when I produced a book, entitled *A Pleasant Surprise*, and proceeded to pour out some ancient Fine Champagne, which sufficed until bed-time.

We were up early . . . had an old-fashioned tub, which amused more than delighted me, and were soon ready to make an early start for BORDEAUX.

The bath reminded me of an occasion during the severe winter of 1891 when I won a wager by going down to the O'Lanyer cellars in Bordeaux and took a cold plunger in the huge bottle washing tank. As I write this I can hear the laughter and shrieks of the 'ouvriers et ouvrières' who persisted in shouting 'le canard' and pelting me with corks. Oh! the joy of wilful youth.

I told Daisy that I had been awakened by a lizard in my room. 'I hope you did not kill it', she said . . . 'for the lizard is "ami de la Maison".' This was the first time I had heard that, nevertheless he is a friend I would prefer to keep at a distance.

We were soon well on our way, finding that the vintage was practically over, and that in places the plough was hard at work . . . here with oxen—there with horses.

As we crossed the stream, 'Le Morou', we saw the patient anglers at sport. I cannot imagine that they would have much success, for, the little water there was, was very muddy, but I don't suppose they minded very much.

At ST. ANDRÉ DE CUBZAC we had to go very slowly on account of a long funeral procession. The number of boys in thin red cassocks added to the brightness of the day.

Over the fine 1879 bridge across the Dordogne, we were soon through CARBON BLANC, and arrived at BORDEAUX on the afternoon of Monday, the 8th October.

SUMMARY OF BRANDY VINTAGES

It must be remembered that the expression 'Brandy Vintages' does not have the same significance as 'Wine Vintages'.

Brandy is stored in casks which, owing to evaporation, require filling up from time to time, and this is done, generally speaking, from younger Brandies of equal grade, which in no way should impair the quality.

Occasionally, some Grande Champagne will be found where the casks have been always filled up from another cask of the identical Brandy . . . this is, therefore, the only perfect specimen.

There have been many years in which fine Brandies have been distilled, and the production—alas ! . . . sold many times over.

1865, 1870, 1878, 1893, 1900, 1904, 1906, 1914, 1928, 1929.

These are some of the very finest. Other good vintages, which, however, we would not class as high as the above, are—

1872, 1884, 1895, 1896, 1899, 1905, 1911, 1916, 1919, 1924, 1926.

The absolute failures were such as—

1887, 1888, 1891, 1894, 1897, 1902, 1907 . . .
since when there has not been anything really bad.

1902 . . . A portion of this was excellent, and the remainder a failure.

CHAPTER VII

BORDEAUX

WE arrived at the Hotel d'Orsay in time for déjeuner, and sat down to a modest repast, accompanied by a bottle of 1923 Cos d'Estournel, second growth, St. Estèphe ; a pleasant enough wine, but much too old for its age.

Some of the 1923 wines, especially of the Graves and St. Emilion, are particularly pleasant, but they will not make 'old bones'.

As usual, when drawing the cork, it broke . . . Oh ! Those corkscrews ! !

On the table was standing a bottle of Ch. Latour, 1930 . . . 12 francs, marked 'for propaganda'. What mentality ! To me, it is almost unbelievable that one should introduce to the would-be drinker of Red Bordeaux wine a Ch. Latour, first growth, Pauillac . . . one of the few names to conjure with . . . of 1930 vintage ! ! ! If ever there was a bad vintage, here you have it. Run through your mind the two together—Latour . . . 1930 . . . and then imagine what the public will think, especially when the vintage 1930 is being used for this purpose.

Latour, which everyone regards as the acme . . . 'This must be good, we will try it !' And then comes the fall—the great disappointment. 'If this is a specimen of the finest Red Bordeaux' (they probably know nothing about the vintage), 'then may I be spared from drinking it again !'

It might be argued that, for 12 francs per bottle of Ch. Latour, what can they expect . . . that is not the point. An inferior wine, even if it is given away, can never create a good impression, much less so when even 12 francs is asked for it. This is not the way to popularise the excellent wines of the Médoc . . . of that I am certain.

After a cup of coffee and a glass of 'Fine' which was quite good, we did a little unpacking and then went out into the noble city . . . Reg to see some old friends, whom he knew years ago when living in Bordeaux . . . I to do a little shopping and incidentally to have a walk past some old haunts.

Still having one hour to spare, I decided to go to my old friend, Monsieur Duret, and glean some information about the recent crop of Olives.

Olive groves and vineyards always seem to go together, and most assuredly the Olive is a great help when drinking many wines. It cleanses the palate, and, to my way of thinking, the natural oil in the fruit absorbs the slight alcohol in the wine.

There are many Oils that masquerade as Olive Oil ; under such designations as Table Oil, Salad Oil, etc., but I think one can be fairly safe to conclude that they are not pure Olive Oil, but that they would contain certain proportions of one or other of the following ingredients—Sesame Oil, Peanut Oil, Cotton Seed Oil, Poppy Oil, Coleseed Oil.

It is not the most agreeable experience to taste a number of samples of Olive Oil, but before making commitments I felt it was my duty to do so.

The one which pleased me best came from Provence, in the South of France, and if I remember correctly, the particular Olives were the Picholine and the Amenlaou, gathered about the commencement of December, the crop lasting sometimes as late as April, when the finest mellow qualities are made from the very ripe Olives.

The Oil from the Spanish Olive did not appeal to me as being so light and elegant.

All round the Mediterranean Coast one finds the Olive . . . Nice, Genoa, Leghorn, Bari, Corfu, Mitylene, etc., etc., and on the North African Coast, so you can understand that there is a great variety.

As with the vines, so with the Olive trees . . . the growers have hard and expensive work in destroying and counteracting the diseases which frequently do so deplorable an amount of harm.

The first one hears of is the 'dacus oleœ', that is the 'Mouche de l'Olivie' and is found in the fruit itself. . . .

The 'Teigne de l'Olivier' (œcophoro oliviella) . . . and the 'Fumagine' (noir ou morphée) . . . these are what cause the greatest damage.

Some trees bear more prolifically than others, but much depends on the soil. In a good year old trees will even produce as much as 500 kilos., whereas the average is from 2-300 kilos. The word 'Virgin' or 'Vierge' is frequently used in connection with Olive Oil. This should indicate that it is the first pressing of the ripe fruit, gently crushed between cloths.

The second and third pressings are of a heavier and inferior quality, and are obtained by the great pressure of mechanical machines.

The moral from these remarks is—'see to it that you have, from a trustworthy source, the first pressings of pure ripe Olives ; and do *not* look for the Oil to be darker than a pale yellow, and with only a slight smell'.

Olive Oil should be kept in a cool place . . . it is, however, very susceptible to the cold, and will readily congeal, but this has no detrimental effect, even if it be frozen : should this happen, uncork the bottle and place it in warm water for a short time.

Always keep the bottle well corked, as exposure to the air is against its good preservation.

Some time ago I had been asked the significance of the term 'premier cru' as applied to Olive Oil. I had not heard of it, so made some inquiries. Monsieur Duret told me that he had not come across it, but 'première pression' or 'premier jet' were spoken of . . . meaning the first pressing of the ripe Olive, such as he is in the habit of sending over to us. He added that he had never seen or heard of Oil being obtained before crushing the Olive, the usual process being to crush the fruit . . . that is the whole fruit with the stone, and then press the 'pate' thus obtained.

There is another process in use, in which the stone is first extracted from the fruit, and the pulp afterwards pressed. The Olive Oil thus obtained is still full of 'pulp' and impurities, requiring careful decanting and filtering before it is ready for bottling.

After this interesting chat, and with the glad assurance that the crop this year would not 'let us down', I left my good friend, almost wishing I could retire like Rosalind, to a 'sheep cote' fenced about with Olive trees. On my way to the hotel the thought passed through my mind, how often Olive groves and vineyards are linked together as possessing a dual capacity for good. I delight in Jotham's parable of the trees seeking a tree to reign over them : their first choice was the Olive, then the Fig, and then the Vine ; all of which declined the honour, because of other duties to perform ; the Olive to give 'fatness' to the people, the Fig 'sweetness' and the Vine to 'cheer' both God and man.

Thinking of this naturally turned my thoughts to other references in Holy Writ, especially of Elijah and Elisha ; when everything was dark for the widows, the tot of oil stood them in good stead, and with the widow of Zarephath, the meal and oil never failed her afterwards, but remained as the essential means of subsistence.

As I crossed over the Cours de l'Intendance, to the hotel, trying to dodge the traffic, I recollected the case of a poor man lying by the wayside wounded, when the good Samaritan poured in oil and wine.

Evidently St. Luke, the physician, realised the virtue of outward application, as well as inward.

At the hotel I met Reg and told him that sometimes I came to the conclusion that one half of the ailments to which the flesh is heir, can be avoided by taking regularly a small quantity of Olive Oil . . . but I added, impressed with my recent visit . . . 'It *must* be PURE.'

My family had enjoined upon me that I must see Edmond, so I thought that, as this was the only evening I might have free in BORDEAUX, I would 'phone through to his office.

Edmond Lestapis ('such a nice boy', all the girls would say) stayed with my family at Great Missenden, and afterwards at Surbiton, some years ago, and I do believe that, by virtue of the joyous hilarity of youth, he was able to improve somewhat his knowledge of the English language. He left behind him a very happy memory, and I had all sorts of messages to give him.

[133]

Now that his father is no more, he and his brother carry on their old and well-reputed business.

Edmond has become quite serious under his responsibilities, and I feel as sure as I hope, that good success awaits him in the future.

Having introduced Edmond to you, I will tell you the result of my telephone call.

Fortunately he was at his office . . . I congratulated him on being there at so late an hour, and then asked him if he would dine with us.

I am glad to say that there was no 'let me see': 'well', etc., etc., but right off the mark—'rather !' That's what I like . . . so the three of us dined together . . . the old fellow, and the two young ones, and a very happy time and good dinner we enjoyed.

Edmond introduced us to a small restaurant at the back of the Café de Bordeaux, the 'ETCHE-ONA', a basque restaurant of some repute. It must be good, I thought, as that gourmet, Rudd, had recommended it to me.

We had an excellent soup, and some oysters. With these, we had a bottle of a White wine . . . new to me . . . Banco Monopole —not too sweet. It served its purpose of drowning the fish.

With a small tournedos, we had a bottle of 1920 Ch. Des-mirail, Margaux, third growth . . . very agreeable. If you find a good 1920, it *is* good. It was brought to us in a cradle ! How I detest those cradles ! !

If I remember correctly, we had a guinea-fowl. It may have been a pheasant to follow, and with this we indulged in a bottle of 1900 Ch. Ferrière, another Margaux, third growth . . . on the condition that it was properly decanted. It was, and it was delectable. I might add that, in drawing the cork, it broke, as usual ! ! !

We were progressing admirably by now, Edmond struggling with English, and I doing likewise with French, while Reg chipped in with one or the other. There is something nice and matey about a good bottle of wine, and this bottle of 1900 Ch. Ferrière was GOOD.

I do not think that BORDEAUX knows anything about the beauties of fine Cognac . . . all one finds is dark, dark, dark . . . so

[134]

I offered the list to Edmond, with 'please, do choose something worth drinking'. I admit he found it difficult, especially as he knew my predilection for the pure, pure pale. However, we had the best, that is to say, the most expensive they had—1858 Fine . . . it wasn't bad . . . quite sweet, and rather dark, but not *the Goods*.

A diner had arrived late. He made up for his time, and when we had finished he was well away, and becoming somewhat quarrelsome. . . . I don't care for that sort of thing, so we left. Reg went straight back to the hotel, and I took a walk along the quay with Edmond.

'Good-night, Edmond, it has been such a pleasure to meet you . . . I shall not forget your messages when I get back.'

The next morning I had had no news from Mr. Clark . . . he had promised to meet me here with his good lady. As I had arranged that we should visit certain places together I thought I should like to know what had happened. Thinking that he must be ill I sent him a telegram, hoping for a reply on my return.

At 9.15, my friend Monsieur Danglade with the indefatigable courtier, M. Damade, arrived as arranged. It was raining, but we hoped from the barometric message that it would clear.

Before starting I had a little commission to leave at the office, and the chef asked me if I knew a certain American gentleman of the name of . . . 'No', I answered, 'I have never heard of him. Why do you ask?'

He replied that most of the representatives of the Bordeaux houses had been making inquiries as to his arrival: all I could say was that I hoped he would select the right ones to give him advice.

Monsieur Danglade took us off to his part of the world, as I had desired. The first property that we visited was Château Nenin . . . a good Estate, and good wine—one of the best Pomerol wines. We tasted the 1933, but I thought I detected a dry finish (which would mean too much tannin), and yet it still seemed to be suffering from a slight fermentation . . . it may come round all right.

We then visited the famous Château Cheval Blanc . . . a fine property is this, and well kept. We tasted the 1933 wine, of which we were able to procure but very little—it *was* good, but perhaps somewhat light. It may easily turn into a fine wine, something between a 1900 and a 1923.

We then tasted the 1934, which of course was not in a proper state to taste . . . it is very difficult to say what it will be like. The sample was fermenting, in spite of which I could detect softness by virtue of sugar, and a certain bitterness by virtue of tannin. I think it will develop well . . . it seems so well balanced. We shall certainly have a say in the purchase of the totalité of this famous wine !

Château Cheval Blanc is one of the most famous growths of St. Emilion.

We tasted the wine with a feeling of pride, while speaking of its fine future, yet realising how very difficult it is to foretell how it will turn out. Young wines, so full of life, and 'noisy' with their fermentation, always lead me to compare them with 'humans': consider babies, they all look much alike, and although we know their 'parentage' we remember that 'good wombs have borne bad sons' . . . so Mother Earth is dependent on the elements, and on proper treatment during her 'travail'; the offspring likewise requires the most patient and studious attention in order that we may enjoy later what we fervently hope for.*

We then passed on to Pomerol again, and called at Château L'Evangile, which one of my clerks persists in calling 'Evanguile ! !' Unfortunately there was no responsible person on the premises and we had to retire without tasting.

We then called at La Conseillante, where fine wines are made, but the proprietors always, in my opinion, ask too much to begin with. The 1933 was a very attractive proposition . . . fruity, perhaps a little more body than the Cheval Blanc, but too expensive. I could not entertain it. It was developing beautifully. . . . I would like to have had that wine !

We tasted the 1934 . . . of course, as with the other 1934's, it was impossible to give any opinion, but I was a little surprised that it did not show more than 12°. I might add that there had been beautiful weather . . . sun, without excessive heat, also a little rain from time to time.

* It is developing into a 'Vin Manifique'.

[136]

Melons, peaches, figs, and table grapes were in fine condition, which is a good 'portent'.

The weather now had commenced to clear; in fact, the sun was beginning to shine. We went over to St. Emilion, and at Yon-Figeac we tasted the 1933. I did not find it very interesting . . . others did, and no doubt they know better than I. I made a point of asking what the 'ac' at the end of the name of so many towns signified (such as Figeac) and I was given to understand that it was an equivalent to 'village'.

While we were at St. Emilion I was anxious for Reg to have a good look around at this ancient and attractive town. The ruins of the old castle are very interesting . . . there are besides, the six gates and the ramparts which deserve every attention, but we were only able to have a quick glance.

The Arch de la Cadène was a picture, dating back to the thirteenth century . . . a fine sight meets the eye at Porte Brunet (I only mention these particulars as worthy of notice, in case any of my readers visit St. Emilion. They must make a point of seeing La Collégiale, which is well worth a visit, and the twelfth century ancient church which is to be found beneath another . . . it is indeed remarkable ! !).

The cloisters of Les Cordeliers are interesting . . . there is a sparkling St. Emilion associated with this.

Before one leaves, time should be found to visit the first manufacturer of the delicious 'Macaroons du pays' . . . do not forget this, they are indeed delightful.

From Ch. Pavie, we enjoyed a very fine view: FRONSAC was pretty country. Here we tasted a Côte de Fronsac, Ch. Jeandeman., a 1933 wine, good, and almost elegant. It showed only 11°, which after all is not far short of an average.

This was the morning's work, and we were glad to accept Madame Danglade's very kind invitation to lunch.

With a 1928 Graves . . . a trifle sweet and sulphury . . . we enjoyed some of the Champignons de la Maison. Monsieur Danglade has some wonderful natural caves in which he cultivates fine mushrooms.

With a pheasant, and a pâté aux truffes, we were allowed to indulge in a St. Emilion wine Ch. Bel-Air, 1923 . . . light, very old, but very pleasant, and also a bottle of 1914 Ch. Haut Brion. This wine still possessed character, but I think its best days are over.

With a paté—a special paté de foie gras aux truffes, we had a magnum of 1895 Ch. Cheval Blanc.

Monsieur Danglade had asked if I would like it then or wait a little. . . . Having heard what the wine was, I remarked—'le plutôt possible ! . . . toute de suite . . . the "tooter the sweeter".'

It was grand ! ! I am glad we did not wait for the cheese . . . in this wise I had a double share !

Madame Auschitzky was seated next to me. Madame is Monsieur Danglade's daughter . . . very charming ! Under the influence of the 1895 Ch. Cheval Blanc (bless the wine), I confided to this young lady that her name was too difficult to pronounce . . . would she teach me her Christian name . . . it was Madeleine. And now, Madeleine, I thank you for your charming company, and the happy conversation we carried on during this sumptuous repast. I only wish I could speak your language as happily as you do mine—au revoir, good friends . . . thank you so much !

We had to be off, as we had work to do in the Médoc.

The first visit we paid was at the Château Palmer Margaux . . . I always like these wines, and I tasted the 1933 feeling sure I would not be disappointed—but I was—it was light and elegant, but there was something I did not quite approve of . . . maybe the influence of the 1895 Ch. Cheval Blanc was still upon me. The others thought it excellent, so I was well in the minority.

There is a fine land-mark here, the Church of Lamarque . . . a guiding star in a wilderness of vines.

We were at St. Julien, and felt that we must call at Château Beychevelle, for had we not purchased the whole output of 1933 ? A grand tasting immediately took place. First of all we had to see the 1933, all the casks of which already bore our name. The sample from the first hogshead was agreed to be very good and elegant, so, in case this happened to be a particularly favoured cask we tasted another . . . it was better ! I turned to Reg, and said 'We're in clover !'

[138]

Although there are such excellent wines of 1933, yet I cannot help but think that they must be bought with considerable discrimination.

The summer was hot, and in the vineyards where the roots of the vines did not penetrate sufficiently deep to retain the moisture, it is feared that the grapes suffered, and that the wine made from them will also suffer.

However, do not worry . . . trust to your Wine Merchant. These are the details of which he should be cognizant.

We then sampled the 1934 . . . as I have already mentioned once or twice regarding 1934 . . . it is too difficult to express an opinion, but it promises well. 1930, 1931 and 1932 we tasted . . . the only expression we allowed to escape us was—'N.G.'

The chais are important and imposing, and I was glad to be able to compliment the maître de chais, Monsieur Branon, on the excellent way in which he kept them.

After leaving Château Beychevelle, we made our way to Château Latour, passing Château Ducru Beaucaillou on the way, where we saw the Tri-color and the Union Jack flying side by side.

We noticed a somewhat remarkable thing when we alighted, which was a number of small pegs in the ground, indicating that certain rows (sillons) in a given vineyard belonged to other vineyard proprietors; for example, here and there we found inscribed on these pegs . . . 'Ch. Latour', 'Ch. Beychevelle', etc., etc.

I omitted to tell you the origin of the word 'Beychevelle'. Some three to four hundred years ago, a Duc d'Epernon, Admiral of the Port of Pauillac, lived here, and when the ships passed his dwelling it was customary to 'Baisse la voile'—lower the sail—by way of salute . . . hence 'Beychevelle' (in the Gascon tongue 'Beyche'=baisse . . . and 'Velle'=voile).

We proceeded to Château Latour, and here tasted the 1933 . . . undoubtedly a fine wine. It had been racked once, and showed up beautifully. There is no doubt that some of the 1933 wines are excellent. Most of the régisseurs are very competent men, but one would have to go far to find a more knowledgeable and enthusiastic man than Monsieur Brugière, who controls the destinies of Ch. Latour, 1er. Grand Cru, Pauillac. Out of 1386 growths there are 60 'classed' growths of the Médoc, including Ch. Haut Brion, Pessac, Graves.

During a conversation with this gentleman I learned the following rather interesting details : that four-fifths of the vines were of the Cabernet, the other fifth—Merlot. Some of the vines were upwards of 100 years old and these he regarded as being the small portion that gave the wonderful character to Ch. Latour. There are upwards of 350,000 vines on the vineyards, and the soil is mostly sandy. The vines are planted at least one metre apart, as also was the distance between the 'sillons'. Monsieur Brugière was very emphatic about the way in which his wines were 'equalisé'. He assured me that on no condition was the wine allowed to touch any metal of any description, and it was not even passed through the cask to the vat by means of a pump, which is usual, but was taken in wooden buckets by hand.

We were not sorry to return to the hotel. We had had a long and somewhat tiring day, and therefore decided to have a bath, a quiet dinner, and early to bed.

I cannot remember the menu, but we had a bottle of Champagne nature, which we enjoyed.

With the coffee we inquired for a really good 'Fine'; the waiter brought us a bottle . . . it looked its part, that of 1875 Champagne, and I thought it the best I had ever tasted in a French hotel.

I asked if they had any stock, being willing to pay, say 30s. a bottle for a few bottles to last me on the journey.

The answer came back that there were only two bottles, and the proprietor desired to keep one for himself. If, however, I would like to have the other, it would be 60 francs . . . did I not ! !

The next morning, the 10th October, we awoke to find beautiful weather to greet us. I was out early for I had no less than sixty casks of wine to taste at 8.30 a.m. . . . in order to agree the condition of the 1933 Ch. Le Prieuré.

In these cellars I met a Mr. Thompson—French however—a very agreeable gentleman . . . a partner of Pierre Cayrou, who had also come from the Prieuré to meet me. Every cask seemed

[140]

to be faultless, which indicated the care that had been taken. The wine had been racked only a fortnight before, so allowance was made for this. My note was 'A very pleasant, pretty, well-made little wine, ready to be shipped in the spring'.

As I left the premises I bought the morning paper, and was dumbfounded when I read of the terrible and dastardly tragedy of Marseille; the horrible murder of the King of Yugoslavia and of Monsieur Barthou. Let us hope that they are now experiencing eternal peace, in place of the transitory peace they were seeking to establish here on earth.

It will not mend matters to repeat the gist of the conversation I had with Reg, and afterwards with others during the day . . . it was the only topic of conversation, and everyone was aghast.

The fact that such a fine man, as well as an ideal monarch, was cut off in that way, makes one shudder. As a slight alleviation to personal thoughts I could not resist at each opportunity to express what a blessing it was for the poor, stricken country, to have such a prince as Prince Paul as overseer of its destinies (since relegated to the high position of Prince Regent). A more gracious, sympathetic, kindly disposition could not hold sway in any man.

I am sure that all those who have ever had the honour of meeting this Prince will join with me in wishing him long life with better health, to instil his virtues into the people of his country.

As arranged I called for my good friend, Christian Cruse, as we were to make a tour in the Médoc. When I met him my sorrowful heart was not relieved, for he welcomed me with a sad note . . . he had just had news of the tragic death of his cousin, Monsieur Durand-Dessier, who had been killed in a motor accident the day before while returning from a day's bear shooting in the Pyrénées.

The guide was also killed, and the chauffeur very badly injured. I trust he recovered, for he had a family of eight little ones to care for.

Christian Cruse wished to call on the mother of the unfortunate man at Château Parampuyre . . . a delicate visit, which no one would be able to pay more sympathetically than he, with his kind nature.

While he was carrying out his unfortunate duty, Reg and I wandered through the park, admiring many things, and in particular the Dutch cattle, which provided excellent cheese, but as I understood, not so good as comes from their native country . . . and the guinea-fowl. I have always had a sneaking regard for these birds, for a great many years ago my father kept guinea-fowl, and we considered them to be the finest 'watch-dogs', with their cry in the silence of the night, sounding like 'go-back, go-back'.

We passed Château Giscours at Labarde, and soon had to wait the convenience of the gates at the level crossing. We waited five minutes, when they were opened . . . although no train had passed.

This reminded me of a time when I was living in Bordeaux. The train in which I was travelling, somewhere about the same spot, pulled up suddenly and we stayed some time while the driver and guard endeavoured to drive a number of cattle off the line. No sooner did they consider that they were free of such obstruction than some of the beasts returned further up the metals !

We passed through CANTENAC . . . there was Château Le Prieuré . . . such clean, elegant wine as a rule—not to be confused with the other Château Le Prieuré, St. Genès, to which I have referred previously . . . then Château d'Issan, with its moat of green water. It may be this which invariably somewhat prejudices me when tasting this wine.

Close by here is a children's hospital . . . nearly always full up, where the little ones are tenderly cared for.

Next we came to Château Rausan Ségla (note that it is spelt with an 's', whereas Rauzan Gassies is invariably spelt with a 'z'). This fine property belongs to Monsieur Cruse . . . the approach is pleasing with a beautiful display of Hydrangeas.

In 1761, La Baronne de Ségla (née Rausan) commenced its cultivation.

We entered the chais with more than usual interest, for had we not purchased the totalité of the vintage of 1933 ?

Louis, with his well-earned ribbons, was there to welcome us, and an excellent maître de chais he is.

Naturally, the first wines we wished to taste were of the 1933 vintage.

The wine had been racked early in September and was on its finings. I was happy to find that it was up to expectation in quality—'11°', said Louis . . . about the average certainly, and why wish for more. In 1875 it was slightly less, and what a beautiful wine that was. . . . If any of you have enjoyed it, you know, and, for the others—you must consider it as 'something missed'.

Yes, we thought we would like to see the 1934, and immediately tasted several casks. I cannot say that I was very much impressed—no wonder (after the 1933). I thought I found some fermentation, and something I did not quite care for, but undoubtedly this will recover in time . . . it was really too early to taste.

Nevertheless, in the hands of such viticulturers as Messieurs Cruse, it will make a good wine.

There was indeed one cuve that Monsieur Cruse did not particularly care for himself, and he informed me as he was tasting it, that if it did not 'behave' itself it would never have the honour of going to the world as Grand Vin Ch. Rausan Ségla.

We left this celebrated place, not without a look around the interesting museum, accumulated by Monsieur Cruse's late father. As we were leaving Monsieur Cruse handed me an envelope, which I keep as a curiosity.

Louis, having no ink at hand, and wishing to write to the firm, had a brainwave and wrote with the new wine. . . . I have the envelope in front of me—it is as plain as anyone could wish.

We continued our journey, leaving Marquis de Terme on the left, and then Château Durfort, Margaux.

We arrived at Château Margaux, with its avenues and 100 hectares of meadows. This is a fine property, but I wonder if it is a paying proposition?

I cannot say that I thought so much of the 1933 as I did of some of the other first growths. The 1934 vintage promises well.

The vines which are mostly planted in this part of the Médoc are the Petit Verdot, the Malbec, Merlot, and the Cabernet. This latter suffers particularly with early pruning.

In 1932, owing to severe frost in the winter and the early pruning in January the vines in the Médoc suffered. In early June there were few leaves and very little fruit on the vines, the wood having been frozen just after the pruning ; those vines that were pruned later would not suffer in the same way.

The Merlot and the Malbec vines were more fortunate, as the wood was not nearly so tender.

We then decided to visit Château Paveil, but found the road blocked by a great coal cart, a mechanic driver on his back beneath the cart endeavouring to make repairs, and using such language that would make the ruby wine blush !

We went by Châteaux Citran and Moulis. . . . I would not like to pass by this road at night ; danger at every half kilometre.

So many names of villages have the termination 'ac', I asked once again what it could signify . . . 'Aqua', said one, but I had heard differently elsewhere, as you will have read.

Around CUSSAC could be noticed much waste land. Owing to bad years the proprietors had scrapped their vines, but when they had done this they were at a loss to know what to do, for nothing else will grow.

Through ST. JULIEN, where we saluted, past Châteaux Branaire, Beychevelle, Langoa, the Léovilles, to Pauillac, we went. Here on the right Château Pichon Lalande, on the left Château Pichon Longueville.

The old Church is falling to pieces . . . no money to do it up, which is a thousand pities. I gathered it was a socialist municipality, the members of which do not seem keen on spending money on repairs to the Church.

We were now on the quay facing the river, which reminded me how busy they must have been in years since gone by.

In the reign of King Edward III, the trade with Bordeaux was flourishing. I remember reading somewhere that in 1372, two hundred merchant vessels from England would be in the river at the same time, and that they would all load cargoes of wine. There were many fees or 'droits' to pay in those days, and these were paid in Cypress branches—the 'droit de Cypress' at

Bordeaux . . . the 'droit de Cypress' at Blaye, and at L'Ermit de Cordouan.

The first Château to visit at PAUILLAC must surely be the Château Mouton Rothschild, so thither we went, and after a good deal of knocking and patience we found an entry and were introduced to the Baron Phillipe de Rothschild, who was living there and taking the keenest interest in everything that went on, making alterations to his chais and his house, and endeavouring to make everything as perfect as possible.

He explained to us that he had acquired the Château Mouton D'Armailhacq, which in future would have his personal attention, and which he hoped in time would be an excellent second to the Château Mouton Rothschild.

He also intended to introduce a wine as Château Mouton Cadet, which he did not expect to be equal to its more august parents, but which he would be proud to offer to the world as a wine worthy of much consideration.

We were naturally very anxious to taste the 1933 wine, a large portion of which we had acquired—we were not disappointed. If ever I was convinced (which is a large word to use) I felt that here was a wine which would do credit to all who handled it, and give pleasure to all who were fortunate enough to drink it in years to come.

In addition to the bulk stock, the Baron has some 100,000 bottles here, of choice wines. . . . Who would ever leave such cellars, where they could so easily obtain liquid sunshine ?

We must now tear ourselves away from these surroundings, and visit another celebrated Château, also of Pauillac . . . a fifth growth by the classification of 1855, but now worthy of the highest honours—Château Pontet Canet.

We immediately went to the chais. The 1933 we found very good indeed, but, harking back to the Rausan Ségla, which we tasted earlier in the day, I think I preferred it. Perhaps it was a trifle rounder or sweeter, maybe not quite so much tannin.

When I tasted the 1934, which was too young to comment upon, I fancied again that I detected tannin, but here no doubt there was a sufficiency of sugar to cover it, and it should prove a well-balanced wine.

After this, Monsieur Cruse suggested (and believe me, it was not a bad suggestion) that it was about time we entered the famous Château, to partake of déjeuner. Of course, as usual he quite spoilt us . . . commencing with 1900 Ch. Margaux, and to follow—1900 Ch. Larose Faure. This latter was amazingly good, one of the finest specimens of 1900 vintage (all so good) ; and when he told me I had sent it to him some years ago I was very soberly happy.

We then had Ch. Lafite, one bottle—1878, and one bottle— 1875 . . . both excellent wines. Somehow I preferred the 1878 to the 1875. What an admission to make ! I cannot but think that the bottle of 1875 must have been slightly ullaged . . . there was something a little amiss. I cannot remember having preferred an 1878 to an 1875 before, but there it is . . . an object lesson—I would advise any fortunate possessor of such wines to have the bins gently overhauled and the bottles divided into three categories :

1. Full bottles.
2. Levels (that is, in which the wine is level with the bottom of the neck of the bottle).
3. Ullages.

The ullages could be thrown away ; the levels would in all probability prove all right, and should be used first . . . keeping the full bottles for special occasions—shall I say, for very special occasions, when the Wine Merchant is graciously invited to dine ?

On our way back we passed by Château Lynch Bages . . . fifth growth, Pauillac, which brought back memories of a few bottles of good wines I have enjoyed from here—not exactly great wines, but agreeable . . . the 1899 in particular.

We then passed Château Grand-Puy-Lacoste, where Saint Legier used to live, and went on to Château Batailley, another fifth growth Pauillac wine . . . a great favourite of mine ; how I have enjoyed the 1888 Ch. Batailley before it commenced to go down-hill . . . one could drink a bottle so comfortably, and it did one good.

(If I stop like this at every Château we pass we shall never reach BORDEAUX.)

[146]

'Over in the woods yonder', said Monsieur Cruse . . . 'is the Château du Taillan, one of our properties, where not only good wine is made, but some of the land is used for excellent pasturage.' 'Do not be despondent', I remarked . . . 'one must eat as well as drink !'

We returned to the hotel promising to join our kind friend for dinner at his palatial residence in the Allée des Chartres.

We found awaiting us news from our good friend, Mr. Sterling Clark . . . apart from the disappointment of not having the company of two such genial and interested companions, we were grieved to learn that a nasty attack of bronchitis had got the better of him, and of us. Perhaps some other time we shall be more fortunate.

I sent him a telegram, by which I felt sure he would understand how sincere were our regrets at his inability to join us, and even more so for the unfortunate cause thereof.

When we arrived Monsieur Cruse was profuse in his apologies . . . the family had just arrived from Château Pontet Canet ; some of the carpets, which had been taken up for the summer, had not been replaced and it quite upset Madame Cruse, but I endeavoured to assure her that we had not come to admire carpets, or necessarily to walk on them, but to greet and admire her, and drink her husband's best wines. I felt very wicked at the moment, and if Reg had only given me support, I should have endeavoured to sing that old refrain :

> 'Ours is an 'appy little 'ome,
> No knocker on the door—
> No carpet on the floor,
> Ours is an 'appy little 'ome—etc.'

We had a delightful dinner, as always, chez les Cruses . . . accompanied by such elegant wines as Ch. Desmirail 1900, third growth, Margaux . . . delicious !

I always know how to enjoy the wines of Ch. Desmirail—all the virtues of great quality, light, easy to assimilate, and not so expensive.

We then had two wines of Ch. Rausan Ségla, second growth, Margaux (a fine property of the family Cruse) 1877 and 1875.

I have so few remembrances of the 1877 that I was mildly excited to taste this—especially here. Perhaps I was a little disappointed, it was drier than I had anticipated. The 1875 was A.1 . . . a very fine bottle of wine . . . I almost preferred it to the 1875 Ch. Lafite, first growth, Pauillac, which followed, because it seemed to have more vinosity. Do not let me decry that beautiful bottle of 1875 Ch. Lafite, but I am trying to be critical.

Monsieur Cruse referred to a dinner which had been arranged for us by the Hon. John Benson, at Brooks' Club. It certainly was, as regards wine, one of the most remarkable I have been privileged to attend.

I ask any Bordeaux magnate to look into his experience, and say if he ever had a dinner during which five Bordeaux wines were to be served . . . when the first one introduced was a wine of the perfection of 1875 Ch. Margaux; yet this is what Mr. Benson treated us to on that memorable occasion.

After a cold consommé, and a glass of delectable Chablis, we had Mushrooms Bechamelle, with the 1875 'Ch. Margaux. I often think that mushrooms will make a poor Médoc taste like a good St. Emilion, so you can imagine the effect here ! It was a delightful bottle of wine . . . a little light, but so very elegant.

To follow, we had Saddle of Mutton (on the menu), but it was so tender, I think it must have been lamb, Pousins, and then a Cheese Soufflé. To accompany these delectable dishes, we were offered by this youthful, yet grossly intelligent connoisseur, the following wines :

> 1870 Ch. Rausan Ségla.
> 1869 Ch. Lafite.
> 1865 Ch. Lafite.
> 1858 Ch. Lafite. . . .

What a wine feast for the dual Bacchus cum Dionysus !

All these wines were in a perfect state of preservation.

The 1870 Rausan, a typical Margaux wine of much breed, had stood the test of time remarkably well. It was still full of vinosity and (if it is allowed to) will last for years to come.

The 1869 was wonderful . . . we were all enraptured . . . full of flavour, soft and silky—one of the finest bottles of wine I remember ever to have tasted, and I have tasted not a few ! What a vintage—1869 ! !

Then the 1865 Ch. Lafite. . . . I can see still how surprised we were at the astounding stability of this wine—granted that it was a little overshadowed by its younger brother but, as sound as a bell . . . no unpleasant dryness on the finish ; in fact, an old wine to give the utmost pleasure.

Then came the 1858. One or two of the guests gave the greatest praise to this wine, but although I did certainly appreciate its virtues I found a little hardness or dryness on the finish, which made it take a back seat in comparison with the other wines we had consumed.

I do not wish to decry this wine—it was very good, and we were all highly gratified in meeting it once again.

There was no doubt of the result . . . when we inquired afterwards as to the choice of the finest wine on the table—1869 Ch. Lafite !

I wouldn't mind going a Sabbath day's journey, even to smell, let alone to taste such another wine !

Mr. Benson, thank you . . . as the French people would say . . . 'mille fois infiniment'.

We raised the glass to you, and could have wished that you had cognizance of it.

I must not omit to mention the Brandy we had . . . a great connoisseur is Mr. Benson. He gave us a delicate, absolutely pure, light Grande Fine Champagne Cognac, 1906, topped up with about one third of 1830 . . . not a so-called 1830, but the veritable article, which had never been touched in any way whatever. It was hardly commercial as it was, for it had become a very old 'gentleman', with all its intellect, but faded in strength, which was between 60° and 70° under proof.

But, what a Brandy ! No wonder we left none in the bottle, and some of us felt like purloining the cork ! !

After dinner at the 'Maison Cruse' we sat down to enjoy a very fine Brandy, 1842 Delamain . . . something to fondle in the glass—it is such a 'dainty spirit' as Prospero would say.

'Do you know Thackeray's works ?' I asked. . . . Of course they did. I will tell you an incident about Thackeray that will

[149]

appeal to you. On one occasion he was obliged to consult his medical attendant, Sir Henry Thompson. Sir Henry inquired about his diet . . . Thackeray assured him that it was all right ; what he ate agreed with him entirely.

'Now, what about your drink ?'

'Claret,' replied Thackeray.

'What quantity ?'

'Oh ! One bottle a day, three hundred and sixty-five bottles a year, mostly belonging to my friends !'

I must admit to a slight blush of guilt in retailing this anecdote.

During the conversation of the evening we deplored the fact that even in France it was almost impossible to obtain at hotels and restaurants a really good bottle of wine at a reasonable price.

Monsieur Cruse told us that at one hotel in the Médoc, the Ch. Latour, 1925, first growth, Pauillac (1925, mark you) was actually listed at 50 francs a bottle . . . enough to damage the reputation of any wine !

This must not be allowed to continue, thought this practical man. He therefore made some inquiries, and found that very little of the wine was asked for (I believe that this was about the least expensive on the list), and he offered to send in some wines which could be paid for when sold, and which would show a reasonable profit. The offer was accepted and he sent in a quantity of 1924, 1923 and 1920 wines of the Médoc, commencing with a selling price of 10 francs. When he called some time later to inquire if there were any success, he was warmly greeted, the host proudly announcing to him that nearly all had been sold, and that he would like to have some more.

I hope this may prove a lesson to many others !

Before leaving I said to Madame Cruse—'I do hope that we have not deprived you of a game of Bridge this evening.' 'Oh dear no', she replied . . . 'but, how do you know I play Bridge ? Has my husband been telling you ?'

'No, no!' I replied . . . 'a delightful little bird whispered it in my ears !'

As you may imagine, I was not allowed to go without divulging the name of my informant—'Madeleine', I said . . . 'Madeleine'—and it took me some time to finish—'AUSCHITZKY'.

From what followed, I gathered that they had very many good games of Bridge together. May they live long to enjoy very many more !

The next morning, at 8.30 a.m., I called on my good friend of five and forty years' standing—Monsieur Jean Calvet . . . one of the most respected and erudite champions of Bordeaux Wine in the district.

Unfortunately I had previous engagements and could not spend the day with him, but he would not allow me to escape (pray do not think for one moment that I would have wished to), without arranging a dinner one evening before I quitted the city.

He gave me invaluable information about my tour . . . where I should go, and how I should go there, and loaded me with introductions to friends of his in the Rhône Valley, which proved not only most useful, but very entertaining, for all of which I was indeed very grateful.

We then went as arranged to meet Monsieur Alfred Schyler, with whom we had promised ourselves a day in the White Wine districts.

Our first objective was the well-known Domaine de Chevalier . . . one of the foremost growths of Léognan-Graves.

On approaching, we passed an old man tending some cows. He must have been a hundred years old—I wondered what he would do in an emergency. The wines from the excellent vineyard would never look so 'upright' even as that old fellow, when they reach his age—I thought.

We entered the chais—fine and cool—where the wines were well cared for. We were privileged to taste a number of different wines, and right through the vintages could be detected the same particular taste, peculiar to Domaine de Chevalier.

1933. Light, little dry—good quality.

1932. Lighter, already a little old and worn.

1931. Somewhat fuller and better, with a little sweetness.

I do not remember a more successful 1931 . . . but the prices were much too high.

1934—we tasted next. There was a large quantity for Chevalier, some 38 tonneaux. It was too early to form a definite opinion, but I am nearly sure that it will develop into a good wine

On leaving the interesting Estate we thought we would call at Château Haut Bailly . . . another fine growth of Léognan-Graves. We inquired the way, and had the usual answer (nine times out of ten we found it the same)—'tout-droit . . . 300 metres'.

I was mildly excited—I had never visited Château Haut Bailly, and I had such an excellent remembrance of a bottle of 1891 Ch. Haut Bailly—not a great year, I grant, but this seemed to be the exception that proved the rule.

Bad luck ! . . . the place was closed and we could gain no admittance.

We continued, leaving Château Carbonnieux (Léognan-Graves) on our left . . . a fine view from here, and Château Smith Haut-Lafitte on our right (second Graves-Cadaujac).

We then noticed Château Bouscaut close by (second Graves-Cadaujac), the proprietor of which invariably sells the wine for consumption in France.

At VIRELADE we passed on a new road over the railway, which had been constructed by reason of so many accidents having taken place at this somewhat dangerous spot.

Through PODENSAC (Graves), we reached CERONS (Sauternes), from where we could see across the river to LA REOLE.

LA REOLE—this name brought to my mind an amusing little episode of my early days in Bordeaux. . . . Monsieur and Madame O'Lanyer and family were paying a visit to relatives there, and had invited me to join them. As we were driving along the country lanes, the little ones suggested 'a great joke' for Tante Mathilde. I was to pretend to be deaf, and, as she was very sympathetic, we would all be able to play up to it.

I must not make a long story of this, but I will tell you that the endeavour to be deaf all the evening brought on a headache, and the sympathetic lady insisted on my going to bed early and staying the night under her roof !

The family returned to Bordeaux. . . . The next morning, Madame inquired in a natural voice, how I was and, forgetting my deafness I replied 'quite well, thank you.'

The fat was in the fire ... instead of sending me in her carriage to Bordeaux, I was shown the way to the station—I have not suffered with deafness since !

To continue our journey, we followed the road to BARSAC. A pleasant smell of hay permeated the air ... was this a second or third crop, we wondered ? But we felt that we must use our handkerchiefs—it does not do to smell the wines with nostrils impregnated with this odour.

Five communes enjoy the right to the appellation 'Sauternes', namely SAUTERNES, BARSAC, BOMMES, PREIGNAC and FARGUES.

With regard to ST. PEY DE LANGON, which is also called ST. PIERRE DE MONS, the question as to whether this commune has the right to be called Sauternes is still before the Court.

We passed through the town of BARSAC, with its quaint market place, and proceeded to Château Coutet ... which is a first growth, Barsac.

My recollection of the wines of Château Coutet is that they are of fine quality, and sweet, but I understood that at present, the proprietor is concentrating on 'dry' wines. I wonder if he will be rewarded with any success ?

There was no one to receive us, so we went on to Château Climens, the other first growth, Barsac. Here, a dear old soul pulled at an ancient bell, and eventually someone arrived who was most anxious to give us every attention.

We tasted the 1933, 1931, 1929 wines. I thought the 1933 excellent ... not too sweet.

The 1929 had been sold ; it was very good indeed.

The 1931, as one would expect, did not compare with the others, but this particular wine was quite pleasing ... we took a bottle away with us for lunch!

It was difficult to taste the 1934 while still fermenting, but I am under the impression that the opinion is—the White wines of 1933 will be superior to those of 1934.

On leaving here we had a pretty view of the country, with ST. CROIX DU MONT on the other side of the river.

Through PREIGNAC to SUDUIRAUT, up a short avenue of Pine trees to the Château. As it was after the lunch hour, we did not find anyone 'at home'.

[153]

I instinctively remembered some wines—'Tête' wines of Château Suduiraut, 1899 and 1900—What NECTAR ! !

The same disappointment was met at Château d'Yquem. It would be better for us to go to lunch and return here afterwards, or else we should lose much valuable time.

At the Hotel du Lion d'Or, LANGON, we stopped for déjeuner, and fared very well. We opened the bottle of 1931 Ch. Climens, and more or less enjoyed a glass with a strong and rather highly-flavoured river fish.

We then had a bottle of 1929 Ch. Beychevelle, fourth growth, St. Julien, with a 'flaming' partridge . . . both were excellent, and suited each other admirably.

The 1929 Beychevelle was the fullest and most robust 1929 I remember . . . certainly more so than what I recollect of the 1928 ; incidentally, the cork broke when being extracted !

The patron came across to our table, and was indefatigable in his desire to please. The next time I am in LANGON I shall certainly pay him a visit.

He insisted that we try his 1908 Armagnac. It was quite good, and no doubt was helpful after the partridge which I had enjoyed so much, and the thought passed my mind that a dog would have scorned me for doing exactly what he would have done—that is, picked the bones absolutely clean.

Before leaving we were shown a copy of an American journal, and read a portion of an article on a visit to the district of a number of interested people.

It is a thousand pities that correct information is not broadcast in this way—my eye caught sight of the following journalistic howlers, as far as I remember :

'The vineyards of Château Pontet Canet are all White grapes !'
'The Marc of Mouton was their finest Cognac !'
Château Latour was confused with 'Latour, of the Ile du Nord !'

After lunch we called at Château Rieussec, first growth, Fargues . . . the proprietor of which rejoices in the name of 'Berry'. He is well served by an intelligent régisseur, at least eighty years of age, and with a broken leg to boot !

The 1931 I thought was poor, and was suffering from sulphur.

The 1933 was much better ... rather coarse perhaps ; owing to a little fermentation it could not be tasted to advantage. Here again I felt the necessity of going to the open to taste.

We then returned to Château d'Yquem (1er. Grand Cru, Sauternes) where the new manager (Mr. Jacob), permitted us to taste some of the young wines.

1932.   This I thought very poor in quality.

1933.   Superior wine, but I imagined I detected a curious after-taste : this may easily pass after the next rackings.

1934.   I think will be good, but it would be foolish to prophesy—80 tonneaux were made ... 320 Hogs-heads, and that after the earlier reports that the severe hail-storms had destroyed almost the whole crop.

From here, we went to Château La-Tour-Blanche, first growth, Bommes. I am always fascinated by this wine ... I like the name, I like the label, I like the Estate, and above all, I find it one of the most pleasant of the fine, sweet wines of the district.

In the courtyard is a statue of Ulysse Gayon, as an 'Hommage de Reconnaisance'. He it was who discovered the copper powder used against diseases of the vines.

We commenced with the 1931 wine ... No, I did not like it— once again, full of sulphur !

1933.   I was not much impressed, it had 14° ... a very good alcoholic strength, but somehow or other I am not in love with the White wines of Bordeaux of 1933 in the same way as I am with many of the Red wines.

1934.   Only 12° ... I believe this might turn out very well.

The late proprietor of this famous Estate was one Monsieur OSIRIS, who began life in the humblest of circumstances, lived to make this purchase, and dying, left it to the State with ample money for its upkeep.

At Château De-Rayne-Vigneau, first growth, Bommes, we tasted :

1934.   Not fit to taste.

1933.   This was good ... yes, very good !

1930.   This tasted of sugar only.

1929.   Very good indeed—sweet and yet of full flavour.

The maître de chais was most obliging, and we thanked him for his attention.

Allow me to offer a word of advice—Should you have the same privilege and opportunity as I have had, do not omit to shake hands . . . never mind how dirty they are . . . they like this little courtesy, especially from a stranger.

Close by is the Castle de Budos, and the fine reservoir which supplies water to Bordeaux.

As I was anxious to visit ST. CROIX DU MONT, we decided to double back over the new bridge at LANGON.

It was a beautiful afternoon . . . we noticed many folks sitting about on chairs they had brought out from their houses . . . some were reading, others dozing, and not a few industrious women were making garments of all descriptions.

At ST. CROIX DU MONT (Clos de la Vertus), the grapes were still being gathered.

Very sweet wines are usually made on this hill side, where the vines are subjected to the hot south-westerly winds.

The Church occupies a very prominent position . . . a few years ago it was struck by lightning and had to be rebuilt.

It is a very beautiful spot, and overlooking the Garonne one can enjoy some lovely views.

Immediately behind is the district known as the Entre-deux-Mers.

The Château de Taste was a fortress during the English occupation—now it is a school, where I trust the virtues of the 'Entente Cordiale' are instilled into the youthful mind.

The rock below is most strangely amazing, for it is formed of millions and millions of oyster shells ; I suppose in prehistoric ages all this portion of the Continent was beneath the ocean.

Climbing the rock I saw a lizard, but missed it. I wished to see if there were any truth in what we were told as boys, when we went lizard-hunting on the meadow banks, between Kemp Town and Rottingdean—'Catch a lizard by its tail . . . it will fall off, and another will grow.'

We followed our road back some way, and came through the

[156]

Entre-deux-Mers district, with vines on either side ; here a good quality inexpensive White wine is produced, excellent for White wine cup.

The important towns in the district are LOUPIAC, LANGOIRAN, ROUQUEZ, BEAURECH, CAMBES . . . a pleasing countryside, very hilly in places. Some good wines are made, and especially at LOUPIAC and LANGOIRAN a good trade is done.

At LA SOUYS we met the Bordeaux trains, and in spite of a slight annoyance caused by the Little Auk we were soon back again in the city.

Passing St. Michael invites me to tell you not to forget to pay a visit here and see the mummies below.

The Cathedral is also well worth a visit. . . . I remember on New Year's Eve in 1892 I attended midnight service there, and on emerging with a friend we saw a great light in the direction of the river ; down we went to inquire of the cause.

A vessel was on fire . . . a great number of people had gathered round. It was all very exciting, even more so when we were collared by gendarmes and made to work the pumps, and pull along the water pipes. It was useless to resist—not that we wanted to . . . we rather enjoyed it.

I understood later that on such occasions the gendarmes had the right to commandeer the services of onlookers ; the argument being that if they had the time to stand there, they equally had the time to assist—very sensible too !

We put the car into the quaint old garage, which is an ancient church converted to other use, and went back to the hotel to enjoy a well-earned wash.

We had promised our kind host, Monsieur Alfred Schyler, to join him at dinner, so off we went in good time.

During the conversation the question of the 'cradles' was introduced. I told our host how I detested them, when to rub it in a little more, he related how, on one occasion, a bottle of old wine was brought to him in one of those atrocities, and immediately after placing it on the table in front of him, the waiter took the bottle out, without any care and, turning it round and round in his hand, proceeded to remove the capsule.

On another occasion the bottle was brought, certainly without the capsule, but it was taken out of the cradle and held by the waiter while he drew the cork : as the majority of corks are broken when being extracted by the corkscrew in use, you may imagine how nicely the sediment was churned up in the wine.

For Fine Bordeaux, Monsieur Schyler offered us excellent wines of the great vintage of 1899 :

Château Palmer Margaux, third growth, now known as Ch. Cantenac, Margaux.

Château Cos d'Estournel, St. Estèphe, second growth.

They were indeed worthy specimens, and very enjoyable. The 1899's have undoubtedly aged of late years. I do not think they will ever live, like the 1870's for instance. I have come to the conclusion that the bottled wines mature more quickly in Bordeaux than they do in the British Isles.

We finished up with a very fine, old, pale Cognac. . . . It was good and reminded me of the 1906 Gabloteau, so of course I 'came again'.

After dinner one of the items of conversation was in reference to old and new wine. Was new wine preferred in olden days to old wine—which some people insisted was the case ?

I championed the old wine, and when asked for my reason, I modified my statement a little by agreeing that even in these days there are some wines which should be consumed when young . . . some Beaujolais and Mâcon are better at twelve months than at two years ; also, some Light Moselles are delightful in the full bloom of their early maturity.

I therefore argued that if it were that the new wine was prefer-able, then the wines could not have been of the higher quality, for immature wine is not good to drink, and this I can safely assert ; to discover this—well, the proof of the wine is in the drinking thereof.

With this thought, and a reference to Holy Writ, from the Gospel of St. Luke (remember St. Luke was a physician) :

'No man also having drunk old wine straightway desireth new ; for he saith, "the old is better".'

I considered I had happily disposed of the subject.

We had had a very happy, interesting and instructive day, and are grateful to Monsieur Alfred Schyler for his kindness.

An excellent glass of Vichy, and a thought for our jovial friend Teddy Gwenn, and we said to each other—'AND SO TO BED'.

The next day—Friday, the 12th October, we awoke to find a bright morning awaiting us. It was cheerful after a night made restless by the attentions of mosquitoes. One had actually bitten me on the sole of my right foot . . . most uncomfortable !

If I had not been leaving on the morrow I think I should have asked for some netting.

Before starting, I went to have a hair-cut . . . which reminded me of how, when I first lived in Bordeaux, the assistant laughed at me when I entered the saloon, and with full assurance requested him to 'coûper ma tête'.

I then called on the Bank, and obtained the correct amount, and more civility than on the occasion I have mentioned previously.

I was anxious to meet Monsieur D. Cordier on the Quai Paludate . . . therefore, called on him with a letter from his friend, Monsieur Claeys, but unfortunately he was out of town . . . no doubt off to his beloved ST. JULIEN. He is the Mayor there, and takes the keenest interest and deepest pride in all that concerns the place.

Before déjeuner, I thought I would drop a card on an old friend—one I had not seen for many years, and one who had written to me such a charming appreciation of my little 'Miscellany of Wine'.

I was fortunate to find Monsieur Louis Eschenauer at his office, but it was easier to get there than to get away from his hospitable entreaties. However, I had other engagements for the afternoon and evening, and really only went to shake him by the hand. But I promised to spend the following day with him instead of leaving Bordeaux on the Saturday.

Seeing 1926 Ch. Parampuyre on the Wine List at the hotel, we decided to have it for lunch and with a simple meal it 'went' very well. I found it lighter than most of the wines of 1926.

I used to be somewhat prejudiced against the 1926's . . . it may have been when comparing them with their older and more refined brothers of 1920 and 1924, but I am coming round to the

[159]

opinion that there are many very good wines to be had and that they are developing very well.

After déjeuner, I went to leave one or two cards and then called on the two famous Bordeaux liqueurists Messieurs Marie Brizard & Roger, and Messieurs Bardinet . . . always on the quest of that Sloe Gin ! neither visit gave any satisfaction as far as I was concerned.

It seemed to me a pity that such quantities of sloes should not be used for this purpose. All the information I received was, that a liqueur called 'Prunelle' was made . . . not much was used, and they had no intention of making any other experiment. But I have not given it up in despair yet !

These visits did not occupy as much time as I had anticipated, so on the way back I called in at a 'Station Uvale' to taste the natural grape juice. I will not weary you with this at the moment, as we shall come into closer contact with it later.

On walking through the Public Gardens, in order to have a sight of the rue Montgolfier, I found myself constrained to watch the children throwing bread to the ducks and fish. (I never realised that there were so many children in the world.)

Many a time have I paused on the little bridge over the ornamental water in St. James's Park, to see the ducks being fed, but it was nothing compared with this, for I witnessed a remarkable performance (tax free). The ducks and the fish actually fought each other for the bread, and when the piece was of sufficient proportions I could see a couple of ducks attacking it from above and the fish from below.

Battles royal frequently took place, and I saw fish, not once but several times, leap out of the water, and right over the duck's back.

I think the fish were carp, and some of them would have turned the scale at a dozen pounds or more, and there were hundreds of them.

This took up so much time that when I reached the rue Montgolfier it was nearly the hour to go to the hotel to make ready for dinner.

Each time I go to Bordeaux and pass the rue Montgolfier, I

think how curious it was that that should have been my first address, in a street named after the first Balloonist, and that in after years I should have been so keen on the same sport.

I went in search of No. 22bis . . . it was not easy to find—new buildings and new numbers—but it was eventually located, and as I stood outside I allowed many thoughts to run through my mind.

This was where old Madame Fleys lived and took care of us . . . that is, Ian Campbell as well. He was a good lad, and was well away with an old spinster who also lived in the house. Mlle. TRÉILHARD was her name . . . that I do recollect. I also remember that she was not very prepossessing, but the wary Scot, who sang 'Do you ken John Peel' to her at the least encouragement, knew how to take advantage of his opportunities, for she taught him French, and being a wise scholar he made the best of it.

I heard moreover, that, years after, when the old lady passed away, she did so, ever remembering her good pupil by leaving him a legacy . . . some of us get our deserts, after all !

I was always on the best of terms with my landlady and, as far as I remember, there was only one occasion on which I forgot myself.

I had invited a number of young bloods to dine with me at 22bis, and Madame Fleys was to provide a simple meal ; she suggested a gigot . . . I agreed that this would be admirable— 'but, if you please Madame . . . no GARLIC'.

I carved the gigot, and having, in those young days, a predilection for the knuckle end I cut this for myself. What was my amazement when, with the first mouthful, I tasted nothing but garlic. I rang the bell violently, and as she came into the room I threw the joint at her. Fortunately, it did not hit her in the face, but there was a terrible row. However, all's well that ends well, and I eventually kissed the old lady good-night, she protesting that she would never have thought that anyone would touch the knuckle, and incidentally that she had had an eye on it for herself !

Returning, I notice the plaque in memory of Montgolfier, which is placed outside the Carmelite Church (now in a sorry plight) ; of Roman Byzantine period, of which the architect was a Carmelite Monk.

As I went back to the hotel it suddenly occurred to me how interesting it would be to have plaques in one's cellar, detailing the names of some 'lovely' tenants ; for example :

Bin 26

This bin contained in

1870.   Ch. Lafite 1858.
1880.   Ch. Latour 1864.
1887.   Ch. Margaux 1875.
1892.   Ch. Haut Brion 1888.
1936.   Ch. Mouton Rothschild 1933.

Before continuing, I must make a confession. I have lost considerable time sitting back in my chair and contemplating some fine bottles of the above wines, which I have enjoyed with friends now and again.

It was now time to go to dinner with our excellent friend, Monsieur Jean Calvet. Even as I write his name I feel a glow of pride run through me, for to know him and claim him as a friend is an honour, a privilege and an asset that all men, let alone those connected with the wine industry of Bordeaux, would be justified in coveting. We had mistaken the way, and were a few minutes late. Our apologies were unnecessary to such a host, and we were made most welcome. Several members of his charming family were there, although we missed the attractive presence of Madame Calvet, who was away in the country. Madame Jack Calvet, his daughter-in-law, did the honours with perfection—in fact, before we parted she almost promised to accompany me on my next balloon trip.

We had some excellent wines I remember—1877 Ch. Margaux (1er. Gd. Cru Margaux) . . . it was a beauty, so light, firm and yet silky. Nothing gave me more pleasure than to taste this. I had so often had faulty bottles of this wine—the reason being that when the wine was bottled at the Château, one of the corking machines must have been badly adjusted, for the needle caused a groove down the side of the corks, with the consequent result of ullaging.

The 1871 Ch. Latour (1ᵉʳ. Gd. Cru, Pauillac) was also delicious, but our host informed us that the first bottle he decanted was maché, which I take to mean—fatigué . . . it may have been a little ullaged.

The 1899 Ch. Cheval Blanc (1ᵉʳ. Cru St. Emilion) was wonderful. It was right that it came after the others for it would have killed them. We must remember that 1877 and 1871 are both very old and have lost any heaviness they once possessed.

We finished up with an excellent Fine 1878. During the conversation I mentioned what a number of old folk I had come across whose lives had been spent in the wine trade . . . for instance, look at the number of octogenarians at St. Julien.

Monsieur Calvet, in order to impress it more fully on my mind, told me that he remembered four agents of his in England who had died at the ages of 78, 94, 88 and 80 (over), and further that his last four head-cellarmen had lived to the ripe old ages of 78, 84, 78, and the present one was 76 and going strong !

What a réclame for Bordeaux wine ! !

While enjoying the glass, or perhaps, in order to be strictly accurate, the second glass, of that excellent 1878 Fine, I could not keep my eyes off a certain fine picture, amongst many, that Monsieur Calvet had hanging in his room.

It was of three men and a boy playing cards . . . I cannot remember by whom it was painted, but it took my fancy immensely. The expressions on their faces I thought admirable.

What with the merry, living faces and these intent painted faces I thoroughly enjoyed my evening with this, the kindest of hosts. I do hope London will see him soon, and that I can open a fine bottle of Bordeaux worthy of the occasion.

The next day I had promised to call on Louis Eschenauer, and see his wonderful establishment—taste some wines and pay a visit to the White wine district again.

We were first shown over the chais by Monsieur J. T. Barkhausen, the indefatigable pioneer of the slogan—'Drink more Wine', especially in the U.S.A.

We saw many enormous vats, glass-lined, and filled with inexpensive wine—White and Red—subjected to knowledgeable treatment, by reason of which, they would keep in condition after being bottled. . . . I was somewhat surprised when I learned that extreme cold ages the wine.

During the course of conversation, the name of Otto Dunker was mentioned. . . . I pricked up my ears. I had often thought of him and, in spite of many inquiries, I had heard nothing of him since 1892 when I left Bordeaux, where we were in the same office. It appears he was killed in the war, serving in the capacity of a balloon observer : what a coincidence !

Coming from the vast chais we proceeded to taste many wines; in fact, with the less expensive White wines of Entre-deux-Mers and Graves, we must have sampled upwards of a score. Many of them were 1931 vintage, which did not appeal to me, but some of the 1929 Barsac and Sauternes were very good indeed. I recollect well the excellence of the 1929 Ch. Rabaud, and of Ch. Guiraud—both first growth, Sauternes.

Out of the kindness of his heart Monsieur Eschenauer allowed me to taste a couple of Bergerac wines—Monbazillac . . . but I shall treat of this wine when we reach Bergerac.

I do not believe it falls to many to have such a galaxy of wine offered at lunch for half a dozen people, as we enjoyed and were privileged to taste and to drink.

To commence with we had—comme dégustation :

1929 Ch. Haut Bailly. Excellent in a few years.

1928 Ch. Lafite, first growth, Pauillac . . . Not bad, after all.

1928 Ch. Mouton Rothschild, second growth, Pauillac. A great future before it.

1928 Ch. Olivier. Much better than I expected.

1896 Ch. Margaux. Was a surprise for its excellence.

1899 Ch. Mouton Rothschild. BEAUTIFUL.

1869 Ch. Lafite (Bought in London). LOVE-LY ! ! ! ! !

1871 Ch. Mouton Rothschild. Monsieur Eschenauer had only half-bottles of this remarkable wine—a rarity. The first one opened was 'N.G.' . . . (this was my note). The second half-bottle was delicious and reminded me of the fragrance of rose-leaves. What a wine to go to bed with, and hope you would never be awakened from your dreams !

For some reason or other, a bottle of that excellent Champagne followed :

1926 G. H. Mumm, Cordon Rouge . . .

I sipped it certainly, out of politeness, which provoked a remark from Monsieur Barkhausen that I thought it was intended to wash my teeth with ! !

What a lunch ! Monsieur Eschenauer had 'promised' me one, and he had more than fulfilled his promise.

I wish I could remember a fraction of the interesting things he told me, but I must admit that I was so much taken up with the beautiful wines that I could not pay proper attention to all that was said, for, do we not know that—'Where your treasure is, there will your heart be also.'

After this sumptuous repast and all the better for it, we decided to pay a visit into the Graves and Sauternes districts.

As we passed by the 'Caves du Médoc' we noticed, standing outside, Monsieur le Comte de Beaumont—a part owner of Château Latour. I sent him a wireless of thanks for the good wine he made in 1933 ; I wish he could have received it, but maybe he will, in this belated manner.

Probably I should not have seen him in the ordinary way, but I always cast a glance at the 'Caves du Médoc' when I pass, for it was there in 1891 that I purchased my first bottle of Allash-Kümmel and I can remember even now the glow of pride with which I was covered on emerging from this establishment with my precious parcel.

Whether it was due to the fine wine, I do not know, but about this time the mosquito bite in the sole of my foot began to irritate so much that I was glad to descend at Château Lagarde, Martillac, and paw the ground like a distressed horse, whose shoe was too tight, or who was endeavouring to release an imbedded stone. I remember hearing a child remark when she saw a horse doing this that it must have 'pins and needles' in its foot! I hate mosquitoes ! !

At this Château we tasted the 1931 wine and the 1933.

The former I thought very poor, but the 1933 appealed to me as being quite good ; although there was something at the back which rather worried me.

At Château Smith-Haut-Lafitte—an exceptional growth of red Graves-Martillac—we sampled the 1933 wine ; this pleased me considerably . . . my remarks were—'very good, soft, developing well'.

From here we went to pay a visit to Château Haut-Bailly, where we had been unable to gain admittance on the previous day. This wine is also classed as an exceptional growth of red Graves-Léognan.

We were privileged to taste the 1933 and 1934. The wines are extremely good, but—Oh ! What a price ! However, it is better to pay a high price for a good wine than a low price for a poor one.

Château Olivier, Monsieur Eschenauer's property, was the next call. Here we tasted the Red and White wines of 1933 and 1934. We found nothing to complain about in the quality of the 1933's—and the 1934's seemed full of good promise.

Before leaving we entered the famous Château, where a note of sadness struck our ears ; for we found a young lady 'listening in' intently to the memorial service, held in Paris, in honour of one of the tragic victims of Marseille—Monsieur Barthou, Minister of Foreign Affairs.

'In the midst of life . . . etc., etc.' we paused . . . and then we continued our way.

Before arriving at Bordeaux, we called on Monsieur Gibert, of Château Haut Brion, first classed growth, Pessac. He was kind enough to allow us to taste his wines of 1933 and 1934.

I cannot truthfully say that I was much impressed with the 1933—nevertheless, it may alter . . . it has a long way to go yet.

It is foolish to pass an opinion on so young a wine as the 1934, but I will risk suggesting that it may conceivably be an improvement on the previous vintage.

We returned immediately after this visit to Bordeaux, having passed a very enjoyable and interesting day with Monsieur Louis Eschenauer, to whom our sincerest thanks are due.

To-morrow morning we were to leave the city, so that night, after the pleasant fatigue of the day, we thought we would take a quiet little supper at 'La Presse'.

This supper did not consist of much more than a well-cooked

Langouste, washed down with the contents of a bottle of Pommery nature . . . the best liquor the Langouste had ever tasted, I ween !

A stroll around the 'Quinconces' where great preparations were being made on account of the coming Fair, and then—to bed !

Summary of Bordeaux Vintages

RED

Should any of my readers possess such old wines dating back from 1858 to 1878—take my advice and drink them . . . they may be very good indeed, but although some of the vintages will continue to hold their own, it is too much to expect them to improve.

A friend of mine told me that the late Lord Herschell, who had a fine collection of old Claret, had been making arrangements for a couple of dinners, in order to enjoy some old Jeroboams with his friends, when, alas ! he died . . . how pathetic !

It is so frequently said that 'I cannot find anyone to drink Claret'. . . . Allow me to suggest in all humility, that where there is a will there is a way. I could find one !

1858.   Rather hard, and dry finish.

1862.   Not bad. Has been better—not of the highest quality.

1864.   Magnificent ! This is indeed a liquid gem.

1865.   Very good, but as with the other vintages, so much depends on how the wines have been kept.

1868.   Very fine, but gradually going down hill.

1869.   'Twin' with 1864—Magnificent wine !

(Of these, the best to keep is the last, but do not allow that last to last too long.)

We will now consider the next decade. . . .

1870.   An extraordinary wine, which developed very late. At present, the wines, well kept, are excellent.

1871.   Very pretty, and also, strange to say—very good ! But do not keep them. They may soon go 'beyond'.

1874. A fine vintage. Certainly a little drier than it was a few years ago. Entertain it, and be entertained by it before it is too late.

1875. Who said 1875 ? Perhaps Mr. Warner Allen out of his vast vocabulary of suitable expletives may find one to fit the beauty of this vintage.

1877. Delightful wine. Little on the light side, but, oh, so delectable. I do not think it will be any better.

1878. A fine wine (or rather, it has been) undoubtedly, but I have been a trifle disappointed with one or two bottles I have been privileged to taste lately.

1879.
to } Phylloxera years.
1887.

1888. Was very good—alas ! *was*.

We will now consider another decade.

1890. Good, but not too pleasant, with its hardness and dryness.

1891. Some good wines—patchy.

1893. For many years these were excellent. . . . But now they are passed their prime.

1895. Not accepted as a great vintage but I have seen some remarkably fine wines; for example—1895 Ch. Lafite !

1896. Good.

1899. Very fine indeed. I almost think it so good that it will not be better.
     (Of these, keep the 1899 and 1895 to the last . . . be quit of the others as soon as you can drink them.)

The next three decades . . .

1900. Beautiful . . . softer, and more fruity perhaps than the 1899—both are delightful.

1904. Very good—somewhat old now.

1905. Pleasant, sound, wine and water.

1906. Fuller, fair quality.

1907. Somewhat like the 1905.

1911.   Fine wine, but will not improve.
1914.   For many years an attractive wine—but no longer so.
1916.
1917.
1918.   All passable, but not 'grandes choses'.
1919.
1920.   Very elegant and of good quality. With some wines a little dryness or bitterness is becoming apparent, owing no doubt to the cochylis.
1921.   Too big. Tastes of burnt skins, owing to the excessive heat. A vintage that will probably keep.
1923.   Good—Old before its time.
1924.   Excellent in every respect.
1926.   Some wines are developing much better than was expected.
1928.   Very fine wine. Excellent.
1929.   Very good, but I cannot think it will be a vintage to last very long. It does not appear to be so well balanced as the 1928.

1930, 1931, 1932.   Of these, the least said, the better.
Of the 1933 and 1934 I have already written.

The short remarks against each vintage will be sufficient indication as to what to use first and what to keep to the last.

1888, 1914.   Drink up quickly.
1905, 1907.   Drink up slowly.
1899, 1900.   Keep for best.
1911.   Good bottle for extra occasions.
1923.   Do not keep too long. Make an excuse to open a bottle.

Supposing a cellar is almost depleted of its stock, and an average consumption of, say, a little every day is used, or approximately 15 dozen—I would suggest that a reasonable outlay would be (not taking into consideration a small quantity of very special wines)—

1 year's supply of 1920 vintage,
2 years' supply of 1924 vintage,
2 years' supply of 1928 vintage,

[169]

(which should be excellent in 3-4 years' time), and then while the going is good, at the opening prices a good large quantity of 1933.

Where only a fraction of the quantity is likely to be used, I would suggest a stock in proportion. Once having started to build in this way, addition can be made as good vintages arrive and, what is so important—at opening prices.

Besides which, what a pleasure to visit one's cellars and longingly cast the eyes over your own 'children' developing for your own enjoyment and gratification !

SUMMARY OF BORDEAUX WINES

WHITE

1847. Excellent.
1852. Good.
1859. Good, but did not keep well.
1861. Very good.
1864. Very good indeed.
1869. Most excellent.
1874. Very good.
1878. Good.
1881. Good.
1887. Good.
1890. Very good.
1893. Very good—sweet.
1896. Pleasant wine, with breed (rather light).
1899. Very good, full bodied, sweet.
1900. Excellent.
1904. Excellent.
1906. Good, sweet, but showed early signs of becoming maderisé.
1908. Good.
1911. Good.
1916. Good.
1917. Very good.
1919. Good.
1920. Good.

1921.   One of the best on record, ranking with the 1869.
1922.   Good.
1923.   Good.
1924.   Very good.
1928.   Very good.
1929.   Good.
1933.   Varies—some good.

When it is noticed that a golden wine commences to be made-risé, then is the time to see that it is used. It will be good to drink, but it gradually loses its subtle characteristic.

CHAPTER VIII

BERGERAC

ON the 14th of October we awoke to a dull morning, but a pleasing incident made things seem brighter. What a great difference a slight thing will make. I remembered that some years ago I was sitting between two brother Knights of the Round Table—Mr. Serjeant A. M. Sullivan, K.C., and the late F. C. Wade, K.C., Agent-General for British Columbia. The one was 'spare' . . . the other, not. We were somewhat crowded and the Serjeant seeing a vacant seat elsewhere, moved to it, whereat the other remarked—

'Isn't it wonderful what a lot of room a spare man will take ?'

This enabled us to turn our chairs and listen in comfort to the classical oration of the Knight Champion, Albert C. R. Carter ; the 'piece de résistance' of the evening.

The little incident which made so much difference at the moment was the fact that the 'femme de chambre', when bringing in my café complet, actually brought my boots into the room . . . no particular person's job, I suppose. The 'boots' would place them outside the door, with a look which suggested—'now fetch them yourself !' The valet usually would bring in the café, and would either kick the boots out of the way or step over them . . . it wasn't his job ! I left a few francs at the 'office' for the maid, adding that I appreciated very much her thoughtful action.

This trifling thing made all the difference and I left the hotel just after nine o'clock quite happy and contented.

We were making for BERGERAC . . . a wine-growing district I had not visited before, and I was full of enthusiasm.

On this Sunday morning we found the streets somewhat deserted, and had an easy run viâ LIBOURNE. Many chasseurs were out, and I wished them good sport. There were vines on either side of the road most of the way.

After passing ST. PEY-D-ARMENS, we noticed quantities of maize.

Just before reaching CASTILLON, we were in time to see the start of a bicycle race . . . these events are taken very seriously.

After CASTILLON we passed through a very pleasant avenue, emerging from which we found meadows, both on the right hand and on the left, several of which were given over to 'le football'.

At MONTCARET the country was more pleasant. It was no longer raining and we had a ridge of wooded hills on either side.

The Little Auk was behaving better, after a little trouble to start with. We arrived at a level crossing which fortunately was opened, for we had caught up with three of the dirtiest unkempt brown camels it is possible to imagine, and whether out of fright or not I do not know, but the Little Auk commenced 'back firing'.

I notice that, in the majority of cases, level crossings in France are at the bend of a road and one has to be on the 'qui vive' for them all the time.

At ST. FOY the village idiot greeted us—we had not met with many of these, but I suppose they exist in the same way as they do in our country villages.

We were nearing BERGERAC, for there were many more vines to be seen.

Crossing over the river at GARDONNE, we nearly ran over a water rat—nasty things, water rats . . . I wish we had killed it.

As we neared BERGERAC we could see the result of much agricultural industry . . . Maize, Artichokes, Marrows, Pumpkins, Vines. But it was the produce of the vine that had brought us thither.

Bergerac is a very old town and one which has passed through many vicissitudes—having been pillaged and destroyed by Visigoths, Saracens, Normans and others.

In the twelfth century, by reason of the marriage of Eleanor of Aquitane with Henry II, the town came under the domination of the English.

[173]

The first name that comes to one's mind on arriving at Bergerac is undoubtedly—Cyrano . . . 'l'enfant terrible' . . . and one can conjure up all sorts of escapades which he must have contrived to carry out in the dismal streets of the town.

The first notice of wine which caught our attention was the following—

> Vin à emporter (=1934).
> Vin Rouge . . . 1 franc,
> Vin Pécharmont . . . 1 franc 25,
> Vin Blanc . . . 2 francs 50 per litre.

This did not look very encouraging.

Pécharmont is a small vineyard on the slopes of the hill outside Bergerac, where only Red wine is made.

We put up at the Hotel de Bordeaux, where we were quite comfortable. For lunch we had some fried gudgeons which were very good, with a bottle of local wine—Vin Rosé, Monbazillac (5 francs) . . . quite attractive, especially on a hot day.

Little crabs were offered as hors d'œuvres, but they looked so red and bashful that it seemed wrong to take advantage of them.

An excellent tournedos, with a yard of bread, which required strong fingers to break, came next.

While we waited for the quail and ceps a rat ran across the floor, much to the consternation of the few people lunching there.

I must tell you of an extraordinary thing that happened one day to my stock clerk ; it is almost incredible, but I can vouch for the truth of it. On a certain day he went out, as he usually did, to lunch at a well-known restaurant in the neighbourhood. He had seated himself at a table opposite a lady and gentleman and was waiting for the attention of the waiter, when he suddenly felt something on his leg immediately above the ankle. He stooped down and grasped it . . . however, he was not quick enough, for it immediately ran up his leg inside his trousers. More or less terrified, he clutched at it, and as he strangled it, it bit him—do not ask me where, for it is too delicate a question to answer ! He was assisted out of the restaurant, still hanging on to his capture, by the help of a couple of waiters, and when they reached an ante-room and lowered his nether garments, lo and behold they found a young rat, or at least a huge mouse, which had bitten him !

Perhaps the dear little maidens can be forgiven now for jumping on chairs when they hear a mouse in the room.

With the quail we had a bottle of Monbazillac. I did not think much of it . . . it was a nondescript sort of wine.

Sunday being a 'dies non' as far as work was concerned, we indulged in a little rest before taking a run around the immediate neighbourhood. We thought we would visit Monbazillac . . . a peculiarity of the soil of Monbazillac lies in the fact, rather rare in France, that one finds often very near the surface, on a foundation of clay and chalk, veins of the stone used for mill-stones. Some of these quarries are still worked—an industry which was far more flourishing in the past.

As we passed some meadows we saw numbers of children gathering mushrooms. This had been a wonderful season for them both.

From Bergerac we began to climb almost immediately, with fine healthy-looking vineyards on the hill-side and beautiful views on the right—although they were somewhat mollified by the rain which had commenced when we reached ROUFFIGNAC.

On the roadside we noticed one grave, enclosed, with tombstone. I wondered what tragedy had taken place here. We passed several ancient churches, particularly one at FLAUGEAC, but we did not feel sufficiently energetic to stop.

Out in the country, away from everywhere, we actually came across a man on point duty. His presence was certainly required, for he was at a cross-road and a very sharp hair-pin bend. I could not help but think that many unfortunate accidents must have occurred here before it was decided to place him on duty.

All was quiet, the road being none of the best, with little to attract attention, so, no wonder we took notice when we saw a man walking along, very carefully, and more carefully carrying in the hollow of his hand a single bunch of grapes, as if it had been the one and only in the district.

Further on, we passed a chasseur. He looked forlorn. I was not surprised, for we had seen neither rabbit nor bird the whole afternoon : except, I might add, a few chicken and turkeys, bearing in mind the goose I have mentioned before !

The roads were being repaired, and we entered a long patch on which broken chalk had been spread. It was not in the least comfortable. . . . How a poor old fellow managed to trundle along on his tricycle, I cannot imagine.

The next village, we understood, should be that of BOUNIAGUES. . . . We came across a church and concluded that that was all the village consisted of.

We were back at Bergerac by 6 o'clock. The cafés were full, and dancing was going on to the melodies of the gramophone.

Leaving Reg to put the Little Auk safely away, I took a turn through the streets . . . a small crowd of people were gathered together outside a café, where much altercation was being carried on. The subject of contention was the result of a 'Grand Match de Rugby'—

A.S. du Midi
contre
U.S. Bergeracoise.

Crossing the road I had a look at the outside of the ancient Church of St. James.

Passing through a narrow street, I came across an old gentleman outside a tobacconist shop . . . he had let fall a 50 cent piece and refused to move until he had found it. We both searched, but in vain and, at last, he gave it up and entered the shop. As he did so I immediately saw it . . . it had been under his foot all the time.

I picked it up, took it into the shop and gave it to him.

First he thought he would, and then he thought he wouldn't— give it to me . . . that is how I understood he regarded me, not knowing what to say.

I left him with a 'pas de quoi', thinking at the same time that had I been a little more shabby I might have earned an honest 50 cent piece.

Before going into dinner we sat in the lounge for a few minutes. Here, the same thing happened as we had noticed before in one or two other hotels. Not only the guests, but the servants were reading aloud the news to each other—they will even stop one another on the staircase and read whole columns in this way !

The dinner was not so successful as the lunch, maybe we were expecting too much.

The soup was cold . . . the plates were cold and—no bread !

The fried sole was very acceptable . . . fond d'artichauts to follow . . . cold and most unpleasant.

The service was atrocious. We put it down to Sunday night, so overlooked it and asked the waitress to try and do better.

We then had a Pintade de la Maison, which was very good and really hot, so the slight reprimand had had its effect.

With this meal we commenced with Monbazillac Vin Blanc. Then came Haut-Marsalet 1929—22 francs. Not being too sweet it was very drinkable. I thought it was a trifle woody—Reg thought it 'earthy' . . . whatever it was I think it must have been its own peculiarity.

There was a wine on the list described as 'Marquis de Fournils', but the boy thought we should find it too sweet. He was a nice boy, and I think he meant well, but he possessed enough sauce to cover all the geese in Bergerac and Toulouse together.

We therefore tried a bottle of sparkling St. Emilion, Clos des Cordeliers . . . it was a little too old, but drinkable. My reason for the selection was a passing thought for an old friend of mine, now away, Leo Rosenheim . . . for it was with him, upwards of thirty years ago, that I sat on a bench at the Clos itself, in beautiful surroundings, and enjoyed a bottle of this sparkling wine, well iced, on a hot day.

The waitress by this time was beginning to be quite attentive ; 'What cheese would you care for, Messieurs,' she said . . . 'I recommend the ROBLOCHON.' 'Very well,' we said . . . 'We will try it" . . . but—never again !

This displeased her very much . . . the poor soul was upset. She dropped the nut-crackers, and then a plate, and finally she trod on the tail of a dog fastened to the leg of the next table. I leave it to you to imagine the pretty Sabbath scene which ensued.

In the lounge we indulged in a glass of Armagnac, 1893 Clos des Princes. We had met this elsewhere and we did not think it could be improved upon. It tasted of good quality, although strong and of a dark colour.

Sitting here was a young lady who was drinking one cup of tea after another. She was rather good-looking and I wondered what she could be doing alone in this out-of-the-way place. She was continually taking up the paper and reading something . . . probably, thought I . . . the details of the trial of Violette Noziere, who had just been condemned to death. I tried to fasten her eyes, but she would have none of it . . . I have never seen anything quite to equal it—and she did not squint !

I suddenly remembered that she had had water with her dinner, when immediately my curiosity was turned into pity, and beneath my breath I exclaimed—'La pauvre'. Something was on her mind . . . at this distance of time I really don't mind what it was—but then . . . ! ! !

A gentle stroll before turning in. . . . At the corner of one street I was able to read by the help of the moonlight, I think it was—it may have been a street lamp—a notice, as follows :

' AIDEZ NOUS
TENONS
LA VILLE PROPRE
NE JETEZ RIEN PAR TERRE.'

As I went back to the hotel I thought how very necessary this injunction was.

The church bells seemed to be ringing at odd intervals all through the night, so I was frequently awakened, and I can remember thinking of the poor fellow who complained to his landlady, cursing Belisha the while, that he could not sleep 'on account of the damn silence'.

I suppose he must have suffered the same sort of oppression that the Egyptians of old suffered when they were subject to a darkness that ' could be felt'.

In the early morning the clouds were breaking in spite of heavy rain during the night, so we looked forward to a pleasant day.

One or two small incidents occurred here which I think I will be excused for mentioning.

Although the bath was, I was glad to see, larger than most, the chain attached to the waste-play was, as usual, faulty. I do not think I am exaggerating when I say that this is the case in seventy per cent. of the hotels in France.

I am more likely to notice this than most people for, owing to good reasons which I need not explain, I wash outside the bath and release the waste before getting in.

The difficulty in fixing this release is really remarkable . . . I have even found a lead pencil used as a wedge.

I have also found string attached to a towel-horse, and when one wished to empty the bath, it was necessary to move the towel-horse further away. I will admit that there was only one occasion when I failed and I had to take the bath, leaving the water in.

On this particular morning there was one other thing I noticed which accounts for an incident which happened to me some time before.

I, probably in common with many others, am frequently guilty of putting my foot on a chair, in order to tie my boot-laces. Twice I can remember finding chalk marks on certain parts of my trousers . . . this morning I discovered the cause. The chalk put by the 'boots' on the soles of the boots comes off on the chair, and, should you sit on the self-same chair, the chalk comes off on your trousers ! ! ! Moral . . .

It is time we made a move in the direction of the house of Messieurs Delpérier Frères, one of the illustrious merchants dealing in the wines of Bergerac.

We were fortunate in having such an introduction, for Monsieur E. Delpérier himself, the senior of the firm is 'President du Syndicat des Vins de l'Arrondissement de Bergerac', also 'Conseiller du Commerce Exterieur'.

Owing to the very kind introduction of Messieurs Cruse of Bordeaux we were received with open arms.

We had a lengthy conversation with these gentlemen and gained much valuable and interesting information which I hope to impart to you.

Being quite ignorant of the wines of this district I took advantage of asking several questions, for example :

Q. What wine districts are entitled to be called 'Bergerac wines ?'

A. Monbazillac-Montravel.

Q. Is there any difference in the quality of these wines ?

A. Monbazillac—the best. . . . Montravel—good, ordinary.

Q. What quantities are made ?

A. In a good year the quantity might reach 20,000 Hhds.

Q. Is it only the wine from Monbazillac which is entitled to the appellation ' Monbazillac ?'

A. No . . . also the wines from the three parishes of—Pomport, Rouffignac and Colombier.

Q. I suppose any vine can be planted in these areas ?

A. No. No hybrid vines are allowed.

Q. What vines are permitted ?

A. The Sauvignon, the Sémillon, the Muscadelle. . . . The usual and most satisfactory proportion is two-thirds Sémillon, and one-sixth each of the others.

Q. What about St. Laurent ?

A. Ah, yes . . . St. Laurent des Vignes has instituted a process in order to obtain the right to the appellation 'Monbazillac' . . . locally it has been decided in her favour, but it is now subject to an appeal.

Q. When do you commence the vintage ?

A. About the time when it is finishing in the Médoc—that is, generally speaking, about the second week in October.

Q. In what size casks is the wine shipped ?

A. As in Bordeaux—Hhds. of about 50 gallons.

Q. With the sweet wines of Monbazillac, do you have much difficulty with the fermentation ?

A. No ; none in the least. Our wines are treated in the same way as the finest wines of the Sauternes.

Q. In Sauternes the 'pourriture noble' is welcome ; do you look for it ?

A. Oh, yes, and we vintage when this is apparent.

Q. What is the difference then between your wines and the Sauternes ?

A. Nothing—only the soil. And without boasting we conder ours as good as theirs.

[180]

Q. What is the alcoholic degree of your wines ?

A. It varies according to the year, from 11° to 14° or even higher.

Q. Harking back to your reference to the soil—what is the soil in this district ?

A. Chalk.

Q. Is there more White wine made than Red ?

A. Much about the same quantity. However, in Monbazillac itself we find three-fourths of White wine and only one-fourth Red wine.

Q. Does the wine bear exportation well—will it keep bright ?

A. Certainly, if properly treated before shipment, that is, by judicious application of sulphur and good racking, according to the vintage.

Q. What are the best known growths ?

A. Le Theulet, Le Touron, Le Fumat, Tirecul, Le Septy, La Borderie, Pintouka, Poulvère : Le Ch. de Monbazillac, Haut Marsalet, La Fonrousse, and Le Peroudier (all 1ers. crus).

Q. How long after the vintage do you bottle the wines ?

A. On an average, three to four years.

Q. What effect does age in bottle have on the wines ?

A. Remarkable. It improves and alters them out of all recognition.

After this very interesting and instructive conversation we accepted Monsieur Delpérier's invitation to taste some of the fine wines from his rich store.

1929 Monbazillac—from the cask, appealed to me as being of fine quality and excellent value.

1928 Monbazillac—I found sweeter and fuller. Both these wines were from the cask.

We then sampled the 1928 which had been two years in bottle—what a remarkable difference ! ! When Monsieur Raoul Jonchères, a partner of Monsieur Delpérier . . . himself 'President du Tribunal de Commerce', 'Conseiller du Commerce Extérieur' and 'Président de l'Union du Commerce et de l'Industrie' —saw my astonishment, he explained that it was not given to all vintages to develop in such an extraordinary way.

[181]

To follow we were shown the 1926 wines, both from cask and bottle ; I think I preferred the 1928.

We had arrived at the highest class of wines—1924 TIRECUL, 14°.... This particular wine was more elegant. It had been four years in bottle, and asserted itself in no small manner.

1918 PINTOUKA. . . . This was an exceedingly fine wine, 6-7 years in bottle. I could not help remarking that at last I could understand the taste of the ladies at the old French Courts, when they sat down to such wines (Monbazillac as we read) at five o'clock, and enjoyed them over a plain cake.

This was indeed a delightful bottle—somewhat different to the fine Ch. Yquem . . . firmer, and more assertive—a real wine !

'Monsieur Delpérier', I said . . . 'You must allow me to have some of this famous wine, and I will be able to give the ladies a treat at home !'

He smiled, and replied that he would see !

The next wine was a little older, but of the fine vintage of 1914 . . . POULVÈRE 1914 . . . it was very, very good, but very, very sweet ; I still preferred the Pintouka.

We spoke of the great vintages of 1921—evidently quite a rarity now. The good people of Bergerac considered their Monbazillac wine of that famous vintage to be superior to the Sauternes—'better balanced wine' they would infer.

I was told of one vineyard that yielded a Vin Rosé, but I had no chance to see what wine it produced.

The wines which I had been allowed to taste appealed to me in spite of their richness. It may be that they were new to me, for I could hardly remember tasting them before ; except on one or two isolated occasions.

I related to Monsieur Delpérier, senior, how, upwards of thirty years ago when I was staying at the Château de Bois-Renard in the Vendée, I had been privileged to taste, among other curiosities, a Monbazillac wine of great age, but at that time I had thought it was too sticky and sweet to be agreeable and—if I recollected rightly—it was quite dark in colour.

'Ah', said Monsieur Delpérier . . . 'probably a fine wine, become too maderisé through age.'

I then ventured to ask if he had any wine of outstanding merit

[182]

and of great age which could be offered at table as 'something exceptional'.

'No', he said, 'they do not exist—yet—yes ! I have a little 1874.' And he kissed the tips of his fingers at the very thought of it—a delicate action.

As we were speaking of many things I asked where was the best outlet for these excellent wines, and I must admit that I was a little surprised to learn—Holland ! It would appear that, after the revocation of the Edict of Nantes in 1685, large numbers (nearly 40,000) of Protestants who were living in and around Bergerac, were forced to exile themselves (Les Huguenots). Those of Monbazillac for the most part made their way to Holland, where they settled down to commerce, in particular dealing in the wines of their native country of Monbazillac, which resulted in a good trade between the two communities ; the Dutchmen as well as the Huguenots taking large quantities of the wine in exchange for the renowned Dutch cheese.

We then accompanied these very kind gentlemen on a tour through the districts. What more could we wish for—and in the company of such people who evidently knew all that there was to know about the wines of Bergerac and Monbazillac !

After passing a very critical hairpin bend in the road, we were shown the famous growths of Touron and Fonrousse on the left, and Pintouka on the right . . . while further on came Le Fumat, also on the right, perhaps not of such fame as formerly.

The proprietor of Fonrousse, Monsieur Domenget de Malauger is 'le President du Syndicat des Vignerons de la Dordogne et des vins à appellation Monbazillac'.

From LE TOURON we had a fine view, revealing many hectares of vines. Here we espied one of those rarities—a white blackbird !

The vintage did not seem to be finished—I gathered that the lack of casks had caused some delay.

We had now arrived at Château Monbazillac itself . . . on the hill, with magnificent views, overlooking the valley of the Dordogne.

The castle is not inhabited, which is a thousand pities ; it is so commanding. It is of the renaissance period, and outside in the grounds are trees, some four hundred years old.

We lingered here for some time, unwilling to quit, but we knew that we must away.

On our way down the hill and over undulating ground we felt constrained to stop and take a last view of the fine castle ; I shall always remember how it appealed to me.

We were now privileged to visit a few of the well-known Estates, the first being Château Rose-Boissière . . . also, Château Poulvère, 1er Cru Monbazillac. Then came another part of the property—the Château Laumont, with its thirty-five hectares of vines.

On looking over the grapes I was grieved to see such a quantity of cochylis . . . big and fat ones too ; the proprietors will probably lose one fifth of their crop on account of this scourge, and it will surely be apparent in the wine.

I noticed that the doors of the chais were heavily covered with straw. This helps to make a more equitable temperature which is very necessary when the wines are fermenting.

We sampled the 1934 wine at Château Laumont. The first cask gave 16° sugar, Gay Lussac . . . the second 17°. One degree makes much difference.

The third was 22° . . . full of sugar—the fourth showed 25° . . . this is very high. The wine probably will not start fermenting until the Spring.

The fermentation lasts from one month to four or five. The more there is of sugar, the slower the fermentation.

We then tasted a sample which showed 28° sugar . . . this is too sugary. It may commence to ferment in March, and it may never finish !

Tasting these extraordinary, sweet wines, I inquired what happened in a bad vintage. I gathered that, although it was contrary to the law, some few unscrupulous people did add a little sugar.

On leaving these chais I noticed a quantity of what appeared to be large casks of earth ; this was the residue, covered with earth to prevent fermentation . . . being kept ready for the public distiller to distil into Marc.

In another corner of a chai the press was being worked, and as the juice exuded from these over-ripe grapes it was as if they were shedding sweet tear-drops. This day it showed 25°... the drop of 2° being due to the moisture and the rain. It would have been better to have had a larger quantity not so full of sugar. We waited a couple of minutes, and tasted it again—25·50°.

On leaving, we offered our hand to the maître, but he humbly apologised in refusing his hand, and extended one finger, which in itself was like a sugar-stick !

This first pressing is not very severe. The grapes are subjected to a second pressing, and even at times to a third, which serves to make the more ordinary wines of the country.

We returned to the office for a few minutes, and selected a little literature on the wines of Bergerac. Monsieur Delpérier, senior, had retired for a moment, when back he came, all smiles, and carrying an ancient bottle in his hands—it was grasped by both of them. 'This', he said—awe, mingled with sympathy in his voice ... 'is a bottle of 1874 Monbazillac.'

I arose to examine the revered bottle, and ventured to suggest that I might purchase a few bottles in order to oblige my very good friend whom I was shortly to visit at Biarritz.

'Impossible!' he said ... 'Impossible—I have but five remaining.' A pause ... I apologized, explaining that I gathered he had a few dozen. At the suggestion of a few dozen he laughed, and by that laugh I felt that I had made a serious faux pas in asking if I might buy some. The moment was a little awkward ... when, what do you think happened ? He gently laid his hand on my shoulder and said—'For you, and you only, Mr. Berry, I will release one of these precious bottles, and you shall give it, with your compliments, to your deserving friend at Biarritz.'

This was indeed a clever move, for I could not have accepted for myself, and equally, I could not refuse on behalf of my friend —'could I, Mr. Levis ?'

'I hope when you open it, you and your company will not forget to raise the glass to Monsieur Delpérier for his sacrifice ; he certainly merits it.'

This little anecdote will, I trust, go far to illustrate the real virtue of wine and its influence on character.

Before we left Bergerac, these hospitable people insisted on entertaining us at déjeuner. We tasted several wines, to commence with an uninteresting wine—Castillon Red (Gironde) and a Vin du Pays (Bergerac)—this was vin compris . . . but I would not have wished for them often.

The Vin du Pays (Bergerac) was drinkable—more like an overloaded sulphurous Graves than anything else to which I could compare it.

A Bergerac Wine from the valley followed—1929 Sorbier (a Dutch mark). It had gained third prize at a recent exhibition . . . the quality was good, but it was too heavy for lunch, resembling somewhat a Tokay Aszú.

We then had a bottle of 1918 Monbazillac—a trifle sweet for me—but it was that extraordinarily fine wine we had sampled during the morning.

With these we had a Langouste, with which the Vin du Pays was tolerable. Then followed a specialité of the hotel, in the shape of Hare, with which the rich wines agreed.

We finished with ceps and a poulet . . . Augustine only smiled when I told her that, instead of 'ail' with poulet, she had given us poulet with 'ail'! . . . and then a glass of 1893 Armagnac to settle it all.

We bade 'au revoir' to our very good friends and, while thanking them most sincerely, assured them that if we were ever in their part of the world again, our first visit would be to them.

SUMMARY OF MONBAZILLAC AND OTHER BERGERAC WINES

1847.	Very fine, but passé.
1865.	„ „
1874.	Merveilleuse !
1899.	Very good indeed.
1900.	Probably the best to be found.
1916.	Good.
1917.	Fair.
1918.	Excellent. Only small quantity.
1919.	Fair.
1920.	Good.
1921.	Exceptional.
1922.	Variable.

1923. Good.
1924. Very good.
1925. Very poor quality.
1926. Good.
1927. Rubbish.
1928. Very good.
1929. Too much sugar—some few very good.
1930. Bad.
1931. Fair.
1932. Bad.
1933. Good.
1934. Promises well—however, some of the wines may suffer from an excess of sugar.

These White wines should be drunk quite fresh—that is, cold.

CHAPTER IX

ARMAGNAC

BEFORE three o'clock we were on our way again through much of the same country where the yellow flowers of the Jerusalem artichokes made a brave show . . . perhaps they were jealous of all the attention bestowed on the vines.

As we passed the Domaine du Fumat it commenced to rain, and by the time we had reached FONROQUE it was coming down very fast . . . we had some shelter from an avenue, the trees of which appeared from a distance to be almost dead, but which was, we discovered, only the outward effect of quantities of dead ivy still clinging to the trunks.

Near LA SAUVETAT the rain came down in a deluge, so we were unable to see much of the quaint old market town of MIRAMONT. From here to SEYCHES are to be seen, so I understand, some fine views, but the persistent rain entirely hid them from us.

Through the town of MARMANDE with its thirteenth century Church of Notre Dame, and on in the driving rain to AIGUILLON, over the river, where there is a pretty waterfall on the left. . . .

We were forced to wait a little further on, on account of a closed railway crossing.

The Little Auk back-fired, which so frightened a horse standing close behind that it nearly caused an accident.

We had to wait about ten minutes, which seemed like ten hours, in the rain.

There was an old couple quite near the car, both thoroughly drenched . . . it was rather pathetic to hear the old fellow begging his dame to go back, else, he felt sure, she would get wet !

After we had been allowed to pass and were continuing along the road I saw something approaching . . . two dark brown oxen

drawing a load of wood. I remarked about this to Reg . . .
'They are not oxen', he said . . . 'They are a couple of donkeys.'
As we passed we could see that it really was—one mule and one
man ! And yet, Reg insisted he was right ! I am relating this in
order to illustrate how bad the visibility was.

At Port Ste. Marie there was a dangerous hill to take, and on
the further side, a very sharp turn under an archway. We were
soon at the river level crossing near MENAUX.

The bad weather continued, and at FEUGAROLLES we encountered such a violent gale that we could see large fields of maize
being laid out flat.

Here, many peasants were carrying their bread home, tucked
under one arm—yards of it. I asked Reg what it would be like
when they got there . . . he suggested that the best use for it
would be to make 'hot bread and milk' of it ! Not a bad idea,
especially if they added a soupçon of local Marc to it.

A curious looking large Château stood on the right, as we
climbed a steep hill. Here we deplored the weather for we were
denied what must be some very fine views.

On the summit the vineyards were neglected . . . I do not
know for what reason, but the sight of numbers of decayed old
roots still in the ground gave us this information ; lower down
the hill we did see some vines, although they did not look very
flourishing.

It may be that this particular area is subject to extremely bad
weather . . . it had evidently suffered from the gale, a part of
which we had experienced on our way, for the road was littered
with debris and even tree trunks.

LAVARDAC was the next town, which Reg persisted in calling
'Love-a-duck'—'A sentimental community here', he remarked,
on seeing the public band-stand. I supposed, although I did not
question it, that he had had a passing thought in connecting the
music with the way he pronounced the name of the place.

We crossed the river again . . . still the wind was howling, and
bringing with it heavy rain. It was amazing to see with what
facility, in this weather, men and women too would manœuvre
their bicycles, while carrying open umbrellas.

I wonder how many times that day the expression 'quel sale

[189]

temps' was said; I agree that there seemed ample justification for it.

When we arrived at NERAC it was almost dark, so we journeyed on to CONDOM without observing anything.

At CONDOM we put up at the Hotel Continental—a small, clean, provincial hotel.

We were making the necessary inquiries as to accommodation, which by the way we had reserved, when the electric light gave out. We were therefore in darkness for a few minutes, while candles were fetched. We were shown our rooms, such as they were, when the lights failed once more, and it was not until the early hours of the morning that it was restored.

The whole town was in darkness—the work of the storm. This reminded me of an occasion when I had been—jointly with my friend Charles Spencer—guilty of placing a town, or a part of it, in darkness. It was at Pourville, some few years ago, when we were taking part in the Coupe Gordon-Bennett: we were making a landing in a field which lay on the other side of a row of Poplar trees. Hidden from view by these trees were several stretches of live wires . . . our trail rope caught them, and as the end was bound with wire, you can imagine the result—one result was the placing of Pourville in darkness.

I did not think that there could ever be so huge a flame. We were just above, with 60,000 cubit feet of gas ! ! ! 'Good-bye', we bade each other, when, by the grace of God, the trail rope broke through the wires (for there was a fair wind) and we were safe.

I remember with what hospitality we were treated—entertained right royally at the large hotel facing the sea, the name of which has escaped me.

When we came downstairs there were many candles alight to illuminate the place—we were met by three comely dames, whom I described to Reg as—Large, larger and largest ; evidently they had been fed on the fat of the land.

Shortly afterwards we made our way into the café, with its marble-top tables and kitchen chairs. LARGEST was doing needlework in the café, and playing around was her baby grandson, being very rude and generally naughty, until finally he was carried off squawling to bed. I gathered that the same thing happens (not the failure of the electric light, but the squawling kid) every day.

I recollect an amusing incident at this moment. The only dame who had been in the café had left with her charge . . . there remained some dozen men. Suddenly, one of these rose from his chair, and touching his béret, said—'Bon Soir, messieurs et *dames* !' . . . force of habit I suppose.

We passed candles placed on the floors of the landings when we went to have a wash before dinner and the same means of lighting was afforded us on the dinner-table.

There were a goodly number of diners, mostly commercial travellers, I think . . . there was one female.

Red and White wine was offered as vin compris ; some of the commercials mixed the two together. On inquiry I learned that the Red wine was 1934 vintage and the White 1933 ; both Vin du Pays.

I tried the White wine, and helped it over the stile with a syphon of Seltzer.

Reg attacked the 1934, with the aid of water, and thinking that it would be amusing to drink so young a wine I poured out a little in another glass—I got it as far as my mouth, but courage failed me !

With these beverages we were served—soup, raw ham, fried egg, and choux-fleurs . . . this last accounted for the strong smell of cabbage-water with which our noses had been offended.

I forget, with the choux-fleurs we had a good and hot portion of poulet.

1893 Armagnac saved the situation.

The waiter wished to impress upon us that Armagnac was far superior to Cognac and that it was only publicity that made Cognac so popular. I am sure I should be forgiven my smile !

After this repast we ventured outside and found that the 'sale temps' had departed and left a beautiful star-lit night, with Madame La Lune showing half her glory.

Wandering through the narrow streets, with no other light than the moon, reminded me of the war days when not a light was to be seen, even in the windows . . . thank goodness the cause was not the same.

Back to the hotel we groped our way to bed, and nearly fell over LARGER, who had stumbled down a stair on the landing.

There were no blankets on the bed . . . this did not concern us, as the night was sultry. I instinctively looked at the clock to see what hour it was . . . As I might have expected, I was none the wiser ! I wonder what percentage of hotel bedroom clocks show the correct time more than once in the day and once in the night ?

A bolster instead of three pillows rather worried me, but I made the best of it and, as I lay in bed before dropping off to sleep, I thought of the two fellows on a long tramp, in the summer. . . . Away in the country, they stretched themselves out in a meadow to sleep. 'I wish we had a pillow', said one. 'Haven't you', said the other. . . . 'I have fetched a drain-pipe from the road.' At which suggestion, his friend did likewise.

In the morning they exchanged experiences—'How did you sleep ?' 'Rotten', was the reply. . . . ' The drain-pipe was so hard, I had to discard it.' 'Stupid fellow', retorted the other . . . 'You should have done as I did'.

'What was that ?' . . . 'Why, you mutt—I stuffed it with straw !'

LARGEST was an agreeable personage, with the face of a full moon—such as is seen in some advertisements—which seemed to say—'Never mind if it has been raining all day . . . I keep smiling.'

LARGER always seemed very pre-occupied, and disdained to look favourably on travellers.

LARGE, the last, but not by all means the least, was the most communicative, and spoke of domestic affairs. I trust she may increase in prosperity, if not in size !

The next morning was fine, and the sun was shining. I enjoyed a bath, in spite of the fact that, as usual, the chain for the waste would not act.

We had a pleasant view, looking across the canal at the old town built on the hill-side opposite.

Shortly after leaving we missed our turning, and took the road to MOUCHAN, instead of going as we intended, through VALENCE s/BAÏSE.

It was an open country . . . we passed by vineyards on either side ; the roads, however, were more or less strewn with leaves, twigs and small branches—showing the effect of yesterday's storm.

We had passed through MOUCHAN, when the Little Auk seemed restive. . . . Reg got out to mend matters, but in touching a loose nut, he unfortunately burnt his fingers, which did not improve things. However, he adjusted this and was quite happy that he had found out the cause.

We then came on to a departmental road, which to our surprise was very good—it had recently been tarred—and made our way to VIC-FEZENSAC.

A brace of magpies foretold of 'le bonheur' and we continued along a pleasant English-country-looking road, with meadows on either side, behind hedgerows such as we are accustomed to . . . geese on the commons . . . mistletoe on the trees, and actually a couple of foxhounds.

I like to see the slow, steady, sedate oxen drawing the ploughs, but they are so slow . . . I suppose it was not the correct thought, but it passed through my mind that that may have been the reason the Old Testament Scriptures forbade the yoking of oxen !

Down a long avenue, which I remembered passing along years before with Jacques Delamain and Monsieur G. Buphomène, we arrived at VIC-FEZENSAC, where we intended to make some searching inquiries as to ARMAGNAC. We were now some one hundred and fifty miles to the south-east of COGNAC, and the Brandy distilled here is entirely different.

As in the Charente, so in the Gers ; there are several growths, the most important being the BAS-ARMAGNAC which, in one sense, can be compared with GRANDE CHAMPAGNE in the Charente.

The other growths—the Tenareze, and the Haut-Armagnac—are in a different category . . . rather coarse, and I am certain that the heavy Armagnacs that we found on our way here emanate from these inferior growths.

The Bas-Armagnac Brandies are somewhat delicate and fine, although they possess a 'terroir' of their own. The first of these

[193]   B.W.

is to be found in the department of Gers, of which the delimitation comprises several communes . . . also a few in the Landes, the principal of which are—NOGARO, CAZAUBON, EAUZE, GABARRET, VILLENEUVE-DE-MARSAN, and a part of RISCLE.

The centre of the Bas-Armagnac is to be found in the commune of PANJAS, CANTON of CAZAUBON.

There is an ancient Cathedral, of tenth and eleventh century, at Panjas, also an old Château, which rejoices in its reputation for choice Bas-Armagnac.

The average output of Bas-Armagnac amounts to between 4000 and 5000 hectos. These Brandies mature rapidly—in oak casks, the wood of which is supposed to be ten years old—due, no doubt, to the fact that they are distilled at a strength varying between 5° and 8° *under* proof, whereas the Cognac Brandies are distilled at between 15° to 20° *over* proof.

It would be inadvisable to distil the Bas-Armagnac at a higher strength—experience shows that it would be detrimental both to the quality and the bouquet. The same would apply to the produce from the Haut-Armagnac and outlying districts.

The famous Piquepoul vine (the 'folle blanche' of Cognac) seems to be the predominant plant; with a fair number of Jurançon and La Blanquette, also Colombard.

I was informed that some of the Piquepoul (ungrafted) plants in the various vineyards of Bas-Armagnac, were actually about one hundred and fifty years old, the wine from them being much sought after for distillation.

The first visit was to the old established firm of Monsieur J. Bouchet Mothe, who welcomed us and gave us much of his valuable time. Monsieur Mothe deplored a falling off in the trade, owing, he said, entirely to the 'crise économique', so he looked for an improvement in the near future.

Distilling had commenced the day before, so everyone was busy—a good quality Brandy, and much of it seemed likely—so this brightened the outlook somewhat.

We were shown several samples of young Armagnac, and then an 1893, which was very good. This vintage must have been good and plentiful, for we found it in most hotels.

Before leaving, Monsieur Mothe's son-in-law presented us

with a bottle of 1878 . . . he desired us to let him know how good it was, and how we enjoyed it on the journey.

Prior to our departure he sprang a surprise on us by opening a bottle of 1830 de Gimat, Bas-Armagnac, which had been seven years in bottle. It was a revelation ! I would have liked to possess it, but the high price put it out of the question.

It was a kindly act to show it to us, and one which we thoroughly appreciated ; I can see Reg smacking his lips over it even now !

On leaving VIC-FEZENSAC we passed through a happy, undulating country, but having once again missed the right turning, we were forced to return about ten kilometres. Passing through VIC, we had to pull up for two reasons at the same place—one, a man struggling with an obstinate mule, and another—a man using a very large tree branch as a broom with which to sweep up the debris left on the road after the storm.

The road we took was a veritable switchback, vines here and there, sometimes on the right and sometimes on the left . . . a number of small woods—'chasse gardée'—being plainly marked.

There was much pasture land . . . in one meadow I saw such a quantity of flowers, which I took to be cornflowers, that it brought back to my mind an incident of my very early days when we were living at Kemp Town, Brighton.

The flower, however, proved to be the meadow-saffron, a kind of autumn flowering crocus . . . the lilac purple flower of which is very conspicuous in the meadows of Southern France.

I could not have been more than six years old, and had gone with an older brother, Arthur, for a walk on the Downs. . . . Seeing a lot of these flowers in the cornfields, we thought there was no harm in picking them to take home to mother, but a policeman who had seen us thought otherwise !

He waited for us and led us off in triumph and, in this humiliating way were escorted home and left in one of the small rooms downstairs to await the advent of father ! ! ! What moments they were, but Arthur was very brave, in spite of the fact that mother, to impress upon us the enormity of our crime, had dressed us in our oldest clothes to be ready to go away with the policeman when he returned for his interview with father.

Mother often laughed over this—the dear old soul.

By the time I had amused Reg with this yarn, we were approaching the little town of DEMU, where we had the misfortune to run over and kill a black cock . . . I must say it was entirely its own hesitating fault.

I alighted, and took the mangled body to a dame who, having witnessed the accident, was coming from her house.

I expressed regret, and offered to pay for it, thinking she could ill afford to lose the bird.

I was surprised when she not only spurned payment, but put the entire blame upon 'the stupid thing'.

She informed me that she, as well as her neighbours, had frequently lost fowls in this way, but so far as she could remember, we were the only ones who had offered recompense !

She inquired of my nationality . . . I was glad to say 'British', for I am sure she will always think well of the British after this.

From here, although we were only some five hundred feet up, we had the pleasure of fine views all around.

At MANCIET, where we turned left to CRAVENCÈRES, we had to pull up on account of a deaf man walking in the middle of the road . . . all the hooting made no difference, and eventually we managed to squeeze past him, on the left. We threw a few gentlemanly remarks at him, but he only grinned.

At CRAVENCÈRES, which we found quite deserted, we made inquiries at the Poste Rurale Correspondante, for the Château de Moussot, but after peeping into two of the rooms we came away, not finding anyone at home.

Eventually we discovered Rebecca's husband, at the village well, drawing water, and after some difficulty in understanding his patois, we left, feeling sure we should soon find the way, as he had been very impressive about some Cypress trees.

We went down a lane where marrows were growing on the hedges, and turning round, sure enough we came across four stately Cypresses acting as sentinels at the entrance of a long avenue—so we ventured. At the end of this avenue was the Château de Moussot and, as I got out of the car a large black and white dog came forward—not with a bound, but quietly forward —and proceeded to take a bite at my coat; I don't think he meant any harm, but it was not quite the greeting one would expect, or wish for.

It was evidently a large property, and the Château was of some pretensions . . . maybe we should find some good Armagnac here.

'Is Monsieur le Comte de Paillerets at home?' I inquired, when the door was opened by an elderly Monsieur who had evidently spent most of his life in the country.

'No', he replied . . . 'my son-in-law has gone on his bicycle to MANCIET' (we must have passed him on the way)—'is there any-thing I can do for you ?'

I explained our mission—the way was then open—'Come in', he begged . . . 'we have been expecting you ; now tell me what I can do.'

'Should you have any fine Bas-Armagnac I would like to taste them, and to know particulars as to prices and quantities', I replied.

At the sound of voices a goodly lady appeared, but was easily appeased when her lord informed her that we were the gentlemen of whom Monsieur Delamain had spoken, as likely to pay Monsieur le Comte a visit. He explained that most of the old Brandies had been sold . . . he had, however, a small quantity of a 1904, which we tasted and found very good—one of the best I have sampled, but the price was not commercial—unfortunately !

We tasted some samples, three years old, which were attractive.

There would be a good quantity, and he hoped, an excellent quality, of 1934. Although interesting, it was much too young for me to understand, or entertain. He allowed us to peep into an ante-room, where from the ceiling were hanging large quantities of table-grapes.

We thanked him for his courtesy and begged him to express our regrets to his son-in-law for not having had the pleasure of meeting him.

We then cut across country, past the aerodrome at MIDOUR, where we saw some ancient-looking, weather-beaten planes, to NOGARO. Here we wished to make use of an introduction of Monsieur G. Buphomène, therefore immediately sought the whereabouts of Monsieur Lafourcade.

We met outside the house a very intelligent and kindly disposed young lady. . . . I think she was either the daughter or niece of Monsieur Lafourcade . . . who at once led us into the presence of one of the Armagnac magnates.

He very graciously placed himself at our disposal, showed us his chais and his stills, and allowed us to taste several different Brandies. . . .

1910.   Very pale, good flavour, and, I thought, of very good quality—46° Gay-Lussac.

1893 (the ubiquitous 1893).   This was very good, with a little more colour—probably through age.

We tasted several others (all Acquit Jaune d'Or) and brought away with us samples of 1910, 1915 and 1929. I was glad to have these for comparison. I passed through the Customs safely, with these small samples, and hope one day before long to make time to give them the attention they deserve.

As we were anxious to reach PAU before dark, we decided not to go back to PONT-DE-BORDES, which place we had missed on our way out.

Nor did we think it would be of any commercial benefit, if we delayed by paying a visit to Monsieur Bedout at CAZAUBON, as we understood he had parted with all his fine Armagnacs.

However, I would very much like to have left a card, as a souvenir of the gracious reception he extended to me some years ago when I called upon him, but not being certain of finding him at home, we decided to lose no time.

From NOGARO to LUPPE we went, passing vines, pampas grass growing by the wayside, and quite a large number of the funereal and stately Cypresses—these trees seem to be a feature of the country.

Through VERGOIGNAN next, with its brand new church, and on to the small town of BARCELONNE-DU-GERS where Reg allowed to escape him the remark that he thought the Little Auk must be a female—'because it wants such a lot of humouring', he added.

Incidentally, I have heard others, ladies by chance, who have asserted that cars certainly have sex !

We now arrived at AIRE,—market day. This is evidently a

flourishing town, for did we not see a few houses in the process of being built ! Over the river Adour, we arrived at the Hotel Commerce for déjeuner. We had a little difficulty about leaving the car—we were first directed 'here' . . . then someone said that that would not do, so we took his advice and parked it 'there'. This manœuvre being seen by an Agent de Police he thought. that he should have a word in the matter, and so, with his kind assistance we moved it 'elsewhere'.

The restaurant was full of people, owing to market day, no doubt.

There was no vacant table, but one for four, with a solitary female partaking her meal—we decided on this as being better than nothing !

Our table companion was indeed an illustration of 'mutton got up as lamb' . . . she wore massive ear-rings, drank water, and suffered with an 'acking cough !

Looking around the tables out of curiosity to see what was being drunk, we noticed that Vin Rouge was practically everywhere, evidently vin compris, so we thought we would taste it. It was on the sweet side, but by the colour it should be made next year . . . I never saw so purple a wine !

We were to have hare, so now it was necessary to decide on the wine ; Jurançon wine was on the list, so we thought we would try it.

It was Jurançon Blanc, demi-sec. We then tried a more expensive Jurançon wine . . . it was sweet, something akin to the cheaper Monbazillac ; I was not much impressed with it, besides which, it was slightly corked.

This luncheon hour was really entertaining, and I am constrained to tell you about it.

Venus, my vis-à-vis had ordered a basket of fruit. Neither an apple, grapes, an orange, nor a banana pleased her, but she must select—having this irritating cough—nuts ! She took up three or four before deciding which one she would have.

Steaming hot hare arrived, but the plates were stone cold. At another table was a little boy, aged about six years, tucking into his meal, enjoying his wine, and looking the picture of health. At this table the dessert course had been reached, and one man wolfed all the grapes, and then proceeded to place the nuts in his pocket.

Looking further afield, my eye caught sight of a woman 'making herself up' at the table. I have seen paste, powder and rouge used, but never before in this way. The woman had consumed the contents of a bottle of Châteauneuf du Pape, which in itself had given her enough colour, so perhaps a little powder was thought necessary.

I told Reg to look, and as he did he remarked—'Don't . . . it'll make me sick—Ugh!'

The waitress was requested to bring a brush to brush the powder from her dress.

After coffee, in a moment of forgetfulness, I presume, she wiped her lips with the serviette—off came the double rouge ! It really looked revolting as she held out her serviette.

A man at the other end of the room persisted in looking over at our table . . . I wonder if he has yet remembered when and where he saw me before ?

Our Venus tenaciously held on to the nut-crackers, so that at another table there was much amusement caused by the diners thumping their fists on nuts which they held on the table, hoping to break the shells in this way. It was an awful row, but yet it was 'the ill wind' . . . for it deadened the sound of the hacking cough.

We were not sorry to leave this pandemonium. Outside we counted upwards of two hundred two-wheeled carts, all more or less in a state of dilapidation, these being the conveyances which bring the peasants into the 'market' from the outlying villages.

The largest business seems to be in haricot beans !

An old soul brushed past, carrying a brace of turkey cocks, in an open panier. She and the dindons all seemed happy and pleased, but what the birds had to rejoice at I failed to see.

We left AIRE, to the braying of an impatient donkey, which we hoped was not a portent for rain ; it however reminded me of an excellent repartee, told by Father Healy against himself. He was about to pass a jarvey with his donkey, in the streets of Dublin . . . the patient beast began to bray—'Do you hear your brother ?' asked the priest. 'Yes, father', was the simple reply.

SUMMARY OF ARMAGNAC

The best succeeded vintages are :

1911, 1906, 1900, 1898.
1893. Very good indeed.
1886.
1878. Very good indeed.
1874. Very good.
1864.
1848. Exceptional.
1830. Very good.

CHAPTER X

AIRE TO CARCASSONNE

(viâ Pau and Biarritz)

A LITTLE after two o'clock we quitted AIRE SUR/L'ADOUR, making our way to PAU ... immediately enjoying some good views on the right ; there were not many vineyards, but instead, we saw a quantity of maize—two cows were loose in one field of maize ; what a time they would have, to be sure !

We did not see a great many Oak trees, for which we were on the lookout, as we had been told that the Armagnac was matured in Oak casks : the oak of the 'pays' . . . perhaps we were misinformed.

At GARLIN we came to some wide, open moorland, full of bracken and gorse. We were happy in some fine views and wooded roads.

At LALONGUETTE we found men felling a number of trees in the avenue, and on inquiry we were told that they had to come down because they were attacked by a curious sort of disease, the name of which I have forgotten.

We continued along winding, wooded, picturesque roads, in parts very steep, until we came to NAVAILLES-ANGOS, where we had the first sight of the Pyrénées. It was not far after this, along a good straight road, passing an aviation camp on the right, that we reached PAU ; as we approached we noticed myriads of midgets . . . we therefore could look forward to better weather on the morrow.

We stayed at the Hotel de France, where Louis Eschenauer had promised us we should be well looked after . . . and he was right.

I had been once before to PAU, many years ago, with Monsieur

Georges Calvet, the brother of my good friend, Jean. I always remember this for four special reasons :

1. His extravagance in insisting on ordering a bottle of 1875 Ch. Lafite. . . . I can almost taste it now ! !
2. A walk along the Boulevard des Pyrénées, enjoying the glorious view across to the mountains.
3. The visit to the Château Henry IV, with its wonderful tapestries.
4. Last, but not least—Georges Calvet's introduction to— instead of tea—strawberries over which we squeezed the juice of a lemon . . . with, if I remember correctly, a little sifted sugar and cream !

This is many years ago, but I recollect comparing this mixture, which was delicious, with the whisky and water, which made one of his countrymen exclaim—

'You are the funny people . . . you do things by contraries— you have the strong whisky, and you put in the water to make him weak : you add the sugar to make him sweet, and then put in the Citron to make him sour . . . then you raise the glass to a friend, and saying "here's to you"—you drink him yourself ! Oh, you are the funny people ! ! !'

We were ready for our dinner, which was well served and well cooked. With the sole we had a bottle of Jurançon, Vin du Pays. . . . It was quite enjoyable—the driest I could select.

To choose a bottle of wine to have with an excellent tournedos, I looked down the list for a good Bordeaux wine . . . a 1924, for instance, but there were very few, and they were terribly expensive ! . . . so we indulged in a bottle of 1893 Ch. Larose Sarget. It was not as good as I expected. . . . I asked to be allowed to see the cork. I found that it was stained with wine right up to the top, so I surmised that I had been unfortunate and had been served with an ullage.

We afterwards had a bottle of Pouilly Réservé . . . it was light, dry and very good.

I had a little chat with the waiter, and would you believe it possible ! it is almost incredible ! it just goes to show how they are almost coerced to sell the wines in stock, which will not sell themselves—He told me, in all seriousness, that with Bordeaux wine 1915 was one of the best years, and that 1922 was far superior to either 1923 and 1924 ! ! !

We had hardly commenced our meal when a lady at the next table, even at the soup course, commenced smoking. This surely should not be allowed in any self-respecting hotel . . . it is an abomination in itself, without considering the effect it has on others dining close by. If it is found to be necessary, pray allow them to have a room apart.

We finished with a glass of Old Cognac—Flavelle, 45 years old . . . it was good, but oh ! so dark !

There were two elderly ladies at the next table . . . one was enjoying a half-bottle of Médoc, and the other a half-bottle of Barsac, and these half-bottles were corked up to be served at the next meal. How much better they would have fared if they had been sensible enough to share a half-bottle of one or the other each successive night.

I remember a Brother Knight of the Round Table Club telling me that on one occasion he was staying with his daughter at the Sheringham Hotel, when they noticed a honeymoon couple (they were there for a week), and for each meal, they had a bottle of wine labelled GRAVES-CALVET, which was placed on the table. Always the same bottle, which by the end of the week still contained sufficient for a couple of meals. Poor Calvet . . . no doubt he was the one who had the blame !

We took a walk around the town . . . it was very cold. The weather had changed indeed ; we were glad of our overcoats, and even in the lounge of the hotel people were wearing overcoats and wraps.

The next morning we took a look around JURANÇON. There were some pleasantly situated vineyards, but we had no introductions, and after a cursory glance around the neighbourhood we made our way to BIARRITZ, in order to accept the generous hospitality of Mr. H. C. Levis who was living close by at Chiberta.

We passed by LESCAR, finely situated on the hillside, to the right. There was an electric railway through here, direct to

[204]

BIARRITZ, which should make this delightful seaside town more accessible to BORDEAUX.

We passed through numerous avenues, all beautiful—quite a feature of the country ; nevertheless, there were so many of them that we became a little weary and longed for the good old English country lanes.

We passed through DENGUIN, where we saw cattle with enormous horns, and through ARTHEZ, where we noticed many vineyards . . . on to LACQ, where, over the crest of the hill, we had a beautiful view.

At ARGAGNON we came to a very dangerous turning, with the warning 'DANGER'—large ; I think, for such turnings as this, a double sign would be advisable . . . one some short distance away from the present one.

Through ORTHEZ, with the prominent 'Tour' which stands on the hill, known as the 'Tour Moncade'.

At BAIGTS we saw many vines, and wondered if Mr. Levis ever countenanced any of this wine in his house, or always went further afield. Of one thing we were pretty certain, and that was, that we should not see it.

At RAMONS the sun was shining through the trees in the avenues, giving a delightful effect.

From RAMONS we reached PUYÔO, where there was a school on one side of the street, and a gendarmerie on the other, so we thought that the little 'gamins' would have to be on their best behaviour !

At a level crossing here, the gates were closed for five minutes. I could not help but notice a painter at work. . . . While doing his job, one hand was in his pocket all the time, and even when he stooped down to paint the base of the gate-post he kept his left hand in his pocket.

Eventually, the electric train passed . . . it quite frightened me to see at what a tilt the carriages were ! I thought it would topple over at any minute, but it passed safely.

I was still thinking of this at LANDES, where I seemed to notice everything awry : the vines were trained like hops, the roads had a terrible camber, the oxen walked all aslantwise, and the trains tilted terribly. After all, perhaps I was at fault !

[205]

It was market day at PEYREHORADE, which accounted for the traffic we had passed on the way. I rather like the white coverings over the poor oxen which are intended for sale.

I was also attracted by the way the ducks were evidently trained to stay in the baskets.

On nearing ST. MARTIN we came across the first quantity of Pines, so we were approaching our destination.

The way in to BAYONNE is not particularly picturesque, with the factory buildings around. We went straight on into BIARRITZ . . . it was good to see the sea for a few minutes.

The rocks reminded me of Dawlish, and the few moments I stayed there helped to remind me of pleasant boyhood holidays, spent with my cousins in the South of Devonshire.

Having taken the fresh sea air for a few moments we made our way to CHIBERTA, in order to fulfil a pleasure to which we had been looking forward for a long time . . . to take lunch with Mr. Howard Levis at his charming Villa Aturus.

In spite of a little trouble with the car, we arrived in good time, and were accorded a gracious welcome by Mr. Levis and his good lady. These hospitable people certainly deserve to enjoy this charming retreat, after many years spent in the hard life of an industrial world.

Surrounded on three sides by the pines of the forest, and on the other by the sea, this palatial Villa was tucked away far from the turmoil of universal strife.

It was here then that we were to sit down in perfect peace to enjoy a déjeuner fit for the greatest epicure, living or dead !

The following is the menu, bound in a delightful cover, on the outside of which was the reproduction of an old woodcut :

' "Cellarman examining a glass of wine."

From the title-page to

"KELLERMEISTEREY"

STRASSBURG

(1536).'

[206]

MENU	WINES

VOL-AU-VENT

FILETS DE SOLE à l'Armori-
caine.

NOISETTES DE MOUTON aux
Légumes.

PINTADE EN TORTUE garnie
cornets jambon.

SALADE LAITUE avec Chablis
et huile d'Olive.

FROMAGE BOULESTIN.

BOMBE PLOMBIERRE.

FRUITS.

CAFÉ.

SHERRY, Choice Amontillado.
(In the library before luncheon.)

CHATEAU CHÂLON, 1915.

CHATEAU AUSONE, 1920.

CHATEAU MARGAUX, 1870.

CONSTANTIA, bottled in 1878.

BAS ARMAGNAC 1900.
Domaine d'Hillet le Duc
1er. Grand Cru.

This was a feast indeed, and I feel sure that I will be excused for making some slight comment on the wines.

The Ch. Châlon, 1915, was an eye-opener . . . clear, brilliant in fact, without any suspicion of age—a wine which will last for half a century.

There is no other wine quite like this . . . a trifle austere per-haps, but an austerity that claims not only attention but admira-tion. I shall, I hope, be able to tell you more of these wines after my visit to the Jura, which should be near the end of this 'Tour'.

The two Red Bordeaux wines could not have been improved upon.

1920 Ch. Ausone, Grand Cru, St. Emilion, is a delectable wine . . . one of the finest wines of this excellent vintage. It is an old friend of mine, for I have a small bin of it at home, and I was glad to 'shake it by the hand' as it were.

There is such a fading suspicion of the truffle in the dis-appearing taste of this wine that it is almost captivating and coerces me to 'come again'—yes, candidly, I like to be coerced under such conditions !

The 1870 Ch. Margaux, 1er. Grand Cru Margaux followed.

[207]

It had taken the place of 1900 Ch. Rausan Ségla, which somehow or other had slipped out of the cellar 'unnoticed'.

I had enjoyed the 1900 quite recently, and so was not altogether sorry that the 1870 should put in an appearance.

I never feel unkindly disposed towards the Red Bordeaux wines of 1870 . . . although, from a wine merchant's point of view, they were the most stubborn and contrary wines he had to deal with. For years and years they refused to develop, but when they did start they made the rapid strides which stand them in such good stead to-day.

I think long after the '77's and '71's, long after even the '99's and 1900's have gone the way of all wine, the 1870's, especially the Grands Crus, will be regaling us with their hidden virtues.

'Mr. Levis, thank you so much for that more than excellent bottle of 1870.'

By saying this I am not endeavouring to belittle the fine quality of the 1920, but there always seems to be a special licence when referring to old age.

The Constantia, bottled in 1878, was most interesting . . . illustrating the fact that some of these Empire wines will last.

So much for the wines . . . but I cannot omit my appreciation and admiration for Julie, the cook-artist. Each succeeding dish made me wonder if she was the re-incarnation of Carême.

The Bas-Armagnac of 1900, from the Domaine d'Hillet le Duc, was much finer and lighter than any Bas-Armagnacs we had recently seen, even though we had come through the Armagnac districts.

When I think of that delightful spot : the charming hosts, and the lovely wines, I feel that it is a pity there are no 'BAINS' in the district to give a 'medical' excuse for calling again !

There was another guest fortunate enough to be invited to this repast—Monsieur Blanchet, the worthy and entertaining secretary of the Golf Club. I remember that he told me that, as an evidence of the virtue of Bordeaux wine, in the Médoc alone there were over 400 couples of old people who had been married upwards of fifty years, and in order to impress this upon me he afterwards sent me the issue of *La Petite Gironde* of 17th June, 1934, in which, at a banquet given to Monsieur Albert

Lebrun, the President of the Republic, these facts are strongly emphasised.

At the time of departure it was found that the car would not go and we were delayed considerably while Reg and Mr. Levis' chauffeur attended to matters.

It appeared, after all sorts of investigations, that the trouble was with the petrol . . . someone had played us false—instead of petrol, they had given us petrol and plenty of water ! When some of the contents of the tank were emptied out, it was found that a lighted match would not start a flame ! ! !

What a lesson ! Mr. Levis advised us, and he had learned from experience, that he always buys E.S.S.O. on the roads.

We were off at last, grateful for much kind assistance, and accomplished the journey to PAU in one hour and fifty minutes.

We had a simple dinner with a bottle of Pouilly (20 fcs.) slightly iced . . . it was enjoyable.

After dinner I took a stroll, and passing across one street I was much amused to see in large letters—

AMERICAN BAR O'BERRY.

What a fall was there ! !

On returning to the hotel I could not help thinking of my good friend Maurice Healy, and his reference to Ch. Haut Brion (O'Brien).

The next morning I paid an early call on Doctor J. A. Doléris, of the Academy of Medicine, whose name and address had been given to me by Messieurs Saüt Frères, of the rue Montpensier. I had entered their office on the off-chance of gaining some information about the wines of JURANÇON.

Unfortunately I was unable to see the learned doctor (who took such a keen interest in Jurançon wines—in fact, was a 'vigneron' himself), but his good lady gave me considerable information, and with the correspondence which passed between us afterwards, I was able to assimilate a good deal of knowledge with regard to these wines of Jurançon, perhaps better described as the wines of Béarn.

In one of the learned doctor's many books on the subject of Jurançon wines, he writes :

'Ils en sont d'ailleurs convaincus, car ils ne le supportent pas. . . . Pourquoi ? Parce qu'ils ne le méritent pas.

'Il faut mériter le vin par une hygiène physique et cérébrale bien comprise et justement équilibrée. Ce fut mon verdict. Je ne m'attarderai pas à nouveau sur la matière.

'Que de mauvais estomacs, que de foies pitoyables, que de buveurs d'eau on supprimerait si, à la place de ces horribles et innombrables drogues, spécialités, thériaques diaboliques et coûteuses, eaux soi-disant digestives, etc., on leur ordonnait des kilomètres de footing au grand air . . . qui ne coûtent rien qu'un peu de temps et de bonne volonté, ou bien l'escrime, la chasse, le mouvement en un mot !

'Il est une maxime antique et sage dont je fais personnellement mon précepte de conduite, celle de l'École de Salerne : "Bois un peu de vin". Cette texte exclut l'abus, il condamne, par contre, les abstentionnistes rigoureux, les buveurs d'eau.'

From which I understand that a good glass of wine, and a good walk every day . . . well, then you may live half the age of Methuselah.

A few wines I sampled reminded me somewhat of an Aszú Tokay, but others that were not quite so 'moelleux' were not only interesting, but when served cold, quite pleasing.

Both Red and White wine is made, but the larger proportion is the White.

This vine-growing area has suffered much in the past ; on several occasions the vineyards have been destroyed . . . on one occasion by the Emperor Domitian, *circa* A.D. 90.

The three principal growths are Jurançon, Vic-Bilk, and Monein.

The principal vines are the Mausenc, the Ruffiac, and the Courbu ; although in these days one sees other varieties, probably with the desire for more quantity rather than better quality.

A sparkling wine is also made for local consumption.

There is not much old wine to be found ; in fact, I doubt if the wines improve very much by extreme age ; in recent years the best succeeded vintages have been those of 1921, 1923 and 1924.

We left about 9.30, in the rain . . . the Little Auk behaving admirably.

I was troubled a little with a sore finger, the result of a mosquito bite, but I think the good wine of the next two days soon subdued any influences of the poison.

We did not go through JURANÇON, where the vintage had not actually commenced, but followed the road on the left to LOURDES —as I was anxious to see the place of pilgrimage fame. . . . There were plenty of vines to be seen in the immediate neighbourhood, especially on the left-hand slopes.

At ARESSY we saw a pretty waterfall just outside the church . . . it was a picture in itself.

It was very misty, and little could be seen for some distance until we reached BETHARRAM, where there was a glimpse of mountain scenery, and the miraculous fountain; the hill tops, however, were enshrouded in clouds.

We passed by some pleasant scenery, reminiscent of Perthshire, between here and PEYROUSE, which is a very quaint, interesting old town.

The weather had cleared somewhat, and we had a most enjoyable run along the top of the wooded slopes that fell down to the river . . . and we were soon at LOURDES.

Being market day, LOURDES was crowded, and in the mêlée we mistook the way and arrived at LEZIGNAN before we realised it.

Returning, we had a long wait while the cliff on the roadside was blown up with gunpowder (widening the road). When this happened, an old woman astride a donkey was nearly thrown off, which caused considerable amusement. It is strange how another's predicament causes amusement.

We eventually found our way to the Grotto, which is well worth a visit . . . it is finely constructed and very impressive.

We missed the road again on leaving LOURDES and struck a bad patch through BARTRES, and on through pretty country to OSSUN, from which place it was easy to make our way to TARBES, where we intended to lunch.

We drew up at the Hotel, where they were so busy with déjeuner that the large restaurant was crowded, and we were ushered in with several others, to a small room apart.

We ordered a bottle of Vin Blanc and a Perrier as we were very thirsty. I inquired what the wine was. 'De Gers' was the reply.

'I do not wish it', I said ... 'if it is "cher".' 'No, no—"Gers",' he said ... 'by no means "cher" ; it will only cost you four francs' (!) and it was quite drinkable.

The civilization in some parts is hardly up to expectation. It may be that I am not accustomed to it, for I never go out to lunch—not more than once a year, and that is on my annual visit to my doctor. I made a note of a few things which appealed to me as being somewhat crude, in this, one of the largest hotels in the town.

(1) The Manager passes the bread to the diners with his hands.
(2) Wet overcoats were placed across the tables ; which were afterwards used for a meal—without a cloth !
(3) One salt-cellar for eight tables.
(4) The greatest difficulty to obtain butter.
(5) The cork used for the bottle of White wine was absolutely black with age and dirt.
(6) The waiter's exit, with empty plates, was through a swing door, which he opened by giving a violent kick at the lower panels. I thought every minute he would kick right through, so I rose and went across the room to have a look at them—they were brass bound ! ! !

We had an excellent poulet, and straw potatoes ; wishing for more wine, the Manager assured us that we would be better off with the White than the Red ; so saying, he took up the empty bottle, and giving it a double somersault in the air, went away with a broad grin on his face, returning after quite an interval with a bottle of Vin Rouge ; Oh, dear no, he could not place this gently on the table, but evidently considered it necessary to subject it to the same Cinquivallian trick.

1893 Armagnac was offered to us. I made the usual inquiry ... 'Is it of good quality?' ... when the Manager (quel type) pushed the top of the bottle against my nose and exclaimed— 'Sentez !'

I think he meant well, for he waited at the door as we passed out, and insisted on shaking me warmly by the hand.

It was very wet when we were ready to leave TARBES, so we decided not to have a look round the city, neither at the Cathedral

[212]

nor at the Museum ; simply to salute silently the memory of Marshal Foch, and make tracks direct for CARCASSONNE.

The country through which we passed was not very interesting—slightly undulating in places—but the rain interfered with the visibility.

We passed over a fine bridge at LANESPEDE and then climbed up to MONTREGEAU, from which to VILLENEUVE it was very steep, which necessitated careful handling of the Little Auk because of the slippery nature of the roads.

At ST. GAUDENS we saw an ancient church, probably Norman, and then passed through some pretty country, but it was too misty to see with any satisfaction, therefore we were happy to notice above us at LESTELLE enough blue sky, as the saying is, 'to make a sailor a pair of breeches'.

After ST. MARTORY, where we had seen, still in use, a fifteenth century public weighing machine, we crossed the river Garonne by a most interesting old bridge, almost adjacent to which was an ancient Château on the water's edge.

Here we were struck by the greenness of the verdure, and that in spite of the recent drought.

ST. GIRONS is an old town with interesting buildings, terraces and ramparts, but we missed our turning, and inquired the way of the first person we met on the highroad.

The inquiry was somewhat amusing, but we managed to understand each other . . . on my side, broken French, and on his side an extraordinary North Spanish patois, mixed with even less French than I was capable of.

On making our way back we came across such a large flock of sheep that we were delayed for several minutes ; further on in a green meadow were to be seen numbers of white cattle. It was beginning to rain again, and the cattle were rising in order to seek what shelter might be offered from a few trees in the hedges. This gave me the opportunity of pointing out to Reg a simple little thing which he had not noticed before. I explained to him that cows always got up on their hind legs first, but horses on the front legs.

At CLERMONT we remarked how like parts of Derbyshire the country was, and a little further on we passed along a pretty undulating road, with small dwellings built in the hillside, reminding one of the habitations on the sloping banks of the Gironde.

There was a variety of scenery here, which made the journey more entertaining. We passed through a tunnel before le Mas d'Azil, and nearly ran into a pig at the far end, which was being urged along with a shovel.

Passing through SABARAT I mentioned that the countryside reminded me of Connemara—maybe that the sight of the pig was still having a subconscious effect on my mind. At PAILHES we had climbed to a good height, and even with the misty and cloudy weather we were experiencing, we could enjoy some beautiful scenery.

From here we immediately dropped to the river level, with good open country on either side, and here and there a small vineyard.

At half past five, we had reached MONTREAL, and were soon to be at our destination.

We had decided to stay at the Hotel de la Cité, therefore made our way through the modern portion of the town with its hotels and business premises, and taking a sharp turn on the right we climbed up until we came to the old Pont-Levis, which we crossed in order to enter the amazing and ancient city of CARCASSONNE. Through the arch, and wondering wherever we were likely to land ourselves we steered through very steep and very narrow cobbled thoroughfares . . . I have never seen anything to equal it . . . until we came to an open space on the summit, with the Hotel de la Cité on the left.

My immediate thought was, why had I never been here before, and as we left Reg confided in me that he had made up his mind to come here again 'one of these days'.

With the kindest attention we could have hoped for, we were shown our rooms, and made as comfortable as possible ; we really felt quite happy, partly maybe, that we had ofttimes heard of CARCASSONNE, and here we were, realising a consummation far exceeding the anticipation.

I could write volumes on this place, but I must put a curb to my enthusiasm.

We were in the province of Languedoc—LANGUE D'OC, Old

Aquitania. I had so often heard of the wines of Languedoc, but was always told that they were not sufficiently interesting to bother about—we shall see !

I was under the impression that all the wine, White and Red, was made from Red grapes, but this was quite incorrect, for the French law strictly forbids any interference with the natural colour of the Vins Rosés (made with grapes of red skin and white juice) in order to make White wines. Nevertheless, there do exist numerous vines in the Midi which are absolutely White, both in respect to juice and to skin. Among these, the best known are the Bourrés, Picpouls, Clairettes, Chasselas, etc.

A general market was held on the Saturday at CARCASSONNE, at which buyers from Paris, and I was informed from Bordeaux, would come to purchase these wines of Languedoc, which they used for blending.

The principal crus of l'Aude, Languedoc, are :

Vins Rouges de Limoux (which is said to rival the Beaujolais).
Vins Blancs—Blanquette de Limoux.
Corbières (rouge) (which the natives compare to the Maconnais).
Minervois 10° and 11°.
Carcassonne.

At dinner we thought we would have a number of wines, purely as a matter of education, but I fear that the Somellier thought we were . . . ! ! !

The first we tried was a Picpoul Sec (6 fcs.) from the valley ; a girl would have described it as 'quite decent', so you can imagine what it was like.

We then had a Languedoc Supérieur (8 fcs.) . . . it was a nondescript sort of wine, rather better in quality, but sweeter.

Then followed a wine called Clos du Pavillon (10 fcs.) . . . this was rubbish !

We then tried Vin Rosé Minervois—this was interesting and curious.

There were several Red wines that we thought we ought to taste ; they were as follows :

Minervois Supérieur (5 fcs.)—my remark was 'all right for children when they drown it in water'.

Haut Corbières, Réservé (7 fcs.)—you could see that this was struggling to assert itself.

We then had another Clos du Pavillon (10 fcs.) and here I was regretfully disappointed.

The Somellier was well drilled . . . he assured us that 'all wine is good' (like the English farmer—'there is no bad beer, etc. . . .') but he knew that the Red wines of Languedoc were the best. He endeavoured to induce us to try a wine of MAURY, either Red or Rosé ; he described it as 'strong, quite unique, and was better for being in bottle five years'. It was known in the district as 'Masdu', that is—'Mas-dieu'—a wine I had heard about many years ago and classed as an inferior Roussillon wine.

We really could not taste any more, but we noticed on the list a goodly number of Sparkling wines—no, we had not the courage. They ranged from 20 fcs. to 30 fcs. the bottle, and the descriptions were—

> Blanquette de Limoux,
> Ch. de Cheminières. . . .

There were a number of local apéritifs—Grenache, Rancio, Muscat . . . at 30 fcs. the bottle, and also several local liqueurs—l'Andoise, Micheline and Jacqueline at 3 fcs. the glass.

Now here was a strange coincidence—Jacqueline liqueur—I had never heard of it before, and only that very morning on arriving at CARCASSONNE I had had a letter from home in which I read that my eldest grandchild Jacqueline was seriously ill with meningitis.

We both ordered one at once, and silently drank to the health of the little girl.

In taste it was like a passable imitation Chartreuse.

After dinner I took a stroll through the quaint streets . . . it was like going through a city of the dead, and reminded me of some works I had read, by Lord Lytton, I think.

After a good night's rest we awoke to a fresh morning, and on looking out of the windows, we were treated to beautiful views over the city.

For petit déjeuner we had a sample of Narbonne honey ; it was very good. The waiter had warned me of its quality, emphasising the fact that in his opinion it was the finest honey in the world.

'Why', I asked. 'Well', he said . . . 'you see, the bees are fed on Thyme ; they are larger, better and more intelligent.' In fact, I think he thought they had come direct from the Garden of Eden, or at least, from the Ark !

I hope he forgave my smile.

We had a busy day in front of us, for we were off to investigate the wines of the Midi, and in particular those of Languedoc—all new ground for me.

We left CARCASSONNE for PERPIGNAN, intending to call at ST. PAUL-DE-FENOUILLET on the way. We motored viâ ROUFFIAC and LIMOUX with a sight of vines most of the way.

At ALET, where there is one well (80°) boiling, and another quite close where the water is icy cold, we passed the well-known Bains. After a delightful run along the course of a pleasant stream I remarked to Reg 'What an enticing river in which to cast a line', when going round a corner we met a number of anglers, complete with equipment, and yet deep in contemplation of the catches they were about to succeed in making.

From ALET we found vines on either side, especially on the rocky, hilly slopes, and they all appeared to be well kept.

It was cloudy, but not raining, and we went gaily along the twisting and winding roads to COUIZA, where we noticed a number of women washing clothes in the bed of the river.

Past this village, the country became very pleasing, with now and then a delightful avenue.

Out in the wilds when all of a sudden we came across a factory, whose chimney was belching forth black smoke to the annoyance of all except those inside.

Over a bridge guarded by four Cypress trees, which appeared to be standing at attention, we reached CAMPAGNE where the soil was rich, and the air was so permeated with new wine that I was forced to echo the words of Isaiah :

'These are a smoke in my nose—
A fire that burneth all the day.'

We managed to pull behind an enormous lorry here, but with the winding roads, we found it impossible to pass. I did not regret it much, for it gave us time to enjoy the lovely scenery; the fading vine leaves added to the beauty, with their varying autumnal tints of copper, golden yellow and the dying red.

We passed through QUILLAN, a town of some importance, famous for its felt hats, and reached BELVIANES, protected by huge white cliffs on the north, quite inspiring in their austerity.

Through cliffs and rocks a way was cut along a wonderful gorge—nothing much higher than a car could pass beneath the overhanging rocks. The river trickled far below on our left.

To arrive at ST. MARTIN-LYS we passed through a tunnel—there had been a drought . . . what would happen in torrential rain?

We will not worry about that though, for the sunshine of the present smile has wiped away all tears.

The slopes were now more wooded than rugged . . . now rugged again; here we actually passed a postman on his bicycle—lucky man to have such an environment of life!

This had been wonderful, and I was reconciled to the disappointment of not seeing the 'Gorge du Tarn'.

Here we were at LAPRADELLE PUILAURENS, more or less famous for its candies.

Comforting sunshine now was apparent, and the mountains were further apart.

Vines were predominant, and the vineyard area was far more picturesque than the Médoc. We had passed Monsieur Violet's BYRRH factory, where a thousand hectolitres a day are produced, nearly all from local wine, and arrived at ST. PAUL-DE-FENOUILLET, where we had to make a stop.

A town crier was blowing a horn and calling out some important news, but evidently not that of our arrival, for no one took the slightest notice of us.

We called on Messieurs Catala Père et Fils, who, on hearing that we had come on the introduction of our good friend Jean Calvet, lost no time in placing themselves wholeheartedly at our disposal.

I inquired if Monsieur Catala spoke English, to which he replied in the negative; adding that his son was an English scholar, and that he would fetch him.

He returned to his office, where we were, and in a few minutes was followed by his son, a tall, energetic, fine-looking fellow, who greeted us with a smile, an outstretched hand, and a hearty 'GOOD-BYE, Sir'. They were a jolly, happy couple, and we got on very well with them in their own language.

I had such a number of questions to ask, that I fear I must have worried them considerably, but they took it in good part, forgiving my ignorance.

It was all new to me; the wines are sold by the 'degree' . . . this is the most important item.

This particular wine district of LANGUEDOC comprises CORBIÈRES, ST. PAUL, PAZULOS, TUCHAN, LE CARTFITOUT, etc. Mostly Red, but some White wine is made, and the department of Pyrénées-Orientales alone accounts for an average output of four million hectolitres. The cheap variety is moved about in those huge wagon-reservoirs one sees so frequently on the railway sidings; the better class wine is kept in Hogsheads.

This year (1934) the vintage is so abundant that the Government have acted as described in the issue of 11th January, 1935, of *The Wine and Spirit Trade Review*:

'With remarkable skill the threatened crisis feared from the superabundant wine yield has been faced by the law of December 24 last. It has passed the Chamber and the Senate, and is now in operation both throughout France (including the Rhine and Moselle Departments) and Algeria. The twenty-four sections meet the conditions admirably. Every grower who obtained 200 hectolitres or more of wine is directed to have a portion of it distilled, or to cause some of the must to be concentrated, by a fixed date. The alcohol so distilled is to be delivered to the State at certain rates of payment, according to its strength and purity. Some 125,000 hectolitres of pure alcohol will thus be bought by the State before May 31, 1935, including alcohol from Cider; and the quantities so purchased will be used for carburation or for fortifying wines. Small growers or those whose vineyards were injured during the war are exempt from this levy.'

'Besides the above relief, the sale and planting of vines is

[219]

regulated, whilst a portion of the excess of new plants will, in due course, be destroyed, the owners being indemnified ; but replacement of vines is permitted up to a certain proportion. From August 1, 1935, the sale of certain quantities of wines is forbidden, except for distilling or for vinegar-making. Wines sold for consumption, whether imported or not, must be approved as fit for that purpose, and wines for blending must reach a strength of at least 9.5 degs. of alcohol, whilst rules concerning 'blocage' will apply to the wine yield of 1935.'

The blocage of the wines does not concern Gironde, Bourgogne, nor Champagne, that is, the countries enjoying what is called an 'Appellation d'Origine'.

I mean by these words 'Appellation d'Origine' a particular name under which the wine has been known, offered and celebrated for centuries, such as 'Bordeaux', 'Pauillac', 'Fronsac', 'Château Lafite', 'Cheval Blanc', and so on. The blocage concerns specially the countries of ordinary wines produced in immense quantities, such as all the wines of the Midi and Algerian departments.

As regards the wines that are blocked up, they cannot be sold in France as long as the total average of the wines existing in France according to the declaration made by each proprietor after the crop, exceeds a certain number of hectolitres, say about sixty million hectolitres. Yet if these wines cannot be sold in France during that time, each proprietor has the right to export or distil them.

The alcoholic strength varies considerably up to 18°. The Corbières wines, according to the vintage range from 10° to 18° ; the Roussillon wines from 8.50° to 13.50°.

The fermentation is quite natural. 'Without sugar ?' I asked very gingerly. 'Oui, oui, oui', was the emphatic reply—'Sans rien, rien, rien.'

There are practically no old wines (that is, table wines, not dessert wines) to be found. One vintage is disposed of within a twelvemonth, and the wines are consumed within one or two years, but Monsieur Catala agreed that he saw no reason why they should not be kept, and improve.

This drinking of new wine might have had some bearing on

the conversation relating to old and new wine, which we had at Monsieur Alfred Schyler's house.

The best succeeded vintages in the near past have been undoubtedly those of 1924, 1925, 1931; and 1934 is looked upon as being another really good one.

I inquired if any quantity of the wine was exported—'Not much', was the reply—'nearly all used for home consumption, or for . . .' here he hesitated, adding—'I should not tell you this.' 'No', I said—'but some firms in other districts find the wines useful for blending !'

'C'est ça !' he exclaimed—'but I didn't tell you so.'

The Carignan was a favourite vine stock, and for the Grands Vins, that is, the dessert wine; the GRENACHE; these White wines, quite natural, will reach at times 23° alcohol.

The Roussillon wines are chiefly consumed by the 'ouvriers', the Corbières by the bourgeois.

We had a self-conducted tour through the fine establishment, and then were ushered into the tasting-room.

The following were my remarks as we sampled one wine after another :

1934 Corbières 12°
1934　　„　　13°　—still sugar; what a difference is one
　　　　　　　　　　　degree !
1933　　„　　12°　—quite good of its kind; smells good
　　　　　　　　　　　and dry (compare Roussillon).
1931　　„　　13°　—good type, but not for England.
1931 Maury　18°　—fine raspberry flavour—but dried off.
1934 Roussillon 8.50°—acid, vinegary.
　　　　„　　10°　—not quite so bad.
　　　　　　(Attractive purple colour.)
　　　　„　　11.50°—might be drinkable with the help of
　　　　　　　　　　　water, in a year's time.
1933　　„　　11°　—Smoother.
　　　　　　(Classed as vin vieux.)
1925 Maury　20°　—Rancio; brown, old vines, dry finish.

When we had discussed these wines, we were introduced to a range of dessert wines, which were very much more interesting.

I can believe of some of these that they would prove most enjoyable, especially as an alternative to such wines as Port, Madeira and Sherry.

GRENACHE - - (8 years old)	Brown, good flavour, without being too sweet.
MALVOISIE - - (10 years old)	Lighter in colour.
MACABEO - -	Interesting, peculiar.
MUSCAT—du Pays (10 years old)	A mouthful of Muscatel grapes—wonderful for dessert.
GALAMUS - - (12 years old)	22.50°. These wines are kept in cask. Rancio style, drier in comparison with the Grenache, and yet its sweetness sticks to the lips, prolonging the pleasure of taste like a lingering kiss, and what is more, when past, you can look back at the bottle with affection !

We did not taste the Banyuls 17°, which is a wine of similar style.

At the end of this fierce tasting I craved a glass of fresh water.

The son offered me the can of water—a curious local vessel of medium dimensions; I looked at him and asked for a glass. 'No occasion for a glass', he said—'a true Catalan requires no glass' . . . and suiting the action to the word he raised the can a full arm's length above his head, and throwing back his head, he poured the water direct into his mouth—never a drop was lost. This was drinking 'à la Regalade'.

He tried to dare me to do it, but I had more respect for my clothes.

I was sorry to leave these good people, and can only hope that my ways may be their ways again one of these days . . . in the meantime, I may indulge in a sip of their remarkable wines; I can still taste that Muscat as I write ! !

We had decided to lunch at PERPIGNAN, for no other reason as far as I could imagine than that the name of the town sounded like 'possibilities'.

What's in a name ? . . .

We passed through MAURY, the streets filled with 'human' children, for they were playing 'Hop, skip and a jump' over chalk enclosures marked on the road.

How I pitied the poor parents who were called upon to provide the little boots and shoes.

The country was more open now, with the hills in the somewhat near distance.

We just scraped through the next level crossing as the gates were being closed. 'Ten minutes, or a quarter of an hour saved !' said Reg, and I have no doubt he was well within the mark.

We looked across the river, or rather at the river bed, for there was but a trickle of water, and yet . . . there he was undaunted—an angler !

Between ESTAGEL and PERPIGNAN there was little worthy of observation, save perhaps, the hedgerows of Cacti.

To the Regina we made our way for lunch, but we were not overpleased. The first wine we asked for was—'Sorry, sir, we are out of stock' . . . and if I remember correctly it was the same with the second, so, being a little piqued I said 'Bring what you like' . . . thinking I would try my luck that way.

Châteauneuf du Pape (Blanc) 1926 was suggested. 'Oh, yes', I acquiesced—'that will do' . . . adding—'I do not mind if it is a bottle of good White wine.'

'Ah oui, Monsieur', was the reply—but when it arrived it was Red wine ; everyone was annoyed.

I forgave her for she reminded me of a mixture of two old maiden aunts of mine—Ellen and Mary, affectionately spoken of in the family as 'Mellin' and 'Hairy', so you can imagine the prepossessing maid we had to wait on us.

We were determined to have a bottle of Vin Blanc, and seeing on the list a wine supplied by our good friend Jean Calvet, we ordered a bottle of Chablis, 1er. cru, 1924, and made a present of the offending bottle of Vin Rouge to the waitress.

The Chablis was very pleasant and we enjoyed it—Reg, neat, and I, helped with Perrier.

The dish I quite enjoyed was one of kidneys, grilled and served on long skewers, very hot and with fried potatoes they just appealed to me.

Before leaving we thought we would have an Armagnac (for experience more than any other reason) . . . there was none to be had !

We then suggested Cognac. When the bottle was produced it was Eau de Vie . . . there was no Cognac ! Is this not unbelievable, that in one of the best restaurants in a large French provincial town it was impossible to find a glass of Cognac !

We thought we would return to CARCASSONNE viâ NARBONNE in order to have a view of the country . . . it was not very interesting, rather flat, with some poor-looking vineyards here and there.

We left RIVESALTES on the left, having heard that there were no old vines remaining, and that the quality as known in days gone by did not exist. We therefore decided to go straight on, in spite of the fact that we would have liked to salute the town that gave birth to that illustrious Frenchman, General Joffre.

At SALSES we passed a village smithy at work. This always seems to give me a slight thrill of pleasure.

The sea, or rather 'un étang', was on our right, and the scenery was more entertaining, with the mountains at our back.

The weather had cleared, and we had a pleasant run to NARBONNE; on approaching which town we easily recognised the many advertisements we had seen, displaying the conspicuous towers. From here we turned to the left, in order to make for CARCASSONNE.

Vines and more vines all the way to VILLEDAIGNE and on to LEZIGNAN-CORBIÈRES ; thousands of acres of them.

At BARBAIRA we noticed the 'Caves Co-opératives' which is so useful to the smaller and peasant vignerons.

At TREBES there is an interesting old church, and from here we caught sight of CARCASSONNE in the distance—it was a fine sight !

At dinner that evening we saw quoted on the Wine List, 1913 G. H. Mumm, Cordon Rouge at 150 francs ; but not for us ! We called for a bottle of Chablis and to follow, a bottle of Claret, 1924 Dom. de Chevalier (40 fcs.) ; the same peculiarity attributed to this growth . . . it was very enjoyable, of excellent quality, but rather lighter than I would have expected.

The cheese of the country, I think described as 'Moun' . . . a little resembling Port Salut, went very well with it.

1870 Armagnac, Domaine de l'Abbaye, was quoted. It was most necessary for us to taste it (10 fcs.) . . . it was very dark in colour ; none the less it was soft and quite good.

After dinner Monsieur Paul Grabette, who took charge of the comforts of visitors to the hotel, very thoughtfully handed me a book to look through : it was an amazing book, and I advise anyone visiting this hotel, to take the opportunity of looking at it.

It is the work of a Monsieur Henri Sivade, Secretary of the Society of Arts and Sciences, of Carcassonne, and it is executed admirably, the whole work of emblazonments, pictures and script being carried out in the most accurate manner.

When I revelled in this work, I thought of Brother Hilarius, and for the first time could, in a measure, understand his desire to be a limner.

It is indeed a great prize—no wonder that Monsieur Grabette smiled when I suggested it might be for sale.

The sequel to this was that, when Monsieur Sivade called in the evening he was told of my admiration, and suggested that he would bring up to the hotel in the morning one of his works, on which he had been occupied for upwards of three months, as perhaps it would interest me.

It did . . . I have it now . . . one of the most entertaining and astounding productions I have seen. It measures three feet eight by five feet, representing an illuminated survey of the Cité.

In exchange for some francs this beautiful souvenir changed ownership, and in addition, in recognition of a copy of my *Viniana*, he dedicated it to me. I was very proud to receive this from the learned and accomplished man.

Should you meet him in CARCASSONNE, stop and speak to him . . . it would be worth while ; he stands about 5 ft. 2 in. ; not overdressed, has a little white moustache, and has the appearance of a 'savant' absorbed in his work.

The next day was Saturday the 20th of October, and by my diary I saw that it was my 'Saturday off', perhaps the second in twelve months, so we decided to spend the morning having a good look around this remarkable city.

B.W.

While we were waiting for an excellent guide introduced by Monsieur Grabette, we were intrigued by two functions taking place at the church immediately outside the hotel. The one was a funeral, the other a christening; so that was all square, we thought.

This church, or one-time Cathedral, of ST. NAZAIRE, is most attractive. The west wall is of the fifth century, and a part of the structure is Gothic.

Along came our guide, so off we went—I will not venture to give a literary description of this city; but simply to place on record in a short and concise form, the interesting items which I remember, or which I jotted down as we went along.

Outside the hotel is yet another smaller hotel, the Carcas; so called from the Celtic tribes who came here from Italy three to four centuries B.C.

The first, or outside wall of the city, built 200 A.D., is nearly one mile in circumference; the inside wall approximately three-quarters of a mile; this second wall was built in 1240 A.D. by Louis IX (St. Louis). The restoration had been in the care of the renowned Viollet le Duc, he who was also responsible for the work at Vézelay.

In the quadrangle, or amphitheatre, with the fine walls as background, is played once a year to crowds of spectators, two performances of a Shakespearian play. Last year it was *Hamlet*, and the guide described it as most entrancing; there could not be a better setting, especially for the ghost, making his appearance down the stone steps of the walls.

As we walked along the ramparts and entered the various turrets we had wonderful views—the one over the two bridges was most pleasing. In fact, with so much to remember I have lost myself, but I frequently think of the wonderful towers, turrets, bastions, barbicans, etc.

One can dream to advantage, as I did that very evening, looking up at the ramparts in the moonlight, reconstructing what the guide had told of the Romans fighting around here 100 B.C., the struggles with the Visigoths and the Saracens, until Simon de Montfort made himself master of the place . . . and pondering over the fact that the English Parliament (the mother of Parliaments) was based on the method of legislature obtaining at CARCASSONNE about de Montfort's time. Rather thrilling, I thought !

With these strange imaginings, in the shadow of such ancient surroundings, I must have been on the verge of a sentimental impulse, for I remembered the words of Wordsworth :

'For I have learned
To look on Nature, not as in the hour
Of thoughtless youth ; but hearing often times . . .
The still sad music of humanity.
And I have felt
A presence that disturbs me with the joy
Of elevated thoughts, a sense sublime
Of something far more deeply interfused
Whose dwelling is the light of setting Suns.'

I would not like you to run away with the idea that I remembered all this, but I knew the sense and most of the wording, so have looked it up in order to give it to you correctly.

We had a simple lunch at the hotel . . . a casserole which was excellent, and a veal steak which also was very good, and with these we had a White Languedoc wine, Hautes Corbières (7 fcs.). It was of a good colour and pleasant to drink.

After lunch we decided on a run around—our primary objective being MINERVE, but we mistook the road . . . nevertheless we enjoyed a pleasant trip over the black mountains ; through TREBES and LAURE, the countryside being well planted with vines.

After this we went quite astray, and had a long run up hill, down dale, over mountain passes ; with hardly a person or a dwelling however humble to see. I enjoyed it, feeling sure we should arrive somewhere.

Eventually we struck the little town of CAUNES, and took the hill to CITOU, where the remains of an ancient fortress still stand.

Here, wine making was progressing on the slopes of the hills ; we ventured still higher to LESPINASSIÈRE, where most of the houses appeared to us to be in a dilapidated condition.

Yet still higher we climbed to SALES. At the summit, about

three thousand feet up there were fine views. The country was wild, and the few odd houses here and there in the rocks helped to make an excellent scenic effect.

Returning from here we found a winding tortuous road, making it incumbent upon us to proceed very warily.

We eventually reached MAZAMET, a busy town at the foot of the hill. This is an important centre for wool and washing ; a large portion of the wool used in Europe, coming from Australia, is washed and combed here. The red roofs of the town could be seen from all angles, and added a touch of colour that was not in the least displeasing.

Higher up we passed CUXAC ; a pretty village, evidently laid out for a summer resort—and on, with a drop, to VILLEGAILHENC, with its remains of ancient battlements.

We were now well on the way back—some of the roads had not been very grand, but the scenery had, and this made up for it.

We could see the Cité of Carcassonne in front of us, glorying in the red light of the setting sun, and we did not hesitate to obey its glowing invitation.

At dinner we had a bottle of Graves, Ch. Carbonnieux (Blanc) 1922. I think we were too fatigued to take much notice of it, however, I made no note of its qualities, for which reason I gather it did not impress me.

After a short stroll, groping through the silent, eerie, cobbled, narrow by-ways, and passing innumerable cats, I returned to the hotel, and was glad to find my bed.

CHAPTER XI

CARCASSONNE TO MARSEILLE

(MIDI WINES)

THE next morning we were happy to see the weather bright, promising a fine day, especially after the sunset which had set the city aglow.

I carried off very proudly my souvenir from Monsieur Henri Sivade, and received a complimentary bronze medal, struck in honour of the Cité de Carcassonne, Bi-Millénaire, from Monsieur Grabette; to whom I was offering (not as a 'façon de parler', but most sincerely) my grateful thanks for all he had done to make my stay in the remarkable place most interesting and enjoyable, and to me—memorable.

We followed the same road as before, passing LIMOUX; where a Sparkling wine is produced, to ALET, a watering place, with interesting ruins of an eleventh century Cathedral, and on to COUIZA. Here we forsook the main road, as we wished to pass by the Gorge du Galamus. The countryside was rugged . . . the remains of a demolished castle stood high up on the hill, and a number of small houses dotted here and there reminded me of the dreary-looking cottages of evicted tenants in Ireland.

We took a turning on the right to RENNES-LES-BAINS; we had with difficulty located this, for the sides of the mountains being so close together, it was almost hidden from view.

The scenery here was grand, offered by a gracious Providence to appease the groanings of the rheumaticy patients who arrive in numbers to take the cure at RENNES-LES-BAINS, which is quite a good-sized town in the wilds.

On we went, in the happiest of moods, for the air and the scenery required it . . . rugged hills alternating with woodlands—

narrow, very narrow roads, up hill and then down again, around corners with a view of a sheer drop of, maybe, a thousand feet below. The very colouring of the rich soil, and of the autumnal leaves, red and gold, added an extra warmth to the heart.

Here and there, through a gap in the mountains, we could discern a humble hamlet, content with such an all-sufficiency of life.

Suddenly the mountains as it were disappeared, and we were faced with an open countryside; actually a small vineyard and a field of maize; perhaps the means of existence for the few inhabitants of the hamlet we had espied.

'Reg', I said, 'we are in for some more of this magnificent scenery, for look ahead at those awe-inspiring mountainous rocks.' 'That must be near the Gorge of Galamus', he said, on referring to the map. I agreed, although we must be at least a dozen miles by road from it.

We passed by BUGARACH, a very ancient village, which as Reg said went back to the year 'dot'.

We nearly ran over some jet black ducks, lazily wandering in the roadway; but we did not, and 'a miss is as good as a mile'.

It was quite fascinating to motor around these winding roads through the mountains; whose very sides seemed to hug together. I would not care to risk it at night time, or through a thick mist, for without any protection there is a sheer drop into the precipice below; surely, if 'Sens Unique' was ever necessary it would be here.

We were travelling down a hill, the sides of which were dotted with small trees and shrubs, in which a number of small wild birds had sought refuge. The next habitation was CUBIÈRES, where on the hill we could see a quaint building, standing alone, without any pretence of another building in the immediate neighbourhood. On making inquiries we learned that this had been an ancient monastery, but now only the church remains.

'Galamus !' said Reg, and here we actually were; an enormous defile; the overhanging rocks threatening like the sword of Damocles.... 'For the land's sake, don't sound the hooter', I begged of Reg, 'for if you do, these rocks could not stand the shock, and would fall on us.'

We stopped to contemplate, but as there could be no passing

[230]

here (the roads being so narrow that the sides of the Little Auk almost seemed to touch the side of the hill and a low protecting wall that had been raised here); we therefore sought a spot a little further ahead, where a cutting had been made for the purpose.

The grandeur of the scenery must be seen, for no poor pen of mine can adequately describe it.

As we emerged from this defile, and gazed upon some of the bare-faced villainous-looking rocks, I hardly knew whether to cry or laugh.

Having passed through a short tunnel, cut through the rocks, we came to more open country, and breathed more freely. Here were the fine vineyards belonging to Monsieur Catala, some of the produce of which we had already been privileged to taste; I really must have a few bottles of this Galamus wine to offer as a sip to grandchildren in the years to come, when inspiring them with the details of this glorious experience.

I have no doubt that there are other gorges as beautiful, or even more so, but this, my first, is good enough for me.

We were now close to ST. PAUL, but before reaching there we had to negotiate with considerable care, some extraordinary, twisting roads—half a dozen hair-pin bends, as it were !

Through ST. PAUL-DE-FENOUILLET, where we gave a thought to Messieurs Catala, père et fils, we then followed the same road as previously to PERPIGNAN.

At PERPIGNAN we had lunch at the Grand Hotel and decided to try the Vin Compris, a young Vin Rouge du Pays. . . . It was quite drinkable, especially with the Perrier, which I added to it. What a quantity of Perrier I must have consumed during my tour ; the dividends should be increased !

We had Rouget . . . very good ! And, to follow, a beefsteak which was equally good . . . a most excellent choux-fleurs au gratin came after that.

I thought I would like to indulge in a few grapes, so helped myself to them. As I was eating them I wished they had had no pips—perhaps one of these days I shall be able to spit them out on to the plate, like the natives, without feeling self-conscious and guilty ; especially when a young thing or a demure dame is sitting opposite.

[231]

After this very comfortable déjeuner, we set off for BEZIERS, viâ NARBONNE ; we followed the same road as before, with a slight exception . . . a wrong turning taking us a little out of the way, past LES CABANES.

At SIGEAN we saw plenty of vines, and what interested us much more at the time was the number of sailing boats making the best of a fair wind—blue sky above and blue water beneath. We were soon through NARBONNE, with its bridges, its taverns and its avenues . . . 'And, thank the Lord for that !' ejaculated Reg. 'Why, might I ask ?' . . . to which I had the terse remark, that it savoured too much of the war-time . . . ' 'NO-BON".'

A straight road took us to COURSAN, leaving by a fine avenue of very old trees, 'peupliers argentés', which looked quite majestic. Over the river Aude we nearly ran into a couple of lovers ; he appeared desperate and she calm. I trust no hole was made in the river, later !

We then reached NISSAN . . . a few hills had relieved the monotony of the flat country through which we had passed, and we soon had a view of BÉZIERS which stands out well in the approach.

We put up at the Midi Hotel, where we were quite comfortable, and happy to say that in spite of the proximity to the station, the trains in no way interfered with our night's rest.

After having safely garaged the car, and as there was some time to spare before dinner, I thought I would have a look around the town, and perhaps find the office where I was to call on the morrow.

I passed up the hill, along a few streets, and eventually arrived at the address for which I was in search. I looked it up and down, and noticing a light in the upper rooms I thought I would inquire if this were actually the place.

In answer to my knock a kindly dame opened the door.

'Is Monsieur Nougaret in ?' I inquired.

'No, sir ; he does not come on the Sunday . . .' Believe me, I had quite forgotten the day of the week.

'A thousand pardons', I offered, and explained. The lady accepted them with grace, saying that a few gentlemen had met upstairs to have a private talk . . . that was the reason of the light burning. She also told me that Monsieur Nougaret was a very,

[232]

very busy man, and if I wished to catch him I must go before nine o'clock in the morning to an address she wrote for me on a paper. . . . With the best of smiles, and an uplifting of the hat, I thanked her and bade her 'Good Evening'.

I took a stroll along the broad walk in the centre of the town. There were literally thousands of people there, simply walking up and down, doing nothing.

It was a motley crowd indeed . . . the air was full of all sorts of aromas, in particular, the offending garlic.

There were chasseurs returning, by the score, all with varying degrees of contentment on their faces, according to the weight of their bags ; some wondering 'how the devil they missed it!'

Pêcheurs returning on bicycles—push-bicycles and motor-bicycles . . . many of them by their looks, deploring the loss of the largest fish they had ever hooked.

'Make way ! make way !' . . . I heard behind me, and turning, saw a goat-chaise, with four children seated in it, wishing to pass. It was pulled along by two parent goats, with a couple of their kids harnessed alongside, evidently being instructed in the work which was to be life's occupation.

Next week was to see the opening of the second Congrès National des Médecins, Amis des Vins de France, Exposition Horticole. . . . This may have had some bearing on the reason for such crowds wandering about the streets.

The enterprising paper *L'Eclair* was announcing in the windows of its office the results of the Rugby football matches ; the crowd here was so dense that it was impossible to pass, so I made my way back to the hotel to partake of a frugal meal.

The fish was 'Daurade', coarse (John Dory) . . . followed by poulet, and to drink we had a Languedoc wine ; Pelure d'Oignon Rosé, 12° (8 fcs.) ; it had evidently, from the outside appearance, been in the bottle for a long time, and this confinement had not improved it. To be candid I noted it down as rubbish'!

With coffee we had Armagnac—I found so often that I could obtain better value and better quality with this Brandy . . . there were a great many Armagnacs figuring in the lists of the provincial hotels.

[233]

The next morning, before 9 o'clock, I started off to see Monsieur Nougaret. His good lady spoke to me and begged me to understand how very occupied he was; but I was able to smile my way through this defence, and was ushered into the great man's presence.

He inquired of my mission, to which I replied by handing to him my letter of introduction from Monsieur Cruse.

This worked wonders, for he said ... 'What you require will take more than a few minutes, and I have not more than a very few to spare ... come and lunch with me at the Hotel Moderne.'

'I have my son with me.' ...

'Of course, he will join us; yes? no!'

'Yes', I replied, with suitable thanks. As he ushered me to the door, with a 'bien entendu' ... 'midi et demi' ... I saw him take up the telephone receiver and ask for the hotel, and, as we passed along the corridor we could hear him emphasising the necessity of having a really 'excellent déjeuner'.

In order not to lose time we decided to take the journey to SÈTE, or CETTE (as 'Cette' was too Roman) so that we might make a call on Monsieur Déjean, to whom Monsieur Delamain had given us an introduction.

SÈTE has been wrongly called 'CETTE' for many centuries. As the Romans, in their galleys, approached this shore, they observed the Mountain of SÈTE, or Mont St. Clair, which from a distance resembled an enormous whale lying in the sea; they therefore gave to this mountain the name of Mount Sétius, whence the alteration in spelling.

The country was not very interesting; some vines here and there. Passing VIAS and AGDE we soon came along close to the sea on one side and the Étang de Thau on the left.

SÈTE appealed to us as we approached it, and on arriving there we were not disappointed, for it is a busy centre, well allocated ... an excellent harbour, founded in 1666 on plans drawn up by de Vauban; with a quantity of shipping ... fishing boats predominant.

There are a number of attractive bridges across the water, which runs between the sea and the étang, over one of which we crossed in order to reach our destination.

Monsieur Déjean gave me a hearty welcome. I had left Reg at the end of the street, which was under repair.

I was anxious to see the making of our special Vermouth, and was introduced to a remarkable chai, where tens of thousands of hectolitres of good Vermouth were in their infancy.

Vermouth is not a modern 'wine' in any sense ; we hear of it upwards of a century ago. I suppose that, as a centre, SÈTE and MARSEILLE were selected by reason of the number of different wines varying in quality in the Midi, and the excellent harbour near at hand.

Of all those who drink Vermouth, it is only a small percentage who know how it is composed.

The principal ingredient is White wine, but for French Vermouth, 'any old White wine' will not do. It is absolutely necessary for a good product to have wines from the Midi, and in particular from such vines as the Picpoul, the Bourrés and the Clairettes.

With the help of a natural alcohol of at least 11° to 12°, the strength of the wine is raised, and the wine is pumped into immense casks—oak casks. 'Cement and glass-lined tanks', said Monsieur Déjean, 'should be absolutely discarded.'

These vats were enormous to look at, but must have been small in comparison with the wine cask at Bad Duerkheim, which, it is said, will accommodate no less than four hundred persons.

After many months the wines in these several casks are tasted, and equalised one with the other.

Muscat wine is then added with the desire of supporting the wine with an agreeable bouquet.

This then, is the basis of good quality French Vermouth, and to it is added a mash of a large number of herbs, of which the quantity and quality is the secret of each merchant. Amongst them we can safely mention the quinquina and the camomile.

After this has all been well mixed up the Vermouth is drawn off and subjected to a number of finings in order to extend to 'Vermouth' its limpidity.

The Vermouth must now remain together in cask for long months, in order to 'get' well together and produce the apéritif that is so well-known the world over.

French Vermouth should always be served fresh . . . I do not necessarily mean—iced.

Monsieur Déjean desired to impress upon me that in winter time it is served as a useful stimulant, and in summer time with aerated water—a refreshing beverage.

When I ventured to cross-examine him about the apparent frauds that masqueraded as French Vermouth, he told me that a very weak alcohol—not a pure natural strength alcohol—was added to the White wine (and very often water instead of wine), to which was also added, sugar instead of the fine Muscat, and a species of essences instead of the herbs.

These substitutes are immediately placed on the market, without any maturity, and are given labels which, to the outside world, lead the consumer to believe that they are the veritable article.

To sum up, I would add . . . Go to a Wine Merchant whom you can trust when buying French Vermouth.

I would incidentally say, I was more than ever strongly convinced of the trustworthiness of Monsieur Déjean, in addition to which he was, a few years ago, a great exponent at Rugby football (one of the French stars), having played for Richmond when living in England. I always look upon those who play this game as 'men' in every sense of the word.

Taking advantage of Monsieur Déjean's geniality, I asked him, with tongue in cheek, how Marius and Olive were. At this he laughed loudly and begged of me not to believe that the *Méridional* was entirely a 'blagueur'.

'I will, however', he added, 'tell you a true anecdote, which neither Marius nor Olive could improve upon.'

I think it better repeated in French as I heard it, so will pass it on in the same way; especially as I failed in translating to my own satisfaction the exact significance of 'un tout petit bonhomme'—

'Mon père', said Monsieur Déjean, 'il y a quelque temps, en se promenant a entendu et vu la petite histoire suivante: "Un homme très grand et très fort marchait sur le trottoir et derrière lui marchait un tout petit bonhomme qui disait des choses désagréables au grand type qui était devant lui. L'autre en ayant

[236]

assez se retourne vers le petit et lui dit—"Ecoute bien, j'en ai assez. Si je souffle tu t'envoles et si je crache tu te noies".'

I reluctantly admit that I had never taken any particular interest in French Vermouth, or any other Vermouth, but I came away properly interested after this entertaining and instructive visit.

I was very much indebted to Monsieur Déjean and I told him so in such a manner that I feel sure he believed me.

We must now hasten back to BÉZIERS to partake of lunch with Monsieur Nougaret (Président de l'A.P.V., Vice-Président de la Fédération Française des Stations Uvales).

As far as I can remember the following was the menu served in a private room at the Hotel Moderne :

HORS D'ŒUVRES	VIN ROSÉ DU PAYS
BARBUE	10°-11° (frappé)
PINTADE DE LA RÉGION	
FROMAGE	VARIOUS RED WINES
DESSERT	OF THE COUNTRY
CAFÉ	

It was indeed an excellent lunch . . . the Vin Rosé was delightful, and I refused to improve upon it. I have tried to obtain some for home use but so far without success. I was thinking how economical and delightful it would be for tennis parties.

The Barbue, which had been cooked by the chef himself, was absolutely IT. I never remember tasting so delicate and delicious a fish, and Reg will endorse this ; I know he had two helpings, and I believe would have wished for another.

The Pintade was equally well served ; Monsieur Nougaret was explaining that they consider the Pintade to be 'demi-gibier', and laughed when I suggested that a cock pheasant 'a fait la bétise' in the farmyard.

During the conversation at déjeuner I understood that the principal White wines came from the Pinot, Marseillan, Pomerols, Paulhan, Clermont, l'Herault, Fontes and Caux . . . and the Red ones from St. Georges Herault, St. Chinian, Roquebrun, Cessenon, Frontignan, Corbières, Minervois, Montredon and Narbonne—both Montagne and Plaines.

For the Rosé wines, it was necessary to go to Bessan, Roujan and Caux.

And last but not least, the Porto de France, that is the Banyuls, from Banyuls in the Pyrénées-Orientales.

However, the topic of conversation which interested Monsieur Nougaret the most, and for which he was the keenest advocate was—

'LE PUR JUS DE RAISIN'
or
'Le Traitement Uval'.

He preaches the virtue of grape juice everywhere, and from the papers I have scanned from the pens of such learned men as Doctor Bondony, Edouard Barthe, Docteur Leon Dieulafé, I have no doubt that he has an excellent basis on which to build his teaching.

Personally, I have a liking for the fermented juice, but I will not deny that there must be much virtue in the unfermented juice, although from my experience in Bordeaux I was not excited on making its acquaintance.

'For all the valuable time you gave to me and the fund of information I acquired, not to mention that most excellent déjeuner, I thanked you heartily, Monsieur Nougaret . . . and I seize this opportunity of doing so again.'

After leaving our good friend we made for NÎMES, taking the road viâ SÈTE, as earlier in the day.

The sand and seashore were so inviting that we were constrained to alight and walk about, picking up shells and throwing pebbles into the Mediterranean . . . it was quite enjoyable—I was almost inclined to bathe, but I had no towel handy, and it would have taken too much of our valuable time.

We therefore hurried on, and coming to FRONTIGNAN I considered it necessary to make some inquiries as to this erstwhile famous wine.

I called at the Co-operative, and after passing a quarter of an hour with three intelligent lady clerks who gave me much information, I was introduced to the manager, but he was a busy man and I had not come to purchase !

However, I will relate what I gathered from the ladies during an interesting conversation.

The wine that made FRONTIGNAN famous was the Muscat de Frontignan, but, alas ! . . . the sale for such wines, they informed me, had fallen off, and not a vast quantity was made.

When bottled it was generally golden in colour, but became darker with age . . . I suspect, very madérisé.

It is certainly true that during the time of the French Kings the Muscats of Frontignan, as also those of Lunel and Rivesaltes were very well known. If the quality, and especially the quantity have suffered it is owing to the laws, relatively recent, which have authorised the 'vendange' to commence at the moment when the fruit is ready to be gathered, whereas in order to have a riper and sweeter grape, one would leave the Muscat grapes on the vines until the end of November. With the existing laws, which allow anyone, whoever he may be, to pick the grapes from the vines after a date, varying according to the year, the Muscat grapes are gathered, to the great harm of the proprietors.

It is for this reason that the renowned Muscat wines have disappeared almost completely ; all fallen sadly from their high estate.

I have tasted a few of these wines, and can readily understand that, for those who know how to appreciate such luscious, sweet Muscat wines they must appeal very forcibly.

These young ladies told me that the wines of FRONTIGNAN had a history dating back to Roman times, although some authorities considered that the particular vines were brought from the East by returning Crusaders.

The soil was stoney, and well suited to these plants, and these two factors together had resulted in the produce of which their countryside was so justly proud.

As a parting shot (as the manager arrived) they told me that one great Frenchman, Rabelais to wit, had the greatest regard for Frontignan Wines, to which I could only reply that I was able to believe it, because I did not think he would say an unkind word about any wine.

I would like to have spent more time here, but neither the

manager nor I had much time to spare, so, raising my hat three times—once each to the three young ladies, I departed.

Reg had been waiting, wondering what had become of me and, in spite of a suspicious tone in his voice I think he believed all I told him !

The days were drawing in very quickly now, in fact, by the time we were crossing La Mosson (5.20 p.m.) it was quite dark.

We arrived at the fine old town of NÎMES, and stayed at the Imperator ; where, once again, the electric light failed, but not for long on this occasion.

With chicken broth, which was comforting, a tenderly produced sole, which was entertaining, and a 'sanglant' tournedos, which was nourishing, we toyed with a bottle of Vin Rosé from the Vallée des Papes (17 fcs.) and a bottle of Sparkling St. Péray, sec ; that is to say, not too sweet.

This latter wine was peculiar—very distinctive in every way. I cannot say I considered it very favourably, however it was drinkable when well iced.

At the next table to ours were three people—Ma, Pa and the Baby once again, and although the Baby must have passed twenty-one, she gave as much trouble and anxiety to her parents as if she were but a few years old : a very unpleasant, pouting and rude young woman, whose good looks in no way made amends for her behaviour.

A walk through this fine city afterwards, with a special look at the Roman Arena . . . it is a wonderful sight indeed, and as the moonlight, jockeyed by a slight breeze, played through the crevices and small openings it was most alluring, and led one's thoughts to all sorts of gladiatorial happenings.

Returning, my thoughts (for what reason I do not know) alighted on the 'enfant terrible' of the dining-room in the hotel, and I quite agreed with myself that we were all prone to spoil our children, which was a bad mistake.

I wondered if the tables would ever be turned in this topsy-turvy world, and one day children would insist on spoiling their parents.

Finding a mosquito net hanging over the head of the bed, and never having used one before, I decided to be a 'devil' (as the parson did when he entered the smoking carriage), and draw it over the bed.

The experiment was not a success, for I found it so oppressive that at 2 o'clock that morning I was obliged to get out of bed and remove it. I have not yet made up my mind whether it would have been wiser to put up with the oppression than to suffer the bites of sanguinary mosquitoes.

On settling the bill next morning I found yet another tax included (Taxe de Séjour and Timbres) . . . it really is becoming the limit ; extras are continually being added to one's account—as the American cousin would say 'they will pass the "buck" every time.'

These little pricks are very irritating—I would much prefer to pay more for the accommodation and know exactly where I am. But no, a franc or two is knocked off the price of the room, and three or four added by way of extras—taxes, or what not !

I was not very happy about it . . . I had to get out and let the cool morning air blow the cobwebs away—then I thought, I should forget it.

The country outside NÎMES was somewhat flat. On the way to ST. GERVASY we passed many Olive groves, as well as vine-yards. The gathering of the Olives was proceeding apace ; some of the Olive trees were apparently of great age.

On we went and, before very long, we had reached the Pont du Gard, of which we had heard so much . . . it is certainly a most imposing spectacle.

I left Reg to have a 'go' at the Little Auk, which was becoming a bit obstreperous, while I wended my way up the tortuous path, beneath overhanging Olive trees, to the heights, the gorgeous view from which justified the climb.

We rested here for a considerable time, during which we could hear thunder rolling in the distance, and wondered whether we should find the storm later.

Lorries laden with Olives passed us in large numbers . . . there appears to have been a very good harvest this year, and I gathered from a few words here and there in the Olive groves that everyone was well satisfied.

Very large grasshoppers were much in evidence near the

Pont du Gard ... one particularly hefty creature I singled out and tried to frighten it, but Oh dear, no ! ... instead of jumping away from me it deliberately sprang at me ... it may be that living in the vicinity of the Saltpetre caves, the nitre had had some influence on its mentality.

We continued our way to COMPS over the crest of the hill to BEAUCAIRE, then finding the lower level we crossed the Rhône by the bridge of Fourques and followed the road to ARLES.

We had not noticed a great number of vines as we came along, but after passing RAPELES we found the public distiller hard at his work by the wayside.

The country was not particularly interesting—the haze no doubt interfered with our views, for we could just discern the hills in the near distance.

At ST. MARTIN-DE-CRAU we went along an avenue of Cypress trees—very stately, making one feel that it was wrong to smile while in their company ; in fact, as if it were due to their condescension we were allowed to pass. All standing to attention ; not a button missing, as it were ; with reinforcements on the left ... some of these, however, were slightly out of alignment —with years !

On our right was a race course, so we knew that we were nearer SALON, where we intended to partake of lunch.

In this town we noticed an extraordinary fountain and also the Church of St. Michele—very old. The outside was very dusty looking, but the inside was fine.

As we wended our way to the Grand Hotel we saw a large number of pretty girls approaching, but distance lent enchantment to the view, for they had obviously plucked eyebrows, and all the other appurtenances relative to 'facial fraud'.

Menders of chairs were on many pavements, and in the gulleys their children were employed in the happy game of making mud pies.

The Grand Hotel—yes, we might emphasise the Grand. ... I cannot remember what we ate, but I made a note of the wine— Vin du Pays, Provenant du Canton de Lambesc ; Ch. de Calavan Rosé (9 fcs.)—nothing to complain about, but with this description, as one might expect, nondescript !

Seated near us was a delightful old dame enjoying her half-bottle of wine, showing that there was no age limit to the enjoyment of wine.

Reg whispered to me—'She must be a hundred years old if she is a day' and I could not help but add—'This is the result of drinking wine.'

It is amusing and interesting to criticise, especially when no malice is intended. We had Savoie cheese of Marseille. . . . Says Reg—'Before you get to the fromage you must eat the knife-polish; but you will not notice this if you help it down with butter and grey "Poupon".'

The waitress was taking some nuts to the centenarian—another evidence of the value of wine to aid digestion : we could not miss seeing the vigour with which she broke them—then a sip of wine. One nut was finished and the shell ignominiously discarded when she lifted the fruit from the basket in search of another. The waitress, we had spoken of between ourselves as 'Skinny Liz'. I asked Reg what age he thought she was. 'Well', he said—'look at the neck ; no teeth, hands nearly worn away with work, legs like spindles—but her hair is tidy. . . . I should say anything between an old thirty and a young sixty.'

The déjeuner totalled 51 francs. I produced 60 francs, which evoked from Skinny Liz the inquiry—'Do you wish for any change, Sir ?' They are happy in SALON !

When we were outside we found the same sense of joyous juvenility apparent. An old gentleman with a huge bunch of flowers . . . where was he off to ? . . . a padre on a motor bicycle, going down the worst cobbled street ever seen.

A number of young women were standing outside a large car and laughing hilariously at an old fellow joking with a couple of girls inside. Hop, skip and jump on the pavement. We had to mind our step.

Outside the cafés, men were amusing themselves with all sorts of games.

Two girls were making eyes at a young Adonis on a bicycle, and he didn't know whether to be tempted.

All this may seem silly and futile, but we noticed it, and you must see what we see as we go along this journey.

'Good-bye—happy SALON—we salute you.'

From here we passed through LANCON, where there is an ancient Cathedral. Near BERRE the country is open, with a view of a large expanse of the Étang.

On the roadside we saw many trees being tapped, as we skirted the lake at ROGNAL . . . then up we went, between rugged hills, and down again into the City of Marseille.

I could not miss seeing an enormous notice on a wall, which read 'VIVE LE ROI', with the Fleur de Lys ! !

Marseille is a very large city, with upwards of 800,000 inhabitants. The streets were crowded, and the atmosphere permeated with garlic. Through this we made our way to the Grand Hotel in the Canebière, where we had excellent accommodation on the fourth floor, but being outside four cross-roads we anticipated much noise during the night . . . and this we had—enough to drive Belisha crazy.

During a short walk before dinner, I was impressed with three things—the difficulty in finding a letter-box, the number of young women carrying infants in their arms and more to come, and the shell-fish stalls on the quay-side—how any self-respecting community could put up with such a smell, such piercing shrieks of the women opening their wares—was to me incomprehensible.

We had a simple dinner at the Canebière, and took the wine 'en carafe,' which answered well to quench our thirst.

I was fatigued, and noticed little about me, save at the next table, a child who was so very plain-looking that, if things go by contraries, her parents will have to be on the look-out when she grows up.

After dinner I took a stroll in another direction, and came to the conclusion that MARSEILLE was a fine city, well laid out.

As I walked along I made a mental note that the men seemed to be absolutely domineered by the women.

Quite tired I returned to the hotel, and asked for the bedroom key ; 'It is upstairs in the door, Sir' was the reply. When I reached there—on the fourth floor—it wasn't ! I am sure you will forgive me what I said, when I had to go all the way down for it and come back again.

Good . . . and now to bed. As usual, I placed my hands in the bed, the idea being to feel the sheets. These seemed to me to be slightly damp—how I wished that I had an oat-beard with me, with which to confront the authorities.

Some of you may wonder to what I refer, when I say 'oat-beard' . . . one hundred and fifty years ago, and more, one would invariably find attached to a barometer—probably at the head of the wood-work, a small circular contraption which contained an oat-beard. Beneath this would be the thermometer, then the barometer, and at the foot a spirit level.

The use of the oat-beard can be readily understood by the following explanation. Supposing you were travelling in these by-gone days with your family—shall we say, from the West of England to London—when it was necessary to do the journey by road . . . you would have to pass the night (one or more) at an hotel, or country inn on the way.

Your good lady would be shown her room, and the first thing she would be in the habit of doing would be to tell her maid to fetch the oat-beard.

This 'instrument' being fastened by a small spring was easily removed and taken upstairs, where it would be immediately placed between the sheets—if they were damp the oat-beard would respond by slightly moving round.

The lady seeing this, would summon, without delay, the hostess . . . no words were necessary ; producing the oat-beard was self-explanatory, and she was convicted out of hand.

No doubt apologies would be forthcoming and the use of the long-handled bed warmers was brought into requisition.

Not having either an oat-beard, or a bed-warmer by me, I felt constrained to sleep between the blankets !

What with the unusual covering, the mosquitoes and the noise, the night's rest was not one of the best. About 5.30 I turned on the light, and commenced to read some of the literature provided by Monsieur Nougaret.

The following are the principal vines cultivated in the Midi :

ARAMON. The 'Plant Riche' or 'Uni Noir' of Provence. The most productive of the Southern vine-stocks ; very fertile, it grows in nearly all the soils ; in the plains it gives a very large yield but the wine is lighter than on the hillsides where the produce is richer in colour and in alcohol. The wine of Aramon is agreeable to the taste.

CARIGNAN—or 'Bois Dur', produces less than the Aramon, but it is more highly valued by the trade because the wines are fuller in colour and alcohol ; very vigorous and fertile, the soil of the hillside suits it admirably. It is well to watch for the appearance of the disease Oidium.

TERRET (Black, Grey, White). The grey Terret is especially cultivated in this region for the production of White wines.

GRENACHE—'Bois Jaune' produces alcoholic wines and sweet, largely used for the production of the Banyuls.

CINSAUT—vine with a double purpose, giving a fruit for the table or a very select wine.

MOURVEDRE OU ESPAR—a vine of Provence giving a wine of deep colour, rich in alcohol.

MORRASTEL—gives a wine with more colour than the preceding one but it is less productive.

ASPIRAN—a table grape, delicate, excellent. Fine wine can be made but little colour.

CLAIRETTE—used in the production of dry, sweet and sparkling wines. The yield is small.

MACCABEO—produces a very sweet wine in the district of Roussillon.

UGNI BLANC—spread over Provence, it is productive and gives a good wine.

MUSCAT DE FRONTIGNAN—sometimes used for dessert fruit, but it gives excellent sweet dessert wines (Rivesaltes, Frontignan)—yield small.

PIQUEPOUL—cultivated in sandy areas producing white wines.

TABLE GRAPES

MADELEINES—(Angevine, Celine, de Jacques, Royale) are earlier than the Chasselas and also bear less.

CHASSELAS—golden, very popular round fruit; gives an excellent table grape lending itself readily to commerce.

MUSCATS—varieties, which one finds with LE JOANNEN in a private garden.

I am feeling aglow with excitement at the arrival of my old friend, the Sec., who changes over with Reg, in capacity of 'chauffeur'.

This delightful individual is no chicken, that is to say, by reference to his birth certificate which gives him seventy-eight years, but otherwise he would hold his own with any perky chanticleer.

Considering all things, however, I must try to arrange a quieter room for him, after his flight from London to Marseille, although he would be the last to acknowledge that he was in the least fatigued.

The morning was fresh and bright, in fact the air was exhilarating. The first call was at the bank, where I received the correct number of francs; what an extraordinarily long time it does take to obtain change at a foreign bank!

From here we proceeded to the office of the Air-France, in order to purchase a ticket for Reg—through to Croydon, viâ Lyon and Paris (changing aeroplanes at Le Bourget). The cost, if I remember correctly, was 1150 francs. The lady clerk, an intelligent creature, handed me the ticket in exchange for the francs, when I noticed that she had finger nails of a natural hue.

Was I taking a liberty, to shake her by the hand and compliment her? I trow not . . . this is one simple way of allowing ourselves to express what the majority of us think.

We had a look around the vast establishment of Messieurs Noilly Prat et Cie; it was quite a revelation of methodical work—everyone industrious, and everything scrupulously clean. To give an idea of the proportion of this huge undertaking, a delivery of from 4000 to 5000 cases each day could be accomplished.

At the actual moment the output was 3000 cases per diem. At times the demand was larger than the supply as the wine used was required to be of an average of four years.

The alcoholic strength for this Vermouth to be used in France, tested 18°, whereas, for England it was necessary to ship it a trifle higher, 19° Gay-Lussac.

We walked back to the Canebière for lunch . . . the noise in the streets of MARSEILLE can faithfully be described as 'awful'. One half of the people who wished to converse together, were obliged either to shout at close quarters, or place a hand to the ear to protect the sound.

After a hurried lunch, taking the Vin 'en carafe' as liquid refreshment, we hurried off to MARIGNANE, to meet our old-young friend.

The plane, piloted by Casanova, arrived safely within a few minutes of the scheduled time, and there was Samuel Thresher, alias Sec., as happy and smiling as if he were enjoying a new experience in the throes of energetic youth.

We commenced bombarding him with questions as to his journey, and then we found out that the old rascal was in reality a dark horse. . . . Instead of coming straight through from London, he had been spending two or three happy days in Gay Paree ! ! He was old enough to know better, at the same time old enough to take care of himself, and' he looked and felt, I am thankful to say, in the best of health.

Instead of taking the somewhat uninteresting way back to the city, viâ ST. ANTOINE, we made a détour through very hilly, in fact mountainous country along the shore of the Mediterranean, and the length of the quay, into the Canebière up to the hotel.

Here, he was allowed a few hours rest before dinner, while I prepared the itinerary which we were to work upon on the morrow.

Bondronnée-Canebière being so close, adjoining the hotel, we decided to dine there again.

The attention I was giving to the Sec helped, more or less, to beat out of my memory what we had at that particular meal. I remember an excellent mutton casserole—the rest has escaped me.

We started with a bottle of Rosé, Pelure d'Oignon (8 fcs.). . . . I did not care for it, although it was far superior to the one we had tasted at BÉZIERS.

We soon left this, and fell back on a delightful White wine, pétillant—I believe it came from Anjou.

The one thing I recollect about that dinner was that the office of reception clerk was filled by an attractive young lady, who was most anxious to relieve us of our coats, and to see that we were well cared for.

She looked too superior to accept a ' pourboire ' but, desirous of expressing thanks in some way, I sent the 'chasseur' for a box of chocolates, which, when I gave it to her encouraged such signs of gratitude that I felt at any moment I should be enveloped in her arms.

The only comment the Sec made was 'I see that I have my work cut out. . . . I did not bargain for this !'

Before turning in I took a walk along the Canebière and adjoining streets; while doing so I came across the railway station, with an hundred steps or more to reach the platform; this sight caused me to heave a sigh of relief as I thought of the two dozen steps I have to overcome at Surbiton station each morning.

CHAPTER XII

RHÔNE WINES

I HAD only one regret at leaving the noisy surroundings of my mosquito-infested room at the hotel, and that was—the bath-room ; the bath was of good size, and was certainly more homely with its hot and cold directions on the taps, instead of 'chaud' and 'froid' or indeed—which has happened to me— 'froid' on the hot tap, and 'chaud' on the cold.

With my café complét, what I took to be marmalade turned out to be Apricot jam. I ate it solely because the memories of 1914-1915 made me smile—Apricot again !

The morning was fine, for which we were glad, not only for ourselves but for Reg, who was soon to be off to the aerodrome to fly back to England. I was very sad at the thoughts of losing him, but when 'the devil (office) drives . . . etc.'

We had had a very enjoyable tour, covering about 2400 miles and I have no doubt that the knowledge he was able to assimilate will stand him in good stead.

We bade him 'bon voyage' outside the bus which took him to MARIGNANE, and then, fetching the Little Auk, we were ready to start on the last lap of the tour.

We were soon well on the way, traversing the same road by which we had originally entered, as far as LES PINCHINADES, where we turned right, in to a good road G.C. 15., and continued along a pretty road to LIGNANE. On the way there we passed such a quantity of heather that would have sent Lorne crazy, in spite of the fact that there were several notices displayed— 'Chasse Gardée'.

The Vitrolles mountains were on the left, and with a wild scenic waste, looked imposing.

At LAFOND we passed an important wireless station, and later, suddenly came across an immense reservoir, from which there is a fine view. Here we saw a couple of magpies, so I had to initiate the Sec into the mysteries of these birds.

At ST. PONS there was a very bad turning which we safely passed . . . 'thanks to the two magpies', said the Sec.

At EGUILLES we had the imposing view of an ancient church, built on the summit of a hill. We had climbed a long way up and were enjoying some beautiful views, when I could not help but wonder if the inhabitants appreciated it or would rather be in MARSEILLE.

From here we entered into some open country which was not very interesting ; at ST. CANNAT we found it necessary to attend to the petrol requirements of the Little Auk.

We now took notice of vines, the first we had seen since leaving MARSEILLE. At LAMBESC where there is a notable clock tower we heard a dog barking furiously, and on looking round we found that the cause was a postman. I made the natural remark to the Sec that, even in other countries, dogs bark at the postmen, and we wondered as we went along whether the 'cause' was the same.

The hilly country, the 'chaine des côtes' on the right and also opposite, provided more pleasant scenery until we reached PONT ROYAL, where we passed through a long avenue of Planes, formed into an archway, which was very picturesque.

Through the town of SENAS, and on to ORGON, where we saw a remarkable building standing alone high up on the top of the limestone cliffs . . . we could not decide whether it was a church or a monastery, but it was not worth arguing about.

At the Plan d'Orgon we were stopped at a level crossing, and after waiting a long time we were mortified to watch the train pass . . . it consisted of one carriage and, as far as we could see, a sole passenger !

As we passed through ST. AUDIOL I commenced to sneeze ; ' Hallo', said the sympathetic Sec—'have you a cold coming?' 'I hope not', I said, 'but I fancy I had damp sheets on my bed at the hotel.' However, I am glad to say that it passed off without troubling me.

After some time we passed over another railway crossing, which was open, but to our dismay, we saw on the farther side a car on the bank, which had evidently tried conclusions with a train !

We crossed the Durance by a fine suspension bridge. The water in the river, as usual, was very, very low.

Through BOMPAS, and we were soon at AVIGNON, where we intended to stop.

Sec had noticed that the brake of the car required tightening, so he insisted that this was the first thing which needed attention ; as I thought all bodily comforts, in the shape of a déjeuner, were more essential, I left him to see to the car while I went in search of the other.

We stayed at the Dominion Hotel, which proved most comfortable.

The omelette aux truffes de Périgord was excellent . . . followed by a delicate 'gibier'—but I cannot remember what it was. To wash these down we had a bottle of Grand Hermitage, Ch. de Thouet, 1928 (16 fcs.) . . . it was of good quality—some body and bouquet.

Now that we were on the Rhône, we considered it the correct thing to order the Vins du Rhône.

After lunch I inquired of the Sec if he were tired. I could see that he was slightly piqued, for he replied that he was 'as fresh as a daisy'. I therefore suggested a run over to the Pont du Gard, feeling sure that this beautiful spot would appeal to his animate nature.

We took the road viâ REMOULINS, passing on the way many hillside châlets, which were pleasing in their aspect, in spite of the clouds which seemed to be gathering.

There were many small vineyards to be seen on the way, and after passing 'La Begude' we encountered numerous Olive groves, in one of which the Sec insisted that he should take my photo plucking an Olive branch laden with fruit.

At REMOULINS we crossed over a suspension bridge, carrying on until we came to the Pont du Gard.

We left the Little Auk to take care of itself and climbed up to the top of the higher bridge ; from whence we had some fine views, one in particular looking towards CASTILLON, which stood up in the semblance of a proud outpost.

[252]

Before dinner at the Dominion Hotel at AVIGNON, we thought it well to sit awhile in the reading room, and read a little of the beauties we had just enjoyed.

We found however that it was hopeless, for a child in the custody of its governess—for so we took her to be—insisted on spelling out aloud the letters of the alphabet.

The flies were very aggravating, and I expressed myself to the Sec as I had done before when similarly annoyed : viz., I have never forgiven Noah for not allowing the spider to have a meal off those two flies which he had taken into the Ark ! !

At dinner we selected, to commence with, a Clos Tavel (14 fcs.) . . . it was very light, as Tavel should be, and was very enjoyable after we had allowed it to remain in the ice bucket for sufficient time to be fresh.

I cannot give the reason, unless it was to do with the damp sheets at MARSEILLE, but I wheezed ; which provoked from the Sec—for which he should be severely censured—the following remark. . . . 'When you w(h)ine, you must be looked after.' And suiting the action to the word, he proceeded to fill up my glass.

With a good hot dish of Champignons Bordelaises, we thought we would have a more substantial wine to go with the extra flavour, and so selected a bottle of good Bordeaux, 1924 Ch. Haut Brion—Larrivet ; it was very enjoyable . . . a trifle browner and older than I should have expected—I wondered if the hotel cellar was too warm.

We inquired for a dessert wine, thinking it was correct to do so, but they had none—neither Rivesaltes, Frontignan, nor Lunel—rather remarkable, but there it was ! And, what do you think we were offered in its place. . . . ' A wine ' for the English visitors—'a good Porto from Marsala' . . . it is almost incredible!

Some time after dinner I took a walk before going to bed, and passing down a street I noticed an extraordinary thing in the window of a restaurant, where the staff were packing up for the night.

A terrier dog was seated on a table looking quite content as he drank out of the gold-fish bowl ! I watched him, and must admit that he did so in a most gentle and considerate manner, so as not to disturb the fish.

The next thing which attracted my attention was the presence of a man in another café—he was haranguing his fellow guests, and was so vehement that he actually tore his handkerchief in pieces and fell into his chair exhausted.

On the other side of the road, further up, stood the Opera House. As I was passing, the people were just coming out . . . you cannot believe the babel of voices—everyone endeavouring to explain to the others the plot and the beauty of the music.

As I returned to the hotel I thought : so this is AVIGNON of which I have heard so much . . . how flat it falls after CAR-CASSONNE.

When getting in to bed, the telephone bell started to ring— 'Yes . . . what is it ?' 'A telegram for Mr. Thresher.' . . . 'Send it up.'

I took it in to him, and waited while he read it. 'Nothing wrong, I trust', I inquired. . . . 'Oh, no', he said . . . 'only from my wife, hoping I am well and telling me she is—God bless her —good night.'

The next morning I awoke refreshed after a good night's rest, undisturbed, for there were no mosquitoes and free from noise, even with the casement windows wide open.

The early morning was slightly misty, but by 7.45, when we were ready to start, the weather had cleared.

The first incident which attracted my attention was a company of poilus marching along and, as they passed an officer, they properly saluted, whereas he took not the slightest notice, continuing to read his paper.

We made our way around the ramparts, the fourteenth-century walls encircling the town, taking a good road to SORGUES, then crossing the Ouvèze we passed through ST. LOUIS to COURTHEZON . . . there to find a Monsieur F. Dianoux, to whom we had an introduction from Monsieur Jean Calvet. Monsieur Dianoux is an important man at COURTHEZON—'un Vice-Prési-dent du Syndicat du Commerce en gros des Vins de Vaucluse,' 'Conseiller du Commerce Extérieur,' 'Membre de la Commission d'Exportation des Vins de France.'

We had no difficulty in finding this gentleman at L'ENCLOS, where he was busily engaged at his office when we arrived, but his niece—one of the most intelligent and charming ladies I was privileged to meet in France—immediately summed up the position and took charge of us.

We were ushered into the private house, where the lady gave us much interesting information about the district, and the prospects of the present vintage.

After some fifteen or twenty minutes, which passed quickly, we were joined by Monsieur Dianoux, who immediately placed himself entirely at our disposal.

On entering his large chais we saw many very large glass-lined cuves . . . these contained the least expensive wines from the Côtes du Rhône.

The wines of the Châteauneuf du Pape were stored in wooden casks.

These chais were actually under the vineyards, in fact, we were literally surrounded by the vine in one shape or other.

We quitted the chais, and were permitted to taste in the open courtyard, (using an empty cask placed on end as a table), a number of wines which interested me immensely.

I made a note of the wines as they were produced ; the simplest way to explain them to you will be to copy out my notes in the rotation of tasting :

1928 Châteauneuf du Pape 15° . . . . Very good.
　　(This came from a small vineyard known as 'Latour')
1930 Côtes du Rhône, 14°. . . . I did not like this, and by the look on the face of the Sec, he was evidently of the same opinion.
1929 Côtes du Rhône, 15°. . . . Very much better ; should make a drinkable table wine at a very reasonable price . . . excellent value.
1929 Châteauneuf du Pape, 15°. . . . Very good indeed—*this is the one* with body and flavour.
1928 Tavel . . . Vin Rosé—was the next we tasted, from the Co-operative de Chusdan, 12.50°. 'Non, non', I said, but the Sec, not desirous of airing so much of a foreign language, acquiesced by a nod of the head.

Monsieur Dianoux then introduced us to his Marc, of which he was very proud—which consisted of skins only, and was placed in large vessels known as 'SILOS'; hermetically sealed, before being distilled at a high strength.

We tasted some of the ten-years-old . . . I can still hear the Sec spluttering ! And then a sample of one—twenty years old ; it certainly tasted of the grape.

At the back of the establishment was a fine vineyard owned by Monsieur Dianoux, and he explained to us the various vines . . . the Morastel, the Conoëse and the Grenache—these grapes gave his Châteauneuf du Pape, the last named being of the best quality, and helped to cause the wine to mature more rapidly.

Some of the wines of COURTHEZON are entitled to the appellation 'Châteauneuf du Pape'.

'Come along', said our indefatigable host—'we will visit some of the actual proprietors' . . . and without further delay, off we were, at such a speed that it put the fear of God into the Sec : we missed knocking over the wall of a bridge only by inches, at which Monsieur Dianoux turned round and facetiously remarked—'We have to be careful when taking these sharp turnings.'

We were informed that the red leaves on the vines were those of the Alicante, and the yellow ones of the Grenache ; by which we gathered that the Grenache was of better quality.

We looked across at the Castle of Château-Neuf du Pape ; it stood out admirably and was a pleasant sight. Near here we alighted and tasted a red wine just made (1934) . . . it was good. I hesitated to place the 'V.' before 'good' . . . there was sugar, and a little fermentation.

We then visited a vigneron of the name of Jean Avril, and sampled his 'Clos de Jean' 1934 . . . this should turn out quite well.

From here we called on an old and delightful vigneron of the name of Sabon. This enthusiast regaled us with several specimens of Ch. Neuf du Pape wine, made by himself on the spot. . . .

1934 . . . Sucré ; lighter, drier than Jean.

1929 . . . Dry finish . . . not so attractive as the wine we tasted this morning.

1931 . . . Did not care for.

1933 . . . 14.50° . . . lighter, elegant—I like this.

1932 . . . Clos du Mont Olivet—I thought this most unattractive.

The language that Monsieur Sabon spoke was, to us, quite unintelligible. I asked Monsieur Dianoux what it was, and he told me that it was the old language of the Province—the 'Langue d'Oc'.

We expressed our best thanks to our old friend for his kindness, and with a hearty shake of the hand, left him in a happy frame of mind : these old vignerons do love someone to come and make a fuss of them and their wines.

Outside the chais, Monsieur Dianoux introduced us to the Baron P. Le Roy de Boisseaumarie, an enthusiastic advocate of the virtues of wine in general, and of Châteauneuf du Pape in particular.

He is Chevalier de la Légion d'honneur, Croix de Guerre, Président du Syndicat des Propriétaires des Côtes du Rhône.

We were fortunate in meeting this gentleman, for he very kindly invited us to call on him at his residence, the Château Fortia, later in the day, when he would be happy to supply us with much literature bearing on the local wines.

After leaving the Baron we made a call on the Réserves des Cardinaux, and tasted the wine from several casks of 1929 vintage.

I was well pleased with them, although each cask seemed to vary considerably. The first was good—that was a wine with body, and yet not coarse, with sufficient bouquet, and not overloaded with sugar.

The sample from the next cask was very much like it, but gave me the impression of its being a trifle more delicate . . . but, with No. 3, the tables were turned. The wine did not appeal to me in the same way . . . please do not ask me to account for it, for they were all supposed to be the same wine.

We then wended our way back to AVIGNON, Monsieur Dianoux pointing out to us the Château de Fine Roche on the left, which stood out so well, and then the very large gunpowder factory on the right. Soon after passing here, we went by a company of Black Troops, which interested me quite a lot.

Arriving at AVIGNON we made for the Palais des Papes for déjeuner . . . there we fared exceedingly well, enjoying an excellent lunch, and some Tavel wine by way of beverage.

Mdlle. Beysson, another delightful niece of Monsieur Dianoux, joined us, and we made a happy party, although I had to keep my eye on the Sec.

A bottle of Châteauneuf du Pape was ordered, and the Chef was summoned to be complimented on his déjeuner.

We all toasted each other in a glass of the 1929 ; but I found that the wine was somewhat 'troublé' . . . no doubt owing to the vintage time and the fermentation in the air.

There were a number of wines mentioned on the Wine List at the Palais des Papes, among them the 'cru de la Nerthe', but I looked in vain for the well-known vineyard of Saint Patrice.

It was a great many years ago—in fact, in the year 1822, that the topographer Jullien referred to the following crus as 'worthy of being considered of the highest class' : Châteauneuf-Calcernier, cru de la Nerthe, Saint Patrice, La Fortia, etc., etc.

I would like to have made an opportunity of calling upon Monsieur Antonin Establet, the proprietor of the cru Saint Patrice, but unfortunately I had not the time to do so.

You will remember that I have already made reference to my excellent friend, Stephen Gwynn. He has a particular weakness for Châteauneuf du Pape . . . perhaps this weakness is underlined in reference to the Saint Patrice, seeing that he is so worthy an Irishman.

We have all heard of the association of Saint Patrick with Ireland . . . I gather from Mr. Gwynn that Saint Patrick was a Briton, but trained in France for his mission to Ireland, and that he lived for many years on the 'Ile de Lerins', near Cannes.

Knowing of my interest in these wines, and having a good recollection of one or two excellent bottles that we had enjoyed together quite recently, my good friend wrote me from his retreat in Dublin, and said that it was James Joyce, the author of 'Ulysses' who heard of this Clos, and then had insisted on having a special label designed, for the honour of Ireland. It is a most attractive label, and Mr. Gwynn sent it to me by special post on St. Patrick's Day.

I must admit that I am already beginning to experience an inward desire to taste this wine and I must certainly lose no time in writing to the proprietor and finding out what he has of it.

The actual label which reached me had been taken from one of a case of bottles sent by Joyce, to Mr. C. P. Curran, the well-known Irish man of letters. Enclosing this label, he described the sender as 'one of the kindest of men and most courteous of friends' and quotes a letter which accompanied the wine :

'I never drink it myself as I dislike red wine, but it is really "wine from the royal Pope". This vineyard is at Chateauneuf du Pape, the oldest in that part of France, and Antonin Establet who inherited it says that before the sojourn of the Popes at Avignon, the wine of the country was known as *"Vin de S. Patrice"*. I never met a fellow-islander who had heard of it, but I mentioned it to Count O'Kelly, the Irish Free State Minister here' (*i.e.* Paris), 'and to Dulanty, the High Commissioner in London, and they said they would get it for dinner, etc. There is another S. Patrice below Tours, but it is only a *"Vin de pichet"*.'

Mr. Curran adds in his letter to Stephen Gwynn, which I consider was excellently expressed, and I am sure I will be forgiven for repeating it :

'I think you and I will agree that this vintage should be our national drink at this season, and should be admitted to this country free of all duty, except that of drinking it. When this objective has been reached it will be our next business to have restored to the Dublin diocese that portion of *Hibernia irredenta* which includes the Archbishop of Dublin's vineyard at Beaune.'

I understand that the Archbishop of Dublin, who acquired this vineyard at Beaune, was a Norman of the thirteenth century. It would be rather entertaining to find out when the 'See' were 'foolish' enough to abandon it.

On leaving the Palais des Papes, Monsieur Dianoux suggested that we should have a cup of coffee at a café that he knew well. On the way we saw large quantities of fruit and vegetables being placed in lorries—these, we understood, were being prepared for despatch to England.

Arriving at the said café we met the Maire of AVIGNON (who is elected for six years) and several friends, all of whom joined us, and for a quarter of an hour or so we were a jolly party.

Leaving here we passed through VILLENEUVE, where there was a fine view on the right. The vintage had ended on the 15th October.

We noticed in the neighbourhood quantities of bunches of grapes on the vines, and it was explained to us that these were late 'table grapes', and required a longer time—about a month—before being gathered. The grapes are known as 'les Gros Verts', the skins of which are somewhat thicker, and accordingly stand the journey better. However, later we saw large quantities all neatly packed in baskets awaiting transportation.

We were now at TAVEL, and some word from the niece who accompanied us, made me note down—'Oh, happy uncle !'

We immediately commenced tasting some wines . . . 1934 Tavel, 12.50°, which appealed to me as being more than one would expect. We tasted several of these wines, which are most agreeable. . . . I cannot understand that, with an alcoholic degree like this, they cannot travel well and be popular in our country.

We had to make a few more calls, and on the way we passed a very large public washing-place, occupied by a dozen or more women : the Sec insisted on photographing them—what a lad he is !

Near LIRAC we came across a public distiller hard at work ; we alighted and had a chat with the officer in charge. He allowed us to taste the spirit as it was produced. I once heard the expression— 'hell fire water at the pit's mouth', and I think it would have fitted in here admirably.

Our next stop was at ST. LAURENT DES ARBRES (Côte du Rhône) where a wine akin to Tavel is made, but without the appellation.

Here we made a call and were allowed to taste a few wines of the Côte du Rhône, 1934 vintage, and almost drinkable now : they are intended for immediate use, and will be worth less in a twelvemonth than they are to-day. We then sampled a wine—'Landun' . . . the price asked was only about 2 francs a litre—it was astonishing value ; but only having 9.1° alcohol, I doubt very much if it would stand a long journey.

The particular vines in the district are : ARAMON, CARIGNAN, GRENACHE.

Leaving here we asked the way. . . . 'Tournez à droite', said the man of whom we inquired, and waved to the left ! It is absolutely astonishing how frequently this happened, or vice-versa.

'This is Mont Faucon Castle', said Monsieur Dianoux, pointing to the left, and certainly it looked most imposing.

We then called on the Baron on our way back to COURTHEZON and collected the books which he graciously presented to us.

We bade adieu to our kind host, and to Mdlle. Marcienne, only hoping that they thoroughly understood how 'thoroughly' sincere we were in our expressions of gratitude and thanks for all the kind hospitality they had showered on us.

The other niece gave us the pleasure of her company to AVIGNON, and when she left the car, would you credit it—that ancient Adonis claimed the privilege to kiss her hand !

After this somewhat strenuous day, we decided to have a very quiet dinner at the hotel, enjoying a bottle of 1927 Château-neuf du Pape with the same. It was certainly the best specimen of any 1927 wine I had met.

A little walk, by myself, before turning in, when the first thing I noticed was the 'PLANIMETRE'; how useful they are . . . and they could be very well exploited everywhere.

The loud-speakers outside the cafés made an awful noise, so deafening that I changed my direction, and a little later found my way near the café where the vehement man had been holding forth the previous evening . . . but, no ! He was not there—he was probably haranguing elsewhere, as the place was nearly empty.

As I arrived back at the hotel, I could see a fog approaching, but it cleared away in the night.

This was a wicked night for mosquitoes—very little sleep ! There was a brilliant light from a street lamp which shone into the room . . . this may have been the cause, so I jumped out of bed and pulled the curtains to : still it shone through them !

[261]

All night my arms were swinging round like the 'arms' of Don Quixote's Windmill; in a desperate encounter against umpteen odds. They, that is, the insects, must have won, for I was sorely treated.

The next day was Saturday, the 27th October, and we decided to have a day off.

By the time we left AVIGNON the last vestige of the fog was clearing and we made our way over the fine suspension bridge at PORT DE ROGONANS for a run into the country.

Unfortunately, rain was threatening, and before we reached TARASCON it had commenced to drizzle. We suddenly came upon a rugged scene of menacing rocks, through which the railway had been cut.

´Having passed here, we entered upon more open country; with plenty of vegetables—cabbages in particular; vineyards and Olive groves.

At TARASCON, the Château du Roi René, of the fourteenth and fifteenth century, is well worth a visit. . . . More flat and uninteresting country in front of us; in fact, nearly all the way to ARLES.

It was little wonder that we took notice of a huge lorry lying wrecked in a ditch, and from inquiries we gathered that the humane driver, in endeavouring to avoid two women bicyclists, had met with this calamity.

We had now arrived at ARLES, which is a very interesting city, especially from the point of view of antiquity.

The Arena is fine, although I preferred that of NÎMES. We entered and had a walk around, the Sec insisting that I should be photographed in various positions, with and without him.

At the Eglise St. Antoine we found a one-armed man endeavouring to erect a tressel stand for a coffin which was due to arrive. As he appeared to be in some difficulty we gave him a hand . . . pleasant occupation ! The Sec seemed to be preoccupied and it was only after some inducement that we left ARLES, and coming across the eleventh century ruins of the Abbey Montmajour, decided to visit them.

It was very wet under foot, but overhead it was brighter. The concierge showed us around, and was most painstaking.

This is a remarkable building, with an even older Chapel beneath. A short time back a gold chalice was found hidden in the walls : our guide assured us that it is of immense value, and is now in the Louvre.

We were led to a corner near the entrance when the guide called out some word—I think it was 'Alloa'—and we listened to the echo, which seemed to double and redouble itself, and to be never-ending.

Outside, the ancient well—centuries old—was still in use for drinking water, in spite of which the old fellow appeared perfectly happy.

We looked in at the refectory, now full of sheep and goats . . . hundreds of them, all baa-ing at the same time ; 'history repeating itself' was a naughty thought that passed through my mind.

What a marvellous echo would be produced if a number of them were placed in that particular angle of the Abbey. . . . I suggested that, for twenty francs we might try, but the ancient would not take it on.

We sauntered across to the parapet, and leaning thereon, were able to contemplate in comfort a fine scenic and historical view.

There stood the Montagne de Corde, with the appearance of a guardian, wistfully keeping an eye over the ruins of this Benedictine Abbey.

Centuries ago, this mountain was the scene of a remarkable victory on the part of Charlemagne when he defeated the Saracens.

It was actually in the sixth century, and the battle is known in history as 'La Bataille de Corde' ; seven hundred of the Saracens were slain, and the remainder fled, mostly on foot, leaving their beautiful, half-savage white steeds as a prey to Charlemagne and his army.

These interesting details were obtained from the concierge, who, having such an honest face, I think must be true . . . I hope so !

We shook him warmly by the hand (which to outward appearance did not suffer with an 'itching palm') and were so effuse in our expressions of thanks that with watering eyes he begged us to receive a modest souvenir, one which I prize . . . a little picture of the sheep.

He was anxious for us to see the Chapel St. Croix quite near at hand. He wished to accompany us, but as it would have necessitated a steep climb for him, we refused to allow it.

The Sec and I agreed that he was a jolly nice old fellow, whom to meet was a considerable pleasure.

We did not enter the Chapel, contenting ourselves with a scrutiny outside, which bore much remarkable specimens of the sculptor's art.

On the ground adjacent, and cut into the solid rock, were hundreds of tombs, so ancient by now and so overgrown that they almost lost their gruesome identity ; however, I had to seize the opportunity—I struck a pose and almost whispered to the Sec, that pretty sentiment of Omar Khayyám :

> 'And this delightful Herb whose tender Green
> Fledges the River's Lip on which we lean—
> Ah, lean upon it lightly ! for who knows
> From what once lovely Lip it springs unseen.'

and all he replied was :
'Who knows.'

The clouds were heavy, and we were passing through a desolate country (the signpost indicating DAUDET MOULINS), until we reached FONT VIELLE which, with the hills and mountains on the left, engendered a more pleasing outlook.

Here were vast olive groves . . . we tasted one or two olives —how perfectly beastly, to be sure. I was forced to light a tiny cigar (the Sec doesn't smoke), although my rule is not to smoke until after dinner ; when I indulge in as good a weed as I can afford—or occasionally two.

When passing MAUSSANE we exclaimed together that the weather was clearing ; at this we were very glad, for the country was beginning to be much more interesting . . . rugged mountains—quite rugged except for a few feet of the slopes, which were wooded.

Round hairpin bends, up and up we sped into the clouds . . . what a pity it was not fine weather, for what a view we missed.

The country around St. Rémy is full of romance and interest. While thoroughly enjoying it we came upon, as it were quite suddenly, LES ANTIQUES, dominating a fine view in every direction.

These monuments are known all the world over : the Arc de Triomphe, raised to the glory of Julius Cæsar B.C. I, is the principal attraction, but also of immense interest is the mausoleum (mécène). Do not forget to make a note to go, should you be in the neighbourhood, a good long distance out of your way in order to visit these super-imposing monuments. We then decided that for déjeuner we would go to LES BAUX ; passing on the way Les Grandes Vignobles ... Domaine du Mas de la Dame.

It was clearer as we approached LES BAUX, and the only word I can think of to describe the scenery is MAGNIFICENT—in capital letters.

From a little stall on which were exhibited post-cards, picture albums and the like, I purchased some for a few francs ; the old man, who was evidently the proprietor as well as the vendor, desired to embrace me, I thought ... but no, only to shake hands, and he added—'Had I but ten customers like you each day I would be able to retire from work.'

In relating this simple incident, I do so not to show up my extravagance, but to illustrate how little these people really desired in life.

We entered the Hôtel Reine Jeanne, to take déjeuner ... a quaint restaurant, but comfortable enough, where Victorine took charge of us and relieved our hunger and thirst.

It was quite remarkable how, in such an out-of-the-way place, we had so excellent a déjeuner :

SAUCISSON D'AILES
    pâté maison
—

OMELETTE AUX TRUFFES   VINS DU PAYS ROSÉ
—

LIÈVRE EN CIVET
—

GIGOT D'AGNEAU RÔTI
—

TOMATES PROVENÇALES
   pommes frites   MUSCAT DE FRONTIGNAN

—

FLAN AU RHUM

—

FRUITS

Each dish was served as it should be. The Vin du Pays Rosé was excellent, and it was for that reason that we did not make a change for the second bottle—(12 fcs.).

The Muscat de Frontignan was very attractive (25 fcs.), but as we only wished a glass and not a bottle, Victorine considerately opened a bottle and served us accordingly.

I cannot understand why these wines, with their beautiful Muscat flavour which is natural to them, have completely gone out of favour in England.

Admittedly they are sweet, but there are many people, ladies in particular, who like sweet wines, and I believe that, with a little judicious working they might be popular again. I am convinced that they are better for most people than the strong liqueurs which are usually served.

We felt obliged to sample the Marc distilled at the property in 1927 . . . they were very proud of it—I wasn't, and I think the Sec was guilty of what is vulgarly called—'turning up his nose at it'.

It was an enjoyable meal, and I advise anyone visiting these parts to go and do likewise.

When no one was looking I gave a piece of hare from my plate to a cat which was purring around my legs. The way it played with it made me think it must have been of the opinion that it was one of its long-lost kittens . . . who knows ! !

It evidently became undeceived for it attacked the bone in it with such ferocity that the Sec actually remarked—'Hark at that dog crunching a bone !'

We were told that at the hotel the proprietors actually made their own Marc, Oil and Wine ; so they deserve the success they are evidently enjoying.

The incident of the cat brought to my mind a little tongue twister that I learned when living, as a lad, in Bordeaux . . . something like this—(to be said quickly)—

> 'Chat vit rôt
> Rôt tenta chat
> Chat mit patte à rôt
> Rôt brula patte à chat
> Chat lâcha rôt.'

I was so pleased at remembering this that I wanted to 'swank' about it. . . . I therefore called for Victorine, and asked her if she would like to earn ten francs. 'Oui, oui, Monsieur', she replied—'what can I do?'

'You can repeat after me the following, and if you do not make a mistake, there's ten francs for you.'

Much to the amusement of other diners Victorine stood to attention and listened very attentively while I recited the words. . . . She tried once, twice, and then gave it up—so did I the ten francs.

On the way out I saw a plate hanging, on which were these words, in English :

'There are no vices that monkeys and women do not know.'

I would like to have known the origin of this ; but all the information I could obtain was, with a smile—'C'est une blague !'

We could not leave these surroundings without taking a stroll around the quaint old thoroughfares. Seated on the roadside we saw an old lady . . . I never saw anyone so near-sighted. She was reading a journal and she held the paper so close to her eyes that as she came to each line she grazed her nose . . . 'la pauvre', I thought . . . I would like to send her a pair of spectacles.

The visibility was not very good—not that this was of much account to us, for the sombreness of the sky added strength to the rugged, bare and menacing rocky surroundings.

There were innumerable objects of vast interest to be seen in this village situated on the height of this almost isolated rock . . . all of which must be seen to be believed and enjoyed.

The ruins of the dungeon ; the gate Eyguière, the King's house, the Hôtel Manville, the 'Lanterne des Morts', and above

[267]

all the Church of St. Vincent, with its many interesting objects, in particular the 'char de l'agneau de la Messe de Minuit', La Chapelle des Pénitents and La Tour Paravelle . . . in fact everything about the place is full of interest, none the least the streets themselves (if they can be described as such).

In spite of the poor visibility we could visualise the marvellous views to be seen on a bright day : maybe we shall be more fortunate next time in this respect. 'That is a poor sentiment: what do you say, Sec ?'

It was sad to leave, but it was necessary, and we wended our way back between the mountains, in parts of which we saw the limestone pits being worked.

Through these wild parts we came to green slopes and, at a lower level, a very pretty road with open country.

At LA MASSANE we passed a railway station, so dilapidated that the worst one on the old Chatham Railway would have been a palace to it ! A picturesque old mill, however, withdrew our offended attention.

Passing through avenues for some distance we arrived at ROGNONAS in the nick of time, pulling up at an E.S.S.O. pump, as our store of petrol had become exhausted.

We were soon back at the Dominion at AVIGNON ; the Sec took the Little Auk to the garage and, as he considered it was not 'preened' as well as he wished, he gave instructions for an overhauling to take place. This was carried out to the utmost satisfaction by an excellent mechanic ; it is a pleasure to put on record such service as this.

We were not particularly hungry, so were content with a very simple meal at the Hiely Restaurant . . . a fried sole, followed by chicken ; and really, if well served, what better could one wish for. We had no difficulty in knowing exactly what we were eating, as there were no 'frills or furbelows' to disguise the main object.

It is such simple dishes as these that give no trouble in the selection of the wine ; any White wine, of good quality, and dry, would suffice.

We selected a Still natural wine, of Wachter (12 fcs.) . . . how good and clean it was, to be sure. We enjoyed it thoroughly.

There was, however, one sad fly in the ointment; a female at the next table to ours was so pungently perfumed that it was not only impossible to taste the wine with discrimination, but equally · difficult to decide what one was eating.

I think it will be charitable not to disclose the Sec's expressed opinion of the lady.

The enemy mosquito made several sorties during the night, particularly in force about 3.45 a.m. and were successful in making a good many direct hits. However, by dint of personal courage and the aid of 'search lights' they were put to flight after some time.

Sunday morning the 28th October was dull as regards the weather, and as regards the Sec he was obstreperous . . . in what way I cannot recall, but he was argumentative.

We were off about 9 o'clock for VALENCE, taking the road viâ VILLENEUVE, where there is an interesting castle.

Even at that early hour many men were sitting outside the cafés drinking the local wine.

It was not long before the dullness gave way to brighter conditions; we passed along a pretty road, hilly to the left, with wooded country on the right. . . . Plenty of vines revelling in their autumnal tints . . . from the reddish bronze of the Alicante to the golden yellow of the Grenache.

A long avenue of Plane trees led us into ROQUEMAURE. We had passed this way before, and remembered the Castle of Montfaucon, to which we gave a nod of acquaintance.

Here we found the railway crossing closed against us, but the Sec thought fit to sound his horn . . . which did the trick, and we passed over.

We travelled along by the side of the railway, and were interested to see a goods train pass. There must have been a hundred, or even more, trucks, on each of which was a motorcar. . . . It was quite a sight !

The next town on our route was ORSAN where the local wine is known as Côte du Rhône. The country was hilly—almost mountainous, the heights being covered in clouds; so much so that our vision was restricted.

I mentioned before the pleasing picture of the autumnal tints of the vine leaves ; here we had a wider range with trees, bushes and olive groves.

We had now arrived at BAGNOLES, where the principal object to arrest attention is the cemetery. This was a place for the disposal of the body, whereas all along the countryside we saw quantities of Marc material, waiting for the public distiller to raise the 'spirit'.

Over La Cèze by an elegant bridge we went, on the other side of which we were greeted with the sight of a quantity of washing hanging out in the rain to dry.

After ST. NAZAIRE the country was open, not very attractive. The many avenues were pleasant enough, but owing to the fallen leaves the roads became slippery. However, my very careful 'chauffeur' knew how to take precaution.

At PONT ST. ESPRIT there is another fine bridge over the Rhône, but the weather spoilt our view.

From here we took the road to the right, and then at right angles to the left through LAPALUD, where we saw an extraordinary steeple on an old church, and round PIERRELATTE, an old market town.

It was noticeable in this part of the country that the men had a habit of wearing their coats over their shoulders, without putting their arms through the sleeves. We wondered how this originated, but could find no opportunity of inquiring.

We were now enjoying more undulating country as far as Donzere, where our attention was drawn to large quantities of snow-white turkeys.

From here to MONTÉLIMAR the country was flat and uninteresting ; the first thing we noticed when we reached this somewhat important town was a large notice 'NOUGAT', and this 'sweet' word was repeated, as far as we could see, on almost every building. We wondered why the name of the town was not altered to NOUGAT.

It was really amusing. 'Look', said the Sec . . . 'Nougat'. 'Look', I chipped in—'Nougat'. Nougat was everywhere, everywhere . . . and after we had left the place, some many kilometres away, the Sec said—'Look, what is that enormous sign yonder ?' And as we approached, and I could see what it was, I exclaimed, in the words of Mr. Hobbs—'Well, I am jiggered !'

I have just read from the morning paper of the 19th January, 1935, that Mr. W. Stuve, the inventor of the famous sweetmeat, Montélimar, has died at Duivendrecht, near Amsterdam.

Some little distance from LA COUCOURDE, up to which town we had been running, along the bank of the river, we encountered one of those pestering young asses who think it funny and clever to accelerate just as another car is about to pass . . . one of the most annoying of petty annoyances.

I feared that he might be the cause of an accident sooner or later, for in addition to his stupidity he was fooling about with a young woman by his side.

A short distance from LES REYS we passed a car smashed to pieces, being towed along. It was not our 'ass' but it might be later on, I thought.

On our way we passed through SAULCE S/RHÔNE and LORIOL. By now it was after 11 o'clock, and we were glad to see the sun struggling to shine through the clouds.

At LIVRON we crossed the river. 'Surely this cannot be the Rhône ?' I queried. The wise old Sec suggested that I consult the map if I wanted to know. This I did, and found we had crossed the Drôme, an important tributary of the Rhône.

It was pleasant to hear the town-crier, complete with drum, at LIVRON, although we understood not a word he uttered. However, it gave a peculiar feeling of old-world satisfaction.

We were soon over the remaining flat and open country to VALENCE, where we were to make a halt.

We stayed at the Hôtel de la Croix d'Or, in the centre of the town, and from the comfort we experienced we did not regret it.

We were in good time for déjeuner, and treated ourselves to a few Portuguese oysters, which brought back thoughts of 'behind the lines'.

We had an excellent sole to follow, and kidneys so good that I told the Sec they might have been mine own ! This was accompanied with Vin Rosé du Pays, which was drinkable— that's all.

A little rest and then we ventured forth to see the town.

Almost the first person we met was a man—a little 'ivre'. In a way it was rather amusing, for he had such a funny face that we were quite undecided as to whether he wished to be friendly or quarrelsome.

It also passed through my mind—foolish things often do—whether the man had been stung by a bee or a wasp, and was endeavouring to cure himself in the way I read of in the August issue of the *Bulletin International du Vin*. It was described as an infallible remedy:

'Take small quantities of wine continuously, about 15° alcohol, such as Burgundy . . . carrying on until properly 'ivre'. The alcohol in the wine will tend to raise the temperature of the body and lessen the virulence of the poison, so much so that, after several hours, without ill effects, the patient will be cured.'

The Moorish officers walking along the thoroughfares were, in their uniforms, quite sightly.

There are many places to visit in VALENCE . . . but during our stay we could only have a cursory glance.

The Maison des Têtes, thirteenth century, is well worth looking at, not only from the outside, but in the courtyard behind.

Not far from here is the Cathedral, with an entrancing view from the front, overlooking the river. Although of an Evangelical persuasion, it passed through my mind that I would like to enter during the afternoon service. I must admit that, in spite of the continued movement of the congregation (the going and coming, in particular) I came out much impressed with the apparent religious devotion and sincerity.

The ruins of an old castle high up on the hill opposite are most impressive.

The Musée is worth a visit, the 'Nymphe Endormie' (Louis Pierre) is a soothing and delightful picture. Some of the sculpture is excellent . . . there was one exhibit which reminded me of that beautiful work 'Latona', of our great sculptor, the late John Tweed.

As I was arranging for the Sec to have his porridge in the morning, a fellow guest was standing at the desk, and gave his assistance, adding—'This young lady comes from Nîmes, and I can assure you that the girls of Nîmes are the prettiest.'

'How about those from Arles', chimed in the Sec . . . and at last I understood why I had found him so reluctant to leave.

For dinner, we had bargained with the maître d'hôtel to have a woodcock, which he said had been brought in a few days ago by a chasseur. The chef was to cook it such as no woodcock had ever been cooked before. It certainly was most excellent.

DINNER

PETITE MARMITE	CH. NEUF DU PAPE, BLANC
—	(26 fcs.) (very good)
EGGS AND BACON	
—	
WOODCOCK	
—	ARMAGNAC (6 fcs.)
FROMAGE	

We were obliged to taste the hotel Marc, out of politeness.

It is said that politeness costs nothing . . . in this instance it cost something in more ways than one.

Our fellow guest, who had been standing at the desk, was seated at a table by himself. We invited him to join us but he excused himself on account of having an early train to catch. Nîmes—I expect ! However, he condescended to accept a bottle of wine with our compliments. His selection fell on 1924 Crozes Rouge, a wine similar to the Hermitage, and I am under the impression that he thoroughly enjoyed it.

There was little else to do here, so after sitting about in the lounge and pretending to read, while one of us at least in reality dozed, we betook ourselves to our virtuous and respective couches.

'Good morning, Sec . . . how did you manage last night ; sleep well ?' I inquired. 'Yes thanks', he replied . . . 'and you ; no mosquitoes, I hope ?'

'A much better night, thank goodness', I said . . . 'although disturbed a little. I found on waking this morning, the result of one struggle which had taken place during the night . . . the sanguinary corpse of one of the enemy stretched out on my pillow, and on the blanket I discovered another, not quite dead,

[273]

for his, or her wings had been enmeshed in the fluffiness of the material, and I took immediate delight in putting an end to its struggles. Now that I have killed the father and mother I suppose I shall have the whole family hunting round for them to-night—but I must not be pessimistic.' So saying, I went back to my room and with joy and pride returned to show the result of my nightly prowess, neatly displayed on a sheet of hotel note-paper.

The day opened propitiously, for the valet de chambre instead of kicking my boots out of the way, actually brought them into the room.

The fresh air of the morning was very pleasant ... this was gratifying, as we wished to be off early in order to call on Monsieur Chapoutier, at TAIN, to whom we had been given a letter of introduction by our good friend, Jean Calvet, and from our experience of such introductions we knew we were in for a 'wonderful' time.

The first part of the run was over an open country, not particularly interesting ; later the hills on the left enlivened the outlook. At PONT DE L'ISÈRE we crossed the river by an excellent bridge, and noticed that there was more water in the river here than we had seen elsewhere.

As we proceeded, we came across a very large number of black and white goats, being driven along the road. I remarked to the Sec—'Look at Buchanan's goat-herd arriving !' 'What do you mean ?' he asked, keeping a steady look ahead in order to avoid any collision.

'Mean !' I said ... 'fancy a man acquainted with whisky all his life asking such a question !'

Then the dear old fellow smiled.

We noticed here that the vines were taller than those we had seen in other districts ; we were at LA MULE BLANCHE, and the country was more hilly and picturesque with the Rhône flowing steadily along on our left. Entirely different to what I had expected—having so frequently heard of, or read of the 'turbulent' Rhône.

At a few minutes before 9 o'clock we had reached TAIN and, in order to inquire the way to Monsieur Chapoutier, we had pulled up at what looked like a natural parking place. We were seated in the car when, without any warning, a man in another car (6655) made as if to turn in front of us . . . fortunately, the damage though aggravating was not serious.

By the time we had alighted and thought of a few, perhaps inadequate, remarks in French to offer him, he had departed.

As was to be expected, the direction we received was 'tout droit'—trois cent mètres.

There we were chez Monsieur Chapoutier . . . and what a delightful welcome. Monsieur Calvet had advised him of our probable visit, and, by the time I have described to you the work of the two days here, you will in some small measure realise how much these good people did for us, placing at our disposal their valuable time, their generous hospitality, and their great knowledge of the wines of their country.

This was the home of the wine known as l'Hermitage. I had never previously visited the district, although for many years I had promised myself that I would do so.

Monsieur Chapoutier and his son told us so much and showed us so many wines that I find it a little difficult to know how to commence to pass on this information for the benefit of others.

The old-fashioned offices, where I am sure these gentlemen would welcome any lover of wine, are interesting, but we were fidgety to get at the chais and the vineyards. We were therefore escorted to the chais . . . Monsieur Chapoutier pointing out to us on the way the Parc Calvet, where were born our mutual good friends, Jean Calvet and the other members of his family . . . Georges, Emile, Octave and Robert.

After a visit to the chais, it was suggested that we have a run around the country and return to taste a few wines before déjeuner.

During this time I took advantage of the opportunity to ask questions.

The tall vines we had noticed are the Syra, and are responsible for the Red Hermitage wine. The predominant White wine vines are the Marsanne and the Roussanne. The Syra is generally planted in the granite soil, and the White wine plants in the chalky soil which abounds.

The soil of the famous Côte Rôtie is of a granite substance ;

in the vineyards are planted a proportion of two-thirds Syra and one-third Viognier, a White variety. No White wine is made, the Syra and the Viognier are all vintaged together for Red wine, giving an exquisite wine, lighter in colour and body than the Hermitage, and with that particular flavour imparted by the Viognier.

The vine for the red Hermitage is mostly the Syra, and this is undoubtedly the reason why these wines require longer time to arrive at maturity.

I asked about Ch. Grillet; a wine one seldom meets with.

I remember so well the 1865 and 1869, which I drank from the caves du Château de Bois-Renard, reference to which I have already made.

Monsieur Chapoutier deplored the present position of things appertaining to Ch. Grillet. The real and fine article such as I had mentioned was no longer to be found—it was finished—last year, 1933, but three Hhds. of wine were made and that was not particularly good. It should be a wine of exceptional quality, by virtue of its soil and position, full of flavour and sugar, and would require twelve months to finish its fermentation.

The property belongs to an 'avocat' who appears to take no pride in this estate . . . a thousand pities, say all wine lovers; but that is his affair.

A wine under the name of Ch. Grillet is sold, but Monsieur l'avocat takes no notice of this and is adamant in his resolve to sell neither the right to the appellation, nor the property.

We must return to the chais, to carry out the dégustation so kindly arranged for us . . . as before, I think that the simplest way to deal with the number of wines tasted is to give a list in the order of tasting and my comments alongside, otherwise I may be guilty of 'talking' so much as to 'blurr' the issue:

1934 l'Hermitage Blanc 14° Chante-Alouette	- fair body; yet quality. Fermenting a little.
1934 l'Hermitage — 12.30°	- not quite finished fermenting. The price would be given in about three years when ready for bottling.

1934 Côte Rôtie - - - 13.30° Nr. 397	very good ... fine. Monsieur Chapoutier explained when asked that the particular flavour I noticed was due to the presence of White grape.
1934 Châteauneuf du Pape - 15° at least	all Grenache. This was in a state of full fermentation. These wines are vintaged a full three weeks later than the Hermitage.
Vin de Recoupe - - -	quite interesting ... this wine is for the 'ouvriers'. It is the result of second pressing, by a hydraulic press, and takes about half an hour.
1929 Hermitage Blanc - - 12.50°. Chante-Alouette Nr. 314	a little after style of Montrachet. Dry but not severe—in fact, quite attractive.
1929 Hermitage Blanc - - 12.50°. Tête de Cuvée. Nr. 360	good—found it softer.
1929 l'Hermitage, Red - 12.2°. Nr. 320	little dry, but good and rather elegant.
1929 Hermitage, Red - - 12.4°. Tête de Cuvée Nr. 361.	very good—I prefer this. Will keep twenty years in bottle.
1929 Côte Rôtie - - - 12.13°. Nr. 321	pleasant wine. More agreeable to me and rather finer.
1929 Côte Rôtie - - - 12.13°. Nr. 362	I found this a trifle stalky and was not so impressed with it. Monsieur Chapoutier, père, thinks that it will be better after a few years in bottle.
1929 Châteauneuf du Pape - 13°. Nr. 364	did not find this as coarse as some Ch. Neuf du Pape.
1929 Tavel Rosé - - - 13.3°. Nr. 135	excellent—light and elegant.
1929 Tavel Rosé - - - 12.8°. Nr. 146	preferable—lighter and smoother.

While the tastings were taking place, considerable conversation was carried on, mostly about the merits of the respective wines. However, I gathered a few items of interest as we passed around this very fine cuverie.

Some new Oak casks for the wine were ready for the new wine. I inquired what percentage of these casks were faulty, that is—those that would give a 'goût de bois' to the wine. 'Very, very small'—I was assured. The principal effect of the wine coming into contact with the Oak wood was to impart a certain amount of tannin to it.

The 'grappe' left in the wine while fermenting would give too much acidity.

When one is not accustomed to the technicalities, it is necessary to be careful . . . several times I was thinking of 'grape' when 'grappe' was mentioned, until it dawned on me that it could not be.

Grappe is Stalk.
Raisin is Grape.
Peau   is Skin.
Pépin   is Pip.
Verdure is Palate (perhaps I should say a little bitterness on the palate).
Fouloir is the receptacle for the fruit in which the men and women tread : still carried on in a few places.
Vin de Coule—First pressings.
Vin de Presse—Second pressings (hydraulic).

Monsieur Chapoutier then introduced us to something I had not seen before, and that was an attractive, in fact pleasant Brandy not Marc . . . (such a thing I had always considered to be impossible). It was so entertaining that I could not refrain from asking for a bottle for my own use—as a curiosity and an alternative.

It was the distillation of the lees of fine Hermitage wines, 42% alcohol, by volume ; distilled once at 51°, and had been maturing in a large vat for the last thirty years.

What do you think we deserved after this ? Yes—correct . . . and we immediately went off in search of the same.

Monsieur Chapoutier and his son invited us to déjeuner at the Hôtel l'Assurance at TOURNON on the opposite bank of the Rhône ; where, as you will see, we lunched very well indeed.

HORS D'ŒUVRES	1921 HERMITAGE BLANC
—	(Chante-Alouette)
LANGOUSTE À LA ARMORICAINE	
—	
HARE	1921 HERMITAGE DE LA
RÂBLE DE LIÈVRE	SIZERANNE
(for jelly we were offered Apple or Gooseberry Jam —not touched)	
—	
BRAISED CELERY AU GRATIN	1929 CÔTE RÔTIE
—	(I found this too young and
GRIVE FLAMBÉE	was glad to return to the 1921.)
—	LANSON CHAMPAGNE
CAFÉ	Ex. Sec.
	OLD FINE HERMITAGE (Marc)

This was an excellent repast and much credit must be awarded to Monsieur and Madame Clément ; the husband being his own Chef.

One thing pleased me immensely . . . this was about the only time we had had reasonable glasses—both in shape and texture, to drink out of.

Out of these glasses we wished to drink to the worthy couple, so they were summoned ; he looking the part admirably and full of justified pride at his success, and she, somewhat robust— slightly red of complexion, and rather short in stature . . . but there, details meant nothing, for her happy smile and indefatigability to please won our hearts as well as our thanks.

They insisted on drinking a toast—'à la santé de l'Angleterre'; and the Sec, not to be found wanting, determined to photograph them outside their premises.

Altogether most enjoyable . . . but now we must get to work again.

Through MAUVES (Côtes du Rhône ordinaires), we came to a level crossing which was closed to us. 'Thank God', ejaculated the pious Sec, for we were doing 63 miles an hour—and after such a lunch !

On we went to CHATEAUBOURG—pretty scenery with the Rhône on our left and hills on the right.

At CORNAS we paid a visit to a vigneron, and were allowed to taste his new wine : Cornas is a third growth . . . decidedly it was not as fine as the Hermitage or the Côte Rôtie.

It was a small vineyard occupying a fine situation, the wine being considered one of the best of the Côtes du Rhône.

We soon reached ST. PÉRAY, the home of the Sparkling wine of the district . . . made from La Rousette vines.

The outlook here was very pleasing. . . . 'What is it that causes an inward smile and a curious sense of interest when one meets twins ?' I asked the Sec as we passed them. 'I'm sure I don't know', he said . . . ' and thank the Lord I was never burdened with any.' Nevertheless, this feeling does exist and I rather like it.

The public still was hard at it making Marc for the local community. Voge, the distillateur, very kindly introduced us to the workings of the machine and allowed us to taste the product ! He was a good fellow.

Monsieur Chapoutier insisted that we should pay a visit to the Restaurant de la Gare—I don't know why, because Sparkling St. Péray is atrocious—at least, to me ; but when we saw the very good-looking dame bring us the bottle, we concluded that there might have been yet another reason . . . he had heard us mention the beauties of Nîmes and of Arles . . . and doubtless he wished to impress upon us what beauty could be seen at ST. PÉRAY.

I will whisper a secret to you . . . it was with the greatest difficulty that I restrained the Sec from saying—'les choses imbéciles'.

The wine was described as 'Grand Mousseux Supr.,' (the 'Mousseux' is correct !). It was very sweet and dark, and I cannot say that I liked it.

[280]

The Restaurant de la Gare is a curious little estaminet, with a great reputation for cuisine.

'You must come back to TAIN with us and taste some bottled wines', said Monsieur Chapoutier . . . not only said so but insisted—'and this evening we will take you to a very interesting place for dinner.'

I tried to stammer out something about his being too kind, etc., but he had his own way, and we were soon en route once more. We decided to take the road through VALENCE and then on to TAIN, the same as that which we had taken that morning.

A donkey and two oxen yoked to one plough appealed to my imagination. Château Crussol on the right, looking very menacing, attracted my attention—but Sec was too far away in another.direction ; perhaps this was as well, otherwise he would have had his mouth and eye glued to the speedometer.

We came to the White Hermitage vineyards—Murets and Rocoules planted with the Roussanne and the Marsanne.

Here a new wall was in process of structure ; to prevent the earth from falling.

The road through the vineyards was pretty, and the vines looked healthy . . . the new grafts, explained our host, had done very well, especially as they had been grafted only in March and April. During the vintage the women who cut the grapes receive 18 francs for a 9-hour day, and the men who carry them —30 francs for the 9 hours. The regular vignerons on an estate earn 25 francs for a day of 9 hours.

In addition, there is a daily allowance for each of one litre of wine.

What a beautiful view there was from these vineyards . . . looking across TAIN and the Rhône—I revelled in it.

The Chante-Alouette is a very handsome vineyard, and we were happy to be able to compliment Monsieur Chapoutier on his fine property, without any suspicion of saying something agreeable which was not strictly true.

While here we were shown the difference between the White and the Red vine leaf.

The White is rounder and stronger . . . the Red has a rougher edge and fine ribs on the back.

[281]

For the Red Hermitage he planted Le Meal to the east . . .
Le Greffieux to the south, and Le Bessard to the west . . . tall
vines, and he was happy in the result.

The first growths consist of l'Hermitage and Côte Rôtie . . .
the second—Châteauneuf du Pape and Tavel, and the third—
Cornas and Crozes. The St. Péray, a Sparkling wine, stands alone.

After this short interlude we made our way back to TAIN to
taste the bottled wines.

1929 Côte Rôtie . . . good, will improve.

1923   ,,   ,, . . . better than the 1929.

1921   ,,   ,, . . . very good and fine.

1929 Hermitage,
    Grand Vin . . . good and typical.

1923   ,,   ,, . . . softer and fuller.

1921   ,,   ,, . . . *very good* indeed.
      Bottle age makes all the difference.

1929 Châteauneuf du Pape . . . 1st bottle slightly corked.
                              2nd bottle very attractive.

1923   ,,   ,,   did not like this.

1929 Tavel . . .   gives me pleasure—very nice
                              indeed.

1929 White Hermitage . . . one year in bottle—very good,
    Grand Vin   attractive, soft.

1923   ,,   ,,   . . . did not like any better than the
                              1929.

1921   ,,   ,,   . . . good, very old flavour.

1895   ,,   ,,   . . . excellent—kept very well, not
                              too dry.

1874   ,,   ,,   . . . wonderful colour and flavour;
                              before the Phylloxera — the
                              Sec rubbed the back of his
                              ears with the wine . . . evi-
                              dently he was well pleased
                              with it.

We also tasted, I remember—but I cannot quite recollect
where it fitted in—a bottle of . . .

1904 Côte Rôtie . . . splendid nose—a joy. Dry on palate
                    and excellent condition.

We deplored the fact that there was practically no quantity of fine old Rhône wine in the country; however, Monsieur Chapoutier knew of one hundred, or one hundred and twenty bottles lying in a nobleman's cellar—of 1893 White Hermitage, Grand Vin; which, owing to circumstances which he foresaw, might be for sale.

Since this time we have received a bottle which Monsieur Chapoutier obtained from the administrator of the estate. We tasted it . . . it was excellent, with no suspicion of 'maderisation'.

I am glad to think that I shall be able to enjoy a few bottles later on, with friends—'cela va sans dire'.

Having a short time to spare before leaving on our expedition for the dinner these hospitable people insisted on, I thought it well to pay a visit to Messieurs Jaboulet-Vercherre.

Monsieur Henry C. Jaboulet-Vercherre I had known as a charming young man, many years ago, and I remembered his courage at the time of the wreck of the S.S. *la Ville-de-Berlin* off the Hook of Holland. He was one of the very few survivors; but alas ! . . . he did not survive the war, having given his life for his country.

With thoughts of my former young friend in my mind I felt I would like to 'pay my respects'.

Henry's brother Ulysse was at POMMARD, and I saw one of the principals, Monsieur Ferrier, whose acquaintance it was a pleasure to make.

When I returned to the office of Messieurs Chapoutier I was flabbergasted to find the Sec—the sober Sec—indulging in a bottle of Champagne with our good friends !

I kept silence . . . I thought it more discreet to do so, but I gave him a penetrating glance—I wonder how deep it entered.

On our way to dinner we took the road viâ ST. PÉRAY and then continued up hill, taking innumerable turnings in the dark, which caused a giddy sensation.

We reached the celebrated restaurant at LE PIN, almost by itself high up in the mountains, of the beautiful views from which we could see nothing, except a number of dancing lights far down in the deep valleys below.

The dinner had been ordered by Monsieur Chapoutier before

[283]

arriving, and while we waited at the table the Baron Le Roy arrived with a party—introducing to us, Monsieur de Launay. He informed us that he had left Châteauneuf at 5 o'clock and was at LE PIN before 7 o'clock—130 kilometres . . . uphill, and twists and turns nearly all the way. I congratulated him, but confessed I was glad that I was not one of the party !

It was an experience to dine away from the turmoil of every-day life, and we thoroughly enjoyed it.

DINNER

PÂTÉ DE FOIE	1929 WHITE HERMITAGE— very good and very pleasant
TRUITE from the mountain streams, served in boiling butter with citron and parsley	
—	
FONDS ARTICHAUTS Game stuffing	1929 RED HERMITAGE— trifle heavy
—	
ALOUETTES, potatoes, eggs in meat (cooked to a turn)	CHAMPAGNE— Armand Limbany
—	
WILD STRAWBERRIES	
—	
CAFÉ	FINE, Bisquit, 1 , years old

A notable dinner, and one which I shall remember for a very long time.

It was curious to note that in this 'recherché' restaurant we were given steel knives with the fish ; I have frequently noticed this. . . . I do not know if it is laziness not to produce a fish knife, or just the fact that they do not possess them. I could not —such is habit—fancy that beautiful trout cut with such a knife, so I asked for another fork, at which the waitress, I think, considered that I was a little worse than stupid.

[284]

We offered our congratulations to the Chef, and then started back to VALENCE.

Marc Chapoutier—he is the son of Marius Chapoutier—took the wheel. He is a careful driver, although somewhat rapid. This night, his speed was curtailed owing to the twisting road . . . no less than seventy-two hairpin bends in about six kilometres . . . in such quick succession are these turnings that it is not a rare occurrence for those who are motoring, to complain of 'mal de mer'. We heard afterwards that there was—near the village of PLAT, which was not far distant—a length of four kilometres in which there were more than one hundred such hairpin bends.

Our host deposited us safely at the hotel, and said he would call for us the next morning as the Little Auk had been left in their garage at TAIN. We were to take further advantage of the wonderful kindness of Messieurs Chapoutier, who were anxious for us to visit VIENNE . . . have lunch at a renowned restaurant on the way, and incidentally pay our respects to their vineyards at CÔTE RÔTIE.

As I bade good-night to the Sec, I whispered in his ear—'To-morrow, my friend—Côte Rôtie. I think he got in between the sheets wondering which side he would find 'roasted' the next morning.

Tuesday, the 30th October, we awoke to find a fresh and pleasant morning, which promised well for an enjoyable day. Indeed we had been favoured with fine weather, for which we were grateful.

Nevertheless, rain is sorely needed, as the continual dry weather holds up the work in the vineyards, the carrying on of which is very necessary.

As I had foretold 'la famille moustique' arrived during the night in search of their parents : it may be that the grief of their bereavement lay heavy upon them, so that their movements were not so rapid.

When I awoke I was able to count no less than three laid out flat . . . it does not seem a large number, but those who have suffered in the same way—where none is supposed to be—will agree that it was a good catch.

It may be that I am becoming more proficient in this particular kind of warfare, albeit somewhat to my detriment. The following is my *modus operandi*, which I detail in the hope that it may prove useful to other sufferers :

On hearing the threatening music, I gently place my hand in position and quietly wait for one of them to alight somewhere on my enticing body—then, and only then do I strike ; this night, you will have read with what success . . . and many another may have retired mortally wounded.

On one occasion during the night I was thus prepared, when one of the brutes thought fit to settle on my nose . . . pray do not think that, owing to the tasting of so much wine, my nose had become a luminaire, for it had not !

However, this was the spot selected, with malice aforethought. It settled when, with that quickness of action—surely to be commended—I struck with considerable force ! In the darkness I missed my nose and hit myself violently in the eye, seeing literally, hundreds of stars ! !

I think if it escaped, it took a warning to others, and I trusted that then, having disposed of the family, I should be at peace for the last night's rest at VALENCE.

I went in to find the Sec and tell him of my adventures, when, taking a chair to sit on I noticed that in the cane of the seat there was a small break. I had seen the same thing so often, and talking it over, we two wiseheads came to the conclusion that these little breaks in the cane were made by the high heels of ladies' shoes. 'They should be more careful', said I. . . . 'So they should', said he.

The telephone rang . . . our friends had arrived—on time ; 9 o'clock.

We lost no time in making a move, and took the same road to TAIN.

We crossed the Rhône, for CÔTE RÔTIE was on the other bank, and our journey was some distance to the north. It was bright and sunny, and we were able to see what the country had to show us.

As we crossed the little mountain river, Le Doux, our host informed us that it was from this river the trout we had enjoyed the night before had been taken.

[286]

On our left was the well-known vineyard St. Jean, Côtes du Rhône. The vineyards of Vion are in the same classification; here the country was more open, but we could see the vines on the mountain slopes in the distance.

At LATOUR D'ARRAS there are, on the left, interesting ruins of a Roman castle.

In this neighbourhood were to be seen numerous orchards, planted with Cherry trees and Peach trees . . . an abundance of them.

Monsieur Chapoutier pointed out the town of ST. VALLIER, on the other side of the river; there are no ruins here . . . it is a progressive and industrial centre, busy with tanneries and potteries.

After SARRAS we crossed the stream La Cance, whose special waters are said to be so good for the working of the skins at the SARRAS tanneries.

At ANDANCE, still on the right bank of the Rhône, we noticed in passing, an old church, with such a remarkable door that we stopped to have a look at it. At the small village of CHAMPAGNE, quite close, there is an eleventh-century church.

At SERRIERES there is a very fine suspension bridge, but our way did not take us across it.

At VERIN-PONCIN we stopped again, in order to have a look at Château Grillet, about which I have already written. As I regarded it I thought how unfortunate it was that it should be so neglected—the Château itself standing well up in such a happy situation.

'This is CONDRIEU', explained our host . . . 'so we must arrange for lunch to be ready on our return from VIENNE' . . . and with that insinuating smile of his, he added—'a wise precaution.'

CÔTE RÔTIE commences immediately outside CONDRIEU, the wines of which are classified as 3me cru; the Tupin is classed as 2me cru.

These vineyards were arranged in terraces and the vines looked pleased with themselves, basking in the morning sun.

Côte Rôtie is, as I have already mentioned—1er cru, and Monsieur Chapoutier is one of the principal owners of vineyards in this world-renowned spot. . . . His first growth is known as 'La Grosse Roche', taking its name from a large barren rock in the vineyard. The vineyard itself is divided into the Côteau de la Blonde and the Côteau de la Brune—both planted with Red and White vines. There was a small portion on the same hillside which was not planted ; it was to be offered for sale about the middle of November, and I have learned since that owing to a process between the heirs of the old proprietor it is still unsold.

This is in reality a beautiful spot . . . in addition to the vines, Pear trees, Cherry trees, Peach trees, in fact fruit trees of all descriptions.

In the vineyard itself the vines are very tall, requiring two sticks (échalats) for support (double labour) whereas, at Hermitage only one is necessary, and at Châteauneuf du Pape none is required.

The work to be carried out on this steep hillside vineyard is very arduous, and when looked at this can be readily believed.

It is planted with one-third White, and two-thirds Black grapes, which are cut and gathered indiscriminately ; this being the usual procedure for the wines of Côte Rôtie.

On coming from this side of the vineyard we called at the house of the chief vigneron, in order to extend an invitation to lunch. He was, however, away at LYON—'tant pis pour lui' !

We then returned to the car and drove to the precipitous road between the Blonde and the Brune, stopping at the rear of the Grosse Roche.

Here we did enjoy lovely scenery, overlooking AMPUIS, which is the name of the town to which Côte Rôtie belongs. The plain below, stretching for some distance, was well worked and set out with fruit orchards and vegetable gardens.

The whole of the area of Côte Rôtie is but small, approximately 60 hectares for the first cru . . . a similar number for the second, and for the third about 40 hectares. As we were standing and enjoying the fine views and chatting about various things connected with the vineyards, we heard a cart approaching and looking round we saw a horse and cart being driven by a woman. 'Look', I said to the Sec . . . 'did you ever see such an Amazon in your life ?' 'No', he replied . . . 'that I never did.'

Later, when we were speeding on, he confessed that he was not feeling too bright (the only time I ever heard him complain). I wondered if it were the fierce, sour face of the woman who had passed us.

We had time to go as far as VIENNE, a city which one should visit . . . so to VIENNE we motored ; past ST. COLOMBE and over another fine suspension bridge. On the further side, facing the entrance to the bridge stood the Cathedral . . . what a havoc the revolutionists had made ! It was a splendid edifice and well worthy of a visit. There are many fine things to be seen here, one of the most interesting being the Temple d'Auguste, 41 A.D. . . . which we walked around, admiring its structure and its beauty.

Monsieur Chapoutier, père, had left us for a few minutes, and out of the kindness of his heart came laden with picture souvenirs of all sorts, which I now treasure.

As we were leaving VIENNE we came across a very heavily laden lorry with one wheel off ; this caused us to lose a few minutes . . . however we arrived in CONDRIEU in time for the luncheon which had been prepared for us.

The Restaurant Beau Rivage (Monsieur R. A. Roullet) of which Madame Roullet is the mistress of the kitchen is well worth a visit and, should any of my readers be in this part of the country, I counsel you to visit the Beau Rivage. The windows of the restaurant overlook the Rhône, and offer beautiful views. . . . In the sunshine which we enjoyed, nothing more could be desired.

From the window we saw the fishermen off—there was no occasion to use the oars as the stream was strong enough to take them, but coming back with a good catch would not be so easy.

Outside in the courtyard were large tanks filled with fish as and when required by the guests. . . . I saw, amongst others— gudgeon, eels, perch and brochets.

We had an excellent déjeuner :

B.W.

SAUCISSON CHAUD
GRATIN DAUPHINOIS
du lait
et
du fromage
(an excellent local dish)
Fonds d'artichauts ; farcis

—

QUAIL
(very good)

VIOGNIER GRAND CRU DE CON-
DRIEU, 1932—must be drunk
young.

—

1921 HERMITAGE—RED. Very
good, fine wine, but a little
extravagant for déjeuner.
Greedy Marc said—'No.'

—

1923 CÔTE RÔTIE 1er cru—
very good. There is some-
thing I rather like about the
wines of Côte Rôtie.

—

1900 ARMAGNAC

I had refused the 'Marc', adding that I had no use for it, at
which the younger Chapoutier rejoined that I was 'septic',
whereas, as a matter of fact I was not even 'sceptical'.

The maid, Marie, who looked after us was a very intelligent
girl, and we fared well.

Madame, who had superintended our luncheon, was anxious
to catch a train for VIENNE, but we talked and laughed so much
that she missed the time and we had the pleasure of offering to
take her there in the car.

When we arrived back at TAIN we found to our dismay that
the Little Auk would not function ; something was wrong
somewhere—the battery had run down. Eventually, by clever
manœuvring, Monsieur Marc drove it to a garage in VALENCE
and Monsieur Marius, that is 'le père', drove me, following quickly
in its wake.

It was left at the garage, with the assurance that it would be
ready early in the morning. This rapid attention was due
entirely to the kind services of Messieurs Chapoutier.

I do hope that these gentlemen thoroughly understood the
depth of our gratitude. We bade them good-bye, and honestly
look forward to the time when we shall see them once again.

[290]

That night at dinner we were content with simple fare . .
Mock Turtle soup, Omelette and Rognons, with a bottle of
1926 Mercurol . . . a wine, rather nondescript, with a good
bouquet but rather hard on the palate.

After dinner I decided to walk along to the garage and make
some inquiries as to the car. On leaving the hotel I noticed a
sweet shop opposite, which was open. I therefore went across
and purchased a box of chocolates to give to little Charlotte
from NÎMES, who had been so attentive on the telephone and with
telegrams, etc.

At the entrance to the garage I found a little dog, full of fun,
and with him I played for so long that I almost forgot my mission,
and contented myself by asking the mechanic if all was in order.

On the way back, a huge motor-bus drew up to the curb just
where I was. I could see that the seats had been removed and
that the accommodation was filled with sheep. 'Pardonnez-
moi ', said the driver to me . . . 'but, can you direct me to
MONTÉLIMAR ?' I was taken aback—why ask me?. . . . My first
thoughts were 'Nougat' and, remembering the answer to similar
inquiries on my own part, I replied—'Tout-droit, tout-droit' . . .
and off he went quite happily.

SUMMARY OF RHÔNE WINES

	White	*Red*	*Rosé* (Tavel)
1865	Very good	Very good	Good
1870	,, ,,	,, ,,	,,
1871	,, ,,	,, ,,	,,
1874	,, ,,	,, ,,	,,
Phylloxera			
1885	Good	Good	,,
1889	,,	,,	,,
1893	Very good	,,	,,
1895	Good	,,	,,
1898	,,	,,	,,
1904	Excellent	,,	,,
1906	,,	,,	,,
1911	Good	,,	,,

	White	*Red*	*Rosé* (Tavel)
1915	Good	Excellent	Excellent
1918	,,	,,	,,
1920	,,	,,	,,
1921	Wonderful	,,	,,
1923	Good	,,	,,
1926	,,	,,	,,
1928	,,	,,	,,
1929	Excellent	,,	,,
1933			
1934			

With regard to the vintages of 1933 and 1934 there seems little doubt but that both the Red and White wines of these years will be successful.

The 1934 Blanc gives a promise of being better than the 1933.

But, of the Red wines of 1934, it is too difficult to say.

The White wines last longer than the Red.

Should you be fortunate enough to possess any 1904 and 1906, keep a jealous eye on them, but do not hoard them up too long.

1915 will probably outlive the 1921.

Some 1928 wines which I have seen are very good. . . . I therefore advise 1928 and 1929 for present consumption and, for the next few years, consider replenishing with 1933 Red and 1934 White.

CHAPTER XIII

VALENCE TO VILLEFRANCHE

(viâ Chavaniac-Lafayette)

THE morning of the last day of October opened dull ; in fact, a few drops of rain were guilty of making their presence felt. The car had been thoroughly overhauled, and while waiting for it to be delivered our impatience was steadied by the passing of a long Salvation Army funeral procession.

Our kind and anxious friend Monsieur Chapoutier, père, had actually come all the way from TAIN to satisfy himself that everything was well with us. Many a time during the day did we make mention of this thoughtful kindness, not forgetting to drink to his health and the prosperity of his firm.

We were well on the way by 10 o'clock, and the Little Auk was behaving splendidly. We followed the road to ST. PÉRAY, giving a passing glance at the Restaurant de la Gare ; then the same winding climb we had taken two nights before.

What a series of fine panoramic views ! We did enjoy them, and when we reached the top, some two thousand feet up, we could only think and exclaim—'Wonderful' !

At LE FRINQUET we could see but three or four dwellings, but the continual twisting may have hidden the hamlet—the Sec described it as 'valsing'.

At LES RISSES there were another three cottages, which looked much like Anne Hathaway's at Stratford-on-Avon.

Between ALBOUSSIÈRE, GROZON and ST. BARTHÉLEMY the colouring of the pines and oaks was delightful. At the last named place there appeared to be two pleasant-looking so-called hotels. It is truly amazing how people live in these isolated places . . . a few buildings here and there dotted on the mountain slopes.

However, use is second nature, and I do not suppose that they would entertain the offer to change places with someone in a city office.

Away up on the hills we came across a fountain evidently erected by some benevolent sympathetic soul, to whom we raised our hats in humble recognition of the deed.

LAMASTRE was by way of being a town, boasting a railway station . . . there was little else to be noticed.

Looking across a dried-up stream to the right we saw a picturesque hamlet. What a place for a picnic, we thought . . . yet the only picnics we had seen had been taking place on the banks of R. N. roads with traffic passing all the time. This was indeed a corner of La Belle France . . . the sun was shining, and the autumnal tints were entrancing. 'Oh ! 'tis the sun that maketh all things shine !'

DESAIGNES boasts of two churches . . . the whole population had evidently turned out to attend a funeral.

Out from here we had a good steep climb, and from the heights had more gorgeous views. There is no doubt of the truth of the old adage—'Beauty unadorned is beauty adorned the most' . . . ladies, please note that nature's own colouring cannot be improved upon !

I remarked to the Sec that I thought no artist—be he painter, writer or poet, could give life-like expression to what we now enjoyed ; certainly, exaggeration would spoil it. I cannot remember if he agreed or not—I think the surrounding beauty was sinking so deep into his soul that my remarks appeared to him as empty words.

We were sorry to quit such surroundings. The pretty country for miles on seemed more or less 'just pleasant'. ST. AGRÈVE on the hill caught our attention ; we now entered into a more open country reminding me of parts of Cornwall from Liskeard to Newquay.

We were confronted here with a howling wind, head on . . . to this we made no objection, as it was apparently keeping off the rain.

At FOURMOURETTE we noticed one of the very few inhabitants sitting on a chair in the roadway. I could not help calling the

Sec's attention to his nose . . . not as a warning, but as an illustration.

I was instantly reminded of old Falstaff's description of Bardolph's nose :

> 'I never see thy face but
> I think upon hell-fire, and
> Dives that lived in purple ;
> For there he is in his robes—
> Burning, burning.'

At LES CESSES the wind had moderated and we experienced slight rain, which soon made the roads slippery . . . this however, did not worry me, with such a very careful chauffeur.

After passing BOUSSOULET we ran into a terrific storm, which the Little Auk stood up to manfully.

Leaves and twigs were stripped off the trees, and the windscreen was covered with them. We were thankful that it was of short duration, especially as we were near the precipice approaching LA PRADETTE.

The rain stopped almost as suddenly as it had commenced, but the heavily laden clouds warned us of what we might expect, as we continued along the mountain range, twisting and turning at every few yards.

As we arrived at ST. JULIEN CHAPTEUIL we noticed the church. It had the curious appearance of being 'squeezed together'; the continual packing of our trunks may have been responsible for such an expressed simile.

Between LA PARAVEUL and NOUSTOLET we met a number of natives. We could visualise the weather to which they were accustomed, by the sight of their hard weather-beaten faces.

From here we struck a bad road, eventually reaching ST. GERMAIN LAPRADE, which I thought much resembled some old town in the wilds of Co. Clare.

Crossing the Loire, and noticing on our left one half of an ancient bridge still standing, we arrived at LE PUY . . . the first object to attract attention here is the wonderful monument to 'La Vierge', erected on the crest of the hill.

We pulled up at the Hotel Dominion for lunch, finding here,

[295]

much to our comfort and satisfaction, a fire brightly burning in the hearth.

Déjeuner

PÂTÉ
(very good)
—

ROUGET MEUNIER
(very good)
—

ENTRECOT MINUET
(very good)
—

FROMAGE
—

DESSERT
—

(in fact, all very good—and
served hot)

1929 HERMITAGE BLANC
(Ch. Latour Blanche) 26 fcs.
Ch. bottled.

Bottles wired, as seen on some
Brandy bottles.
This was certainly good, and
we enjoyed it, but not so
good as to warrant the excess
of bottle dressing.

The Wine List was quite good, but the prices asked were too high.

All through, we found the same thing—hotel proprietors, in their own interest, would do well to consider this.

Immediately on leaving LE PUY, we commenced to climb and, on looking back—fearless of the salt reminder—we gazed upon the town nestling so happily and pleasingly in a hollow of its own, with St. Michael and Ste. Vierge dominating all.

'Here is a ticklish job', said the Sec, as he manœuvred to pass dozens of circus horses, four abreast. However, after a little wavering this way and that, and with the help of a few 'Sunday School' remarks which I need not repeat, he won out at last.

We were well on our way towards BLEU, when we noticed heavy clouds approaching us, and almost before we could realise it, we were once more in the midst of a terrific storm, such as we had experienced during the morning.

Passing the next two villages, we saw men who had the appearance of drowned rats . . . they had evidently been caught in the storm, a part of which we had just come through.

[296]

At GURMILHAC the rain ceased, and we were favoured with a fine view on the left; the red tiles of BOISSENGES giving a very pleasing effect.

We had now reached our goal, Château Chavaniac-Lafayette, where we were to inspect a cellar of ten thousand bottles of wine.

The task was made somewhat difficult by the absence of any cellar-book, but the 'régisseur' and a very intelligent young lady (not forgetting the Sec) gave such assistance that we were able to leave before it was too far into the night. As this was a private cellar I am not at liberty to discuss it—it was, however, pleasant to find such a good stock of wine tucked away in the recesses of an old French château.

Long subterranean passages led to the different cellars, the doors to some of which were fastened with no less than six locks.

LE PUY was reached without mishap; it was dark, and we had lost no time in sight-seeing. The only incident which occurred was when a horse dashed across the road in front of us. . . . I don't know how many times it had had so lucky an escape; probably, like the cat, it has the proverbial nine lives.

We were greeted with a roaring fire, and made as comfortable as anyone could wish.

We enjoyed a simple meal, the particulars of which I forget, and had no hesitation in ordering a bottle of the same good quality wine which we had had that morning.

After dinner I inquired of the Sec if he felt brave. . . . 'Always brave', replied he—'and ready for anything !'

'Then we will venture on a glass of the Liqueur du Pays' . . . known as 'Verveine du Verlay'.

Over the fire and a cup of coffee we drank this Liqueur and came to the conclusion that it was like a mixture of Yellow Chartreuse and Aniseed.

It had been a long and busy day for us. . . . I therefore urged the Sec to retire to bed while I finished a cigar and then took my usual constitutional.

Thursday, 1st November. . . . Rabbits to everyone ! I think the Sec was a little 'désolé' because I said it first—only for the reason that he was anxious to wish me all good things before

[297]

I had done so to him; but it is necessary to be up very early, to be 'one up' on such a juvenile.

A good night—no mosquitoes, for which I was truly thankful. I took the precaution to hide the illuminated face of my watch, thinking that it might have attracted the brutes. 'The proof of the pudding was in the eating' . . . on the other hand there may not have been any about owing to the change in the weather, although the Sec complained in the morning of a couple of bites.

I feel constrained to relate a small incident which tends to show how the sub-conscious mind is affected. About two o'clock in the morning I was awakened, no doubt by the light of the moon shining full on my face; as I awoke a part of a dream was still with me, and two words came to my mind repeatedly, viz., 'Parker's Piece'. It all seemed so strange—I could not connect 'Parker's Piece' with anything I had heard or seen, or done . . . when it suddenly dawned on me that some forty years ago I had been to Cambridge to examine a cellar of wine, and yesterday I had been to Chavaniac-Lafayette to do a similar work. I must have heard of 'Parker's Piece' in connection with Cambridge, but surely these two words have never been through my mind since, although I may have been in the university city on two or three occasions after the war, always with the object of advising about a cellar of one or other of the colleges.

The more I think of this, the more remarkable it seems; perhaps for this reason I may be forgiven for enlarging on this slight incident.

I saw a note in my diary under this date that my little friend, Norah Park and her husband were sailing from Marseille, by the Bibby Line, S.S. *Oxfordshire*, on their return to India. I therefore called the 'chasseur' and gave him a telegram to send off, wishing them 'bon voyage'.

It had actually been trying to snow, but by a quarter to nine when we were ready to start, it was brighter, although decidedly cold.

Our route took us through BLAVOZY—a dreadful looking place, on to MONTOING, where there was a huge rock that stood up like a church steeple.

[298]

At ST. HOSTEIN we found it necessary to re-fuel, and we were served by a man who resembled for all the world the pictures of Charlie Chaplin . . . but unfortunately he had a split nose.

Through each town and village that we passed we saw numbers of women, all in their best white caps . . . then it dawned on us that it was All Saints' Day.

At LE PERTUIS we noticed in a meadow a number of piglets, asleep—all in a bunch. They particularly attracted my attention for they looked like a number of bottles in a packing case.

From COL to YSSINGEAUX we were astonished at the number of people carrying bread . . . we had never noticed such a thing before. I imagined that it had some reference to All Saints' Day.

'Another car has passed us', said the Sec—'with the lights on.' It is extraordinary how often one sees this.

At ST. MAURICE we found the market in full swing, outside the church door . . . the populace all appeared to be wearing black.

Further on we were to have a treat of beautiful scenery, past CUBLAIZE to the Gorges de Lignon . . . it was magnificent; wooded slopes and exquisite colouring.

This was evidently a favourite spot for we met much traffic.

From the height, about 1500 feet, we looked upon such entrancing glens that the Sec was constrained to take some photos.

Descending the hill we saw large quarries on the right, crossing a most interesting, ancient bridge. Further on, on the left, was a large factory and a new bridge to meet modern demands.

Up the hill we climbed again to MONISTROL, with mountains on either side. At CROUXET we had reached some two thousand four hundred feet, and revelled in a beautiful scene, in which the light made silver streaks across the tops of the mountains.

After ST. FERREOL we commenced to descend a very steep hill, seeing far below an attractive bridge of eleven arches, and another of five.

We continued through the town of FIRMINY, which name brought back memories of the early days of the war when I was stationed at FIRMINY near DUNKERQUE, where, on one occasion in the early morning, in a dug-out, the late Dick Hoare complained that a rat had run over his face, adding—'I know it is an unhealthy one, for its feet were cold. . . . I think it might be beneath the straw.'

I gave myself the order to 'fix bayonets' and then, moving about very carefully, I disturbed the beast, which ran past me. Not waiting for the order, I charged, and, although almost incredible, I stuck it through the ribs. As a souvenir of such prowess, Maxwell Ayrton, the well-known architect, drew a picture of the event—'Seaman Berry and his rat'—which I still have and prize.

Another incident I recalled and related to the Sec was, how dear old Harry Brickwood (not so old, believe me) affectionately known as SPUDS rushed limping all the way across an open and hotly shelled field to a lorry, in order to fetch some iodine to put on a nasty gash I had made on my hand while 'carefully' opening a sardine tin.

'Poor little man' said this mass of sympathy, and off he went, and back he came safely, for which mercy the whole crew uttered in relief 'Thank God'.

'Sec', I added . . . 'it is small wonder that I never think of iodine without a thought for Harry Brickwood, and I never think of him without my mind returns to iodine.'

I shall ever remember that expedition to FIRMINY . . . how proud I was when walking, fully equipped, along the Strand to Charing Cross station, adorned like a pukka A.B. I think the little brown gaiters appealed to me most.

When we returned, I invited my company comrades in arms to dine with me . . . my good lady making a fine show with red, white and blue colours.

Excuse me if I introduce these excellent fellows to you by means of a few lines I perpetrated for the occasion . . . such is life. . . .

'Tall, keen and firm, but of a gentle disposition
Was our C.P.O.
Davison by name, and by nature kind and thoughtful
Thoughtful for the comfort of those around him
Many a time in the silent watches of the night
We thanked our lucky stars that 'twas with him we worked

To have him near us was a sort of balm
Which lessened any hardships we had to undergo.

Perhaps it will not be thought much amiss
If we introduce the seamen of this gallant crew
And in the limelight emphasise in each
The particular trait which surely is his due.

On Seaman Ayrton first we throw the light
And we find beneath that outward seeming piety
A real good sort, ready to do and willing to oblige
But sad to tell, through contact with another seaman
The language that he used by day and night
Would make the devil cringe with shame.
He is an artist of no mean ability
And the able sketches he has had produced
Will prove a welcome souvenir to all.

To Seaman Crawfurd next we would approach
And point to one who grasped the mean of all around
On 'sentry go' his sense of duty was so very keen
That a wand'ring Belgian had a fright and ne'er again was
    seen.
'Twas with equal force he would conclusions try
With Binks by name, a politician cute and dry
But now we know that this misguided rating
Will read the Chronicle and love Lloyd George with wisdom
    unabating.

We all have seen the happy morn a-dawning
And felt the better for it
'Tis just a simile to express the feelings we possessed
When first we looked upon the smiling happy face
Of Seaman Cripps.
It's wicked to be envious, but who is there
That could not envy such a disposition,
We thank thee Seaman Cripps right truly
For those rays of sunshine
The warmth of which we never can forget.

He was a merry fellow ; right merry, but saucy all the while
His chaff and chatter ever with us did the time beguile
Brave as a lion was Seaman Cutbill, and none so bright
Provided he had washed and brushed and put his toilet right.
'Twas a man of many parts, as witness his demeanour in
        Dunkerque
With falling bombs he never thought of danger or of hurt
But simply had déjeuner with appetite and zest.
And treated Seaman Berry to two bottles of the best.
Again at Firminy Hotel he was the one alone
To meet with much success with Jeanette or Yvonne
And his prowess met its zenith in the Royale Rue
But what the gallant fellow did there
Is nought to do with you.

He was not fond of humping, nor do we blame him
Yet he showed us with what will it could be done
The work of orderly did not more appeal to him
Than it did to us.   Yet greasy plates
And knives and forks looked as they did before
Under the careful skilful hands of Seaman Hoare.
We have to thank him for the promise of the photos he has taken
And will keep them ever by us with pleasure and with pride.
In saying this I know I'm not mistaken
We would have liked a snap of Little Tich beside.

Was he slow and was he sure, or was he just a mug ?
If you will only "Follow me"—I refer to Mr. Bugg.
He told us once a giant trod upon his face.
To do a thing like that was surely a disgrace.
But we have our suspicions that the giant he was Rum.
The least said the soonest mended, and so the word is "Mum".

The month has quickly fled
And all the crew are back again
At work in London.
The White Star Searchlights are in their care
Therefore no German Zeppelins ever dare
Approach these shores.

In years to come without the slightest doubt
We shall remember the happy days we spent together
And whether times be hard or bright and merry
You still will have the thoughts of
Seaman Berry.'

The town of FIRMINY which we had just left is of some importance ... the Sec tersely remarked that the only thing which shone in the dirty hole was the sun. However, we were amused by a man regulating the traffic with a red flag, for each time he moved he not only waved his flag, but danced a jig.

To all motorists I give a warning ... avoid the road between FIRMINY and ETIENNE, by hook or by crook. This was the only uncomfortable part of the journey, nevertheless the dear old Sec stuck to it like a trojan.

I heard him mutter on one occasion—'Mon Dieu' ... I thought he had said 'Mon Dewar' and chipped in—'I always thought you preferred Johnnie Walker.'

'No', said he ... 'I seldom indulge, and would rather have "Old Q" or "Blue Hangar" any time—they are the right "spirits"'.

Allow me to skip ST. ETIENNE ... it was a horrid part of the journey—until we come again into the open, near LORETTE. Here there are terraces of vineyards on the left, the view being somewhat spoilt by factories on the right.

Onward we climbed, and with some fine open views, the depression of the towns was almost forgotten.

We were nearing TALUYERS and espied on our right, more or less isolated, a restaurant, called 'The Café des Acacias'. We had passed it, but I persuaded the Sec to return, for it seemed a likely spot to obtain a good lunch.

It was a commodious place, but it appeared deserted; however, I ventured in and spoke to the young woman who presented herself.

'Can you serve lunch for two?' I inquired.... 'Oh, no, Sir', she replied ...'our season is finished.'

A little altercation then took place, which was evidently overheard by the 'patronne' for she came out of an adjoining room, and chipping in, said—'Of course we can manage something for these good gentlemen.' I treated her to the smile she richly deserved.

While déjeuner was being prepared we took a look around. There was a large dancing place railed in, with dancing floor—and a large notice . . . 'Men are forbidden to dance together.' There were also many divergencies for the young and for the amorous.

We went in to lunch, and this is what we had on the spur of the moment :

DÉJEUNER

HORS D'ŒUVRES
(to while away the time waiting for the hen to lay an egg for the omelette, we looked through a window and saw a child bring two eggs from the nest) —

1925 MEURSAULT (2 bottles)

Much better than I would have thought a 1925 could be.

OMELETTE
—

LETTUCE SALAD
—

CANARD
(alive this morning — no doubt killed for their 'All Saints' Day lunch. With chestnuts cooked with the parson's nose)
Haricots Verts
—

JAMBON
Foie du Canard
with
milk, eggs and herbs
(exquisite)

VIEILLE CURE LIQUEUR
(At the Sec's special request)

—

ST. MARCELLIN
Goat Cheese
(something like Brazil nuts)

Except for the fact that I had to curse Noah a few times for allowing the flies to live, I thoroughly enjoyed it, and so did the

Sec. The Ritz could not have done better; in fact, we were without the flunkey standing behind to steal away our plates before we had finished.

We noticed on coming out, some writing on the wall:

> 'Un vieillard m'a dit
> Et il avait raison
> Si tu fais crédit
> Tu perdras ta maison.'

We therefore paid up, and looked genuinely cheerful and grateful to our hostess for her wonderful performance.

After this excellent repast we made our way to VILLEFRANCHE. Ruminating on the good salad which was offered, I suddenly thought of a slug; I suppose—a very natural combination of thoughts . . . when an incident occurred to me, told by my mother when we were very young, but I have never forgotten it. I rather think it was a dark threat in case we did not take our cod liver oil properly.

We were told of a little girl who lived near my grandparents at, I believe, Brent . . . in fact, I am under the impression that the child was a school companion. Unfortunately, the little one developed consumption, and after many weary months, the medical attendants gave the parents to understand that there was little hope of ultimate recovery. In the quiet of the evening, saddened by such news they sat silent, when an old friend called on them, and during the conversation and exchange of ideas which followed, she said (of course, this is as near as I can remember what, and how my mother told us). . . . 'If the darling child were mine, I should give her some slugs !' The mother was horrified. . . . 'I would, in truth', she continued—'good, big, black slugs. Yes, yes ! I know what I am talking about : roll them in some sugar ; she will swallow them, taking them for jelly, and she will then get better.'

To cut this long history short, these slugs were procured and given to the child, so that her health improved out of all knowledge. I recollect my mother, on being asked, did not remember if the child afterwards knew what she had taken by way of medicine. I think I should describe it as 'Black Magic'.

As I related this to the Sec, I think he became more and more sceptical until I represented to him that it has recently been discovered that the sputum of angry or frightened TOADS contains a very large average of ADRENALIN, that marvellous drug which instantaneously invigorates its recipient. The natural exudations of the slug might possibly be found on analysis to give the same effect.

The weather was warmer, but the country was not very attractive.

At BRIGNAIS we saw a hundred boys being escorted to the cemetery . . . in honour of All Saints' Day, we imagined.

We passed by some ancient aqueducts, through TASSIN and ANSE, to VILLEFRANCHE.

Here we deposited our baggage at the Hôtel de l'Europe, and then made our way to VILLE S/JARNIOUX in the hopes of finding Mlle. Coulon at her vineyards at BEAUJOLAIS.

From VILLEFRANCHE we saw vines on either side ; this was evidently an important wine-producing area. At JARNIOUX we found every house unoccupied . . . we understood that the whole populace had followed the priest to the cemetery.

Eventually, by dint of perseverance we came across two ladies who knew Mlle. Coulon, and they informed us that she had left only yesterday for Paris. This good lady had given us the address of a Monsieur Dost, of whom she spoke well, and who she felt sure would look after us well.

We had therefore written to him to meet us at the hotel early the next morning.

VILLEFRANCHE is a pleasant town, and with the Fair in progress, was in a particularly lively mood.

DINNER

SOUP	
—	POUILLY-FUISSÉ (good)
TROUT	
—	
PARTRIDGE	BROUILLY-BEAUJOLAIS
—	(very pleasant, agreeable— light)
CHEESE	1893 ARMAGNAC

CHAPTER XIV

BEAUJOLAIS

THERE had been a severe frost during the night, and the thousands of bunches of flowers, etc., placed upon graves in the cemeteries, were frozen stiff.

The night's rest was thus spared from the invasion of the mosquito, for which we were both grateful. I thought, however, that I had a cold coming, as my lips were dry, nose moist, head heavy . . . so I was glad to be out in the clean, fresh, early morning sunshine.

There was no bath available at the hotel. Missing my morning bath may have had some influence here. . . . I promised to take two the next morning !

What creatures of habit we are !

We were ready to be off at half-past eight, with Monsieur Dost who, true to his appointment, had come to fetch us at the hotel.

Our road lay through the village of ARNAS . . . the country was pleasing, with a wintry aspect . . . the night frost still covering the ground.

As we proceeded, Monsieur Dost gave us useful information —such information culled in the country itself always seems more interesting and more lasting.

The Crus Classés of BEAUJOLAIS, generally accepted, are :

1. Moulin-à-Vent ⎫
2. Fleurie   ⎬ Grands 1ers crus.
3. Morgon   ⎭
4. Brouilly   ⎫
5. Chiroubles   ⎬ Crus Classés
6. Julienas   ⎭

The second crus are Regnie, Quince, St. Amour, Odenas, St. Etienne-les-Oullières, St. Etienne-la-Varenne, Lancie, Corcelle, St. Joseph, Chanes, Chasselas, etc.

The average alcoholic strength of Beaujolais is from 10° to 13° . . . and for the appellation 'Beaujolais' the wine must be produced from the GAMAY jus Blanc.

We were in the Commune du Perreon, and called at the Hospice de Villefranche where we sampled several wines of the 1934 vintage. They tasted good, light, and one might say—elegant. These wines mature quickly, and can be bottled within twelve months, and put into consumption IMMEDIATELY after that.

Yet, is it not extraordinary that at TAIN-HERMITAGE, not a great distance away, the wine must be kept in cask several years before it is ready to bottle ?

We were then shown a wine of 1933 vintage . . . grown by a vigneron of the Hospice, a Monsieur Perros. It had good colour, but was a trifle hard.

Another wine of St. Etienne-la-Varenne we found very similar.

All the good wines of Beaujolais come from the Côteaux . . . in the same way as the Côte d'Or applies to Burgundy.

On our way to BEAUJEU we could see the Chapelle de Brouilly on the summit of a hill, looking most important. The wines of BEAUJEU are not considered in as high a category as those of Brouilly.

We called at the Hospices de Beaujeu, and presented a letter of introduction to Monsieur Rampon who very kindly made arrangements for us to visit the chais of the Hospices, near REGNIE, some distance away from the town.

In the course of conversation the word 'old' was used. I inquired what was considered as old, when to my surprise, Monsieur Dost informed me—' Last year's vintage, 1933', . . . 'with us is "Vin vieux".'

We passed by JULIENAS, the wines of which district when made with jus blanc (Gamay) are entitled to the appellation 'Beaujolais'.

The soil is composed mostly of limestone and sand. If the wine requires any assistance, the law allows it by the addition of sugar.

The law of 27th July, 1929, modified that of 1926 in relation to chaptalisation.

The word 'chaptalisation' is derived from 'Chaptal', the name of a French chemist (1756-1832), who, by his work, reinstated an old process which had been abandoned, which consisted of adding sugar to wine in order to improve it.

The vines of Mâconnais and Beaujolais are : Gamay à jus blanc (Gamay de Vaux, Gamay de Bouze, Gamay-Charmont and some Gamay-Dormoy) . . . this last is a 'precocious' plant, being vintaged three weeks earlier than the others. The wine from these Gamay enjoys the right to the appellation 'Mâconnais, or Beaujolais', and also to that of 'Burgundy'.

The Gamay à jus rouge . . . give a deep-coloured wine ; for this reason they are often referred to as 'teinturiers'. The best known of them are the Chaudenays, Freau and the Moureaux. The wines are much heavier than those of the Gamay à jus blanc. Although they have the right to be called Beaujolais or Mâconnais according to their origin, they do not enjoy the right to the appellation 'Burgundy'.

While speaking of the vines of the district we must not forget to mention the Hybrides, mostly met with in the plains ; the principal varieties being the Siebel, Conderc, Berhyl-Seive, Gaillard, and also the white NOAH ! Many of these vines are doomed to be 'grubbed up' in order to prevent the over-production of wine of bad quality. The law of 24th December, 1934, provides the date 1942 as the latest time for the 'grubbing up' of the NOAH vines.

Let us hope that the Patriarch's name will be re-introduced and allowed to be associated with some other specie more worthy.

We called at the chais of the Hospices. The surrounding vigneron's cottages are most attractive—each family has a picturesque cottage, and these form a large quadrangle, the chais completing the western side.

The régisseur was most obliging, and with the assistance of his little daughter, helped us to consider several wines. . . .

No. 1.   1934 . . . I cannot say I cared much for this—too dry and hard, although a fair amount of colour.

No. 2.　—　Rosé and Gris, 13° . . . quite agreeable.

No. 3.　1934 . . . filled up two days ago—better and softer.

No. 4.　1933 . . . dry finish, good colour, fruity.

The vintage of 1934 commenced on the 15th September . . .
in some years it is later.

The Vin Rosé was only made to order.

We passed through ODENAS on our way to ST. ETIENNE DES
OULLIÈRES, having some glimpses of fine views on the way.

At ST. ETIENNE we partook of déjeuner at the Hôtel des
Oullières.

PÂTÉ
(good)

—

HARE
Potatoes (no)

—

CHICKEN
(good)

—

FROMAGE

—

DESSERT

—

CAFÉ

MOULIN-À-VENT, 1929.
(quite a big wine)

I think it a mistake to 'Chambre' the Wines of Beaujolais ;
this was very pleasant straight
from the cellar.

ARMAGNAC

What a corkscrew !　The handle was like a broom handle ;
evidently the proprietor, Monsieur Lafond, did not intend that
anyone should inadvertently put it in his pocket.

I had been much intrigued during the morning over the expressions frequently used . . .'jus blanc' or 'jus rouge', for I had
always been under the impression that the juice of all grapes is
white, often explained to me by the simile that the blood of all
humans is red—be they black or white.

We know full well that Champagne is made with the largest
proportion of black grapes—yet here was my host continually
emphasising 'jus rouge'.　At last I said—'I wish that I could see
some grapes with red juice.'　'Unfortunately', said he, 'the
vintage is over, or I could have shown you vineyards of them

[310]

. . . however, we will continue our journey, and when we come
to a vineyard which, by the leaves of the vines, I know will yield
"jus rouge", we will jump out, and by going along two or three
rows, we will find a few odd grapes overlooked.'

We did so, and after a few minutes I heard a voice—'Here
you are . . . I have some.' And sure enough there was a bunch
of grapes in his hand.

Offering them to me, I took grape by grape, and squeezed
them. . . . Out fell drops of blood, for that was what it looked
like.

The wine from these grapes is, as you may imagine, full of
colour but lacking in quality, and is used chiefly in blends.

From here we passed one of the second crus, Salles, and continuing, saw the Château de Montmélas on the top of the hill.

At DENICÉ was a distillery, which we had not the time to
visit.

At COGNET, another Hospice de Villefranche . . . but the
wines were inferior to those of PERREON.

At ST. LYERGUES, we came to the 'Co-operative', and here set
to work to inspect the excellent establishment and to taste a few
of the wines. . . .

No. 1. 1934, 11° - - poor.
  „ 2. 1934, 12° - - lighter and paler . . . perhaps
                                  the colour will develop.
  „ 3. 1933, 11.6° - - Vin Gris . . . not nice.

We gathered that the impression was that the 1934 wines
would not be as well succeeded as those of 1933.

Monsieur Dost then showed us a sample of his own 1934
vintage, 13°. . . . We found it to be quite promising, though
not extravagant in its pretensions.

With protestations of sincere thanks to Monsieur Dost for
all his kindness and attention we left him and the district for
MÂCON, at 3.45 p.m.

We had intended to stay at the Hôtel Europe et Angleterre,
where Monsieur Burtin's cooking is so famous, but unfortunately the hotel was closed ; we therefore made for the Terminus,
where we were very comfortable, arriving about 4.30 p.m.

The exhilarating air, and the smelling of so many wines had

completely dispelled the cold I had felt coming on in the morning, and for this I was truly thankful.

At the hotel, having advised the Post Office of the change of address, I found a notice requesting me to collect a registered letter. I took this notice with me and produced it, but was absolutely refused the letter . . . in spite of producing other letters addressed to me, and visiting-cards, etc. But no, nothing would suffice, I had to go back in the rain all the way to the hotel to fetch my passport.

I mention this as a warning to others . . . that it is always better to carry one's passport in one's pocket.

With a sole and a tournedos, cooked excellently, we had a bottle of Pouilly, 1929, which was very good, although a trifle sweet.

CHAPTER XV

MÂCONNAIS

THE next morning was foggy and frosty, and we waited for Monsieur Jambon, who had been asked to call on us.

He arrived before 9 o'clock, although we had expected to see him by 8 . . . evidently the telephone message was at fault.

Monsieur Jambon immediately placed himself at our disposal, and off we went to investigate the district responsible for the world-known wines of MÂCON.

As we proceeded we learned that the wines of MÂCON usually possessed 10° to 11° alcohol . . . rather less than the neighbouring BEAUJOLAIS. They had, in the most part, a slight 'goût de terroir', and were mostly produced from the Gamay-Teinturier . . . the Chaudenay, Freau and the Moureau for the red ; these have no right to the appellation 'Bourgogne', but are called 'Mâcon Rouge'. The soil was chiefly clay and limestone, inducive to larger quantities.

We were taken to one of Monsieur Jambon's properties, and tasted several wines, the most interesting of which was—1934 Précoces (No. 5), gathered three weeks earlier than any other. This would be bottled in the Spring . . . it is not a wine to keep.

We then tasted a Gamay, jus blanc, 10° . . . it was inclined to be acid, and it did not appeal to me.

The next was a Hybrid (Siebel), full of colour and used for blending . . . for this purpose it was sold.

We then sampled a White wine of Hurigny which was pleasing and of good quality.

After this we paid a visit to Monsieur Rabuel, a hard-working vigneron of seventy-one years, who thought that the Sec was my father. . . . We argued afterwards as to which one of us was entitled to the compliment !

We entered his small chais—kept in good condition. The bung-holes of the casks were covered with vine leaves, on which was placed a large stone. . . . He explained that he had found this method the most successful: we had seen this method employed in the Champagne district.

We tasted one wine, which was rather 'sucré' . . . maybe a little more fermentation would correct this.

The wine from the next cask was drier, but I should think he has good wine in store.

Leaving here, we passed by the Château du Teil, where the late proprietor, a retired Colonel much esteemed, died in 1933. He had been the president of the Société Hippique de France. Monsieur Jambon himself is the president of the Aero Club (Mâcon) and a pilot.

We passed by CHARNAY and LA PATTE DOIE, before reaching POUILLY, in which place I seemed to feel a particular interest . . . probably for the reason that I have, from time to time, given oysters their last bath in this delectable wine.

POUILLY is MÂCON, although on the borders of BEAUJO-LAIS. The only districts entitled to the appellation 'Pouilly' are, POUILLY, POUILLY, FUISSÉ, SOLUTRÉ, VERGISSON and CHAINTRÉ.

The soil is mostly limestone, with a mixture of red stone.

I had told our host that I was particularly interested in the wines from this district, and he took infinite trouble to introduce me to various vignerons; in fact, asking children by the roadside if their parents had made any wine and, the answer being in the affirmative, off we went with them to pay a visit.

POUILLY is in fact a portion of POUILLY-FUISSÉ, and the good people of POUILLY consider that the wine is 'IT'.

We called on Monsieur Renaud, where we sampled the 'vrai' POUILLY, 1934 vintage. It was very good—I thought, superior to the 1933.

The next cask, another cuvée as it were, did not please me so much.

I was so pleased with the first that I felt constrained to bargain for what they had made. Monsieur Renaud was away, but Madame I found a hard business nut to crack.

This wine should be bottled within eighteen months, or else will prove a little troublesome with its deposit.

These good people were the régisseurs of the proprietor, a Monsieur de la Cour, and their pay was a certain proportion of the récolte.

The next chais we visited—the name of the proprietor I forget—contained Pouilly-Fuissé, 1934. . . . It was slightly different and coarser.

We then visited a Monsieur Cante—

1st Cuvée—trifle sweet, not fine.

3rd   „   —did not care for . . . unpleasant after-taste.

2nd   „   —better than the last, but not so attractive as No. 1.

4th   „   —not good at all, in my opinion—slightly bitter ;
            we must, however, remember that these wines
            were very young.

Monsieur Denageon was the next, with much the same experience.

From here we went to Monsieur Blanc, at SOLUTRÉ, who showed us a wine that was pleasing, but nothing out of the ordinary.

The chais of another vigneron we visited smelt so offensively that we did not stop to taste any of the wines.

SOLUTRÉ . . . I cannot pass by here without a simple reference to this remarkable place.

'SOLUTRÉ ! . . . Why', asked Monsieur Jambon . . . 'is this the most musical town in France ?' 'Because', said he . . .'it is composed entirely of three notes of music—"Sol ut ré".'

For archaeologists, this place must be a paradise. I gathered, from my conversation with our host, that the rock of 'SOLUTRÉ' consisted of no less than five prehistoric geological periods. To appear quite learned and interested I wrote them down at his dictation—

'MAGDALÉNIEN',
'SOLUTRÉEN',
'AURIGNACIEN',
'MOUSTÉRIEN',
'ACHEULÉEN'.

[315]

We entered the Musée, where a kindly soul showed us over. She beamed so pleasantly that the Sec felt obliged to photograph her.

The view from the Musée was very fine, and inside we saw exhibits that seemed to me incredible.

I was much impressed by the sight of complete skeletons of human beings, dug up at the foot of the high hill, after having been buried some six thousand years.

I purchased a little book, illustrating some of these extraordinary things, but I must refrain from commenting on them, or part of the tour will be a reproduction of what can be found issued elsewhere, and that is what I wish to avoid ; I would, however, remark that, if to a layman it made such appeal, it surely must be more so to interested scientists . . . most of whom, however, probably know all about it.

The vines on the slopes of the hill looked entrancing in the sunlight, in their dying garb.

Two kilometres from POUILLY-FUISSÉ, we crossed the other side of the hill into BEAUJOLAIS . . . CHASSELAS at the foot, and further on—LEYNES, where we visited a Monsieur Cortot and tasted his wine, at 11.30°, which was pleasant and light, but rather difficult to handle for the English trade, as it should be bottled in a year and consumed straight away.

We visited Monsieur Bellicaut and tasted several wines . . . the first I thought almost attractive—not in the least hard or dry, but the second cuvée was decidedly 'sharp'.

We then went on to taste other wines in the same chais. No. 5 was superior to No. 2, but the after-taste was not particularly agreeable.

The next sample, No. 4, was decidedly better—all the same price, and sold on the lees. Monsieur Bellicaut then showed us his White wine, of which he was proud. It was good, but coarser than the Pouilly.

We tasted the wine at JULIENAS . . . much of the same description, but as Monsieur Jambon said— with 'plus de race'.

There is one thing to remember about the two vintages of 1933 and 1934 ; in the first year the cochylis was very prevalent, which has much bearing on the result, and wines must be bought with considerable discrimination.

We halted at JULIENAS to take lunch at the Coq au Vin. . . .

PÂTÉ TRUFFE	
(more truffes than Pâté)	POUILLY-FUISSÉ, 1926
—	(very good)
STEAMING HOT SAUSAGE ROLL	
—(glorifie l)	
—	
POULET DE BRESSE	
(Coq au Vin)	
bearing the metal medal in its	1923 MORGON FAYE
joints.	(brown colour—old and
—	enjoyable)
FONDS D'ARTICHAUTS	
AUX TRUFFES	
Hot as H . . . ! and very good	
—	
SARMENT ENTRECÔTE DE BŒUF	
—	
RHUM OMELETTE	GRAND MARNIER
—	
CHEESE	
—	1914 ARMAGNAC
FRUIT	

Chicken from LA BRESSE for many years had the reputation of being the best in the world ; in fact, the poultry farmers of the district used to send their chicken to London poultry shows, and invariably met with success.

The most noticeable thing about this restaurant was the number of unkempt, dirty-looking people who sat down to their meal—unwashed, unshaven, and in their shirt-sleeves . . . but this was provincial France. Nevertheless, the meal was most excellent.

During this repast Monsieur Jambon interested us very much by giving a full description of how and when the wine of Mâcon was first introduced into Paris, somewhere about the year 1660.

I will endeavour to pass on the details as near as possible as I received them, hoping that my memory will not be very much at fault :

Before that time, that is to say 1660, the good wines of the Côte d'Or were already famous, due no doubt to the monks of Cîteaux who had done very much towards popularising them and giving them European reputation. There is a legend about the first appearance in Paris of the Mâconnais wines.

Paris, owing to the example of the City and the Court, at that time consumed practically only the wines of Auxois and Orléanais. There was a vine-grower of Charnay, which is a little village quite near Mâcon, who was the cause of the introduction of the Mâcon wines to the Court in Paris, and his name was Claude Brosse.

About this time, the middle of the seventeenth century, the wines of Beaujolais and of Mâconnais were only drunk in their native districts, that is to say, in their native land, and in the adjacent 'environs'. The cultivation of the vine was more or less neglected, and there was no demand for it, but Claude Brosse who, himself a wise man, had a well-furnished cellar, boldly determined to travel to Paris in order to find some customers for his good wine.

He loaded two casks of the best, and placed them on a cart which was drawn by the strongest oxen from his stable, and off he set for Paris.

He was a very tall man, and he was very strong minded. As he proceeded, on more than one occasion he thought he might lose his wine, but being so strong, his clenched fist proved the best argument on the highways, and at the end of the thirty-third day he safely arrived in the city of Paris.

Within a week of his arrival, the King's Mass, which was celebrated at Versailles, was disturbed by a curious incident. When the psychological moment of the ceremony arrived, when all the congregation should have been kneeling, His Majesty perceived a man's head which rose above all the others. His natural thought was that one of the congregation had remained standing. He sent an officer to this person, whom he looked upon as being most disrespectful, and ordered him to kneel.

The officer soon returned and he told the King that the man to whom his attention had been drawn was in reality kneeling, but his stature must have been the cause of His Majesty's mistake.

Louis XIV ordered that this man should be brought to him as soon as the Mass was at an end.

An hour later, our friend, as you may have already guessed, Claude Brosse was brought to the King. He was clad like his countrymen of the Mâconnais, wearing a broad-brimmed felt hat, his chest was covered with a large apron of white leather reaching down to his knees, and his legs were encased in long leggings of a grey coarse linen.

'What do you come to Paris for', inquired the King. Claude Brosse made a low bow and he answered without being in the least disconcerted, that he had just arrived from Burgundy with a cart drawn by oxen, bringing two casks of his Mâcon wine with him. He said he knew the wine was so excellent that he hoped to sell it to some of the noblemen in Paris. The King immediately wanted to taste it. He found it far superior to the wines of Suresne and of Beaugency that were then being drunk at the Court. All the courtiers forthwith ordered from Claude Brosse his wine of Mâconnais, and the clever vigneron spent the rest of his life conveying to, and selling in Paris, the produce of his vineyard.

Such was the beginning of the trade—one might almost say, the famous beginning of the trade of the wines of Mâcon.

With such dissertations the time passed all too quickly, and off we had to be. We were then taken by our host to taste some of his own wines . . . 1934 vintage :

No. 1. 13°   —not very attractive.

B. 13.7°—I liked this—clean.

T 1.   —quite good.

T 2   —much the best . . .

by law, the 'chaptalization' already referred to is allowed.

We then tasted 1933 wines, which will be put into bottle in March (1934).

No. 1—rather dry, good colour, good nose. Monsieur Jambon says that the dryness will disappear in bottle.

T 33—much better.

We were then introduced to the Eau de Vie, of Moulin-à-Vent, distilled in 1900. It was good and it was interesting, but it emphasised the fact that Eau de Vie is not Cognac!

Monsieur Jambon informed us that his grandfather had distilled it, as in the year 1900 he had such large quantities of wine that he did not know what else to do with it.

At CHENAS we sampled the 1934 Moulin-à-Vent (Roche Gres), one of the best we had seen.

ROMANACHE THORINS comes under the appellation of 'Moulin-à-Vent'.

We then went on to FLEURIE, where we struck rain, but were recompensed with good views of the country.

At LABOURONS we tasted 1934 Fleurie, 12° . . . not very attractive. Then, calling on Monsieur Bartier we sampled a Fleurie of 1934, which we did not like, as the taste was disappointing, and then a sample of another Fleurie, 12°, of the same vintage. This was far superior, although somewhat 'anaemic' in colour.

At FLEURIE itself we tasted, chez Monsieur Jacquet, a wine of which he had made 9 pièces, which appealed to us as of good quality—12.50° . . . and much more colour and body. All these wines are sold on their lees, which from a purchaser's point of view is a serious item.

We then made our way to see Monsieur Chervet, who introduced us to his wines of 1934. . . . He had made 20 pièces with the astounding alcohol degree of 14.4° Malligand.

You can imagine how surprised we were when he informed us that his 1928 wines actually reached 15°!

One of two instruments is employed, by which the alcoholic degree is determined—the Malligand, and the Salleron. The Malligand is the one generally to be found in use, particularly between proprietors and merchants.

It might be said that the former gives the 'commercial' degree, and the Salleron, the 'legal' degree. The difference of the degree given by the two processes varies but little—not more than 0.2°, which is insignificant.

The Malligand gives the stronger, and is always understood to be referred to unless the word Salleron is indicated.

His 1933 wine was inclined to be slightly dry . . . however, that did not worry him, for he had sold it all.

'Now', said Monsieur Jambon . . . 'I will take you to see an old friend of mine . . . a Monsieur Daniel of Morgon. . . . I frequently buy his wines, for he is a wise old vigneron, and knows what he is about.'

Unfortunately, in 1934 he had suffered with a visitation of hail, which had done much damage . . . but he kept on smiling. I made a note, after tasting his 1934, that if I should consider a purchase of Mâconnais, here was the wine. It was so clean, and one almost used the adjective—'Fine'.

This ended an enjoyable and an industrious day's outing . . . we returned to the hotel, Monsieur Jambon promising to call for me later when we would drive out into the country for dinner ; while we left the dear old Sec to rest after the physical fatigue of the day.

I shall always feel indebted to Monsieur Jambon for taking me all the way (especially in a torrent of rain) to VONNAS, to dinner at the Grand Hôtel Moderne—pray make a note of this . . . it was excellent—yes, *excellent* underlined !

DINNER (22 fcs ! ! !)

TERRINE DE CANARD À LA GELÉE —	1928 POUILLY very good
ESCARGOTS BOURGUIGNONNE (exquisite—each in a separate earthenware pot) —	1926 MOULIN-À-VENT very good—rather old
BROCHETONS MEUNIÈRE —	
POULET À LA CRÈME —	1815 ARMAGNAC
BEIGNETS VONNASIENS Fromage frais —	soft and pale—really excellent
TARTE MAISON —	
FRUITS	

B.W.

The chef, Monsieur Perrat, who joined us afterwards over the Armagnac in order that we could compliment him on the dinner, was an artist to his finger-tips. I shall ever remember him . . . his soul-like feeling for wine was almost pathetic. I can see him now as I write this—with uplifted eyes, and hand on heart (having listened to a few remarks on the excellence of wine), softly uttering, with profound depth . . . 'Ah, oui Messieurs . . . LE VIN QUI EST MYSTÉRIEUX.'

I have promised myself that if ever I go to these parts again, I will return to shake him by his honest hand.

I took away with me one of the delightful little escargot pots . . . each time this catches my eye I feel the glow of a smile of pleasure.

I thoroughly enjoyed this, but it was not until the next morning that I was able to tantalize the Sec on what he had missed. However, being of a charitable turn of mind I did not think fit to rub it in too far.

It rained all through the return journey and all through the night, but I was able to improve the darkened hour with conversation with Monsieur Jambon : the following is the gist of what he told me :

That, in France, the Red wines of the Mâconnais, and the *ordinary* wines of the Beaujolais, are not *generally* kept for any long period as likely to make 'fine wines in bottle'. They are consumed even in the year of their production as 'bottled wines'. As a matter of fact, their degree of alcohol does not permit them to give a lasting quality, and at the end of one year, or even two, their colour becomes that of 'Pelure d'oignon'. They sometimes lack aroma, but have an excellent taste of 'fruit', recalling that of the raisin. This character might disappear at the end of a year, therefore look to it that the light wines of Mâconnais or of Beaujolais are consumed before eighteen months, and don't dream of keeping those which do not contain at least 12 degrees of alcohol. On the contrary in the good years like 1929, 1933 and 1934, one can keep, without any fear or misgivings, the wines of the growths of Beaujolais, such as BROUILLY, MORGON, FLEURIE, CHIROUBLES, CHENAS, JULIENAS and MOULIN-À-VENT. All these wines have more than 12°, and will give an admirable bottle at the end of about three years.

Monsieur Jambon then related to me the manner in which the wines of these growths are matured :

When the wine comes from the vats and presses it remains on its heavy lees until the Spring, that is to say until the end of February or the beginning of March ; it is then racked, and the time of the last quarter of the moon is chosen for this operation because it has been observed for a very long time that the racking can be effected very much better and with less deposit at this period than if it were carried out during the first quarter, or at the full moon ; for the state of the atmosphere has a real influence on that of the wine. It is also well to remember that when the wind is in the south the racking is less successful than when there is a northerly wind blowing. Next year (1935), the last quarter of the moon ends on the 5th of March, by which date the racking will certainly have been finished. In the month of June, that is to say, at the moment when the vine is in flower, a second racking takes place in order to avoid the fermentation occasioned by the approach of warm weather. Then, in the month of September, immediately before the vintage, the wine is given a third racking, and from this time should be entirely free from impurities. Therefore, during the first year the wine may have received three rackings—in March, in June and in September.

Now is the moment to consider the bottling.

There are two alternatives :

(1) To bottle the Red wine at the end of two or three years ... this method has the advantage of giving a bottle of wine in which there is not much deposit ; nevertheless it will require decanting. The wine is at the same time, more worn ... it has lost its vivid red colour and some of its bouquet, and has taken on 'pelure d'oignon'.

(2) To bottle the wine after it has been a year or eighteen months in the cask ... this is the method most recommended for the better wines. By this method of early bottling, the fruity character and the aroma will be retained and will develop in bottle.

The fermentation of the White wines is always much longer than that of the Red wines, seeing that the White wines do not remain in vats before pressing, and that directly they come out of the press they are run straight into their hogsheads where the fermentation takes place.

The rackings of the White wines are undertaken at the end of January or at the beginning of February, as soon as the cold weather has been able to precipitate and cause to fall to the bottom of the cask, the lees in suspension. Then following the same method as for the Red wines, the White wines are racked again in June and September. The most convenient time for the bottling is also from twelve to eighteen months, seldom later because of the risk that the colour, through 'oxy', might change from white to yellow.

'In fact,' emphasised the enthusiastic Monsieur Jambon, 'in good years, the Red wines of Beaujolais and the White wines of Mâcon can rival the great Burgundies. They have just as much finesse and aroma.'

I left my good friend at the hotel, and can only hope that he understood how much I felt indebted to him for all the kind attention he had given us. He was of the utmost valuable assistance, knowing every niche of the country; I was indeed fortunate in having fallen under the auspices of such an erudite and painstaking personality.

The following is an appreciation of the vintage years in the region of—

BEAUJOLAIS AND MÂCONNAIS.

1910—Small vintage year of mildew . . . bad quality.

1911—Remarkable year for its quality and finesse. Complete wine with good alcohol.

1912 ⎱
1913 ⎰ Two years of mediocre quality.

1914—Could not be appreciated at its true value on account of the War and the deplorable conditions in which the vintage was gathered.

1915—Gave good wine.

1916 ⎱
1917 ⎰ Could not be appreciated.

1918—More important quantity, but only passable quality.

1919—Very good wine ; have been very much inquired for.
1920—A hard wine.
1921—A soft wine ; fruity but very fine ; very good year.
1922—Quantity but no quality.
1923—Well made wines but hard ; they deceive buyers very much.
1924—Good . . . medium quality.
1925—Full bodied wines, but lacking in finesse.
1926—Grand year . . . grand quality.
1927—An abundant year but very inferior quality.
1928—Very great year ; full bodied wines ; generous wine of the most remarkable years since the opening of the century.
1929—Equally a very great year ; wines less complete than the 1928, but developing finesse.
1930—A year of mildew ; bad quality ; small vintage.
1931—Very mediocre quality.
1932—Quality hardly passable.
1933—Very great year ; small production but excellent quality.
1934—Appears as though it would well follow 1933, but in view of the very large production, a careful choice is necessary.

CHAPTER XVI

CHÂLONNAIS

AND A VISIT TO MONTRACHET

THE next morning, Sunday the 4th November, we drove to CHÂLON S/SAÔNE. . . . It was raining all the time, not allowing of the happiest disposition.

When we arrived at the hotel it was nearly time for déjeuner. I was hungry, and possibly slightly disgruntled.

The hors d'œuvres were a number of 'messy' looking vegetables. The fried sole was tough and dried up. . . . 'Probably left over from the night before', said the Sec.

The petit pois smelt of vegetable water, and the bread was stale and damp !

To assist this on its way we indulged in a bottle of 1928 Chablis Moutonne, the nose of which was better than the taste.

The knife even refused to cut the potatoes.

The one redeeming feature was the oil, which was undoubtedly pure olive oil ; none of the mixtures so frequently masquerading as such.

For cheese, I mixed the delectable Rocquefort-cum-butter-cum-Armagnac, and practically made my meal off this.

To add to our discomfort we had facing us, at a near table, a black-bearded man, who looked for all the world like a communistic villain !

The waitress was attentive, and appeared discomforted at our discomfort : she spoke English very well, and told us that in her younger days she lived with a French family in England, and learned English by attending evening classes.

After lunch the rain ceased and we took a walk around the town, being much interested in the barges going through the locks, and watching the anglers, none of whom caught so much as a weed.

I remember one very long barge, which took up the complete space of the lock ; the dwellers on the barge came out to exercise themselves, together with their dog and even their chicken.

One dirty little infant was bent on chasing a cockerel, which reminded me of the old saying 'if you want to catch a bird you must put salt on its tail'. When I was a youngster, I should think about six years of age, this was very forcibly impressed upon me. I had frequently heard this, and on an occasion when my mother was out I thought it would be fun to catch a bird in this way. I went to the store cupboard, and taking all the salt I could find I placed it in a pail which I filled with water, and thought I would throw some on the tail of any stray bird that came into the garden . . . this was not successful—what should I do ? I then had a brain-wave. I fetched the syringe, and by this means tried to squirt it on the tails of the little feathered ones.

It was painful sitting down during the next few days ! !

At dinner we fared considerably better :

CONSOMMÉ	
(very good)	1928 CHABLIS VAUDÉSIR
—	
ŒUF MORNAY	
—	
ROAST CHICKEN	
—	
CAMEMBERT	1924 CHABLIS, MONT DE
—	MILIEU
BISCUITS	

The eggs evoked from the Sec the commonplace query, which I endeavoured to explain to the waitress—'Which came first ; the egg or the chicken ?'

She was an intelligent girl, for when she arrived with the next course, she remarked—'You are answered now!'

The biscuits were Huntley and Palmer's and, in order to support home industries, we ordered a second portion.

Of the wines I preferred the freshness of the 1928 ; by the look of the Sec's glass I gathered that he was of the same opinion

... so we were extravagant enough to leave most of the 1924, and order another bottle of the younger wine.

I do not think that the Sec was any more comfortable than I was here, for he expressed himself in no measured terms about the ... lift, and the ... bell !

The next morning it was raining. I enjoyed a good bath, but as usual the waste chain would not function—these trifling things are most annoying.

We left for GIVRY about 8 o'clock, passing through Chatenoy le Royal, and Dracy la Forêt.

We had arranged to meet Monsieur Bonnot, the régisseur of the Baron Thénard—part owner of the 'Grand' Montrachet.

We did not know where to find the chais, but having reached GIVRY, and proceeded a short way into the town, I suggested that I should make some inquiries. I asked the first person who came along, and received the welcome information—'ici, Monsieur' ... and true enough we had stopped outside the gates !

Simonet, the cellar-man, was busy coopering, and informed us that Monsieur Fonchet, the maître de chais, would shortly arrive ... but we wanted to see Monsieur Bonnot, and were told that he would certainly arrive before long. It was raining hard, so we jumped over a pool of water at the entrance, and took shelter inside the chais.

In good time, Monsieur Bonnot put in an appearance, and showed us marked attention, for had we not bought considerable quantities of 1928 and 1929 'Grand' Montrachet from the Baron's estate ?

These wines of 'Grand' Montrachet which are grown on one particular well-favoured hillside, are remarkable ... I agree with the opinion so often expressed that they are the finest White wines of France.

Monsieur le Général, le Marquis de Laguiche owns a similar hectarage to the Baron; in fact, between them they possess the largest portion of the whole hillside, which, after all, is not very extensive.

At GIVRY we tasted the following wines, which I give, together with my own impressions :

[328]

1930 Gd. Montrachet . . . very poor.

1932 „ „ . . . quite good—not a giant.

1931 „ „ . . . seems good—some body, still fermenting.

1933 „ „ . . . I did not like this as much as the 1932, maybe because of the fermentation . . . the others did not agree with me.

1934 „ „ . . . very young to taste, but I believe (in upstairs chais—which it will prove an excellent wine. is rather warmer. This 13.8° to 14°—can bottle (with assists the fermentation racking), in two years. somewhat).

By way of diversion we were shown—

1933 Givry Rouge . . . a very pleasant wine for early use.
(Hill slopes) Pinot
—Clos St. Pierre

1933 Boix-Chevaux . . . did not like this so well.
(Rouge)

1934 „ „ . . . hard and fermenting.

1934 Pouilly-Fuissé . . . quite attractive, but I remember to have tasted more agreeable wines at Pouilly.

With many thanks for the kind attention, we bade Monsieur Bonnot 'good-day', and went off with the generous gift of a bottle of the delectable 1929 'Grand' Montrachet.

From here we went to CHAGNY, through MERCUREY and LES FONTAINES. It was raining all the time; in fact, the whole country-side seemed full of rain. We thought—this rain will surely keep Monsieur Colin Bouley indoors, so if we call on him at CHASSAGNE, we shall find him at home, and no doubt he will allow us to taste the wine made from the estate of the Marquis de Laguiche—probably the most famous Montrachet in the world.

Yes, our luck was in . . . there he was, and ready to be more than obliging.

We sampled the 1934, 15°.... I thought it was excellent. 'Surely', I said to the Sec ... 'we must have some of this.'

The fermentation was going on, in fact will continue probably for two or three years : the Marquis will allow nothing to be done which in any way will interfere with the true and straight line taken by nature ... no doubt this is accountable for such a success and such a wonderful reputation.

Tasting this wine reminded me of—

'O Montrachet, divin Montrachet, le premier, le plus fin de vin blanc que produit notre riche France, toi qui es resté pur et sans tache, entre les mains de ton honorable propriétaire, M. le Marquis de Guiche, je te salue avec admiration.'

I was listening to the fermentation, when Monsieur Colin Bouley remarked that the noise was called in the district, the 'Bruit des Grenouilles'.... You will perhaps remember that, somewhere else on the Côte d'Or it had been described as the 'Chanson du Vin'.

The vines on this renowned vineyard are the Pinot-Blanc.

We then had a few more to sample :

1934 Bâtard ... this had nearly finished fermenting— 13° ... but what a fall from the other.

1934 Chardonnay... 13.50°—more sugar. I preferred this to the Bâtard.

Aligoté ... a very ordinary wine.

1933 Clos St. Jean... 12.50°—quite a pretty little wine, but de Chassagne too costly.

As we were tasting and chatting about the wines our attention was called to the sound of a bugle.... 'This', said our good friend ... 'is only the bugle-boy, who is announcing to the villagers that he has arrived, and that they can buy some cheese from him if they so desire.'

We expressed our gratitude to Monsieur Colin Bouley and his good wife, and then made our way back to CHÂLON S/ SAÔNE, en route for LONS LE SAUNIER, where we intended to have our lunch.

Summary of Vintages of Beaujolais, Mâconnais and Châlonnais

Old wines, as we think of them, do not exist . . . it is only on the rarest occasions that a bottle of old Beaujolais, Mâconnais or Châlonnais is produced. When this happens, one is invariably prompted to remark—'What a pity such a wine was not consumed before !'

Such vintages as 1878, 1885, 1895, 1898, 1899, 1904, 1906, 1911 and 1915 are spoken of in hushed tones . . . a token of respect to the long departed.

Every now and then a bottle of 1919 will put in an appearance . . . very good, but should be used.

The—

1923's are excellent ; but drink them while they are so.

1926's I have been fortunate to have a share of several bottles . . . they are in their prime, and surely that is the time to show them off !

Since then, the best wines produced were those of 1928, 1929 and 1933 . . . and those of 1934 promise very well.

For those who like and appreciate the lighter variety of wine produced in these areas, as compared with the Côte d'Or, attention should be given to these last two vintages. Let them fill their bins during the next twelve months, at a low cost, and look forward to good, young, healthy beverage wines, for early consumption.

CHAPTER XVII

ARBOIS AND CH. CHÂLON

WE were now intent on visiting the JURA . . . in particular, ARBOIS and CHÂTEAU CHÂLON, of world-renown, owing in part to the association of the famous Dr. Pasteur with them.

At CHAMPORGEUIL the weather had cleared a little, but as we arrived at CHÂLON S/SAÔNE, the rain arrived with us.

We found it necessary to refill with petrol, and were somewhat intrigued by a notice, which read—

'POURBOIRE INTERDIT.'

This was the only place where we had noticed such a thing !

I was much amused here for, when leaving, the attendant bade us—'Bonjour, Monsieur et Dame' . . . no doubt a matter of habit . . . but this had happened so often that I was wondering whether it was the Sec or myself who was beginning to look so effeminate as to be mistaken for a 'dame'.

Down a long avenue of Poplars, we were at ST. MARCEL, and once again remarked what adepts the natives were at riding their bicycles, in wind or rain . . . it mattered little. On they went, with umbrellas open !

In this part of the country, the maize hanging under the eaves of the house was quite a feature.

The country was flat and not interesting. After passing LA ROUGÈRE, we had considerable difficulty in passing a lorry . . . any chauffeur but the Sec would have been furious, but he, dear old fellow, took it almost philosophically, being perhaps a trifle annoyed.

At VELARDS, I exclaimed—'Two magpies', and sure enough before we reached ST. ETIENNE the clouds were breaking and there seemed a possibility of better weather conditions.

However, this did not last for long, for on reaching the further side of MONTRET, it commenced to rain again.

We were now entering more hilly surroundings and more interesting country.

At LOUHANS, the market was in full swing, in spite of the rain ... everyone and everything in the market and streets was drenched. It was all so pitiable—even the cows shook themselves like a wet dog does under such circumstances.

Before arriving at RATTE, we had to pull up at a level crossing. After waiting some four or five minutes a P.L.M. train passed, consisting of both passenger carriages and goods trucks.

It appeared to be clearer over the JURA ... we therefore felt more confident of finer weather during the afternoon. At RATTE we were much amused at the quantities of pigs being taken to market—two layers in each van ; how they squeaked when they were put in. . . . I could not help but hum 'This little pig ... etc.'

At BEAUREPAIRE we were disappointed at a continuance of rain. Near COURLAOUX, some ruins of an old castle presented a pleasant sight.

We were soon at LONS LE SAUNIER—a quarter past one, and quite ready for déjeuner.

We stayed at the Hôtel de Genève et Paris ... and for our meal we had—

PÂTÉ	ARBOIS ROSÉ, en carafe—good to drink in the country, probably 1933—pretty to look at, but on the taste, slightly casky.
—	
MUTTON HASH very good and hot	
—	
CHICKEN (good) Brussels Sprouts	1921 CH. CHÂLON—with that special characteristic which we expected.
—	
CHEESE	

No wonder, I thought, that the editor and 'farceur' of 'Mr. Clerihew' approves of this wine, for it assuredly must rise to his head, and enable him to offer to the public such misrepresentation of my amorous activities ; even should he in some measure

[333]

make amends by virtue of agreeing that I am somewhat inclined to share a bottle of good wine with a good friend.

After lunch it had ceased to rain, and we wandered out for a few minutes. The first thing which caught our attention was a statue to Rouget de l'Isle . . . he who wrote 'La Marseillaise'.

LONS LE SAUNIER is a very interesting old place, with its curious bridges, its fine restaurants, and many ancient associations.

I had the misfortune to lose one of my gloves, therefore thought well to seek a shop where I could replace them.

I took advantage of the opportunity of having a chat with a couple of intelligent young women in the shop I had entered, and during the conversation they gave me the name of a certain Professeur Monot, who could give me much information on the subject of the wines of the district . . . unfortunately he was 'out'.

I then made my way to the Syndicat d'Initiative and found an elderly lady there, who was extremely helpful.

As I left this office I was caught in a violent storm . . . so violent that the streets were empty in less than a minute. I rushed for shelter. . . . I won't tell you where ! The very vivid fork-lightning lasted for a long time.

As I write this I can almost see how a car was struck by a gust of wind, in the hurricane, and almost turned over . . . how it managed to right itself was a miracle.

This, the fifth of November, was 'Guy Fawkes' day, and we had the fireworks, with a vengeance !

When I got back to the hotel I found the Sec in a state of despair, wondering what had become of me . . . however, my unharmed bodily appearance soon put his anxious mind at ease.

DINNER

POTAGE (vegetable)	1921 VIN JAUNE DE JURA (old cork) 30 fcs.
SOLE MEUNIER (too much grease)	Did not appeal to me, reminded me of Ch. Châlon, when not very good.
MORILLES À LA CRÈME (rich—very good)	1929 ARBOIS, Extra Fin. 18 fcs. fuller and softer.

BÉCASSE S/CANAPÉ
Plain salad
(very good)
—
ÉCREVISSES
—
GRUYÈRE DU PAYS
—

DESSERT
—
CAFÉ

1893 CH. CHÂLON—over 30 yrs. in bottle (too madérisé) As dark as Pale Brown Sherry — strong, good flavour, dry. Would not care to drink this very often —much preferred the 1915 which Mr. Levis gave me.
1865 MARC DU PAYS—As the Scotsman would say—'Nae sae bad' . . . but his throat is seasoned.

When I went out for a walk I found a starlit night ; most pleasant after the storm . . . no wonder that the Sec thought I was a long time gone.

The hotel (provincial) arrangements were not quite up-to-date . . . there was no place to put the toilet accessories. The bedroom-light had to be turned on from the outside ; this may have its advantages but imagine what was said when it was realised that the same thing happened when the light had to be extinguished !

The next morning, at 6 o'clock, it was dull, but not raining. At 7.30 it commenced to rain, but it was necessary to make a start.

On the way we noticed a number of small vineyards and, at L'ÉTOILE, came across the buildings of the local Co-operative, which concern evidently takes care of the produce of these small holdings.

From here we climbed to PLAINOISEAU . . . many vines were here, and we arrived at a pleasant approach to the foot of the JURA hills.

Near ST. GERMAIN we inquired of a cyclist the route for Château Châlon. . . . He gave us the direction and volunteered the information that there was a fine vintage of Ch. Châlon wine this year.

After we passed VOITEUR we came upon a very pleasant winding road to the summit of the hill—and here was Château

Châlon, offering some beautiful views in recompense of the climb.

This quaint village is built on rocks . . . a very ancient place ; such roads and curious houses, and boasting a thirteenth-century church.

What soil there was appeared dark and rich, and with some wooded country in the close vicinity it lent a pleasing aspect.

At Château Châlon itself there were no vines—we continued our way down the opposite slope, past the Granges de Ladaye, with deep ravines on the right.

The roads reminded me of our good English country roads . . . we were soon at PLASNE, revelling in fine views overlooking the valley on the left.

The old rusty tiles of the houses of POLIGNY were picturesque, but the beauty of the situation was spoilt by the rain.

We had now arrived at ARBOIS—market day and raining hard. What a spectacle !

We immediately sought out the whereabouts of Monsieur Déjean de Saint-Marcel, to whom we had been given an intro-duction by our good friend, Duncan Shaw.

This gentleman immediately placed himself at our disposal. . . we were indeed fortunate in having such a valuable introduction.

During our interview we learned many things that were quite new to us. The first thing which surprised me, because of my ignorance, was that the particular wine 'Jaune' which we had come across, was in reality entitled to the appellation 'Ch. Châlon'. Pupillin was Arbois wine from another side.

The veritable Château Châlon wines are from Ménétrue and Voiteur et L'Étoile. Blanc sec is another variety, not made as Ch. Châlon.

The wines of ARBOIS must not be confused with those of Ch. Châlon. The 1934 vintage gave 14° sugar for the Vin Jaune d'Arbois, and also for the Vin Blanc (Merlon) ; these are strong wines, and it will be necessary to wait four years before bottling them.

The Château Châlon will be kept in the cask ten years before being bottled ; the lees are left in the casks so that the wine can be fed by them.

The Sparkling wine, with 6 to 8% dosage, is bottled within a twelvemonth. At ARBOIS there is a larger quantity of Red wine than White.

There is also a Sparkling Pink wine, made on the slopes of the JURA—brut, sec, or sucré.

The enthusiasm of Monsieur Déjean de Saint-Marcel for the wines of ARBOIS was catching, and during the few hours I was privileged to be with him, I was caught in the same vein.

I wish I could remember one half of the interesting things he told me of the history of the wines and the wines themselves.

He spoke of the vineyards as being the most ancient in France, and of the wines as having a great reputation from time immemorial . . . adding that the Romans were well pleased with them, and later, the Emperor Maximillian found them so good that he allowed them free entry into all his domaines.

'This being so', he went on . . . 'it is small wonder that you will find reference to their excellence in the works of such men as Rabelais, Voltaire, and Rousseau—this last saying that he would not stop at theft in order to procure them ! Let me assure you', said he . . . 'that these wines, apart from being so very agreeable to drink, are decidedly "hygiénique".' This will be readily understood when we know of the immense care and knowledge that is brought to bear on the viticulture, in particular with the choice of vines. The Ploussard, Pinot Noir, Savagnin, or Naturé (Traminer of Germany), Chardonnay, Trousseau Noir.

The dominating position is east-south-east at a varying altitude of from 300 to 400 metres, with massive rocks affording much shelter from the north and east winds.

From the Red and White wines, we spoke of the 'Vin Jaune' or 'Vin de garde', and Monsieur Déjean told me a very interesting anecdote. Not trusting myself to remember the detail, I asked him to write it down, so I can give it to you, *in extenso* :

'Un jour Napoléon Ier vantait le Johannisberg au ministre autrichien Metternich qui lui répondit :

' "Sire, vous avez en France un vin qui vaut mieux encore, c'est le vin jaune."

' "Vin de garde", il peut se conserver en bouteille plus d'un siècle sans rien perdre de ses qualités. Lors du voyage du Président de la République à Arbois, à l'occasion du centenaire de Pasteur, deux vignerons, âgés l'un de quatre-vingt douze ans, l'autre de quatre-vingt neuf, lui offrirent chacun un panier de vin jaune dans lesquels il s'en trouvait parmi les bouteilles de bien plus vieilles qu'eux, puisque l'une était de 1811 et l'autre de . . . 1774.

'Écoutez d'ailleurs ce qu'un vieux moine (et les moines sont gens qui s'y connaissent) dit du vin jaune :

' "Vos lèvres y baignent-elles, vous éprouvez je ne sais quel aiguillon qui vous poinct ; vous espérez le trouver au fond du verre et vous avez bu jusqu'à la dernière goutte que vous le cherchez encore. En auriez-vous abusé, laissez-lui du repos ; dormez un moment, il maintiendra dans votre estomac la chaleur convenable, en chassera les 'humeurs nuisibles, poursuivra jusqu'à votre cerveau les humeurs rebelles et les dissipera : vous vous lèverez gai et dispos.' " '

Vin de Garde.—One of the most interesting wines of this district is that of the Château d'Arlay . . . the ancient associations spread a halo around the wines as well as around the place.

Monsieur Georges Tournier very kindly supplied me with much interesting information about this famous wine and this equally famous Château.

The Vin Jaune of 1928 is the best since 1921. This is not only shown when tasting, but also by the complete analysis of the Oenological Institute. This wine (Vin Jaune) of 1928 gave 14.6° at the end of 1928 ; 14.1° in 1931. Having a strong predilection for the 1928 vintage in general over the 1929, I was much interested to learn that M. Tournier considered that of the 1928's and 1929's the former is undoubtedly the better—finer bouquet ; less hard and not in the least 'madérisé', whereas the 1929 is already somewhat madérisé and has not developed in accordance with expectations.

Certainly these wines of Château d'Arlay are remarkable . . . there is nothing in the world to compare with them. I was privileged to taste the 1928 which will shortly be bottled, and is considered to be of the highest quality . . . and should last, without becoming madérisé, a hundred years or more.

When you taste it for the first time, you will be nonplussed. First you will say 'Sherry'—then perhaps—'Marsala'; then—'no, it's like a cross between the two.' But, it is entirely a species of its own.

It would do well to serve, on very special occasions, at the commencement of dinner . . . dry, clean and something out of the ordinary; moreover, if what I heard is true—most health-giving. Something to talk about as well as to enjoy.

There is made also, Vin Rouge, but this did not appeal to me in the same way, and I am under the impression that it does not live so long.

I will admit, however, that some of the lighter, more elegant varieties are useful at the commencement of a meal (even with fish) and do well to lead up to the finer wines which follow; or perhaps I ought to say—which *should* follow.

Château d'Arlay is the name of the Château which has been re-built many times during several centuries B.C. Its vineyards, called 'The Vines' of Château d'Arlay, also existed B.C. It is from this source that occasionally one comes across the celebrated Vin Jaune, or the Vin de Garde; the right soil, the right vines, and an ideal position; that is, south-east, such as one finds in the 'Grand' Montrachet—the property of the Marquis de Laguiche.

It was the Lords of this Château who founded, two leagues from Arlay, the Abbey of Château Châlon in the year 670 of our era, at a time when Château d'Arlay had already been destroyed, reconstructed and transformed, and had been in existence for several thousand years.

The Romans, under Julius Caesar, sacked the manor and the vineyards, which were replanted under the Emperor Probus about the year 278 A.D.

We read that in the history attaching to this place, one Gérard, who had married the grand-daughter of Charlemagne, made the Château d'Arlay the capital of all his possessions; the very heart of the Franche Comté: from which time down to the present, the greatest pride has been taken in the production of these unique and almost marvellous wines, which, given a good vintage, will last (and not become 'maderisé') for upwards of half a century.

[339]

We read with regard to the Vin Jaune, that it was the Princes of Châlon, Lords of Arlay, who had, in the course of their long campaign in Hungary, on the Bosphorus, in the Lebanon and in Palestine, brought back amongst others, the Imperial plants of Tokay which have become at Château d'Arlay, the Savagnin which produces the Vin Jaune. It was at Château d'Arlay that Vin Jaune first appeared, and it was only later that it extended itself to its surroundings, of which Château Châlon is an example. The wine of Château d'Arlay bears only the name of Château d'Arlay and not the name of Château Châlon. The name of Château Châlon is carried, not only by the wines of Château Châlon but also by the wines of the surrounding communes where the Abbey owned vineyards such as Nevy sur Seille, Voiteur, Ménétru and Domblans.

On the other hand the name of Château d'Arlay has remained for, and only for, the wines of Château d'Arlay, without its name being used for wines from other vineyards, which the Lords of Arlay, Princes of Châlon-Arlay actually owned in neighbouring communes.

One might reasonably ask why the name of Château Châlon is known so much better than that of Château d'Arlay. The fact that the name of Château Châlon is borne by the wines of several communes is one of the reasons. The principal reason comes from the fact that the abbesses sold a part of their wines, and further used them to make presents to powerful people, and even to their Sovereigns in order to obtain such favours which they, as ladies, could scarcely obtain otherwise. The Princes of Châlon, who often treated the suzerains and kings as their equals, invariably kept for themselves the greater part of their wines from their Château d'Arlay, but it did happen that at times monarchs would cause, by treaty, to be sent to them personally, Château d'Arlay Wine which they coveted. This was notably so in the case of William III, King of England by the Treaty of Ryswick in 1697.

The Marquis de Vogüé, in whose family the estates have been for 700 years, has at the Château some ancient and extraordinary wine . . . surely, I must discuss the matter with him.[1]

[1]The deed has been accomplished.

[340]

We must, however, continue our search for good wine, and follow our kind host who urged us to taste some of his wines. . . .

1926 Vin Jaune—Savagnin . . . very good quality.

1923 „ „ showed the age ; not exceptional.

1921 „ „ very good indeed.

1929 Vin de Merlan—White wine of Arbois . . . quite pleasant.

Demi-Sec Mousseux rosé—A. Déjean—3% . . . clean, little too sweet. The next sample of similar wine—cleaner and drier—rosé. My remark was—'How the girls would love it !'

Jaune-Sec, 15.50°—White . . . good and fruity, 15.50°. These wines were all quite attractive but the initial cost, plus English duty, on these strong wines, put them out of court.

To finish—

1926 Vin de Paille . . . 17° ! ! (exposed to the sun on straw for a couple of months).

Very good indeed, resembles Tokay but stronger. The price asked was under 10s. for a half-bottle.

Before going to déjeuner, our hospitable host thought we would like to see the old Church of St. Just . . . it certainly was very old ; very old indeed, and very smelly. Here, we noticed a statue to PASTEUR, with the words—'Pria dans cette église', which we thought savoured rather of worshipping the creature instead of the Creator.

The seats certainly appeared to be suffering from dry rot, and the whole place was dreary . . . this is to the Glory of God.

We made our way to the Restaurant Marle ; with its very curious and somewhat attractive entrance through a courtyard. Here we partook of déjeuner.

Déjeuner

SAUCISSE (hot)	ARBOIS BLANC 1929 (absolute
Mortrau	type of the country)
(the best the Sec has had)	

—

PÂTÉ DE BÉCASSE
aux truffes
—
LIÈVRE (jugged)
—
CHAMPIGNONS À LA CRÈME
(very good—not so rich as
the Morilles)
—
GRIVE (excellent)
—
GRUYÈRE (Franche comté)

1893 VIN JAUNE D'ARBOIS (fine,
strong—same vines as at
Ch. Châlon.... I compared
it to a Manzanilla or Mar-
chanudo Sherry)
1904 VIN ROUGE D'ARBOIS
(light in colour, 'exquis' in
flavour—excellent wine of
fine vintage)
MACVIN (a very curious liqueur,
made with new wine, and
cooked with aniseed, corri-
ander and cannelle. Inci-
dentally it is becoming quite
a rarity.)

Yvonne brought us another Marc, 1911, which she thought would please—not me ! However, the girl, who had a good honest face, had the most captivating smile, which easily took the place of the Marc !

I told Yvonne a little histoire of how, when a young man (with no knowledge of French), I had been introduced to an admiral's daughter—Yvonne B . . . and, referring to her quite by accident as 'Yvrogne' she approached me, in a dance-room, and smacked me across the face. 'What would you have done ?' I asked. . . . 'It depends how it was said', she rejoined . . . 'it may be that I would have embraced you.' Do you wonder that this cost me ten francs ?

After this lavish déjeuner, Monsieur Déjean insisted that we should return to his house to meet the ladies. 'With pleasure', said the Sec (he is a rascal !) and I willingly acquiesced. So off we went and met the most charming society.

We were all, very soon, seated around the mahogany table, tasting various liqueurs, twelve different kinds—amongst three ladies and four gentlemen. What a host !

We were then introduced to SUZE—*No* ! . . . this was not another lady, but a liqueur—nevertheless it had its charms . . . to wit ; its aid in cases of indigestion.

One hundred kilos of Gentian root are required in order to produce one litre of this liqueur. It is made chiefly at a place called PONTARLIER, which stands higher on the hills than ARBOIS, from the roots of the yellow Gentian which grows on the mountain.

Mr. Duncan Shaw, who knows this country so well, has told me many interesting details, in particular the legend which states that 'so high as the yellow Gentian grows, so deep will be the snow in the winter'. This, he assured me, he had himself proved correct.

We were loath to leave such genial company, but we had to be off, and with profound expressions of gratitude, which we trust were thoroughly understood, we made our way, still in the rain, back to LONS LE SAUNIER.

After such a remarkable feast as we enjoyed at ARBOIS we were not in the mood to spread ourselves at dinner time, so were content with much the same menu as we had had the night before—good and simple.

We ventured on a wine described in the list as 1928 Ménétru (in the Ch. Châlon dumpy bottle). It was characteristic ... strong, of good quality.

The Sec did not care for it, so we invited the chef to have his share, while he contented himself on Perrier.

The chef and I drank to him—deeply !

After dinner the conversation veered round to the subject of 'Pasteur', and we discussed this illustrious man until it was time for me to take my 'constitutional'.

What I have heard of Pasteur from Monsieur Déjean de St. Marcel and more particularly from Mr. Warner Allen, who has made so great a study of the curious and somewhat rare wines of Arbois and of Château Châlon, I will set forth for the benefit of those who feel sufficiently interested to read it.

Pasteur, born in Arbois, naturally turned to the Jura wines when he began his researches into acetic and vinous fermentation. He was a fervent believer in wine as a food and stimulant and, chemist though he was, held that nature provided exactly the right proportion of alcohol for man.

'Our object', he writes, 'should be to provide for workman

and peer alike at a low price with the wine of France which is a food, the natural wine, with which God so lavishly endowed the fair land of France.'

About 1860 just when phylloxera was on the point of ravaging the vineyards of the world, Pasteur penetrated the mystery of fermentation and discovered that it was the work of living organisms. As it happened, the Jura wines provided him with perfect material for his investigation of the transforming of wine into vinegar which was his jumping-off place.

From the first he suspected that vinegar was due to the work of a microbe 'mycoderma aceti' and he soon found that this organism had a twin which he called 'mycoderma vini', known in all wine-growing countries since the days of the Romans as 'flower' (flos vini). When most wines are left on ullage, freely exposed to the air, the vinegar microbe forms a film on their surface and by the combination of two or four molecules of oxygen with one molecule of alcohol, forms acetic acid.

Jura and Jerez wines do sometimes turn to vinegar. Occasionally, the vinegar microbe establishes itself and wages war with the 'flower'. If it wins, they turn to vinegar just as Burgundy or Bordeaux would do.

This very brief summary of Pasteur's inquiry into Jura wines may give an idea of the way in which that great scientist pursued his investigations into the diseases of wine. Nearly all of them proved to be due to microscopic organisms.

The Jura wines are distinguished by the quality of producing not the vinegar microbe, Tweedledum, but Tweedledee the 'flower'. The 'flower' is a more vigorous organism than the vinegar microbe, for it takes eight or twelve molecules of oxygen from the air and completely transforms the alcohol, reducing it to water and carbonic acid gas.

The vinegar microbe is an obvious foe to the wine-grower since it ruins the taste of his wine. It requires large quantities of oxygen and for that reason wines which breed it are never left on ullage, and are kept as much as possible from the outside air.

The 'flower' is neutral and does not affect the taste of a wine beyond making it rather flat and reducing its alcohol. As such, it has little to recommend it to the wine-grower, yet everything

[344]

is done to encourage it, not only in the Jura, but also at Jerez. The wines which breed 'flower' do not usually turn to vinegar when they are exposed to the air. As a matter of fact the 'flower' is so greedy for oxygen that none of it reaches the depths of the wine at all. Beneath the film of 'flower' a kind of second fermentation takes place which gives to certain wines of the Jura—Château Châlon in particular—and Sherry a quality and savour which is peculiarly their own.

SUMMARY OF ARBOIS AND CH. CHÂLON VINTAGES

Owing to the small quantities of wine made in this district, one seldom meets with old wines, and then the price asked is so fanciful that they are not often indulged in.

During the last forty years the wines of some few vintages stand out most prominently for their excellence :

1893, 1895, 1904, 1906, 1915, 1921, 1923, 1924, 1926, 1928, 1929.

1933 and 1934 both promise to be very good.

The three outstanding vintages were 1915, 1921, and 1926.

In my opinion those wines which retain their limpidity, and do not become maderisé, are infinitely to be preferred to many of the older ones which, more often than not, are dark, heavy—and I am inclined to think—indigestible . . . the only 'virtue' perhaps, being the high price asked !

Therefore, do not keep them too long—and thus avoid disappointment.

Note.—Contrary to all usage with White wine, it is permissible to slightly chambré the wine of Château Châlon.

CHAPTER XVIII

FROM THE JURA TO THE COAST
(viâ Chambertin, Ch. de Chaumont, and Paris)

IT had rained consistently through the length of the night, but at 7 o'clock the next morning there was actually an encouraging sample of blue exposed to view.

We were away at 8 o'clock and, passing along one of the roads outside the town we noticed a remarkable thing, the explanation of which I have never been able to find—a dog suspended by a wire, hanging from the roof. I suggested that it may have been a dummy dog, placed there to frighten 'cat' burglars.

At BELLEVESVRE there is an interesting old church, but once again we remarked on the dilapidated condition of the doors.

The road we took was not particularly interesting through VARENNES, FRONTENARD, SEURRE . . . here we mistook a signpost and continued to POUILLY S/SAONE before turning back. We crossed the river and came in sight of the first vines near LABERGEMENT and CORBERON.

We did not stop at BEAUNE, but gave a salute and a very sound, well-meaning one as we passed Château de Corton Grancey, the home of our very good friend, Monsieur Louis Latour.

As we passed into the little village of MOREY ST. DENIS we had a puncture—the first—I alighted from the car at the very moment when a young lady came from a house on our left. Raising my hat I inquired if she could direct me to the gentleman I was in quest of.

'Here !' she replied . . . 'you have stopped exactly outside his house.' Looking up, I saw my old friend standing in the garden.

[346]

Greetings took place, while his most obliging son attended to the changing of wheels, etc., for which we were very truly grateful . . . the nuts being screwed on so tightly that neither the Sec nor I could move them.

I was after making a bargain for those casks of 1933 Chambertin, to which I referred during our previous visit here in September.

We had mapped out a considerable distance to go, so urged our friend to allow us to taste a few wines without delay :

1934 (No. 9) Chambolle-Musigny, 13°
  good colour—trifle dry.

1934 (No. 12) Charmes-Chambertin
  has quality—fermenting slightly.

1934 (No. 16) Charmes-Chambertin
  more body.

1934 (No. 4 & 8) Gd. Chambertin, 13°
  in spite of fermentation we found these very good.

I shall be very interested to see how these wines have developed in two or three months.

1933 Chambertin
  the wines we had come in search of; on this tasting
  I liked them even better than on the previous
  occasion, which may have been accounted for, after
  tasting the 1934 samples.

1928 Charmes-Chambertin, 13°
  good quality, but should have been already in
  bottle.

We then left the chais and proceeded into the courtyard, where there were literally dozens of cats prowling around the three hundred years old house.

To begin the proceedings, the Sec thought it well to take a photograph—'Garibaldi' (for so we nicknamed the old gentleman) and his son Armand, standing in the entrance of the door, with two large dogs between them, slightly in the background. It was quite a successful effort. Garibaldi, but more so, his son, would have wished a higher price for their wine, but here I was firm, and as a result, honest tenacity won the day.

We bade the old fellow 'bonjour', complimenting him on his

wonderful good health ; his hard-working and obliging son ; his charming daughter-in-law, and above all, on his business acumen.

The Sec remarked to me as we drove away up the wrong turning—'I think he's pleased ?' 'Yes', I replied . . . 'he looked so as we parted.'

I had promised myself, the next time that I was in the neighbourhood of NUITS ST. GEORGES, to have lunch once more at the Hôtel de la Croix Blanche, where we had fared so well on a previous occasion.

We duly arrived at the hotel, making it our first duty to inquire about the possibility of finding a garage open at this hour, where someone would attend to the puncture.

Madame Legendre, the wife of the proprietor, immediately took the matter out of our hands. . . . 'Leave it entirely to me,' she said . . . 'and while you have your déjeuner this will be attended to' . . . and it was !

As I enjoyed my meal here, and the surroundings as much as at any place I had visited, I feel it incumbent upon me to introduce to you Madame Legendre, and Mariette, both of whom took such good care of us.

Madame, naturally, is not so young as once she was ; but could not be more attractive . . . a charming personality. If Gerald Kelly, R.A., had been with me I should have lost him for the rest of the journey, for he would have kidnapped the good lady for the next year's Academy.

Mariette was attractive and 'comme il faut' ? Yes, but very attentive and anxious to assist two strangers. However, I was surprised when she inquired of me—'Where is the "jeune homme" ? ' 'Oh, naughty Mariette', I said . . . 'fancy that you should remember him.'

'I do, most certainly', she added . . . 'you both sat at the table over there', indicating the right one, and, as a final touch —'Wasn't he nice.' (Or that is how I translated it !)

I have particularly mentioned this as it goes to bear out a simple remark I made in introducing Lorne to you all. Oh ! Lorne ! ! I fear I did not keep my eyes open sufficiently.

One other little incident which amused me much in connection with this conversation I will relate to you :

'Well, Mariette', I said . . . 'you now see me accompanied by an old gentleman—the young ones have deserted me.'

'What', said the Sec, pricking up his ears at 'vieux'. With the most gracious smile, she bent towards the Sec, and said— 'Monsieur "dit" that he has now the company of a gentleman of "moyen âge" !'

If I had not restrained him I think the Sec would have endeavoured to embrace her !

I must not delay the serving of this excellent déjeuner longer :

DÉJEUNER (25 fcs.)

GAME PÂTÉ (Maison)
(excellent)

—

JAMBON FUMÉ

—

TRUITE DE RIVIÈRE MEUNIÈRE
(very good—cooked and
served beautifully)

—

JAMBON BRAISE NUITONNE,
QUINNELS : CHAMPIGNONS
Sauce Gd. Vin de Nuits
Pomme Paille
(This was one of the most delectable dishes I have ever enjoyed)

—

POULET FROID
SALADE

—

CHEESE

—

DESSERT

—

MONTRACHET PULIGNY
LES FOLATIÈRES, 1929—
16 fcs.

CHARMES CHAMBERTIN, 1929
good flavour—rather too young : has not lost the 'purple'. 35 fcs.

ECHEZEAUX—very good—light ; brown in colour. 35 fcs.

We had a little discussion about this wine. Madame preferred the 1929, but my predilection was for the 1923. Mariette confessed that she was of 'mon avis'.

CAFÉ	After such an excellent meal

CAFÉ	After such an excellent meal
—	I would have been happier
FINE	with a better 'Fine'.

We left, I hope with properly expressed French politeness, promising to return at the first opportunity . . . no empty promise, if occasion offers.

It was pleasantly sunny and we were feeling bright as we passed through BEAUNE on the way to CHAROLLES, where we intended to pass the night.

We left MEURSAULT, CHAGNY and GIVRY, all of which brought back happy memories.

The company of vines remained with us until nearing GERMAGNY, but it was not until JONCY was reached and we commenced to climb, that we came across some pretty wooded country, which was particularly pleasant after the flat expanse.

Owing to a fault in our map, we made an error about here, which cost us a valuable twenty minutes at least.

We were out in the wilds, with no possibility of meeting a passer-by. I therefore determined to venture across a meadow to a farm-house to make necessary inquiries.

The dogs were, I am glad to say, on chains ; but three children outside the dwelling were so astonished at seeing a stranger, and hearing their language treated with such scant respect, that two of them commenced howling at the top of their voices, and the other stood dumbfounded.

I tried to appease them . . . this made the dogs more furious, when, having made up my mind to depart without having gained any information, I saw a goodly dame hastening across another meadow. I went to meet her, and having apologised profusely for being the unwilling cause of so much noise, she smiled broadly, saying 'sont bêtes' !

She then accompanied me to the roadway, and indicated the direction we should take.

After a circuitous route, we eventually arrived, in the rain, at ST. BONNET . . . at five o'clock and still raining, we reached CHAROLLES and put up at the Hôtel Moderne, opposite the station.

[350]

DINNER

FARM SOUP

—

HARE—
petits pois

—

LAMB

—

CHEESE

—

DESSERT

1928 POUILLY-FUISSÉ, 25 fcs.
(this was an excellent bottle
of wine).

ARMAGNAC

A simple little meal, quite enjoyable.

Then a short stroll, while I left the Sec, in order to explore the town; fortunately the rain had ceased.

A very curious old town is CHAROLLES, the river-ways through the streets, requiring endless small bridges, are very intriguing. I strolled about these dark and somewhat dirty streets for some time before returning to the hotel, where I found that the Sec had retired to his roost.

On going to the bathroom the next morning, I found that there was no key, nor any fastening to the door ; a little disconcerting for a shy Englishman, but if you go to Rome, etc. . . .

This is where I found the waste-plug fastened by a piece of string to the towel-horse ! ! Almost incredible.

I looked out of the window at 7 o'clock . . . the weather was not very promising ; the clouds looked full of rain.

Almost touching the window shutters as I pushed them open was the red-tiled roof of an adjacent building, probably the hotel garage, on top of which was a weather-cock, which had evidently done service, and collapsed under the strain.

Before starting for the Château de Chaumont, we had the car cleaned . . . it sadly required it after yesterday's experience. Whilst this was being done we took a walk into the town. I was anxious to show the Sec what a quaint place it was.

Outside the church, in fact, adjoining it, was a Bowls Club. The green (excuse the word) was full of puddles of water from yesterday's rain ; several 'woods' were actually lying almost as they were left after the last game . . . benches were placed around, and electric light supplied for play after dark !

It was truly a remarkable spectacle.

We then hastened back to the hotel. . . . On the way we were much amused at seeing three men trying to induce a bull to move from one cart to another—we did not stop to the finish. . . . When we left, the men looked angry, and so did the bull ! !

At 10 o'clock, slight rain began to fall, but we had to be on our way. The hedgerows were black with sloes . . . this fruit seems to have a fascination for me.

At LA FOURCHE we entered a wooded road, and continued through delightful woods, spending quite some time in enjoying them.

About half-past eleven, we arrived at Château de Chaumont . . . the weather had cleared somewhat.

Monsieur le Général, le Marquis de Laguiche, who had so graciously extended to us an invitation to visit him, greeted us on arrival.

We were proud to enter so famous a place as the Château de Chaumont, and to meet the illustrious owner, whose name is justly immortalised in connection with the wonderful wines of the 'Grand' Montrachet. Of these wines I have spoken before—you may therefore understand my pleasure and pride at being here.

The Marquis had promised me some excellent wines if I could come to lunch . . . the following is the lunch—judge for yourselves:

DÉJEUNER

EGGS (daintily served)	1906 GD. MONTRACHET LAGUICHE (excellent)
—	
BEEF STEAK (melted in the mouth)	1915 GD. MONTRACHET LAGUICHE (lighter, but oh ! so good)
—	
CHICKEN —	1904 MORGEOT (rouge) (brown in colour—excellent on the palate. After many years in bottle it was relinquishing its vinous secrets).

[352]

APPLE TART
—

CHEESE
—
CAFÉ

1888 MORGEOT (white)
Pinot
(This was the best White
wine made on the Morgeot
Estate.)
CONSTANTIA, 1839,
1923 MARC DE MONTRACHET.

The beef steak was so excellent, that I have regretted ever since that I was too shy to take a second helping. When the dish was offered, I noticed but a single portion remaining, and I must have unconsciously remembered my upbringing —'Never take the last cake, or piece of bread and butter off a plate. . . . someone else may wish for it.' On one occasion I recollect my youngest sister, Mabel, having her eye on the one remaining orange on a fruit dish . . . she knew she should not ask for it, and yet she would have liked it. The artful young monkey, aged about eight, solved the problem this way—'Mother, please may I have one of those oranges ?'

This was a most interesting lunch, and one which I shall remember for years to come, and from what the Sec confessed afterwards, I feel sure that he will also.

The Canton of Morgeot, from whence came the Morgeot wines which we had enjoyed, is quite close to MONTRACHET, and here the family of the Marquis had two acres of vines, which produced a Red wine, much sought after. The quantity, however, was very small, and taken by various members of the family.

It was an eye-opener to me, and I feel very guilty that I almost coerced this very genial aristocrat to allow me to have a small quantity of the 1904 . . . the delectable wine we had indulged in at lunch.

Of the Montrachets from his private cellar, I am to have a little assortment. I gathered that, owing to present circumstances, the Marquis does not think he will be able to use them

B.W.

all before they have passed their prime . . . a worthy sentiment, which I encouraged.

1848 was a great vintage, as was also 1865 ; I have never tasted the former, but on two or three occasions it has been my good fortune to share a bottle of the 1865 ; some years ago, certainly, but it had already commenced to change its character.

Of the 1870, he had only a few bottles, which he kept as a curiosity, and these, he confessed, were a little 'maderisé'.

'The 1906 was a remarkable wine,' said the Comte de Laguiche—the eldest son of the Marquis . . . 'this, to me, is perfection.'

I asked about the 1904 . . . he shook his head—'Not so magnificent as the 1906.'

What a pleasure it is to be in the company of such knowledgeable enthusiasts !

I must not forget to tell you that the idea of showing the 1839 Constantia, which was wonderfully preserved, was to impress upon us the fact that this particular wine from South Africa was made from the Montrachet PINOT vines, sent there by his predecessor.

The Count very kindly took the trouble to show me the library, some of the priceless early tomes, printed about the middle or end of the fifteenth century . . . with what pride did I handle them . . . with thoughts directed towards Malory and Caxton !

We indulged in some excellent Liqueur Cognac, 1864 Grande Champagne, before taking a walk around the estate.

I believe, if it had not been for the Sec, I should have made some excuse to eke out this delightful visit, but he was adamant —'Walter !' said he—and took out his watch.

The views from each side of this Château are entrancing ; to me the whole atmosphere, not omitting the cellars of the Château, would be paradise indeed !

The stables, now used mostly as garages, formerly stalled ninety-nine horses.

A very fine building. . . . Over the doorway is a fine sculptured work—a former Marquis mounted . . . he who was Master of the Horse to King 'Henri Quatre.'

It was time we left, but before doing so, the Sec had his camera out, and I had the honour and privilege of being photographed with Messieurs le Marquis and le Comte de Laguiche. I am keeping with pride this happy souvenir of a most enjoyable occasion.

I (in fact, I might say—we, for the Sec was highly gratified) endeavoured to impress on our hosts what we felt, and our sincere thanks for their gracious kindness . . . then we reluctantly left by that very pleasant wooded road that was to take us away from such delightful environment.

Our intention was to reach NEVERS and stay there the night.

We took the road through DIGOIN, where we smiled a greeting to a passing hiker, along flat and open country to GILLY S/LOIRE, ST. AUBIN, LESME and VITRY, which last town was situated further from the banks of the river.

At CHARRIN we commenced to climb, and had a few glimpses of pleasant views until after we had passed DECIZE, at which town we rejoined the river, cutting across to BEARD and ST. OUEN, where the country was certainly more interesting, arriving at NEVERS rather before 5 o'clock.

Here we stayed at the Hôtel de la France, with excellent accommodation and good meals :

DINNER

VEGETABLE SOUP
—

BARBEL SAUCE MOULES, CHAMPIGNONS
—

SPINACH À LA CRÈME— (served properly—and to be properly vulgar—'hot as hell, green as envy' !)
—

GRILLED CHICKEN (excellent)
—

CHAMPAGNE NATURE (very slightly corked) 15 fcs.

1929 POUILLY-FUISSÉ (slightly corked) 26 fcs.

Another bottle as the 1926 on the list was not in stock.

CAMEMBERT	The second bottle was very
—	good—light and clean.
DESSERT	FINE

The Sec fancied Cordial Médoc with his coffee. This again (and it happens so often, not only in France but in England) was not in stock, although on the list.

I much regretted the slight disappointment, for this liqueur, which he enjoyed, was new to him when we had had it on a previous occasion.

The strain of continually speaking a language of which I know very little had the curious effect of causing me to carry on a conversation in French in my dreams. This occurred to me twice during the night . . . it might have been due to the Moules and Champignon sauce, of which I think I helped myself somewhat liberally.

At 6 o'clock the sun was rising, but at half-past 7 it was looking very sorry for itself—moist and almost faded ; however, we were off by 8 o'clock for PARIS.

I expect you are all glad thus to see the end in view . . . please bear with me a short while longer, and we will be back in dear old England.

We drove up-hill most of the way to POUGUES, from which town we had some excellent views, on to LA MARCHE, with the Loire still close to our left . . . we continued hugging the river through LA CHARITÉ, to POUILLY S/LOIRE, where we drew up outside the residence of the charming old Countess de la Chesnaye, in order to raise our hats in recognition of the kind reception she had afforded us when Lorne and I called on her some weeks before.

On the roadside between POUILLY and COSNE, we passed what had been a large trolley . . . it was burned out to a cinder !

At MYENNES we used the new bridge over the railway, which saved passing over the level crossing.

We then had to negotiate long, uninteresting roads as far as BONNY S/LOIRE, where the country was more undulating.

At BRIARE the market was in full swing . . . we could not stop to enjoy the interest or amusement, but, crossing the canal, we turned sharply to the right through LE BUSSIÈRE, to NOGENT.

Near here we witnessed a hawk pounce down on a small bird . . . it was caught, and the hawk mounted with it. We hooted —it may have been for this reason . . . I will not venture to say . . . but the little bird fell and before touching the ground flew away ; the most interesting little episode we had seen for some time.

The tower at NOGENT is a land-mark which can be seen miles away, standing at the end of this long, dead straight, road.

There were a number of apple orchards here, but the fruit had not been gathered.

The blushing sun of the morning had hidden behind the clouds, and the rain had commenced to fall ; this, combined with an uninteresting road, made us glad to hurry on, as quickly as possible, through MONTARGIS, SOUPPES, to NEMOURS—the birthplace of Mirabeau.

After BOURRON we found it very pleasant passing through the beautiful Forêt de Fontainebleau, reaching the little country town of CHAILLY-EN-BIÈRE about 12 o'clock, just in time for lunch.

We halted at a wayside restaurant, the Lion d'Or . . . it did not look very interesting, but we did not fare badly.

DÉJEUNER

HORS D'ŒUVRES	1928 POUILLY S/LOIRE, BLANC
—	FUMÉ. 18 fcs.
MACKEREL	Very good indeed—dry and
—	good flavour ; we may
VEAL—Spinach	have been thirsty, but we
—	did enjoy it.
CHEESE	
—	
DESSERT	

It was a noisy place, but amusing. . . . At one long table a company of chasseurs were having their meal—seven men and two women—some in their shirt sleeves ; two or three of whom would persist in singing.

At the small table next to us sat a Parisian gentleman with his companion—presumably from a cabaret.

The only other diners comprised a family of four—Ma, Pa and the ubiquitous infant, and one other female . . . we could not decide whether she was an aunt or a governess. They were all undoubtedly quite ready for their lunch, but French people always seem to be so—perhaps this is only natural, considering the meagre breakfast they take.

As we came through the doors of the restaurant we saw that the sun was trying to break through the clouds. We were happy at this prospect as we were anxious to enter the gay city under the best conditions, particularly for the reason that it was to be the first occasion on which the Sec had ventured to motor through Paris. Courageous fellow—I thought, but I kept such remarks to myself until he had safely accomplished the feat.

We arrived most comfortably, without hitch or hindrance at the Hôtel Astor.

The Sec garaged the car, and coming back we enjoyed a well-earned rest, wash and brush-up.

At the hotel we met several friends, and passed the time of day with them. As they were booked for dinner, we wandered out to the Laurent, knowing full well that there we should have a good meal, besides which I had a vivid recollection of what Mr. J. Edward Johnston had told me of its excellence.

Unfortunately, there were but few diners . . . but after the rush of the day, we were not averse to the quietude.

Dinner

CAVIAR	VOUVRAY NATURAL—en carafe. Very pleasant, clean, elegant.
COLD CONSOMMÉ	(This wine had actually been in bottle about one year and had been decanted into the carafe.)
JAMBON BRAIZÉ	
BRIE	RILLY ROSÉ (natural) 1928 (casky) . . . So we had another carafe.

DESSERT

—

CAFÉ

FINE 1911—
FINE 1863.

The morning of the next day, Saturday, the 10th November, was dull and it was trying to rain.

As I was dressing, the telephone bell rang. . . . It was Mr. Sterling Clark, in his genial way, inviting us to dine with him that evening . . . so we knew that we were in luck's way !

It was so good to know that he was well again. I promised to call on him during the afternoon as I had several interesting things to tell him which might escape me during the evening.

When we arrived in the hall of the hotel a note was handed to us, informing us that a front spring of the car was broken.

We therefore hurried to the garage, and prevailed upon the good man there to do his best, in spite of Saturday being only half a day . . . to do the necessary repairs so that we could be off early on Monday morning. He did, bless him . . . for which he deserves full marks.

I did one or two commissions in the morning, and the Sec did likewise ; we returned to the hotel about 12 o'clock, and then went off together to partake of déjeuner at the Griffon Restaurant.

We were enjoying an excellent sole, and a bottle of Vin Nature Champagne, when who should enter but Christian Cruse. We prevailed upon him to join us, and were happy to have his cheerful company.

After the sole, we were served with a particular dish of kidneys sauté . . . and intended to have a bottle of Red Burgundy with them.

Such is the generosity of this Bordeaux magnate that he insisted on ordering a bottle of wine for us, oblivious of the fact that he had showered 'beautiful bottles' on me during my recent stay with him.

However, he would not give way, and I overheard him say that he would have a bottle of Ch. Haut Brion, 1899. Here I felt thoroughly justified in objecting—'If you order that wine you can drink it yourself. . . . I flatly refuse to taste it !' I said.

He was astonished. . . . 'What do you mean ?' he asked . . . 'isn't it good enough for you ?'

I said—'Because you are having a simple lunch with us, you feel it necessary to offer us one of the most famous and expensive wines to be bought. . . . I won't have it, and that's that !'

'I wish you would let me', he replied. . . . 'Not another word, please', I said. With that he handed me the wine list—'Be good enough to choose one yourself.'

I did so, and we had at his expense, for which we thank him again, an excellent bottle of 1920 Ch. Latour, after the first one had been returned as badly corked ! ! !

In the afternoon I called on Mr. Clark, and enjoyed an interesting chat with him, making an opportunity of tasting some Madeira, bottled in 1852. . . . It was very good and soft, but as I was asked to be quite candid, I added that it might have been 'finer'.

I was also shown a curiosity in Calvados, 1875 . . . very dark, strong and full of flavour ; probably the best Calvados to be found anywhere, and for those who know how to appreciate, something to sit down and enjoy.

I asked permission to have a look at some of his beautiful works of art, and regaled myself for a short time enjoying such Masters as Degas, Sargent and Renoir.

I left, promising to be back with the Sec in good time for dinner.

Passing down the Champs Élysées, I remembered that Monsieur Cruse had told me that he was staying at the d'Orsay Hotel, so I directed the taxi-man to take me there, as I wished to tell him of something that had suddenly come into my mind.

I arrived, and inquired at the reception office, to learn that he had just left to catch the train for BORDEAUX.

The hotel porter overheard the conversation and as I was leaving, stopped me and said that he had put the gentleman in his seat, and knew exactly where to find him in the train . . .

[360]

would I come with him ? There were two minutes before the train was due to leave !

Off we went, as the saying goes—'like a streak of greased lightning' from the hotel to the station. Here, the hotel porter explained the circumstances to the ticket collector as he rushed through the barrier—I following.

He tapped at the window of the carriage—Monsieur Cruse looked up, and seeing me, came to the door. We had just under a minute to discuss important business, which was finished on the telephone the next morning, from BORDEAUX.

I felt grateful to an intelligent hotel servant, and told him so.

On account of a special memorial service for the late King Alexander of Yugoslavia, it took us forty minutes in a taxi to go from the Madeleine to the Arc de Triomphe . . . we must have gone all round Paris. . . . We were therefore somewhat late in arriving for dinner, and naturally very apologetic. However, the gracious hostess very quickly, in her pleasing way, put us at our ease.

In detailing the excellent dinner, I do not do so in any sense to make you jealous, but to allow you, if you will, to join me, while I enjoy it over again.

DINNER

CONSOMMÉ
(elegant)
—

TURBOT
(solid and excellent)
—

TURKEY
(something to 'gobble')
—

FRESH PÂTÉ
Truffes
(very rich ; very delicious
—a dish to be proud of)
—

1921 AVIZE
(a magnificent specimen of
White grape Champagne)

1911 CH. HAUT BRION
(excellent and well-
preserved)

1899 CH. HAUT BRION !
(a dream—I would like to
be Rip Van Winkle, and
take a bottle of this to
bed with me)

FRESH CHEESE—
(Goat's)
—
DESSERT
—
CAFÉ

1900 CH. YQUEM
(probably the finest Ch.
Yquem in existence)

1830 BAS-ARMAGNAC
1834 GDE. CHAMPAGNE
OLD CALVADOS

I do not wish to be unkind to anyone who has read through this menu, but truly—don't you envy me?

What an extraordinary thing it was that Mr. Clark should have so generously spared a bottle of the 1899 Ch. Haut Brion!

After my refusal at luncheon—to find it again at dinner! Well! Well! I said to the Sec afterwards—'Virtue at times receives her due reward!!'

I feel sure that I will be pardoned any indiscretion, but I would like to take advantage of this opportunity of referring to an action of great sacrifice and generosity. The facts are as follows:

I remembered that a valued client had said some years ago that the finest bottle of Claret he remembered to have enjoyed was 1899 Ch. Haut Brion, and he wondered when he would taste it again.

As I remembered this, I ventured—'Please do not think I am rude, Mr. Clark. . . . No, I am not going to ask you to sell me any of this fine wine, but for a very particular reason I am going to ask you to give me two bottles; I will give you, in London, two bottles of the best I have in exchange.'

'I don't want any in exchange', he immediately said . . . 'and you shall have the two bottles, but what is the particular reason?'

I then told him, as I have related, and asked him if he would be good enough to send them to this gentleman, by air-mail. He was surprised when I wrote down the name and address, for it was that of a reigning Prince.

I have since heard how, at the Palace, this wine was enjoyed and how the guests on this occasion 'were unanimous in their praise and gratitude.'

'Mr. Clark, do please accept my sincere thanks once again.'

[362]

We indulged in a further soupçon of the 1834 **Grande Fine**
. . . *very* good indeed, very—underlined !

The 1830 Bas-Armagnac was a disappointment . . . it did not
belong to Mr. Clark, but had been left for me at the hotel,
together with a wonderful history, and during the afternoon I
had mentioned it, when Mr. Clark said—'Bring it along, and we
will taste it this evening.' I wish it had been fine, but it was NOT.

Sunday, the 11th November, was Armistice Day . . . this is
exactly what happened.

I got out of bed, looked out of the window—RAIN ! I went
to the bath-room . . . the handle of my patent shaving brush
had been smashed. I turned the water on for a cold bath and
continued to shave . . . on returning to the bath to stop the
supply of water, I found it empty and, on examination, discovered
that the bath-waste—'ouvert' was in reality 'fermé' and vice-
versâ !

I was annoyed, and looking round I saw the bath-towel just
as I had left it the day before. I *am* getting along nicely on this
day of Peace-Remembrance, I thought. However, after a cold
bath it was soon forgotten, except the broken handle of a gift
my wife had given me three Christmases ago, and one which I
prized considerably.

Monsieur Roditi, who had called to see us at the hotel, very
kindly extended an invitation on behalf of his mother, to go to
her house in the rue Presbourg, in order to see the ceremony at
the Arc de Triomphe, and the march past of the troops.

Here, we met many members of M. Roditi's family and many
of his friends, and we were a merry party who enjoyed the
privilege which Madame Aide had granted us ; for which we
were extremely grateful.

We found it difficult to pass down the Champs Élysées to go
back to the hotel . . . we therefore took one of the roads on the
left, and, about half-way down I called out to the Sec for his
camera . . . such an amusing incident, which would have made
a delightful snap, was taking place. A car had been left, while
the occupants were evidently making a call, and in the car was a
dog. This young rascal had found his mistress's umbrella—one
of the short ones, and he was fighting with it for all he was worth.

Not much umbrella left. . . . He suddenly realised that he was being watched, when he made a dart at the window, barking furiously. This brought up another dog from under the seat; we left them to it.

Monsieur Renauleaud who was staying at the hotel, and whom we had met previously over a bottle of good Ayala Champagne, brought us an invitation from Madame Prunier, to lunch with her at the rue Duphot. She was soon to be a neighbour of ours in St. James's Street, and had had this happy thought of making my acquaintance.

It was a great pleasure to meet this charming lady and also her husband. I thank her once more for the trouble she took on a very busy afternoon to give us her time and an excellent lunch.

If anyone knows all there is to know about oysters, Madame Prunier does . . . the only child of the most famous oyster merchant that ever was.

Hearing her speak of oysters led me to perpetrate a parody on a few lines from 'King Henry V'. . . .

> 'Hear her debate of mollusc—
> You would say . . . "it hath been all in all her study" . . .
> List her discourse on bi-valves and you shall hear
> A delightful subject rendered you in music.
> Turn her to any crustacean dish
> The delectable knot of which she will unloose—
> Familiar as her garter. . . .'

I am certain that all Londoners will join with me in extending to her a right good welcome, and wish her success in her courageous undertaking.

DÉJEUNER

HUÎTRES   POUILLY-FUISSÉ 1928
——

HOMARD GRILLÉ
——   CH. CHEVAL BLANC 1906
FAISAN RÔTI,   (excellent)
SUR CANAPÉ,
Pommes Chipped

FROMAGES
—

MOUSSE AU KIRSCH	1915
—	CHAMPAGNE, BOLLINGER
FRUITS	
—	LIQUEURS
CAFÉ	FINE

Hearing that Mrs. Baylis was in Paris, I got into touch with her, and asked her to dine with us at La Tour d'Argent. Happily, she was able to give us the pleasure . . . a most attractive, erudite, and pleasant companion, and we passed the evening to our utmost content. The dear old Sec simply beamed with pleasure.

DINNER

VEGETABLE SOUP	CHAMPAGNE NATURE
—	(very good)
FILET DE SOLE CARDINAL	
—	1923 CH. CHEVAL BLANC
CANTON TOUR D'ARGENT	(excellent—little older than
125.980 —	one would expect)
canard	
FROMAGE	1875 ARMAGNAC (good)

The next morning we left for the coast, passing by ALLONNE, where, close by the village, the ill-fated British air-ship, R. 101, crashed and was consumed in flames, in the early hours of Sunday, the 5th October, 1930. She was on her way to India, with many distinguished men on board, most of whom perished —the death-roll being 48.

We noticed a café on the outskirts of the village, named Café de R. 101.

At ABBEVILLE we had lunch . . . everything on the menu was 'of the pig'. . . . I cannot understand the reason ; look at this :

TRIPE À LA MODE
SAUSAGE
PIG'S TROTTERS

BLACK PUDDING (pig's blood)
PORK CHOP
CÔTES DE PORC
JAMBON FROID. . . .

almost unbelievable ! !

I inquired if we could have anything else . . . yes, a beef steak. This we waited for, and washed it down with a bottle of Mâcon Blanc.

On the way to the coast we saw hundreds of cart-loads of parsnips. We stopped to inquire the use—commercial alcohol ! This made me think that, on more than one occasion we had been served with 'celery' which was, in reality, stripped parsnips.

We stayed at the Terminus, at CALAIS, very comfortable, and not too noisy. Having some hours to spare in this city I thought I would like to see the place where Beau Brummell once lived, for he used to be a regular 'habitué' at 3 St. James's Street.

I went to the public library. . . . I went to the Town Hall, and made endless inquiries, without success. I went back to the library to ask permission to look at a book, and curiously enough, got into conversation with an elderly gentleman, who gave me the necessary information . . . so off I went to the rue Royale and entered a furniture shop. A new building, but undoubtedly on the site of where the illustrious Beau used to live ; the lady in charge told me that she frequently had such inquiries . . . surely this is a place for an identification plaque.

The following is an extract from my firm's register of weights, showing the various items against the name of Beau Brummell :

GEORGE BRUMMELL, ESQR.

Book 5—Folio 123				Date		Weight			
Boots and Frock	-	-	-	23rd January,	1798	12 st.	4	lbs.
Half-boots	-	-	-	3rd Sept.	,,	12 ,,	9	,,
,, ,,	-	-	-	23rd January,	1799	12 ,,	9	,,
,, ,,	-	-	-	4th April,	1800	12 ,,	12	,,
Boots	-	-	-	5th March	,,	12 ,,	7	,,
Half-boots	-	-	-	24th ,,	,,	12 ,,	9	,,
,, ,,	-	-	-	1st June,	1801	12 ,,	10	,,

Book 5—Folio 123				Date		Weight		
Half-boots	-	-	-	7th August	1801	12 st.	10	lbs.
,, ,,	-	-	-	25th ,,	,,	12 ,,	9	,,
,, ,,	-	-	-	26th Sept.	,,	12 ,,	9	,,
,, ,,	-	-	-	19th Octr.	,,	13 ,,	1	,,
,, ,,	-	-	-	20th April	1802	12 ,,	5	,,
Boots	-	-	-	13th May	,,	12 ,,	7	,,
,,	-	-	-	24th ,,	,,	12 ,,	3	,,
Shoes	-	-	-	5th July	,,	11 ,,	13	,,
Boots	-	-	-	20th August	,,	12 ,,	9	,,
,,	-	-	-	23rd ,,	,,	12 ,,	10½	,,
Shoes	-	-	-	24th Novr.	,,	12 ,,	11	,,
Boots	-	-	-	11th July	1803	12 ,,	13	,,
,,	-	-	-	26th August	,,	12 ,,	10½	,,
,,	-	-	-	29th Octr.	,,	12 ,,	10	,,
,,	-	-	-	13th Janry.	1804	12 ,,	12	,,
,,	-	-	-	17th ,,	,,	12 ,,	10½	,,
,,	-	-	-	30th May	,,	12 ,,	9	,,
,,	-	-	-	2nd July	,,	12 ,,	10	,,
,,	-	-	-	18th March	1805	12 ,,	7½	,,
,,	-	-	-	21st June	,,	12 ,,	8	,,
,,	-	-	-	17th July	,,	12 ,,	8	,,
,,	-	-	-	29th ,,	,,	12 ,,	8½	,,
,,	-	-	-	5th Novr.	,,	12 ,,	13¼	,,
,,	-	-	-	18th August	1808	13 ,,	3½	,,
Boots and Great Coat			-	17th Novr.	1809	13 ,,	4	,,
,, ,, ,,			-	28th ,,	,,	13 ,,	7	,,
Boots	-	-	-	25th Janry.	1810	12 ,,	0	,,
,,	-	-	-	30th April	,,	12 ,,	1	,,
,,	-	-	-	30th July	,,	13 ,,	0¼	,,
Boots and Great Coat			-	16th Novr.	1811	13 ,,	10	,,
,, ,, ,,			-	6th July	1815	12 ,,	10	,,

Also Book 2, Folio 735—

Boots	-	-	-	26th July	1822	10 ,,	13	,,

You will notice that the last weight recorded is in 1822 . . . he fled the country in 1816, and, as far as any books, writings and history are concerned, he never returned.

[367]

But here is evidence of his appearance in London in 1822. I read—unfortunately I cannot remember where—that, about this time, owing to distressed circumstances, he had written a treatise on dress, and had tried to sell it to a publisher in Brompton.

It would therefore appear that he had slipped across the channel himself, to try and fix the business unknown to anyone, and before returning had paid a visit to his old haunt to see what his weight was.

When I related this to the Sec, he appeared so interested that I felt constrained to tell him another episode connected with the office, and thinking that it might interest you, my readers, I feel I will be forgiven for copying out the following from an interesting volume which recently came into my hand, entitled— *Ye History of Ye Ancient Society of Cogers*:

'Shortly before Louis Napoleon quitted London in 1848, on the enterprise which ultimately raised him to the throne of France, he paid a visit to the Cogers at Bride Lane.

'It may be asked how the exile of Leicester Square came to hear of the orator of Bride Lane; but Sherer, it must be remembered, was reputed to have been editor of the *Standard*, and during that period, being a man of refined and elegant tastes, was well known in literary circles west of Temple Bar. Sherer's nature may have been naturally secretive, but even if it were, it was so dominated by his vanity that I had not known him long before he told me the story of his meeting with Louis Napoleon, who had then founded the Third Empire.

' "After I had spoken," said Sherer, "Napoleon came and seated himself next me, and after a few commonplaces, asked if he could speak to me in private. On reaching Fleet Street, we got into a conveyance and drove off to his lodgings, in a street off Leicester Square, once a tobacconist's shop. After a few jesting remarks on the lack of imagination in English writers, he opened a bottle of Champagne, and before the bottle was empty had me at a table hard at work drawing up a manifesto to the Irish people, calling on them to throw off the English yoke."

' "The Irish people!" I exclaimed. "What were the Irish people to Louis Napoleon?"

' "Nothing, of course." Before entrusting me with the work he had in view he wanted to test my literary suitability, and being by nature profoundly distrustful and cautious, he substituted Irish for French. The composition I drew up, if I remember aright, was distinctly champagny in character—it foamed and frothed, but it pleased Napoleon, for he gave me a sovereign for it. But as more manifestoes were required and the hour was growing late, I arranged to meet him on the following evening. Just before I took my leave Napoleon altered the place of meeting. The landlady's daughter had come in once or twice during my stay ; though I, of course, attached no importance to the girl's coming and going, yet it so filled Napoleon with suspicion that he arranged that I should meet him at the Coffee Mill, a wine-room kept by a Mr. Berry at the bottom of St. James's Street. "We shall be quiet there," said Napoleon, as we parted.

' And quiet we were. Napoleon, who seemed quite at home at Berry's, met me at the entrance at the time appointed, and after weighing me in a pair of enormous scales in the shop, and showing me an entry in a book recording his weight (the entry may still be seen), told Berry to bring a couple of bottles of wine into the cellar. The cellars of the Coffee Mill must be of great extent, for we traversed several passages before Napoleon came to a halt. We were evidently in the middle of St. James's Street, for I could distinctly hear the sound of traffic overhead. As soon as Berry, who had preceded us with the wine, had fixed up a table with candles and writing materials, we were left to our own devices. Even then Napoleon's caution did not desert him, and it was not till he had thoroughly searched the cellar, tapping the casks and peering into the empty ones, that we got to work. It was no light job with which I was confronted. Beside appeals to the French army and people, there was over a score of proclamations for distribution in the chief towns of France. The proclamations were devised to suit the tastes and feelings of the inhabitants of the different cities. During the whole time I was at work Napoleon never once left my side. Suspecting all, trusting none, even at this period in his career he evidently thought that were he to turn his back I should pocket one of the copies.'

[369]

It is a fact that the Emperor was very friendly with the old Mr. Berry, for they were both sworn in at the same time, as Special Constables, during the time of the Chartist riots : we have in our possession the special police baton issued at the time.

We had no difficulty in leaving CALAIS, especially with the car, under the auspices of the R.A.C. I cannot say too much in praise of the very kind services rendered by Mr. E. L. Farquharson. I advise anyone travelling this way to seek him out, and then they need have no misgivings . . . he was thoroughness and attention personified.

We had decided to have lunch on board . . . how fooled we were. We went to the first-class dining-room—'Have you reserved seats ?' 'No'. . . . 'Sorry.'

We tried the second-class—same results . . . it appears that all the accommodation had been allotted to a number of people who were coming over to England to witness a football match.

We went upstairs to the bar, and contented ourselves with a sandwich and a Brandy and Soda ! What a climax !

HOW ARE THE MIGHTY FALLEN !

By the time we reached Surbiton the Sec, who must have driven me approximately 1900 miles, was maybe a wee bit tired, but still happy and smiling. To me, in the words of Albert Chevalier—'It ain't been a "mile" too long.'

To my three excellent chauffeurs who took me over some 5600 miles, in fair weather or foul, I have nought to say but praise and sincere thanks.

INDEX

[371]

Autun, Bishop of, 56.
Auxerre, 36, 39, 40, 42, 43.
Auxois, 318.
Avallon, 40, 42, 72, 73, 77.
Avignon, xxiv, 252, 253, 254, 257, 258, 259, 260, 268.
Avize, 13, 22, 361.
Avril, Jean, 256.
Ay, 15, 27, 28, 29, 33.
Ayala, MM., 29.
Ayala (champagne), 29, 31, 364.
Ayrton, Maxwell, 300, 301.
Azay le Rideau, 95.

Bacchus, xiii, xiv, xv, xxv, 148.
Bad Duerkheim, 235.
Bagnaux, 104.
Bagnoles, 270.
Bahèzre, MM., 65.
Baigts, 205.
Bailey, M., 47.
Banyuls, 222, 238.
Baptistère, St. Jean, 108.
Barbaira, 224.
Barcelonne-du-Gers, 198.
Bardinet et Cie., 160.
Bardolph, 295.
Bari, 131.
Barkhausen, J. T., 163, 165.
Barry, xix, xx, xxii.
Barsac, 117, 153, 164.
Barthe, Ed., 238.
Barthélemy, 293.
Barthou, M., 141, 166.
Bartier, M., 320.
Bartres, 211.
Bas-Armagnac, 193, 194, 197, 207, 208, 362, 363.
Bassac, 119.
Bataille de Corde, 263.
Batailley, Ch., 146.
Baule, 92.
Baylis, Mrs. H. Paxton, 365.
Bayonne, 206.
Beard, 355.
Bearn, Royal, 209.
Beau Brummell, 366, 367, 368.
Beaucaire, 242.
Beaugency, 92, 319.
Beaujolais, 158, 215, 306, 307, 308, 309, 313, 314, 316, 318, 322, 324, 331.
Beaujou, Hospices de, 68, 308.

Beaune, 54, 70, 259, 346, 350.
Beaune (see Côte de Beaune).
Beaune, Hospices de, 54, 55, 56.
Beaune (wine), xxiv, 68.
Beaurains, 7.
Beaurech, 157.
Beaurepaire, 333.
Beau Rivage, 289.
Beauvillain, M., 99.
Bedout, M., 198.
Bees, 217.
Beine, 44.
Bel-Air, Ch., 137.
Bellevesvre, 346.
Bellevue, Auberge, 29.
Bellicant, M., 316.
Bellvire, 124.
Belnot, Marc, 38
Belvians, 218.
Benson, Hon. J. R., 148, 149.
Bergerac, 164, 172, 173, 174, 175, 176, 186.
Berhyl-Seive, 309.
Berre, 244.
Berry, Mr., 369, 370.
Berry, A. H., 195.
Berry, Barbara, 125.
Berry, C. W., viii, 32, 85, 120, 184, 300, 302, 303.
Berry, Mrs. C. W., 31, 363.
Berry, Ellen P., 223.
Berry, Harry P., 122.
Berry, Mabel, 353.
Berry, Margaret, 31.
Berry, Mary P., 223.
Berry, R. W. (Reg.), 86-250, 370.
Berry, Mrs. S. H., 107, 122, 125, 195, 353.
Berry, Mr. (at Ch. Rieussec), 154.
Berry-au-Bac, 9.
Bertha (gun), 8.
Bertin, M., 52.
Bertin, M. (Cointreau), 98
Bertin, Champ de, 52.
Bertrand, 55.
Bessan, 238.
Bessy, 41.
Betharram, 211.
Bethune, 6.
Beychevelle, Ch., 138, 139, 144, 154.
Beysson, Mlle., 258, 261.
Beysson, Mlle. M., 255, 261.

[374]

Cortot, M., 316.
Cos d'Estournel, Ch., 130, 158.
Cosne, 84, 356.
Cosy Corner, 7.
Côte Chalonnais, 68.
Côte de Beaune, 53, 57, 63, 68.
Côte de Fronsac, 137.
Côte de Nuits, 53, 57, 63, 64.
Côte d'Or, 46, 48, 51, 53, 57, 71, 117, 318, 330.
Côte Rôtie, 275, 277, 279, 280, 282, 285, 286, 287, 288, 290.
Côtes du Rhône, 255, 260, 269, 280.
Cottenham, Earl of, 32.
Cotton, Dr., xv.
Couiza, 217, 229
Coule, Vin de, 278.
Coulon, Mlle., 306.
Courbet, 4, 5.
Courbu, 210.
Courlaoux, 333.
Coursan, 232.
Courthezon, 254, 256, 261.
Courtisols, 26.
Coutet, Ch., 153.
Cramant, 11, 13, 14, 16, 18, 25, 28, 30, 31.
Cravencères, 196.
Crawfurd, Seaman, 301.
Cremant de Cramant, 10, 37.
Crépy, 8.
Cripps, Seaman, 301.
Croix Blanche, La, 69, 348.
Crouxet, 299.
Croydon, 247.
Crozes (wine), 273, 282.
Crusaders, 75, 239.
Cruse, Christian, 141, 142, 143, 146, 147, 148, 150, 178, 234, 359, 360, 361.
Cruse, Mme., 147, 150.
Cruse et Fils Frères, 143.
Crussol, Ch., 281.
Cubières, 230.
Cublaize, 299.
Cumières, 18, 31.
Curran, C. P., 259.
Cussac, 144.
Cussay-les-Forges, 73.
Cutbill, Seaman, 302.
Cuvée de Famille, 17.
Cuxac, 228.

Cyder, xxvi, 3.
Cypress, 144, 145, 242.
Cyrano de Begerac, 174.

Damade, M., 135.
Damocles, 230.
Dampierre, 99.
Dauglade, M., 135, 137, 138.
Dauglade, Mme., 137.
Daniel, M., 321.
Darby and Joan, 124.
Darius, xviii.
D'Arlay, Ch., 338, 339, 340.
Daudet Moulins, 264.
David, xvii.
Davidson, J. R., 300.
Dawlish, 206.
D'Ay, Ch., 29.
De Beaujeu, 308.
De Beaumont, Comte, 165.
De Bois-Renard, Ch., 276.
De Boisseumarie, Baron P. Le Roy, 257, 261, 284.
De Budos Castle, 156.
De Chalon, Princes, 340.
De Chaumont, Ch., 346, 351, 352.
De Cheminières, Ch., 216.
De Chevalier, Dom., 151, 224.
De Citeaux Abbey, 52.
Decize, 355.
Decoppet, Robert, 87.
De Corton Grancey, Ch., 56, 60.
De Cournon, Vicomte, 93.
De Fine Roche, Ch., 257.
De Fournils, Marquis, 177.
De Garde, Vin, 338, 339.
Degas, 360.
De Gimat, 195.
De Grancey, Le Comte, 58.
Déjean, A., 234, 235, 236, 237.
Déjean de Saint-Marcel, 336, 337, 341, 342-343.
De la Blonde, 288.
De la Brune, 288.
De la Chesnaye, Comte, 80, 356.
De la Chesnaye, Comtesse, 80, 82.
De la Cour, 315.
De la Croix d'Or, 271.
De la Gare Restaurant, 280, 281, 293.
De Laguiche, Comte, 354, 355.
De Laguiche, Marquis, 65, 328, 329, 330, 339, 352, 353, 355.

[381]

Noir de Noir, 31.
Noiriens, 53.
Noisot, Parc de, 51.
Notre Dame de St. Lazare, 42.
Nottingham, 125.
Nougaret, M., 232, 234, 237, 238, 245.
Nougat, 270, 291.
Noustolet, 295.
Noziere, Violette, 178.
Nuits (wine), 63, 69.
Nuits St. Georges, 53, 63, 69, 348.
Nymphe Endormie, 272.

Oat-beard, 245.
O'Berry Bar, 209.
Oddonino, 38.
Odenas, 308, 310.
O'Kelly, Count, 259.
O'Lanyer, Louis, 6, 125, 127, 128, 152.
O'Lanyer, Louis, 126.
O'Lanyer, Mlle., 125, 128.
O'Lanyer, Mme., 126, 152.
O'Lanyer de L'Estaing, 126.
Old Q., 303.
Olive, 236.
Olive Oil, 131 et seq.
Olives, 78, 131 et seq., 241, 252, 262, 270.
Olivier, Ch., 164, 166.
Omar Khayyám, xxiii, 264.
Orgon, 251.
Orléanais, 318.
Orléans, 86, 87, 91.
Orsan, 269.
Orthez, 205.
Osiris, M., 155.
Othello, xxv.
Ouvèze, River, 254.
Ouzouer s/Loire, 85.
Oxfordshire, S.S., 298.

Pailhes, 214.
Palais des Papes, 258, 259.
Palladius, xxiii.
Palmer Margaux, Ch., 138, 158.
Panama, 62.
Pangloss, xxvi.
Panjas, 194.
Parampuyre, Ch., 141, 159.
Paris, 8, 9, 23, 38, 41, 47, 80, 81, 87, 95, 247, 317, 318, 319, 346, 356, 358.

Park, Norah, 298.
Parker's Piece, 298.
Parnay, 99.
Pasteur, Dr., 332, 338, 341, 343, 344.
Pau, 198, 202, 209.
Pauillac, 130, 139, 144, 145.
Paul, Prince, 141.
Paulhan, 237.
Paveil, Ch., 144.
Pavie, Ch., 137.
Pazulos, 219.
Peau, 278.
Pécharmont, 174.
Peckham, 5.
Peel, John, 161.
Pelure d'oignon, 322.
Pepette, 31.
Pépin, 278.
Pepys, 31, 32, 33, 36.
Pequignot, M., 95.
Perch, 78.
Perignac, 123.
Perignon, Dom., 15.
Perigord, 252.
Perpignan, 217, 223, 231.
Perrat, M., 322.
Perreon, 311.
Perrier, Dr. E., 70.
Perrier-Jouët & Cie, 10, 11, 13, 14, 16, 17.
Perros, M., 308.
Perthshire, 211.
Pessac, 140.
Peter, 77.
Peter the Hermit, 75.
Petit Verdot, 144.
Petite Champagne, 121.
Petite Chapelle, 62.
Petra, xx.
Petrarch, xxiv.
Peugeot-Helyett, 86.
Peyrehorade, 206.
Peyrouse, 211.
Philippe, Duc, 56.
Philippe le Bon, 68.
Philippe le Hardi, 68.
Philippotte, 56.
Pic, Albert, 45, 93.
Pichon-Lalande, Ch., 144.
Pichon-Longueville, Ch., 144.
Picpoul, 215, 235.

[385]

[387]